I0109799

Minorities and the Modern Arab World

Middle East Studies Beyond Dominant Paradigms
Peter Gran, *Series Editor*

Minorities and the Modern Arab World

New Perspectives

Edited by
Laura Robson

SYRACUSE UNIVERSITY PRESS

Copyright © 2016 Syracuse University Press
Syracuse, New York 13244-5290

All Rights Reserved

First Edition 2016
16 17 18 19 20 21   6 5 4 3 2 1

∞ The paper used in this publication meets the minimum requirements of the American
National Standard for Information Sciences—Permanence of Paper for Printed Library
Materials, ANSI Z39.48-1992.

For a listing of books published and distributed by Syracuse University Press, visit www
.SyracuseUniversityPress.syr.edu.

ISBN: 978-0-8156-3452-2 (cloth)   978-0-8156-3433-1 (paperback)
978-0-8156-5355-4 (e-book)

Library of Congress Cataloging-in-Publication Data
Names: Robson, Laura, author.
Title: Minorities and the modern Arab world : new perspectives / edited by Laura Robson.
Description: First edition. | Syracuse, New York : Syracuse University Press, 2016. |
    Series: Middle East studies beyond dominant paradigms | "This volume originated
    in a conference held at the Middle East Studies Center at Portland State University in
    2013, Minorities of the Modern Middle East."—Acknowledgments page. | Includes
    bibliographical references and index.
Identifiers: LCCN 2016010724| ISBN 9780815634522 (cloth : alk. paper) |
    ISBN 9780815634331 (pbk. : alk. paper) | ISBN 9780815653554 (e-book)
Subjects: LCSH: Minorities—Arab countries—Congresses.
Classification: LCC DS36.9.A1 M55 2016 | DDC 305.0917/4927—dc23 LC record
    available at http://lccn.loc.gov/2016010724

Manufactured in the United States of America

Contents

Acknowledgments

ANY BOOK REPRESENTS a collective effort, but this is perhaps especially true of an edited volume encompassing the work of a number of participants. It is a pleasure to acknowledge the many people whose help and support made this collection possible.

This volume originated in a conference held at the Middle East Studies Center at Portland State University in 2013, "Minorities of the Modern Middle East." I thank my workshop co-organizer, Yasmeen Hanoosh, and the then director of the center, James Grehan, for their hard work putting the event together. The center's staff members Elisheva Cohen, Karen Lickteig, and Tam Rankin provided invaluable assistance, and the conference received funding from the Portland State University Speakers Board and the Internationalization Minigrant Program. Further sponsorship came from the Portland State University Departments of History and World Languages and Literatures and from the Portland Center for Public Humanities.

Besides the contributors to this volume, the conference's other participants were centrally important to shaping the conversation and helping to clarify the ideas that appear here. I would like to thank Juan Cole, Jennifer Dueck, Lina Khatib, Roberto Mazza, Laila Prager, Paul Silverstein, Keith Walters, and Keith Watenpaugh for their participation and incisive comments during the course of the conference and its aftermath.

Syracuse University Press has been an enthusiastic and involved publisher, providing invaluable editorial support and assistance throughout the process. I thank Deanna McCay and Suzanne Guiod for their editorial acumen and commitment to the project. I also thank the two anonymous readers for the press, whose thoughtful and thorough reviews much strengthened the final version.

Minorities and the Modern Arab World

Introduction

LAURA ROBSON

In 1947 British Lebanese scholar Albert Hourani—later to be famous as the author of *Arabic Thought in the Liberal Age* and *A History of the Arab Peoples*—published a slender volume entitled *Minorities in the Arab World*, in which he attempted to outline the histories and characteristics of the religious, linguistic, and ethnic minorities in the Ottoman Empire's former Arab provinces. He defined "minority" quite simply, as a community that was either non-Sunni Muslim or non-Arabic-speaking or both, existing within a Sunni Arab majority, and with a long-standing presence in the region (thereby excluding Ashkenazi Jewish settlers in Palestine). There were, he explained, "a number of communities which have long resided in these countries, or in other parts of the Middle East before they came to these countries, and most of whose members possess their legal nationality, but which are not Sunni Moslem by faith, although they are Arabic-speaking; there are others which are Sunni Moslem but not Arabic-speaking, and others again which are neither Sunni nor Arab. It is to these communities that the term 'minorities' refers."[1]

This idea that minorities in the Middle East are clearly identifiable, separate, long-standing communities persisted for many decades, even as scholars began to acknowledge the flexible nature of such communal categorizations. As Gabriel Ben-Dor put it in 1999, "The authentic ethnic approach . . . emphasizes both the dynamics of change in ethnic identity and consciousness and the more or less objective variables that define majorities and minorities, which tend to endure over time."[2] Equally long-lived has been Hourani's approach to defining the primary characteristics of these "minorities," who are described by their theological systems first

1

and their linguistic-national attributes second. His Christian minorities are characterized by their theological points of origination: the Eastern patriarchates' split from Rome in the eleventh century, the Nestorian controversies over the nature of the Trinity in the fifth century, the Monophysite doctrines about the oneness of Christ and Jesus. Muslim minorities appear as defined by the Sunni-Shi'i split over the caliphate in the seventh century, by the 'Alawi belief in a "Divine Triad," by the Druze theology of transmigration of souls. Similarly, Hourani's linguistic minorities are sorted by the strengths of their claims to nationality: the Armenians "have a continuous history as a national entity in this homeland since ancient times," while the Kurds have a "group of dialects" spoken by "a number of Moslem tribes, scarcely united enough to be called a nation."[3] This approach to the question of minorities in the Arab world dominated the public perception of non-Muslim and non-Arab communities in the region for decades and sometimes entered into a public realm already primed to view Sunni Islam as a monolithic entity engaged in various forms of institutionalized discrimination against non-Muslim or non-Arab communities.

But over the past twenty years, a new picture of minorities in the Arab world has begun to emerge in the scholarly literature—one that eschews the picture of static, clearly defined, predetermined minorities in a permanent state of tense relations with an equally predetermined Sunni Arab majority. Increasingly, scholars have begun to think about the modern phenomenon of "minorities" as the consequence of a *process* of minoritization, beginning in the late nineteenth century and continuing to unfold through the present day.[4] Rather than offering a definition of "minority," then, the chapters in this volume seek to examine the processes by which minority identities in the Arab world have been constantly formed, practiced, and altered. They challenge the idea that ethnic, religious, and linguistic minorities stand permanently outside majoritarian states across the Arab world. Collectively, these essays make three central arguments: that the category of "minority" became meaningful only with the rise of the modern nation-state; that in this new political landscape, groups labeled minorities often sought simultaneously to project an essential cultural "authenticity" and a nationalist commitment through specific and focused types of political engagement; and that Middle Eastern and North African minority identities owe much of their modern self-definition to developments within diaspora populations and other transnational frameworks.

The Historical Development of the "Minority" Concept

The concepts of "minority" and "majority" were essentially meaningless in the context of the Ottoman Arab world before the nineteenth century. In late Ottoman practice, Christian and Jewish communities in the Arab provinces were categorized as *millets*, a word indicating a non-Muslim community that had the right to a certain degree of communal autonomy (most centrally, separate courts for issues of personal law like marriage, divorce, and inheritance), in return for certain institutionalized disadvantages (like special taxes). This system, which had been highly localized and unevenly applied through the empire in earlier periods, underwent a process of institutionalization and centralization in the context of empire-wide political, economic, and military reforms in the mid-nineteenth century, though it was still practiced and interpreted in variable and locally conscious ways. This move toward institutionalizing the millet system meant that the Ottoman state now identified and differentiated certain religious communities in more formalized ways. It did not, however, map those communal distinctions onto a state framework of political rights. As Aron Rodrigue has put it, "Nothing in the political system of the Ottoman Empire called for different groups to merge into one. . . . That particular arrangement, therefore, renders invalid all our terms for debate about minority/majority, which are all extraordinarily Europe-centered."[5] The Ottoman Empire's rule depended not on claims to represent its subject population, but on political and military will and on claims to religiously sanctioned power.

The idea of minorities (and, for that matter, majorities) arose outside the Middle East, in a post-Enlightenment Europe where the desirability of assimilating identifiably separate internal communities into a theoretically universalist nation-state framework became a paramount concern. By the nineteenth century, these ideas were beginning to make their way into the Ottoman sphere. Under political, military, and economic pressure from the European imperial powers, the Ottoman state's series of reforms known as the *tanzimat* began to make nods toward the concept of representation and to move toward a national political identity. This development coincided and interacted with the rise of nationalist and separatist movements on the edges of the empire—particularly in the Balkans, where political nationalism was often organized and deployed through Orthodox church institutions, thus fusing political opposition to the Ottoman state not only with irredentist national feeling but also with Christian institutional self-definition. At the same time, Ottoman military losses in Europe and the dispossession and expulsion of hundreds of thousands of Muslims following nationalist rebellions in places like Greece, Serbia, Bulgaria, and Macedonia made for a demographic shift within the empire toward what was for the first time a definitive and overwhelming Muslim numerical majority.[6] This shift also saw a move on the part of the Ottoman authorities toward the use of Islam as a unifying concept representing the empire, moving away from earlier Ottoman imaginings of the polity as essentially pluralistic.[7]

In the late nineteenth century, early European colonialism in North Africa began to develop the concept of treating certain communities as minorities, with differentiated sets of political rights and types of representation vis-à-vis the state. In Algeria, which the French occupied in the 1830s and declared legally a part of France in 1848, colonial governments began to investigate the possibilities of bestowing special citizenship rights on Algerian Jews. In 1870 the French Jewish lawyer Adolphe Crémieux—a longtime advocate for the rights of Jews in Europe and the founder of the Alliance Israélite Universelle—successfully pushed through what became known as the Crémieux Decree, which gave French citizenship to approximately thirty-five thousand "native" Jews in Algeria without altering the second-class "indigenous" status held by Algerian Muslims and Berbers.[8] This decision foreshadowed decades of colonial decision making across North Africa and the Middle East that would tie religious community to political representation via a minority-majority framework.

Even by the 1920s, though, the term "minority" had not become common currency in the ex-Ottoman provinces. Rather, it emerged as a central concept in European discussions of these territories, and especially in the discourse and organization of the League of Nations. The international framework of "minorities treaties," begun with the promulgation of the Polish minority rights agreement in 1919, marked the beginning of a new phase of international political jockeying in which the minority-majority distinction would be central to definitions of citizenship and sovereignty. The mandate system offered the opportunity (and, in many cases, the incentive) to clearly define ethnic and religious minorities and majorities in the new Arab states being folded into a colonial system. And once these categories were in place as institutionalized conduits to national and international representation, groups that had hitherto not thought of themselves as minorities began to claim that status on a global stage.

Following the First World War, much of the Arab world was brought under European colonial occupation. The postwar treaties created the newly defined states of Syria, Lebanon, Transjordan, Iraq, and Palestine, declaring them "mandates" under British or French authority. Technically, these new mandate states and their European rulers fell under the international jurisdiction of the League of Nations and were supposed to be moving toward eventual sovereignty. In practice, they were mostly governed as additions to the British and French colonial empires.[9] In this context, both the British and the French mandate governments across the region made use of practices of ethnic, religious, and communal categorization that they had developed in other imperial contexts, creating new paths for religious identity to carry legal, political, and administrative implications. The new British mandate government in Palestine, bound by international agreement to encourage mass European Jewish immigration there, created new, separate legal institutions for Muslim, Christian, and Jewish subjects, thereby carefully dividing the Arab population along sectarian lines and making possible the emergence of state-like institutions for the Yishuv.[10] In Iraq British colonial officials hoped that careful alliances with Sunni urban elites who had constituted a political leadership under the Ottomans would allow them to forestall the emergence of a secular Iraqi nationalism by firmly assigning the Iraqi Shiʻi communities a distinctly separate and generally unfavorable set of economic and political circumstances.[11] French interests drew the new Lebanese borders with the specific intent of engineering a particular demographic mix of

Christians and Muslims, on the theory that Lebanese Christians would need to ally with the French in order to maintain political control over the country and emerge as the region's only Christian-dominated nation-state.[12] The French mandate government in Lebanon consistently privileged Christian communities over either Sunni or Shi'i voices through discriminatory practices of educational funding, government hiring, and political representation.[13] In Syria minoritization took on a physical aspect, as the French mandate government drew borders between Sunni, 'Alawi, and Druze "statelets" and declared them separate, communally determined political units. French mandate policy also encouraged a sectarianization process in the military, which by the 1930s was primarily made up of 'Alawis and other non-Sunni populations and thereby took on a "minority" association. Egypt, while not under mandate supervision, remained under a strong British colonial influence and military presence throughout the interwar period and experienced a similar politicization of its Coptic community, treated as a distinct legal, administrative, and political entity.[14]

This heavy-handed process of colonial sectarianization met with considerable resistance from both sides of the minority-majority divide, particularly among urban elite and middle-class populations committed to emerging concepts of secular nationalism. In Palestine Arab Christian journalists, activists, and writers insisted that they were not a minority but full and committed members of a vibrant Palestinian Arab nationalism. Coptic leaders in Egypt similarly resisted the label of minority, proclaiming their commitment to Egyptian nationalism and placing their community at the center of Egyptian historical identity. In Syria the fragility of the French hold became apparent in 1925 when a Druze uprising in the southern province of Jabal Druze quickly became a mass rebellion against French imperial rule that included Muslim, Christian, and Druze communities and lasted for more than two years.[15] In Morocco French attempts to isolate the Berber community through the imposition of a "customary" legal code (the *dahir*) to apply only to Berber communities and regions met with considerable resistance from Moroccan nationalists, both Berber and Arab, who saw this development as an imperial attempt at divide and rule and protested accordingly.[16] Nevertheless, legal codification of sectarian identities reified and hardened communal divides across the region, as colonial subjects found themselves trying to carve out political, economic, and social opportunities for themselves in very restricted circumstances.

Further, there were some minorities for whom this colonial sectarianization process seemed to open up new political opportunities. Ethnolinguistic minorities who had suffered displacement during the war—particularly Armenian and Assyrian populations, who had been victims of genocidal massacres and mass deportations from 1915 on—saw in the new European focus on minorities an opportunity for national statehood, or at least some form of local autonomy. Engaged with a large and vocal diaspora population, Armenian and Assyrian communities argued in the international sphere that they could not be successfully integrated with hostile Muslim and Arab majorities. Their appeals to international Christian opinion, aligned with emerging humanitarian organizations like Near East Relief and the Red Cross, helped to solidify a narrative of ethnic Christian minorities persecuted by Muslim Arab majorities, a message warmly received by Western audiences who donated enormous amounts of money to their cause. Similarly, British colonial support for Zionist settlement in Palestine opened up the specter of an ethnoreligious minority hoping to alter the demographic realities on the ground to become a majority, with the support of the British mandate government, practical help from the European Jewish diaspora, and political assistance from the international community in the form of the League of Nations.

The minoritization process unfolded on two levels in the interwar period: on the ground, in the context of colonial governments committed to sectarianization, and in the international sphere, as ideas of minority rights and communal nationalisms mingled with older European concepts of Muslim and Arab despotism in an emerging international legal regime dominated by the League of Nations. Following the collapse of the mandates system in the 1940s and the emergence of a series of unstable postcolonial governments across the region in the 1950s, the situation for minority communities took on a new color. The states that eventually emerged in Egypt, Syria, and Iraq were all secularist national regimes under authoritarian leadership. In the cases of Syria and Iraq, they were dominated by a small and insular group of people who shared a sectarian and regional affiliation (Latakian and 'Alawi in the case of Asad's Syria, Sunni and Tikriti in Saddam Husayn's Iraq), lending a degree of minority shading to what were avowedly secular pan-Arab regimes. Across the Mashriq, questions of pan-Arabism gave rise to new conversations about what constituted Arab identity and how "minorities" fitted into it. In Egypt, dominated by a secular nationalist authoritarian regime that sought to accommodate certain aspects of Islamist thought to preempt opposition, Coptic leaders struggled to articulate their nationalist commitment to the state. In other parts of North Africa, Arab nationalism competed with visions of Mediterranean "cosmopolitanism" and Berber separatism as exclusionary nationalisms emerged out of the toppled British and French empires.

In this secularist but often highly identitarian era, many Christian and Jewish intellectuals across the region found themselves drawn to leftist movements. Palestinian and Lebanese Christians dominated the Marxist-oriented Popular Front for the Liberation of Palestine; the first Arabs in the Communist Party in Israel were Christians, who continued to be the dominant Arab element in the party until its split in 1965; the leftist opposition in Iraq and Syria was similarly disproportionately Christian. Around the same time, as the economic and political failures of these regimes became increasingly evident following the 1967 war and into the economic doldrums of the 1970s, the rise of Islamist political organizations contributed to a further sectarianization of the political landscape.

This period saw a significant engagement with questions of minoritization from diaspora groups, some of which were intent on demonstrating their essential separation from Muslim and Arab interests for purposes of easier assimilation within their new homelands in the United States and Europe.[17] It also witnessed the rise of increasingly vocal Middle Eastern and North African immigrant communities in the West, who often suffered various forms of both institutionalized and informal discrimination and consequently began thinking of themselves, in explicit and self-conscious terms, as disenfranchised "minorities." This trend was especially pronounced following the dual Palestinian disasters of 1948 and 1967; during and after the long Lebanese civil war that lasted, on and off, from 1975 until the Taif Accords of 1989; and among Iraqi Assyrians in the

Detroit and Chicago areas in the 1990s and 2000s, following the first and second Gulf wars.

The movement from Ottoman rule through European colonial occupation through anti-Islamist, secularizing authoritarianism meant a shifting landscape of political, economic, and social affiliations that led some communities to strongly self-identify as national minorities, while others rejected the label in favor of incorporation and assimilation into other forms of political identity, from pluralistic nationalism to communism. The process by which minority identities were constructed and deconstructed has thus involved multiple levels of contact and confrontation with the state, international agencies, diaspora populations, and emerging secular and religious opposition elements, as well as internal negotiations.

In the current evolving situation across the Arab world, the position of "minority" communities is once again an open question, and the unfolding of revolutions and counterrevolutions appears in many places again to be reformulating religious and ethnic identities as essentially political. The ongoing sectarianization of the civil war in Syria, for instance, stands as a clear contemporary example of how economic, political, and military upheavals can reify or even create newly identifiable minority communities apparently at odds with majoritarian movements. The recent and continuing upheavals across the Arab world demonstrate the ongoing relevance of thinking about the mechanics of historical and political processes of minoritization in the modern era.

Chapters, Arguments, and Themes

The first part, "Conceptualizing Minorities," comprises four chapters intended to shed light on the problems of defining the category of minority in the modern Arab world. It opens with Peter Sluglett's essay, "From Millet to Minority: Another Look at the Non-Muslim Communities in the Late Nineteenth and Early Twentieth Centuries," which investigates the expansion and remaking of the millet system through the nineteenth century into an institution that cast religious identity as simultaneously national and political. Sluglett argues that the millet system, which described the position of particular religious communities within the Ottoman context of a pluralistic imperial subject body, went through a period of expansion in the late nineteenth century that both reflected and institutionalized changes in ethnoreligious identifications occurring in the Balkans and the Arab provinces. In this period, religious communities were redefined both as nations of sorts—an idea with considerable European purchase, as Britain, France, and Russia all searched for ways to exert influence in the Ottoman state—and as "minorities" that represented a problem for majoritarian nationhood. With the collapse of the Ottoman Empire in the First World War, the additional problem arose of encompassing non-Arab and heterodox Muslim groups into states whose borders were defined largely by the external mandatory powers and whose political commitments were intended to be primarily nationalist. The movement "from millet to minority" constituted a series of specific local processes that changed religious communities from a flexible "feature" of the multiethnic Ottoman Empire to "an often problematic component" of the modern national states that succeeded it.

Jacob Norris, in his essay, "Across Confessional Borders: A Microhistory of Ottoman Christians and Their Migratory Paths," fleshes out Sluglett's argument, looking at a specific case study of precisely how the blurriness of communal categories played out in the lives of particular Ottoman Arab Christians. Following the life histories of two Arab Ottoman subjects, Roman Catholics from Bethlehem engaged in merchant activity that took them to Russia and France and back, Norris argues that denominational commitments were much less central and more flexible in the lives of mobile Levantine Christians than has often been thought. The trajectories, both geographical and cultural, of the merchant cousins Elias and Yaqub Kattan suggest that they viewed themselves as part of a pluralistic Arabic-speaking Ottoman Christianity that could find common currency (both figuratively and literally) with Arab Christians from other parts of the Ottoman Empire and belonging to other denominations and faiths.

My own chapter, "Becoming a Sectarian Minority: Arab Christians in Twentieth-Century Palestine," looks at the transformation of these blurred and flexible visions of communal identities into hardened, formalized, institutionalized "minorities" under the auspices of the British colonial government in Palestine, suggesting that this was a process that occurred across the British and French mandate states during the interwar period. Sectarianism, and the recasting of nationalist Palestinian Arab Christians as a beleaguered "minority," brought with it the advantage of dividing an Arab population unified by its simultaneous opposition to Zionist immigration and British rule. Even more centrally, it offered a legitimization of British rule over what was cast as a deeply divided society fractured by ancient and primitive religious disputes. These policies, I argue, were essentially adopted without much alteration into the new Israeli state, which early on began to govern its Palestinian Arab citizens as members of religious "minorities."

The fourth chapter dealing with this theme, Joel Beinin's "Egypt and Its Jews: The Specter of an Absent Minority," examines the recent resurgence of interest in the historical experience of the Jewish community in Egypt. He suggests that this explosion of material—encompassing press coverage, fiction, and films, among other things—is not actually about the Jewish community at all, but represents a mode of talking about other issues. Most centrally, Beinin argues, this new discourse makes a veiled argument for some form of return to what is conceived as the more pluralistic, cosmopolitan, and democratic period of the Egyptian monarchy and cloaks concern for Coptic interests in stories ostensibly about Egyptian Jews. Such uses of minority historical narratives in service of other domestic agendas often render the actual lived experiences of Egyptian Jews invisible. Even more important, they demonstrate that the popular conception of Egyptian Jewishness has risen not from immutable essential "minority" identities, but through specific public discourses with identifiable interests and political commitments in the Egyptian domestic sphere.

Taken together, these essays suggest the essential modernity of the concept of minorities in the Arab world. A discourse of "minorities" emerged in embryonic form with the upheavals of the Ottoman Empire's territorial disintegration and subsequent collapse from the mid-nineteenth century to the First World War. With the appropriation of most of the former Ottoman Arab provinces into the British and French empires, new colonial governments further encouraged the emergence of "minority" identities for their own purposes and enforced them through specific legal and political mechanisms backed by the threat, and not infrequently the actual use, of military force. Once in place, these "minority" narratives often came to stand in for discussion of other issues in a fractured and uncertain postcolonial political landscape.

In the second part, "Minorities, Nationalism, and Cultural 'Authenticity,'" contributors look at the multifarious ways that ethnic, linguistic, and religious communities have sought to define themselves as central to the modern state and the national project in a variety of circumstances. Aline Schlaepfer's "When Anticolonialism Meets Antifascism: Modern Jewish Intellectuals in Baghdad" challenges the received wisdom that Baghdadi Jewish intellectuals were dependent on British government protection during the mandate years and consequently disappeared from the scene after Britain's withdrawal in 1932 and Faysal's death the following year. Instead, she argues, a core group of influential Jewish writers and thinkers began to head up a public discourse that adhered to a strong anticolonial position while also objecting to an Iraqi-German rapprochement on anti-Nazi and antifascist grounds. Schlaepfer's uncovering of this late Baghdadi Jewish discourse suggests multiple processes of remaking minority identity: first, an attempt to move away from minority affiliations with colonial states and, second, deliberate efforts to craft a secular, democratic, leftist political landscape in postindependence Iraq in which Baghdadi Jews could participate actively and fully.

In "Assyrians and the Iraqi Communist Party: Revolution, Urbanization, and the Quest for Equality," Alda Benjamen examines how Assyrians engaged with communism to forge new political spaces for themselves in Iraq from the 1940s to the 1960s. She argues that Assyrians in Iraq were originally attracted to the party for its pluralistic membership and its emphasis on secularity, offering the possibility of full Assyrian integration into Iraqi national identity. When their labor activism within the context of the Iraqi Communist Party on behalf of oil workers in and around Kirkuk and membership within ICP-affiliated organizations began to be seen as a threat to the new Ba'thist state following the 1963 coup, the new regime targeted Assyrian ICP members along with thousands of Iraqis for court-martial trials and imprisonment, at times impugning Assyrians' nationalist commitments and suggesting that they were not committed Iraqi citizens. This alignment of economic and political commitments, clashing with the fragile Ba'thist state, caused the Assyrian community to feel isolated and targeted, ironically increasing its sense of communal separation.

Hiroko Miyokawa likewise focuses on the ways in which a minority community sought to insert itself into the modern state and reinvent—perhaps circumvent—its minority status. In "The Struggle over Egyptianness: A Case Study of the Nayruz Festival," she investigates the Coptic Christian remaking of a Coptic religious holiday, the Nayruz festival, into a national display affirming Coptic commitment to the Egyptian state. Locating the beginnings of this idea in nineteenth-century Pharaonism, Miyokawa argues that Coptic leaders engaged in nationalist discourse deliberately "de-Christianized" Coptic public displays like the Nayruz festival with a view toward promoting Pharaoic visions of Egyptian national identity and arguing for the essential cultural "authenticity" of Copts as Egyptians.

Finally, Samuel Liebhaber looks at the attachment of concepts of cultural and linguistic Arabness to the Mahri language spoken in Yemen. In "From Minority to Majority: Inscribing the Mahra and Touareg into the Arab Nation," he examines a body of literature that claims a "Himyarite" (Yemeni) origin for the Berber languages of North Africa, particularly among the Berber-speaking Touareg. Liebhaber suggests that this narrative is built not on linguistic evidence but on premodern historical intersections between the Touareg and the Mahra, perhaps focused around camel trading—an activity that by the modern period carried positive connotations of Arab and bedouin cultural authenticity. Despite its evident falsity, then, the linguistic theories linking Berber and Mahri allow both minority groups to claim a kind of cultural "Arabian authenticity" that carries political benefits in both the Yemeni and the North African contexts.

The final part, "Minorities in the Transnational Sphere," argues that many Middle Eastern minority identities have been forged in essentially transnational rather than local or regional contexts. Here again the focus is on processes rather than definitions, looking at how minorities have been constituted and entrenched not only through events in the homeland but also through the particular interests of diaspora communities and transnational institutions. In the post–World War II period, some expressions of minority identity have also been influenced by the rise of a disenfranchised and economically disadvantaged immigrant Muslim community in Europe, a designation that has helped shape a general narrative about "minority" troubles in an undifferentiated global landscape.

The first chapter in this part, David Bond's "Tunisia's Minority Mosaic: Constructing a National Narrative," examines the emergence of a carefully constructed narrative of Tunisia as a "harmonious mosaic of communities" reflective and inclusive of a pluralistic Mediterranean history and identity. He traces this idea both through the scholarly literature on Tunisia, which often implicitly suggests a romanticized pluralistic Tunisian colonial history prior to the authoritarian rule of Ben 'Ali (an idea with parallels in Beinin's analysis of the uses of historical narratives of Egyptian Jews), and in the Ben 'Ali regime's own advocacy for this framework, which presented Tunisia as an open, tolerant, and modern nation-state adhering to European standards and norms. Focusing particularly on the Tunisian state's determination to create a built environment reflecting this pluralistic "Mediterranean" history, Bond suggests that the rebuilding of Tunis over the past twenty years, and the architectural emphasis on a multiplicity of flourishing minority communities, suggests "a 'restorative nostalgia' that patches up the past and restores it in the form of architectural projects and financial investments."

Liora R. Halperin uses a linguistic lens to examine the relationship between political power and minority status through a case study of Hebrew in mandate Palestine. In her essay, "Majority and Minority Languages in the Middle East: The Case of Hebrew in Mandate Palestine," she argues that European Jewish educators in Palestine approached the process of reinventing Hebrew as a modern and hegemonic language through treating it as a majority tongue long before it actually became one in a demographic sense. Alongside this idea, though, remained an anxiety about Hebrew's status as a minority language—not vis-à-vis Arabic, which many Zionists believed they could overcome via mass immigration and political takeover, but vis-à-vis English, against whose literary and political range Jewish educators frequently compared Hebrew and found it wanting. Besides examining the active refusal of Zionists in Palestine to be consigned to the category of minority, this analysis suggests that the concept of minority was nevertheless relevant, albeit in a much broader context of global power.

In "The Chaldean Church between Iraq and America: A Transnational Social Field Perspective," Yasmeen Hanoosh argues for a new understanding of Chaldean identity as a conceptual ethnoreligious site with active transnational affiliations. She traces the development of what she calls a "transnational social field" for Chaldean Iraqis in the diaspora, suggesting that the strength and apparent permanence of Chaldean institutions even among second- and third-generation immigrants are a consequence of the deliberate construction of these spaces as simultaneously religious, ethnic, national, and social. Chaldean social fields, then, simultaneously transcend the territorial and political boundaries of Iraq and the United States and forge alternative, region-flexible sites for the expression of loyalties and a substantive global network of social and economic support. This represents a practical and even a materialist approach to understanding how minority identities are consolidated and maintained over long periods of time despite exile and dispersion.

Finally, in "Permanent Temporariness in Berlin: The Case of an Arab Muslim Minority in Germany," Lucia Volk reconsiders the definition of "minority" within the context of Palestinian and Kurdish refugees from Lebanon now existing on temporary protected status in Germany. She suggests that dual minority discourses emerge in this situation: the discourse of Muslim minorities in Germany, which has struggled to envision ways to assimilate Middle Eastern immigrants into what is strongly conceived as a majoritarian European Christian state, and a further minority of stateless refugees within the broader "Lebanese" community. The patchwork of German, European Union, and international law means that these refugee communities are subject to an ongoing status of temporary resident, without being able to move toward a permanent settlement of their status. In Germany, then, the legal frameworks of migration, refugee status, and citizenship have created this particular class of minority, defined less by actual origin, religion, or ethnicity and more by the national and international frameworks surrounding their documentation.

Taken together, these essays make the case that minorities in the Arab world should not be defined as clear-cut communities with inherent collective commitments, even with an acknowledgment of the flexibility of such arrangements. Rather, they argue for examining issues of minority status and identity in the Arab world by unearthing the multifaceted processes by which such communal formulations are created and maintained. This approach makes it possible to look at all angles of minority formations—particular pressures and interests within communities, but also local, national, and global pressures that merge to create new understandings of "minorities" and their relationships with the modern state.

PART ONE

Conceptualizing Minorities

THE MODERN SHIFT toward understanding non-Muslims in various parts of the Arab world as "minorities" had relatively little to do with the individual historical experiences or self-definitions of these communities themselves. Rather, it reflected how *states* across the region became more and more centralized, nationalized, and majoritarian during the course of the nineteenth and twentieth centuries. This part explores the modern construction of the "minority" concept, emphasizing how new state-level reimaginings of communal identity had their own rationale and logic that rarely corresponded to actual practices of communal identity on the ground.

Peter Sluglett takes a bird's-eye view of this process, tracing how non-Muslim communities recognized as *millets* moved from inhabiting flexible but established roles within a pluralistic Ottoman polity in the eighteenth and early nineteenth centuries to rather less well-defined and integrated positions as "minorities" in the fragile nation-states that emerged after the First World War. This process represented a consequence of the pressures of nationalist movements across Europe, imperial intervention in Ottoman and ex-Ottoman territories, and the uneven and unequal institutionalization of communal identity in the political structures of the colonial and postcolonial Middle East. These new state definitions often failed to resonate in individual lives; as Jacob Norris shows, Christian merchant families of nineteenth-century Bethlehem viewed themselves not as part of a disadvantaged "minority" but as part of a successful transnational merchant class for whom communal and sectarian identification was flexible and often subject to economically convenient reinterpretation. During this period, then, the minoritization process taking place in the Ottoman Empire largely failed to touch Palestinian Christian self-definitions or individual experiences. But as the reach of the modern state increased with the imposition of European colonial government in the ex-Ottoman Arab provinces after the First World War, the impact of state policies of minoritization grew more dramatic. My own chapter shows that the British government in Palestine, for instance, had particular commitments to the concept of sectarian divides and enforced a program of minoritization through the legal and political institutionalization of communal identity, with significant and ongoing ramifications for the region's newly defined minorities and majorities. Similarly, Joel Beinin suggests that recent reimaginings of the Egyptian Jewish experience as a "minority" have emerged not from the specificities of actual Egyptian Jewish experience but from the pressures of creating a viable Egyptian national identity encompassing both Muslims and Copts in a tense postcolonial environment. The conceptualization of Egyptian Jews as a "minority" has had little to do with the actual historical experience of the community and much more to do with concerns surrounding the consolidation, centralization, and nationalization of the Egyptian state.

In all these essays, we find evidence that the growth and centralization of state power across the nineteenth- and twentieth-century Middle East were the central pillars for establishing the political categories of "minority" and "majority"—and that this categorization largely failed to reflect the self-definitions and historical experiences of actual Christians and Jews in Arab settings, from Syria to Palestine to Egypt.

1

From Millet to Minority

Another Look at the Non-Muslim Communities
in the Late Nineteenth and Early Twentieth Centuries

PETER SLUGLETT

The whole question of "minorities" and "sectarian and ethnic groups" in the recent history of the Middle East is fraught with complications, many of which result either from problems of loose definition (lumping together disparate groups as if they were part of the same phenomenon) or from essentialism (the assumption that a group does not change significantly in either composition or context over time). In addition, the official discourse of Middle Eastern states sometimes projects the notion that "national" or "ethnic" minorities are foreign-invented concepts that attempt to divide the intrinsic unity of the nation, so that the whole notion of "minority" becomes politically incorrect rather than functioning as a straightforward statement of demographic fact.[1] Further oddities are the minority-which-behaves-as-if-it-were-a-majority, like the Sunnis in pre-2003 Iraq or the Maronites for most of the period since the foundation of *Grand Liban* in 1920, and the majority-which-becomes-a-minority because of demographic change over time, the current fate of the same Lebanese Maronites vis-à-vis their Shi'i compatriots.[2] In this chapter I shall try to trace the trajectories of some of the (mostly non-Muslim) religious communities in the Middle East from the millet system in the Ottoman Empire to the minorities that they became in the 1920s and 1930s, after the collapse of the Ottoman Empire. Some of these trajectories are reasonably well known, while others are less familiar. Much of what follows combines a survey and a critical analysis of the literature.

In this context, the "minority experience" in Europe, especially in the Balkans, since the Treaty of Westphalia of 1648 has some relevance for the history of the region that is now the Middle East. Perhaps the main point of similarity between the history of the two regions is the utter inadequacy and impracticality of any international arrangement for the effective protection of "peoples in danger," whether Muslims in the new states of southeastern Europe after 1878, Armenians in the last few decades of the Ottoman Empire, Jews and Gypsies in Europe in the 1930s and 1940s, Bosnian Muslims in the 1990s, and various groups of Kurds for much of the twentieth and twenty-first centuries. Also, it is sometimes assumed—probably because of the general atmosphere of the Versailles and post-Versailles period—that the treaties ending the Middle Eastern mandates in the 1930s and 1940s contained specific guarantees for the protection of minorities, which they did not.[3] And the specter of the League of Nations "protecting" the Coptic minority in Egypt had been raised in the Egyptian press after Britain's unilateral declaration of Egyptian independence in February 1922.[4]

For our purposes, the most relevant part of the Treaty of Westphalia—which embodied and enlarged upon the notion of *cuius regio, eius religio*[5] set out in the Peace of Augsburg in 1555—was the principle mandating the provision of protection and cultural and other rights for Catholics who found themselves in Protestant territory and vice versa.[6] In the same vein, Austria, Prussia, and Russia agreed to allow their Polish populations to preserve their nationality at the Congress of Vienna in 1815, but it was not spelled out either in 1648 or in 1815 what sanctions might or could be brought into play if these agreements were not honored.

After the First World War, the victors considered it important to address the question of minorities in the context of the creation of the new states of eastern Europe on the ruins of the Austro-Hungarian, German, and czarist empires. They were particularly concerned about the national and educational rights of, effectively, the several million Germans and Hungarians who found themselves outside the borders of the newly reconstituted German and Hungarian nation-states, as well as the religious rights of the Jews of eastern Europe. The new states, especially Czechoslovakia, Hungary, and Poland, were obliged to "sign undertakings to the League that they would extend educational, linguistic, religious and other protections to their minority populations, who in most cases were either Jews or ethnic Germans."[7] The Sudeten Germans would become a cause célèbre in the late 1930s, but Germany was equally active on behalf of the *Auslandsdeutsche* in Poland and elsewhere over the same period.[8] In addition, after the expulsion of between ten and twelve million Germans from various parts of Eastern Europe after 1945, members of various regional associations in the Federal Republic, often wielding a fair amount of political clout, devoted themselves to irredentist projects demanding the "return of German territory."[9] These efforts were generally abandoned after the fall of the Berlin Wall, the collapse of the Soviet Union, and the reunification of Germany, when the line formed by the Oder and Neisse Rivers was recognized as the permanent border between Germany and Poland.

"Ottoman Tolerance"

In the early sixteenth century, when the Ottomans conquered the Arab world, the non-Muslim communities in the region had long been suffering various waves of persecution under the Mamluks, which had resulted in large-scale conversion to Islam, particularly in Egypt. In contrast, during most of the roughly six centuries of Ottoman rule in Europe (and the somewhat shorter period of rule in Asia and North Africa), the state tended at worst to tolerate the non-Muslims and at best to afford them a considerable degree of autonomy in the conduct of their affairs. In general, the non-Muslim communities were known as millets, a term that long remained quite fluid, as is discussed below. Essentially, provided the communities agreed to pay the *jizya* (the canonical tax on non-Muslims, which dates from the first century of Islam) and made appropriate arrangements to collect it, they were largely self-governing. Furthermore, apart from members of the large Jewish communities in Aleppo and Baghdad, who had their own distinctive Arabic dialect, Christians, Jews, and Muslims were largely indistinguishable from one another in most of the cities of the empire. Again, in the more remote parts of eastern Anatolia, northern Syria, and northern Iraq, village or tribal Armenians, Assyrians, and Jacobites would have lived in ways very similar to their mostly Kurdish

Muslim neighbors.[10] In these more remote communities with no regular urban connections, the clergy often had scant knowledge of their own religious traditions, although the arrival of Christian missionaries in the latter part of the nineteenth century would have an important influence on their education and outlook.[11] In general, although Christians and somewhat fewer Jews continued to live in villages in Iraq and the Levant, there was a broad tendency (discernible from the *jizya* records, among other sources) for non-Muslims to migrate to the cities between the sixteenth and nineteenth centuries.

The Balkans in the Late Nineteenth and Early Twentieth Centuries

Various European states (particularly Britain, France, and Russia) had been encouraging ethnic nationalist-separatist movements within the Ottoman Empire since the 1820s, whose first fruits were the formation of an independent Greece at various stages between 1827 and 1830.[12] According to Kemal Karpat, Muslims formed about 43 percent of the population of the (still mostly Ottoman) Balkans in the second half of the nineteenth century.[13] The Treaty of Berlin determined that Bulgaria, Montenegro, Romania, and Serbia, all of which had been, broadly speaking, "fully fledged" Ottoman provinces until the middle of the nineteenth century, would immediately, or soon, become independent states, in which entitlement to full citizenship would be based on membership of the majority religion. After Berlin Bosnia-Herzegovina remained part of the Ottoman Empire until its annexation by Austria-Hungary in 1908, while Greece would obtain Thessaly in 1881; by the end of the Balkan Wars (1913), it had acquired most of the territory in the north of what is now the modern state, together with Crete and the larger islands off the west coast of Anatolia.[14]

As a result of these and other conflicts in northeastern Anatolia and the Caucasus between about 1870 and 1914, several million Muslims died, fled from their homes, or were forced out of them and eventually found themselves in the Asiatic part of the Ottoman Empire.[15] For example, the Muslim population of Crete, 43 percent of the total in 1832, fell to 8 percent by 1910. Although noted and deplored by some commentators at the time, this series of tragedies never formed the subject of any substantial international concern. Karpat comments: "The uprooting of the Muslims from the Danube and Edirne provinces in 1877/78 is described in the grimmest detail in the reports of the British consular agents stationed at Philippopolis, Rusçuk, Varna, Burgas, Edirne, etc. [which are] available in the British Public Records [*sic*] Office."[16] Later political developments served to complicate the "minority" situation further. Thus, in the 1890s, when Bulgarian Muslims formed about 20 percent of the population of the recently created Bulgarian state, the government created a kind of millet system for them, in which a district mufti was made "responsible for a Muslim congregation, the maintenance of mosques and the supervision of *waqf*s [pious endowments]."[17] With the advent to power first of the Young Turks and then of the Kemalists in the 1920s, the Bulgarian Muslims became divided into generally pro-Turkish, anti-Bulgarian state "secular-ists" and anti-Kemalist, pro-Bulgarian "Muslims," with the various bewil-dering and opposing connotations of loyalty-disloyalty and of competing notions of citizenship that can be imagined—how "truly Bulgarian" could a Muslim be? After one coup in 1923, the chief mufti exhorted the Muslim population to keep calm and to obey government orders, in terms oddly reminiscent of the injunctions of loyalty to the Ottoman state issued by Armenian patriarchs in the nineteenth century. The community slowly lost its major territorial assets, *waqf* properties, most of which were gradu-ally privatized, a process facilitated by the fact that such land was commu-nally owned rather than registered as the property of individuals.[18]

The Population Exchange between Greece and Turkey

In January 1923 a convention was concluded on an official exchange of population between Greece and Turkey, with religion rather than resi-dence, ethnicity, or mother tongue as the sole criterion defining who would go and who would stay. Since the convention had retrospective effect to the first Balkan war of 1912, it involved some two million people; nearly a million Greeks had fled western Anatolia as a result of the Greco-Turkish war in 1922. Emigrants from both sides lost their property and their livelihoods as well as their original nationality and acquired their new one when they arrived at their destination. Perhaps with reference to what has happened elsewhere in southeastern Europe, the resulting "ethnic homogenization" in Greece and Turkey is sometimes regarded as "positive and stabilizing," since it helped strengthen the nation-state structures of the two countries.[19] This state of affairs seems to pose a number of moral dilemmas, particularly for Turkey, where another factor in "ethnic homogenization" (in addition to the "departure" of the Greeks) was the expulsion or massacre/genocide of between one and one and a half million Armenians in the years before and during the First World War.[20] In addition, for much of the period since its foundation, the Turkish state has regularly resorted to violence against its "other" major minority, the Kurds, who have sought forms of autonomy or self-government that have been unacceptable to the authorities in Ankara in the regions in which they form a majority. Excluding recent labor migrants from the Middle East (or elsewhere in the Muslim world) to Greece as a member of the European Union, less than 1 percent of the population of modern Greece (around 120,000) is Muslim, almost all of whom live in the northeastern part of the state adjacent to Turkey; only about 3,000 mostly elderly Greeks still live in Turkey.

"From Millet to Minority" in the Arab World: Some Misconceptions

There is a degree of terminological confusion in any consideration of the notion of "religious minority" in the latter years of the Ottoman Empire. In the first place, the word "millet," which is generally taken as being equivalent to "religious community," also has the connotation of "nation," as in "the Frankish nation," "the Bulgarian nation," as well as the less immediately familiar "the Greek Orthodox nation." The "national states" that emerged in the Balkans at various times in the nineteenth and early twentieth centuries (and the "Armenian national movement")—entirely new developments, of course, in the context of the multireligious and multiethnic Ottoman Empire—all came into being as part of movements with a strong "church" component (the Bulgarian, Greek, and Serbian Orthodox churches and the Armenian church in much the same way).

However, given that the Christians living in the Arab Middle East formed a much smaller proportion of their local societies than in the

Balkans, the religious minorities of what are now the states of the Mashriq have a somewhat different history, although they form part of their coreligionists' history until the last years of the Ottoman Empire. The non-Muslims were organized into communities or confessional entities generally called millets, although the word "*ta'ifa*" (sect) was also used to describe these same entities. There is, to say the least, a fair degree of controversy about the origins, nature, and history of the "millet system," although it is now generally accepted that until about 1800 there were only three millets: the Greek Orthodox, the Armenians, and the Jews.[21] In her wide-ranging survey of Ottoman history, Karen Barkey dates the recognition of the Orthodox millet to 1454 and the Armenian to 1461,[22] but it is not clear what this designation meant in practice, since, according to Benjamin Braude, "there were no systemic [*sic*] empire-wide institutions which dealt with non-Muslims" until the early nineteenth century.[23] Given the likely limitations on the capacity of a premodern empire to exert any kind of standardized authority over its far-flung provinces, the absence of a uniform mechanism for regulating the affairs of the non-Muslims does not seem particularly surprising. The reality seems to have been a series of local arrangements, which resulted in the creation of a degree of autonomy for the non-Muslims, who almost certainly formed the majority of the empire's population before the Ottoman conquest of the eastern Arab world in the early sixteenth century. However, communal control seems to have been fairly weak, as evidenced by the fact that Christians and Jews regularly sued each other (as well as Muslim defendants) in the shari'a courts.[24] While it seems most likely that the communities had their own courts for intracommunal disputes, none of the records of such courts have survived.

Recent authors have taken issue with some of Braude's contentions, especially his notion that the term "millet" was widely used to refer to the "community of Muslims."[25] Hidemitsu Kuroki's research shows that the terms "millet" and "*ta'ifa*" were sometimes used interchangeably (the latter conventionally used to signify "sect," "religious community," or "confession"),[26] but it is clear from the shari'a court records that the word "millet" was indeed used in the sense of "separate religious community" by the 1800s.[27] Kuroki's work also highlights the economic significance of the *jizya* and the considerable lengths to which the Ottoman authorities went to collect it in the late eighteenth and nineteenth centuries.[28] For non-Muslim travelers and temporary visitors, their *jizya* receipt functioned as a proto-identity card, as well as furnishing proof that the bearer had already paid the tax (and thus would not be taxed twice).[29]

Changes in the Structure and Nature of the Millets

Let us return to the "three millets." By the mid-eighteenth century, the sectarian situation was already becoming more complicated, for a number of reasons. In the first place, a relatively substantial number of Greek Orthodox, who formed the majority of the Christian population in the Arab provinces, had converted to Catholicism, particularly in Aleppo and Damascus, and it became a matter of great concern to the Orthodox hierarchy that many of the wealthier members of the community had "gone over to Rome." Second, "by the middle of the eighteenth century those [Ottoman] Christians who were neither Orthodox nor Armenians—Copts, Jacobites, Nestorians, and Maronites—were understood to be under the political, if not spiritual, direction of the Armenian Patriarch." The Coptic and Maronite hierarchies do not seem to have made use of this "facility," but the Jacobites and Nestorians regularly appealed to the Armenian patriarchate to complain that Catholic missionaries were "poaching" their flocks. Eventually, these and other tendencies found expression in the considerable expansion of the millet system in the nineteenth century, partly, but not entirely, as a result of pressure from foreign powers: "[In 1848] the Melkite [Greek in this context] Catholic Church joined the ranks of the Orthodox (the *Rum* in Ottoman Turkish) and the Apostolic Armenian Churches that had long enjoyed *de facto* recognition and the more recently legitimated Catholic, later to be known as the Armenian Catholic (1830), and Jewish (1835) communities. . . . Having recognized the Melkites, the sultan opened a floodgate of repressed aspirations for autonomy from the empire's myriad Christian denominations, with the result that the list of officially sanctioned Christian *millets* had expanded to twelve by 1900."[30] Even an incomplete roster of these new millets (which included the Armenian Protestant millet of 1846) shows that most of them were Catholic offshoots from other (broadly speaking "Orthodox") communities. The

Catholics who split from the Nestorians in eastern Anatolia, western Iran, and northern Iraq in the eighteenth and nineteenth centuries were known as Chaldeans; members of both the Armenian Catholic millet (1830) and the Armenian Protestant millet (1846) had split off from the Armenian Apostolic Church, and the Syrian Catholics, who had been in communion with Rome since 1781, were given their own millet in 1845, separate from the Syrian Orthodox "mother church."

The transformation from three millets to a plurality of millets had a variety of causes. Although it seems doubtful whether the great upheavals in southeastern Europe that have been described had much to do with the change, the increasing aggressiveness of France and Britain vis-à-vis the Ottoman authorities was important, although not always crucial. The Russians, who had gained the right to protect the *Orthodox Christians* of the empire under the terms of the Treaty of Küçük Kaynarca in 1774, seem to have been more interested in promoting nationalism and secession/ separatism in southeastern Europe than promoting Orthodoxy *as such*, and relations between the various autocephalous Orthodox churches (for example, Bulgarian, Greek, Serbian, Russian) were often quite strained. Again, intermittent French protection of Ottoman Catholics had been part of the politico-ecclesiastical landscape since the late sixteenth century.[31]

Furthermore, although various European powers certainly lobbied the Sublime Porte on behalf of their protégés at various times in the nineteenth century, the case of the Greek Catholics shows more complex (and quite different) influences at work. Briefly, in addition to the labors of Catholic missionaries and the influence of France, an important part of the motivation for the schism that produced Greek/Melkite Catholicism as a separate sect was the rejection, on the part of substantial numbers of the Orthodox congregations of Syria, of the traditionally "foreign" ecclesiastical hierarchy, who were both Greek speaking and ethnically Greek. The bishops and patriarchs were imported into Syria, mostly from the monasteries of Mount Athos; locals wanted Arabic speakers (that is, "Syrians") to fill these senior positions, which would (incidentally) enable some of their Vatican-educated sons and nephews to play a more prominent role in the affairs of the church.[32] It was not until 1899 that the first Arab was appointed as Orthodox patriarch of Antioch, and the passionate quarrels between the (Arab) Greek Orthodox laity of Jerusalem and the (ethnically Greek) Orthodox patriarch of the city reverberate to this day.[33]

In a recent treatment of the subject, Maurits van den Boogert considers the *tanzimat* era, especially the Hatt-i Hümayün of 1856, as forming a watershed, but he also points out, following Kuroki, that the term "millet" was widely used by the local authorities and the imperial authorities, as well as by the communities themselves, at the beginning of the nineteenth century.[34] He also suggests that the widely trumpeted notion of the "protection" of various communities by various powers (the French of the Catholics, the Russians of the Orthodox under the terms of Küçük Kaynarca, and so on) was rather less universal than it would become by the late nineteenth century. Before that time, France (for example) gave special protection to *some* Catholics, rather than *all* Catholics.[35]

Hence, if one looks at the numbers of *berats* (certificates of consular protection) issued in the nineteenth century, they cover only a fairly small fraction of the overall number of non-Muslims. Thus, Issawi noted that "in Aleppo 19 Jews were granted British protection between 1848 and 1861, and by 1881 their number had risen to nearly 40. . . . In 1850 a list of British *protégés* in Baghdad showed 7 Jews, all merchants trading with India, and 4 Christians, one of whom was a trader." It is not clear whether Issawi thought that these numbers were or were not substantial, but in 1900 there were about 6,000 Jews in Aleppo and as many as 25,000 in Baghdad. By the latter part of the nineteenth century, however, "the foreign protection of minorities had greatly widened. Not only holders of *berats* but all aggrieved members of *millets* within reach of a foreign consul looked to him for protection and redress."[36] Unfortunately, Issawi gives no examples, although there is a lot of anecdotal evidence to this effect. In fact, while some non-Muslims may have benefited economically from foreign protection, it is not clear how much Muslims and non-Muslims actually competed with each other in the same economic spheres. In Aleppo, for instance, Muslims always dominated landowning and the wholesale grain trade, while Christians and Jews controlled various kinds of imports, banking, finance, and the manufacture and sale of textiles in northern Syria. In general, trade with the city's hinterland (in northern Syria, northern Iraq, and southeastern Anatolia) rather than trade with

Europe dominated the commerce of Aleppo between the opening of the Suez Canal and the First World War.[37]

Issawi and van den Boogert interpret the effects of the *tanzimat* rather differently: Issawi regards the reforming decrees of 1839 and 1856 as an attempt to remove some of the disabilities suffered by non-Muslims, while van den Boogert sees "equality" as effectively subjecting the non-Muslims to a raft of new and unfamiliar administrative requirements. These conditions included greater control over permits for the construction and repair of places of worship, the implementation of state-ordained internal reforms of the various communities, and fixing the salaries of members of the various religious hierarchies. In addition, the much-vaunted "equalizing effect" of the abolition of the *jizya* in 1856 was somewhat dampened by the obligation on non-Muslims to pay the *bedel-i ʿaskeri*, or military exemption tax, which, coincidentally, came to the same amount. Finally, in another somewhat perverse attempt to promote equality, the Hatt-i Hümayün of 1856 imposed Islamic inheritance laws on the non-Muslim communities, apparently for the first time. But van den Boogert cautions against regarding Christians and Jews as "victims"; relations between the minorities and the state were "characterised by constant negotiations and renegotiations," and the non-Muslim communities "were not powerless to resist the state."

After 1918

The process of transition out of "millet status" after the First World War was uneven and differed considerably among the various newly created states. It was probably most immediately complex in Lebanon, Palestine, and Syria, particularly in Lebanon, where the changing demography of the various communities from the time of the foundation of the state as well as the inequalities built into the system from its inauguration were some of the principal causes of a long and ferocious civil war.[38] The mandate authorities either did not fully understand or willfully misunderstood the nature of the millet system that they had inherited, causing much misery in the process. It is worth reiterating that, along with many other administrative arrangements that the Ottomans "bequeathed" to France and Britain in Iraq and greater Syria,[39] the roots of the millet system as the Allies inherited it at the end of the First World War lay in the relatively recent past (that is, in the previous fifty to seventy years) rather than "back in the mists of antiquity."

Heterodox Muslims and Non-Arabs in the Arab World

Before discussing the situation of the non-Muslim minorities after 1914, it is important to raise the topic of the heterodox Muslim communities and the non-Arab communities in the last decades of the Ottoman Empire and the years that followed its demise.

First, given the world of national states, populated primarily by Arabs, into which the ex-Ottoman territories outside Anatolia had been transformed after the First World War, the assimilation of fairly substantial numbers of non-Arabs (mostly Kurds) turned out to be not the least of the many "challenges" that these new states faced. As far as the Kurds were concerned, "national feeling" had existed only in very embryonic form in the late nineteenth and early twentieth centuries. In addition, before the First World War, for many, especially the more educated, the best way forward out of poverty and isolation was "to become Ottoman subjects in the fullest sense of the word" and cast aside their "ethno-national identity" by turning themselves into "Turks."[40] Kurdish nationalism would develop more thoroughly in the period after 1918, when modern communications and military technology allowed national armies (and their foreign allies in the case of Iraq) to penetrate into the hitherto largely inaccessible parts of Turkey and Iraq where the Kurds were concentrated and to try to turn them into Iraqi or Turkish citizens, attempts that always aroused bitter and sustained opposition.[41]

In theory, of course, ethnic differences had not been supposed to "count" in the multireligious and multiethnic Ottoman state, and heterodoxy, the second of the categories considered in this section, posed a more serious threat to the polity than ethnicity, especially Shiʿism in the sixteenth century, when the Ottomans and Safavids were fighting each other.[42] In general, however, "the Ottoman Empire was ideologically too heterogeneous and politically too pragmatic [so that] . . . instances of persecution by state authorities should be seen in their specific temporal and political context rather than assumed to be part of a universal anti-Shiʿi impulse."[43] Again in theory, neither the Twelver Shi'a nor members of the various *ghulat*[44] Shi'i sects, particularly the 'Alawites, Druze, and Isma'ilis, were officially recognized as separate communities in the empire in the way that they identified themselves, although the "Shi'i" roots of the beliefs of the Druze and Isma'ilis seem to have been understood and accepted even by their detractors.[45] In contrast, the 'Alawites, who were largely concentrated in tribal communities in the mountainous north-west of what is now Syria, were often treated with contempt by Ottoman administrators[46] and by "Sunni Muslim scholars and chroniclers who placed this minority beyond the pale of . . . formal Shi'i doctrine."[47] Every so often, the state would send punitive expeditions into 'Alawite territory to collect taxes, but just as often it would negotiate with a compliant leader who would collect the tax from the tribes on the state's behalf. In the first "modern" census in Syria taken in 1943, the smaller non-Sunni minorities (Druze, Isma'ilis, and Twelver Shi'i) amounted to 4.3 percent of the population, while the 'Alawites constituted about 11 percent. These percentages are comparable to the figures in a survey taken in 2012, except that the Christians, who formed about 20 percent of the population in 1943, have dropped to about 8 percent because of a process of out-migration that had begun long before the recent upheavals in Syria.[48]

The trajectories of the Shi'a of Lebanon and the Shi'a of Iraq were very different, perhaps reflecting the political institutionalization of the religious sects in Lebanon but not in Iraq. The Lebanese constitution of 1926, which is still largely in force, recognizes eighteen different sects (including 'Alawites, Druze, Isma'ilis, Sunnis, and Shi'a), while Iraqi censuses have always followed (and still follow) the Ottoman practice of lumping all Muslims together, making it impossible to arrive at more than a commonsense estimate of the numbers of Sunnis and Shi'a (or Kurds, for that matter). In the most recent Lebanese census, taken as long ago as 1932, the Sunnis formed 22 percent of the population and the Shi'a 20 percent. Subsequent statistical sampling suggests that the Shi'a are now the largest single community.[49] In addition, their influence has increased immeasurably since the 1932 census, partly owing to demographic growth and partly owing to a deliberate process of institution building that began under the French mandate, with the official recognition of the Shi'a as a *madhhab*[50] in 1926 and the subsequent development of a Ja'fari court system. This was followed by the gradual political mobilization of the Shi'a in the 1960s, the gradual decline of the powers of the "feudal" leaders (the Asads and the 'Usayrans), the dynamic role played by Imam Musa al-Sadr, the formation of Amal and Hizbullah, and the immense impulse given (to Twelver Shi'a everywhere) by the Iranian Revolution.[51] So here we have a community that was once a minority but is no longer. The overall demographic picture of Lebanon, as presented in the *CIA World Factbook* (2014), is that the Christians (as a whole) form 39 percent of the population and the Muslims (including Sunnis, Shi'a, and Druze) 59.7 percent.

Mandatory Syria

Benjamin Thomas White's *The Emergence of Minorities in the Middle East: The Politics of Community in French Mandate Syria*, a particularly thoughtful analysis of the topic, examines how notions of "minority" and "majority" in Syria developed directly in response to Syria's novel status as a nation-state—albeit under mandate—and to the state-building activities of both the French and the Syrians.[52] A form of communal representation in Mount Lebanon had been in place since the institution of the *mutasarrifiya* in 1861,[53] which meant that the "millet-to-minority situation" in Syria was probably the most tangled in the region; about 65 percent of the population were Sunni Muslims, 15 percent non-Sunni Muslims, about 19 percent Christians, and 1 percent Jews. Both the French and members of a variety of Syrian communities sought to exploit the situation of the (generally non-Muslim) minorities to meet their particular needs. For instance, the French "colonial party" considered that one of the main purposes of the French "mission civilisatrice" was to deter the "latent persecuting fanaticism on the part of Syria's Muslims," and of course some members of the "minorities" (including the 'Alawites) did not hesitate to articulate similar views. The French authorities consistently "tried to order Syrian society along religious lines," since they regarded the divisions as "irremediable."[54] Among the more obvious manifestations of these policies was the creation of separate "états" in the Jabal Druze in 1922 and the "territoire des Alaouites" in 1924.[55]

In fact, the term "minority" (rather than "community") began to be used in the Syrian context only in the early 1930s, after Iraq had been admitted to the League of Nations and the French first began to give serious consideration to Syria's eventual progression toward independence.[56] Naturally, the massacres of Assyrian Christians in several villages in northern Iraq by the Iraqi Army in 1933, only a year after Iraqi independence, became a rallying point for calls for the inclusion of minority guarantees in any future Franco-Syrian treaty.[57] White has extremely interesting analyses of notions of belonging and citizenship, the idea of the "national community," and the state and the extension of state authority to more remote regions, especially those areas where the Ottoman state had rarely if ever penetrated. He also discusses the attempts of various ethnic minorities, particularly the Circassians (whose efforts are well documented), to obtain "minority status" as well as linguistic and other privileges. The various ethnic and religious minorities wanted a guaranteed number of seats in parliament and access to state employment in proportion to their numbers.[58] All this activity, it should not be forgotten, was taking place against the background of the gradual creation of an essentially secular nation-state.

Perhaps White's most interesting chapter is his discussion of personal-status law reform, in the course of which the French decided to treat the Sunni Muslims as "another sect among many." This change, perhaps more than anything else, would doom the new law to redundancy. Handily, White has provided his own summary of the argument of his thesis: "The nation-state form creates the objective conditions in which people begin to consider themselves as majorities and minorities: however, these remain subjective categories." So, minorities in their modern form are a product of the nation-state, which has redefined the relationship between population and state: "Because the state now claimed to represent the population, whichever group could constitute itself as the majority could claim the right to define that relationship. Others had more limited rights (whether formally or informally defined), and were constituted as minorities."[59] Although the book is an empirical study of Syria, it evidently has a wider application, both within and outside the Middle East.

Iraq

In the late Ottoman period, the area that is now Iraq consisted of the three Ottoman provinces of Basra, Baghdad, and Mosul, ruled, at least after 1831, by governors sent out from Istanbul. Especially in its farther-flung and less urbanized provinces, the Ottoman state as an institution always relied substantially on informal partnerships with the local land-owning elite.[60] As the Ottoman bureaucracy expanded in the nineteenth century and hereditary landownership gradually became the norm after the introduction of the 1858 Land Law, members of the Sunni Arab nota-bility became part of a bureaucratic and military "aristocracy of service," acting as intermediaries between the Ottoman state and its subjects. As a Sunni institution, the Ottoman Empire had, as has been noted, a some-what ambivalent attitude toward Shi'a, and especially the Shi'a of Iraq, given their growing numbers (largely a consequence of the expulsions of "disobedient tribes" from the Arabian peninsula at the hands of the Wah-habis),[61] their demographic concentration, and their links with Iran.

When the educational reforms of the *tanzimat* arrived in Iraq in the last decades of the nineteenth century, few Shi'a enrolled in the newly established "modern" schools. If they could afford it, Shi'i parents pre-ferred to send their children to private schools run or supervised by the clergy. Again, many Shi'a had a degree of ambivalence toward the state as an institution, and very few of them joined the ranks of the burgeon-ing Ottoman bureaucracy (still less the Ottoman army) between, say, 1870 and 1914. Hence, when the Anglo-Iraqi state was created in 1920, Sunnis continued to supply the main cadres for the administration and the officer corps. They were recruited from the old notable families (which included both urban absentee landlords and tribal leaders in central and western Iraq) and from the ranks of more nouveaux riches (or newly educated) ex-Ottoman officers and officials. The result would be the gross underrep-resentation of Shi'a in proportion to their numbers both in government service and in all the cabinets of the pre-1958 period. It is perhaps worth pointing out that given that 95 percent of the population of Iraq was Mus-lim (in the 1957 census), there were few opportunities either for British or for the non-Muslim minorities themselves to play the "minority card," although in a different context the "Kurdish question" has been one of the constants of recent Iraqi history.

It was also the case that, in their desire to control Iraq, the British (to simplify a much more complex reality) generally found the Sunnis more congenial partners, and for their part both the Sunni aristocracy and the Sunni arrivistes seemed happy enough to transfer their loyalties almost seamlessly from the Ottomans to the British. Faysal, the new king of Iraq, came from a leading Sunni family in the Hijaz, and his principal Iraqi supporters were all Sunnis, recruited partly from the service aristocracy and partly from the ranks of the Ottoman officers and officials who had gathered around him first during the Arab revolt and later during his time as king of Syria. Shi'i interest, or participation, in these activities was of a rather different order and is perhaps best described as "anti-imperialist."[62] Apart from the authority exercised by the tribal leaders, those individuals who molded "Shi'i opinion" at that time consisted almost entirely of members of the clergy. The fact that many Shi'i clergy had been profoundly opposed to the secularizing ideology of the Young Turks did not stop them from rallying to the Ottoman cause as soon as the British landed in southern Iraq at the beginning of the First World War. The 'ulama' of the 'atabat (the holy cities of Karbala and Najaf) declared a jihad against the British and British Indian invaders in November 1914,[63] although it is fair to say that regular Ottoman troops (rather than Arab tribesmen) were responsible for the bulk of the fighting in Iraq.

In the aftermath of the war, the Shi'i leadership was far more interested in "getting the British out" than their Sunni counterparts. Such sentiments were expressed in various petitions submitted to the British occupation authorities in the run-up to the "Revolution of 1920," where the words "independent Arab and Islamic state" or "independent Islamic state" crop up again and again. For their part, British reports routinely portrayed the Shi'i *mujtahids* as extremists, fanatics, and reactionaries, irrevocably opposed to progress and so on, presumably in an attempt to deflect attention from their core demand for *independence*. Eventually, the British and Iraqi authorities prevailed, and the Shi'i *mujtahids* gradually lost their influence, returning to the political arena only in the late 1970s.[64]

However, the struggle for national independence in Iraq under the mandate and monarchy became embedded relatively quickly in a largely secular way of thinking, whether "socialist" or "nationalist." An important by-product of this secularism was that within the new parameters of the nation-state, such people gradually came to feel more conscious of their identity as "Iraqis" than as "Sunnis" or "Shi'a."[65] This sense of national identity gathered increasing momentum with the spread of schools to all parts of the country; after the Second World War, and especially after the Revolution of 1958, sectarian identity began to have much less political and social significance. More specific examples of this "melting pot" tendency are the huge national demonstrations against the Portsmouth Agreement of 1948 and in favor of 'Abd al-Karim Qasim in 1959 and the fact that it was the Shi'a of Kadhimayn who were most prominent of those people who rushed into the streets of Baghdad to defend Qasim's (almost entirely Sunni) government against the Ba'thist coup of February 1963. What would soon distort or destroy the general sense of largely harmonious intersectarian relations would be the growing influence of pan-Arabism and Ba'thism, after the overthrow of the government of 'Abd al-Karim Qasim in 1963, but especially after the Ba'th takeover in 1968.

In some sense, the fact that the Sunnis continued to hold the reins of power during (and long after) the mandate and monarchy in spite of the obvious demographic imbalance—there were always far more Shi'i Arabs than Sunni Arabs—was initially not especially irksome. This was partly because it had long been the case under the Ottomans and partly because, for quite a long time, "the Sunnis" did not, on the whole, discriminate against "the Shi'a."[66] In addition, the surge in the numbers of the educated middle- and lower-middle classes (throughout the 1940s, 1950s, and 1960s) coincided with an equally explosive growth in state employment, the civil service, the teaching profession, and the military. In these circumstances, which coincided with the general process of secularization described above, an individual's sectarian affiliation mattered increasingly less than his or her qualification for any particular job.

In brief, sectarian discrimination of an oppressive kind began to rear its head only in the 1970s, to a greater extent after the Iranian Revolution, and through the war between Iran and Iraq. Things deteriorated further in the 1990s and early 2000s, to the extent that one of the idées fixes of those individuals in charge of the US invasion in 2003 was the determination to order matters for the future in such a way that the Sunni minority would never be able to dominate the Shi'i majority in the way that it had under the Ba'th. As always, the truth was and is rather more nuanced, but this particular obsession led the Americans to create a more or less "Lebanese" sectarian system that had little or no resonance in the experience of modern Iraq.

Millets and Minorities

The main difference between a millet and a "religious minority" in the Arab world is that the first is a feature of the multiethnic Ottoman state that disappeared after the First World War, and the second is an often problematic component of the modern national state. This chapter has attempted to describe some of the pitfalls that took place during the process of transition between the two and has also touched upon the problems of coexistence between orthodox and heterodox Muslims as well as between ethnic majorities and ethnic minorities in the post-Ottoman Middle East. That so many of these problems are still with us can be grasped by comparing the tragic ethnic cleansing that took place as a result of the emergence of new states in the Balkans in the late nineteenth and twentieth centuries with the remarkably similar chain of events that happened in Bosnia only twenty years ago. Both events, alas, were characterized by general international indifference or helplessness or both.

Minorities are not simply a figment of the imagination of their members or of those persons who sympathize with their situation, for whatever reason. The violence in Sri Lanka, or Myanmar, where the ethnic majority persecutes ethnic minorities, shows that such events are not confined to the Arab world; the situation of the Roma in many western European countries shows how very pervasive the problem is. How can the Syrian 'Alawites be protected if Asad is overthrown? How can the remaining Iraqi Christians and Mandaeans be persuaded that they have a future in Iraq? It is difficult to take comfort from previous attempts to "solve" these problems—the Dayton Accords for Bosnia, the Good Friday Accord for Northern Ireland—since none of these states has unified their educational systems, an essential first step if "unity," or even a measure of tolerance, is to be achieved. In addition, the Dayton Accords effectively legitimized and legalized the ethnic cleansing that had recently taken place and upheld the principle of ethnic separation. At the moment, there does not seem to be much light at the end of this long, dark tunnel.

2

Across Confessional Borders

*A Microhistory of Ottoman Christians
and Their Migratory Paths*

JACOB NORRIS

In the year 1880 a young man named Elias Kattan arrived in the city of
Kiev. He had traveled alone from his native town of Bethlehem, leaving
behind his newlywed wife, Negme, and extended family. He had made the
long journey to Kiev, via Istanbul and across the Black Sea to Odessa, in
order to assess commercial opportunities in the Russian Empire. The trip
would prove a great success. Elias quickly opened a shop selling religious
objects on Petchersk Nicolskaia—one of the streets in the major Orthodox
pilgrimage site known as the "Cave Monastery." In the ensuing years Elias
and his sons would establish a permanent presence in Kiev, paving the
way for a small but thriving Palestinian Christian community in the city.

Five years after Elias arrived in Kiev, his cousin Yaqub appeared on
the other side of Europe, in Paris. Along with three other merchants from
Bethlehem, Yaqub's name appears in a petition submitted to the French
Foreign Ministry requesting permission to open a Greek Catholic (or
"Melkite") church. The campaign was eventually successful, and in 1889
the ancient Parisian church of Saint-Julien-le-Pauvre was consecrated as a
Melkite place of worship, complete with a priest appointed by the Melkite
patriarch in Damascus. Today Saint-Julien-le-Pauvre still thrives as a Mel-
kite church, serving a sizable parish of Lebanese, Syrians, and Palestinians.

The curious thing about these two episodes is that the cousins were
neither Orthodox nor Melkite. Rather, they were Roman Catholics, baptized and confirmed in the Latin rites. What had led these two men to Kiev

and Paris, and how did they thrive in religious communities to which they did not belong? In the tradition of the *microstoria* of the 1970s and 1980s, this chapter recounts the experiences of one merchant family as a means of reassessing the role of denomination in the lives of Ottoman Christians.

Since the publication of Edmund Burke and Nejde Yaghoubian's edited volume of nonelite biographies in 1993, historians of the Middle East have been eager to adopt the methodologies of microhistory.[1] Little of this scholarship, however, has focused on Christian life in the Ottoman Empire. As a result, we are left with a rather old-fashioned approach to studying Ottoman Christians—an approach that places denominational politics at the center of the picture. In this paradigm Christians appear as pawns in the wider struggle among Western and Ottoman powers to cement influence in the region.[2] By contrast, relatively little attention is given to the interactions that occurred across denominational boundaries. Studies of the mandate period have begun to break away from this paradigm,[3] but scholarship on the late Ottoman Empire still tends to be organized around the various confessional groupings, examining how they responded to changing sociopolitical circumstances *as discrete communities.*[4]

The expansion and formalization of the Ottoman millet system in the nineteenth century provides the essential historical backdrop to much of this scholarship. Legally, Christians in the empire were now tied more closely to the church authorities of their particular denomination. At the same time, a countervailing pull of nation-based politics became increasingly strong as the nineteenth century wore on. Consequently, when studies of Christians in the Arab provinces of the Ottoman Empire do move away from a denomination-based approach, they tend to do so within the prism of an emergent Arabism, emphasizing the struggles against "foreign" control over various church hierarchies in the region. While this brings to light significant new currents at that time, the daily rhythms of Christians' lives are often subsumed within a picture of elite politics. For most Arabic-speaking Christians in the late nineteenth century, the idea of an Arab nation was an alien concept, irrelevant to their everyday concerns. Nor were their horizons defined by rigid denominational affiliations. Rather, their lives were marked by fluidity across confessional and national borders, by a looseness of identity and a sense of pragmatism in the face of changing economic and geopolitical circumstances.

Examining the uniqueness of this human experience helps further unsettle the category of "minority" as a rigid, age-old form of community in the Arab world. By loosening the historical bond between ecclesiastical-imperial politics and the realm of everyday life, we are able to unburden Ottoman Christians of the principal institutional mechanism that produced them as "minorities": the millet system. Not only were the people studied in this chapter from an area of the Ottoman Empire in which Christians were numerically in the majority (*nahiyat bayt lahm*, or the Bethlehem subdistrict), but it is also futile to characterize their lives in terms of the denominational identities prescribed by the millet system. To the contrary, they actively sought to blur confessional boundaries as a means to achieve their social and economic ends. In the very period in which sectarian identity and rivalry are supposed to have reached new heights in the eastern Mediterranean,[5] this study highlights the increasing irrelevance of church identity to the lives of many Ottoman Christians.

To achieve this uncoupling of people from institutions, we must adopt a more ethnographic approach to history that examines the lives of non-elites at a microlevel. In this regard, the chapter takes its cue from the recent work of Akram Khater, whose illuminating study of one woman, Hindiyya al-'Ujaimi, and her struggle against both the Maronite Church and the Vatican in the eighteenth century has broken new ground in the historiography of Middle Eastern Christians.[6] Echoing Carlo Ginzburg's depiction, in the context of sixteenth-century Italy, of "a peasant religion that had very little in common with that preached by the priest from his pulpit," Khater's study demonstrates microhistory's potential to recast our understanding of Christian practice and identity in the Ottoman Empire.[7] Following Khater's lead, albeit in a later historical epoch, this chapter zooms into the lives of two obscure individuals as a means of reassessing the worldview of certain Ottoman Christians. In the case of nineteenth-century merchants like Elias and Yaqub Kattan, the microhistorical methodology must be combined with a transnational one. In other words, it is imperative to follow the movements of these merchant migrations across imperial and national borders in order to shed light on dynamics within the Ottoman Empire. Rather than representing a world entirely divorced from Ottoman society, the migratory communities in Paris, Kiev, and elsewhere can in fact tell us much about the attitudes of Ottoman Christians. It was precisely when the bonds of authority were loosened in faraway territories that these people displayed a clearer sense of their own self-understanding.

To bring out the individual agency of these actors, the chapter will first need to describe the social conditions that shaped their trajectories. Late Ottoman Bethlehem was marked by an unusually large Roman Catholic population and high rates of migration—conditions that will be explained in order to contextualize the cases of Elias and Yaqub Kattan. The second section will then describe the rise of these two men as successful merchants who traveled the world in the late nineteenth century. The chapter then changes gear to examine the specific campaign to open a Melkite church in Paris as an example of these merchants' very flexible approach to denomination. In this vein the third section focuses on Yaqub Kattan and the motivations that drove his involvement in the campaign. It will be shown that Yaqub and his fellow Bethlehem merchants were part of an emerging "Syrian" Ottoman community in Paris that privileged linguistic and mercantile identities over denominational belonging. Finally, the fourth section switches perspective to Alexis Kateb, the man appointed as the first priest of the Melkite church in Paris. Through Kateb's story we gain further insights into the Syrian community in Paris and the ways it attempted to defy high-church authority. As agents of their own history, these Ottoman Christians understood religious affiliation in their own terms—terms that revolved more around communal belonging and mercantile interests than official church doctrine.

Bethlehem under Ottoman Rule

It is easy to see how Bethlehem's unique status in Christian mythology has rendered it a focal point for sectarian rivalry. If Europeans could reimagine Bethlehem as a place of the mind,[8] then so too could they remake the earthly Bethlehem in their own image. Unlike nearby Jerusalem, the majority of Bethlehem's inhabitants remained Christian from early in the Byzantine period until late in the twentieth century. Bethlehem's status as a Christian stronghold meant the town and its residents became a battle-ground for competing Christian claims to represent the "true faith"—a place where doctrine could be legitimated and reinforced. These tensions frequently assumed international proportions, as witnessed most dramatically in the early 1850s when a series of quarrels between Orthodox and Catholic monks over access to the Nativity Church provided one of the immediate sparks for the Crimean War. Underpinning such disputes was the prestige that control over Bethlehem's holy sites could bestow upon audiences thousands of miles away. The Franciscans' unbroken presence in Bethlehem since the 1300s, for example, was used as an important tool of propaganda in the Catholic struggle to contain the Protestant Reformation in Europe.[9]

The history of Bethlehem in the modern period could, then, be read as the archetypal story of Middle Eastern Christians and their embroilment in wider denominational conflict. But Bethlehem's prominence in the Christian imagination has also produced a very unusual demographic and social picture that renders it unique among Middle Eastern towns. This distinctiveness is manifested in two major and interconnected ways: the diffusion of Roman Catholicism in the town and the extraordinary mobility enjoyed by its inhabitants. Both of these factors impacted heavily the lives of Elias and Yaqub Kattan.

To begin with the first of these features, Bethlehem is unique among Middle Eastern towns in having a Roman Catholic majority since at least the eighteenth century, thanks in part to the proselytizing efforts of the Franciscan order.[10] The Kattan family was undoubtedly caught up in this process of "latinization" in the eighteenth century. The family is held to have migrated in the early Ottoman period from Lebanon to Palestine, settling first in Lydda (al-Ludd) and later in Bethlehem and the neighboring town of Beit Jala. Today those Kattans who trace their roots to Beit Jala largely define themselves as Greek Orthodox, while the Bethlehem branch is Roman Catholic. The Latin Parish archive in Bethlehem is a valuable source for tracing this denominational divergence. The first Kattan to appear in the parish records is Yusef Elias Kattan, born in Beit Jala, 1738, and married to Maria Kattan (the patriarchal lineage of the records means less information is given on women). The fact that neither Elias's marriage nor his baptism was recorded by the Bethlehem parish suggests he moved to Bethlehem in adult life and thenceforth became affiliated with the Catholic Church. Elias and Maria's embrace of Catholicism appears to have been gradual and hesitant: the birth of their first child, Yaqub, was not registered at the Latin parish, but he was later baptized there in 1754. From that point the family seems to have been more closely integrated into the Catholic fold: the births of all seven of their subsequent children are recorded in the archive, as are their baptisms.[11]

Why did the Kattans and many others like them make this switch to Catholicism? A number of localized factors determined this process,[12] but it must also be placed in a wider regional context. Farther north, a major denominational break with the Greek Orthodox (*rum*) Church was occurring in and around the city of Aleppo at exactly the time the Kattans were embracing Catholicism in Bethlehem. As has been well documented, the resulting creation of a separate "Melkite" church (*rum katholik*) produced a distinctly Syrian and Arabic institution that nonetheless felt it expedient to ally with Rome in its struggle against the Greek-dominated Orthodox patriarchate in Istanbul.[13] The new Melkite establishment fostered a local, vernacular form of Eastern Orthodoxy, allowing their members to take mass in Arabic and opening the clergy to local representation.

The Melkites went on to establish major bases in northern Palestine, particularly in Acre and the Galilee region, but their penetration of the southern half of Palestine has remained limited to this day. In Bethlehem a Melkite church was not established until 1964, and in the British census of 1922 Melkites in the town numbered only 155, compared to 2,696 Roman Catholics and 2,285 Greek Orthodox.[14] In the early eighteenth century, therefore, Christians in Bethlehem disgruntled with Greek-dominated Orthodoxy had no homegrown alternative. Instead, the most obvious option would have been the well-entrenched Franciscan community and their specifically *Roman* Catholic rites.

As with the Melkites in Syria and northern Palestine, the ability to use Arabic as a language of prayer must count as an important factor in the Franciscans' success in Bethlehem. Franciscan correspondence confirms that prayers were being conducted in Arabic in the Roman Catholic chapel as early as 1678.[15] Viewing this use of vernacular as the key to attracting further converts, the Franciscan friars fretted over the lack of Arabic skills possessed by their clergy, requesting greater training be provided by the Propaganda Fide in Rome.[16] One priest in particular, a Bosnian named Marc'Angelo di Seraglio, was highly esteemed by the local population in Bethlehem and appears to have played a key role in expanding the Catholic congregation in the late seventeenth century, precisely because he was well versed in the Arabic language.[17]

Although it would be wrong to see in this process the seeds of Arab nationalism, the attraction of the Catholic Church in Bethlehem can nevertheless be located as part of a wider drive to establish greater local autonomy over Christian life in the Ottoman Empire. More specifically, this process conforms to Bruce Masters's description of "the pull of localism" in the context of the emergent Melkite community in eighteenth-century Aleppo: the belief among the merchant middle class that local representation in the church would further their political and economic interests.[18] In Bethlehem the late seventeenth and early eighteenth centuries saw an increase in European, particularly French, involvement in Ottoman economic affairs. In Bethlehem, as well as elsewhere in the empire, lucrative rewards were on offer for local merchants as interpreters, or dragomans, of European consuls and traders. Under the emerging system of capitulations, these local intermediaries could themselves be granted extralegal status as subjects of the European powers. In Bethlehem the adoption of Roman Catholicism was a route to gaining such status. It was in this period that the *tarajmeh* (translators) quarter of the town emerged as one of Bethlehem's seven "historic quarters." Although the spread of Roman Catholicism was not confined to this quarter, a disproportionate number of the town's increasingly affluent merchant class were drawn from the *tarajmeh*.[19] But this chapter goes one step further than the localism thesis, arguing that denomination was an altogether more pliable concept for Bethlehem's merchants. Examples exist from as early as the 1690s whereby the same individual is classified as *rum* in Ottoman surveys while claiming membership in the Latin Catholic Church when corresponding with the Franciscan friars.[20]

By the late nineteenth century, the tendency had become decidedly commonplace. The second most noticeable feature of Bethlehem society, its high rates of migration, was in full flow by this stage. Fanning out to all corners of the globe, Bethlehem's expanding merchant class enjoyed remarkable success in the late 1800s. Typically, they began by selling religious objects produced in Bethlehem: crosses, rosaries, and a host of other devotional goods. Once a foothold in a new market was established, they often branched out into a bewildering array of import-export lines, many of them accruing considerable wealth in the process.

Merchants on the Move

At this point we pick up the story of the cousins Elias and Yaqub Kattan, first introduced at the start of the chapter. Like so many of their Bethlehem brethren, they both started out their merchant careers by trading in religious objects produced in their hometown. This point should be placed in the wider context in which Ottoman Christians had risen to economic prominence through the eighteenth and nineteenth centuries as intermediaries in the empire's increased trade with western Europe. Frequently, this trade had entailed a subsequent decline in the older Jewish and Muslim merchant families who had occupied the middleman position in many of the older overland trade routes through the Ottoman Empire.[21] Importantly, Christians' new role as facilitators of international and interreligious trading also helped break down many of the denominational barriers that had previously governed their lives—exactly the process that is described here at the microlevel.

In Bethlehem the route into a merchant career in the eighteenth and nineteenth centuries would almost certainly involve trading in locally produced religious objects. A particular specialty of the Bethlehem artisans was carving in olive wood and mother-of-pearl—practices with long roots in the region that had been gradually adapted to European tastes under the Franciscan influence. By the nineteenth century mother-of-pearl had become the dominant raw material in the Bethlehem industry, imported mainly from the Red Sea.[22] Importantly, the highly specialized artisanship that produced these items was unique to Bethlehem and carried the added attraction of the "made in the Holy Land" label.

Before he made his long journey to Kiev in 1880, Elias Kattan had already established himself as a successful merchant in Bethlehem with a shop just off the Manger Square, selling religious objects to tourists and pilgrims. His status at this time can be gleaned from his mother's *shat-weh*—a form of female head wear unique to Bethlehem into which were sewn coins and other valuable items as "family insurance." Still preserved by Elias's descendants today, his mother's *shatweh* includes twelve gold pieces as well as a Polish coin dating from the 1870s.[23]

It was thus as a relatively successful trader in Bethlehem's mother-of-pearl religious objects that Elias traveled to Kiev in 1880. Once arrived there he quickly sought to replicate the formula that had brought rewards in Bethlehem. Just as his store in Bethlehem was located next to the Nativity Church to catch pilgrims on their way in and out, so too did he set up shop in the vicinity of Kiev's most visited shrine—the Pechersk Lavra (Cave Monastery). What is most interesting about this enterprise is that Elias was now catering to an exclusively Orthodox market. Raised as a Roman Catholic, it might be imagined he found this switch problematic, both in commercial and in spiritual terms. But all available evidence suggests the contrary. Surviving records of his business dealings in Kiev show how he adapted his trade to the Russian market, commissioning the Bethlehem artisans to produce items such as icons that catered specifically to Orthodox sensibilities.[24]

As the business in Kiev flourished, the Kattans further adapted and ingratiated themselves into Orthodox Russian society. Evidence of their doing so can be found in the Russian-style icon given to the family by the Orthodox patriarch of Kiev in 1910, which today hangs on the wall of Elias's great-grandson's home in Amman. By 1910 Elias's eldest son, Yaqub, had taken the lead role in the business, greatly expanding the range of products they sold. Among the thousands of items listed in the Kattan and Son catalogs are various kinds of incense designed for use in Orthodox churches. The incense was imported from Singapore and Yemen, purchased from the famous al-Sagoff (or al-Saqqaf) merchant family—one of the most successful Hadrami Arab trading dynasties in Southeast Asia.[25] It can be speculated the Kattans utilized the expanding networks of Bethlehem traders in Southeast Asia to establish these connections with al-Saqqaf.[26] But the salient point for this chapter is the ease with which a Catholic family could move between denominational identities to further its economic standing in the Orthodox Russian Empire.

How did the Kattans make this switch to the Russian market with such apparent ease? The answer lies in Bethlehem's status as a magnet for foreign visitors. When Elias Kattan first arrived in Kiev, he would have needed a ready supply of Bethlehem goods that appealed to the Russian market. Rather than start a new trend in Russian-style carvings in Bethlehem, it is likely he took with him to Kiev a sample of goods that had already been adapted to Russian taste. A considerable literature on the growing Russian presence in late-nineteenth-century Palestine documents the exponential growth in Russian pilgrimage to the Holy Land in that period.[27] Contemporary accounts such as the memoir of Bertha Vester, resident in Jerusalem's American colony in the 1880s, show the impact this influx exerted on the local economy: "[Russian pilgrims] created a demand for all kinds of trinkets, and many kinds of industries in the manufacture of souvenirs gave occupation to the inhabitants of Jerusalem and Bethlehem. . . . Then there were the makers of ikons and mother-of-pearl and olivewood trinkets."[28] By reconstructing the pathways of individuals like Elias Kattan, the very top-heavy historiography of Russian influence in Palestine can be balanced out with a better appreciation of how this heightened foreign presence was received and exploited by a local population eager to seek out new economic opportunity.

By the 1910s the Kattan family business in Kiev had diversified into a wide array of import-export lines and was making the switch from retail to wholesale. Prominent among the products they now stocked were glass lenses, fabrics, and jewelry. They still sold numerous types of Christian devotional objects, but they were now mostly imported from manufacturers in Europe and Paris in particular. Indeed, the French capital looms large in the business dealings of Bethlehemites in this period, seemingly replacing Bethlehem as the trading "center" of the various merchant "colonies" around the world.

In the case of the Kattans in Kiev, the family utilized the presence of family members in Paris to cement these trade links. Yaqub Kattan, the cousin of Elias who was introduced at the start of this chapter, appears to have played an important role in that process. The surviving business records of the Kiev shop show dealings with a number of companies and individuals with whom Yaqub shared an intimate acquaintance. Included among them was the Maison Picard—one of the most successful jewelers of late-nineteenth-century Paris, which will be discussed below.[29] The Kattan family records also include fragments of correspondence between Yaqub and Elias in the 1890s in which they discussed new lines of Paris jewelry, presumably for sale in the Kiev shop.[30]

There is no evidence, however, that Yaqub ever settled in Paris on a long-term basis. Rather, he pursued a more complex migratory path, constantly moving between locations in the 1880s. In 1886 he appeared in Paris as one of four signatories on the petition to open a Melkite church in Paris. Having received this petition, the French Foreign Ministry asked the Police Prefecture in Paris to provide further information on the signatories.[31] The resulting reports provide important information on the individuals involved and the very global world of commerce they inhabited. All four of them were from Bethlehem, yet none of them belonged to the Melkite denomination.

Yaqub Kattan was listed in the report as married with one child and permanently domiciled in his country of birth (Ottoman Palestine). The report states he was a "trader in religious objects" who was "travelling on business." He had arrived in Paris from New York on April 13 that year and then left again on May 23 for Liverpool. Through the reports on the other three petitioners we learn they were headed to Liverpool to sell their wares at the International Exhibition of Navigation, Commerce, and Industry, held in the English port city that month. Finally, the report on Yaqub concludes, "The information collected on M. Cattan was not unfavourable to him."[32]

These snippets of information are brief yet revealing. At this time, most migration out of Bethlehem was temporary and transient. Typically, it consisted of young men like Yaqub leaving their wives and children in Bethlehem to carry out business reconnaissance trips. Yaqub was clearly on one of these extended trips in the spring of 1886, leaving his wife and child back in Bethlehem while he sought new markets for the trade in religious objects. This business travel follows a similar pattern to his cousin Elias's early forays into the Russian market. There is no evidence that Elias's wife ever visited Kiev, and it was only over the next two generations that more permanent settlement can be detected.[33] When Elias's eldest son (also named Yaqub) took over the family business, he gradually began to relocate his family to Kiev, to the extent that the youngest of his four children, Nicola, was born there in 1909.[34]

We also glean from the French police reports that in 1886, Yaqub Kattan, cousin of Elias, was on a journey that took in New York, Paris, and Liverpool. It was the age of the transatlantic steamships, and in the 1880s competition between the various lines had intensified considerably.[35] The French Compagnie Générale Transatlantique put four new "super steamers" into action the very year Yaqub made his journey (1886), all of which plied the New York–Le Havre route.[36] It was on this route that Yaqub traveled to Paris in April that year, indicating the extent to which the mobility of these merchants intersected with the new age of steam travel. The inclusion of Liverpool in his itinerary, meanwhile, confirms one of the most frequently voiced explanations of this migration among Bethlehemites today: that the numerous world's fairs of the period provided a key point of entry into new markets. First among the fairs is held to be the 1853 Exhibition of the Industry of All Nations in New York, attended by the Bethlehem brothers Jiries and Ibrahim Handal, who are today celebrated as the first Bethlehemites to sell mother-of-pearl abroad.[37] From this point, subsequent exhibitions in Philadelphia (1876), Chicago (1893), and St. Louis (1904) are said to have provided a springboard for the larger-scale Arab migrations to the Americas, particularly Latin America in the case of Palestinians.[38]

The value of the Paris correspondence lies partly in reorienting our understanding of these activities away from an overly American-centric perspective. The exhibition at Liverpool was part of a circuit of European trade fairs that included Antwerp the previous year (1885) as well as the Colonial and Indian Exhibition held in London earlier in 1886. Most famously, the circuit incorporated Paris in 1889 in the form of the Exposition Universelle, an event attended by a number of Bethlehem merchants. The mobility and transience of these early Bethlehem migrants cannot be understood within purely national (US) or even continental (North American) boundaries. Yaqub Kattan was not traveling westward across the Atlantic to find a new home; rather, he was moving in the opposite direction, traversing the globe in search of new trading opportunities.

The First Arab Church in Paris

Yaqub Kattan's sojourn in Paris in 1886 was clearly not his first time in the French capital. He felt sufficiently affiliated to a wider community of Christian "Syrians" (in today's terms, Syrians, Lebanese, Palestinians, and Jordanians) to act as one of their spokespeople in the campaign to open a Melkite church in the city. His address in Paris was listed as 11 rue des Quatres Fils in the Temple District, where the Syrian community was clustered at that time. In the petition itself, the Bethlehem merchants state: "There are many of us orientals here in Paris and we carry out much business in your city, buying a great deal for export to all the countries of the world, and this obliges us to stay in Paris."[39]

Within this community Yaqub belonged to a distinct subgroup of Bethlehem merchants, bound together by ties of kinship and profession. The other three petitioners, all from Bethlehem, were also listed as "traders in religious objects," and more specifically those items made from mother-of-pearl and olive wood.[40] One of the other signatories, Giries (Georges) Kattan, was a distant cousin of Yaqub's, while the other two, Yaqub Abu Za'rur and Yaqub Jacaman, were brothers-in-law residing at the same address in Paris, 5 rue Chapon, near Yaqub Kattan's residence.

This sense of a tight-knit community incorporating family bonds helps explain the specific connections between Paris and the Kattan business in the Russian Empire. Elias Kattan used his cousin's connections in Paris to help establish new trading partners for his business in Kiev. The importance of this networking was particularly evident with the Parisian jewelry Elias began to sell in his Kiev shop in the 1900s, as will be seen below. But the question remains: why did Yaqub Kattan, a Roman Catholic, front the campaign to open a Melkite church in Paris?

In answering this question, we might adopt the traditional historical approach that sees these Ottoman Christians as pawns in a greater game of politics and denominational rivalries. We might well choose to focus on the French Foreign Ministry and its consistent emphasis on the "political interest" of the project.[41] The Melkite Syrians in both France and the Ottoman Empire had long been viewed as a wedge for French interests in the eastern Mediterranean, and the opening of a church in Paris was viewed by the Foreign Ministry as an opportunity to wield greater influence over the community.[42] When it became clear the Melkite patriarch in Damascus was backing the project, the project acquired further appeal in the eyes of government ministers. As one letter from the interior minister in 1888 stressed, "This affair has been recommended by the foreign minister who sees a great interest in granting the request of the Patriarch."[43] But such a perspective overlooks how the Melkite church campaign was understood by those individuals who proposed it. When viewed from their perspective, the affair takes on very different meanings, showing the extent to which these Ottoman Christians could slip across denominational boundaries.

The obvious way this confessional elasticity was manifested was in the fact that none of the Bethlehem petitioners were themselves Melkite. In response to this point, it might be said that they were nonetheless part of the same broadly "uniate" church. In this explanation the Bethlehemites in Paris defined themselves as much by who they were not—that is, Orthodox—as by their specific church group. But such an explanation does not fully capture the fluidity of these merchants' religious identity. We have already seen that Bethlehemites from the same family in a different context—the Kattans in Kiev—were quite willing to adopt Orthodox customs and motifs to further their business interests and ultimately settle in the Russian Empire. Furthermore, there were no shortage of Latin Catholic churches in Paris for the Bethlehem merchants to choose from. Instead, they chose to identify with a different church altogether, to which they did not formally belong. Why?

Part of the answer lies in a sense of wider community among Syrians in Paris at that time. Within this community it would have been natural and easy for men like Yaqub Kattan to gravitate toward the Melkite Christian population. As Ian Coller has shown, Melkites were found in disproportionate numbers among the early Arab migrants to France, and especially those individuals who accompanied Napoleon's armies back to Europe after the failed campaigns in Egypt and Syria of 1798–1800.[44] From that time onward, they had established a well-entrenched presence in France, particularly in Paris. Not only would Bethlehemites like Yaqub have related to this community through religion (Christianity) and language (Arabic), but the Melkites also had a long and successful history as merchants whose trading networks stretched all over Europe, the eastern Mediterranean, and as far as South Asia. Indeed, like the Bethlehemites, they had been traveling and trading in France long before the Napoleonic campaigns of the late eighteenth century.[45]

It was these common experiences that made the Melkite community a natural base for merchants passing through Paris like Yaqub Kattan. Little has been written about Syrians (or Arabs more generally) living in Paris in the late nineteenth century. There currently exists a historical gap between the early-nineteenth-century community described by Ian Coller and the Arab political meetings that took place in Paris in the wake of the Ottoman Constitutional Revolution of 1908.[46] From the French police reports, we learn that a discernible Syrian Arab community existed in Paris in the 1880s. Geographically, this population was centered in the Temple District in the Third Arrondissement. The Bethlehem petitioners were resident in that same area and in particular on rue Chapon, from where the petition itself was written. These geographical details give a sense of a small but well-defined Syrian community in Paris into which the Bethlehem merchants inserted themselves. It was logical, then, that the initial petition proposed that the Melkite church be located in the Temple District.[47]

By the 1890s better documentary evidence exists to show that Bethlehem families were settling in Paris on a longer-term basis, particularly on the boulevard de Strasbourg—again just a short walk from the Square du Temple.[48] Back in the mid-1880s this community was still taking shape and was largely indistinguishable from the wider Syrian population. In the French police correspondence, the Bethlehem petitioners are intriguingly described as *marchands Homans* who were "originally from Palestine." In reality, all four of the petitioners were born and brought up in Bethlehem, and there is no evidence of any connection to the Syrian city of Homs. In the eyes of the French police, these individuals had merged into a wider group of transitory merchants that may well have included people from Homs. "These merchants," continued the same letter, "number around 25 or 30. Their stay in Paris is relatively short, usually lodging in the Temple district. It is believed that they would prolong their stay in Paris if they managed to build a chapel of their communion which would serve as their central meeting point."[49]

In these lines we find the central factors driving the petition for a Melkite church in Paris. Here was an emerging community of merchants who saw their religious identity in fluid yet highly practical terms. Whether the majority of the twenty-five to thirty individuals in question were Melkites is not clear. What is certain, however, is that the Melkite denomination, with its affiliation to Rome and long-standing history of cooperation with French interests, was highly acceptable to the French government. Lobbying for a Melkite church would therefore have been an obvious way for Yaqub Kattan and his associates to formalize their presence in Paris and thus further their commercial interests.

Looking at the explicit arguments made by the Bethlehem petitioners, we gain further insights into their willingness to identify with the Melkite denomination. The campaign was framed specifically within a linguistic context, as the petitioners urged the need to conduct church services in "our language" (meaning Arabic). As evidence they gave the example of a recent death in the community, leading to the problem of not being able to find a priest who could conduct the funeral service in Arabic.[50] This situation again demonstrates the parallels between the emergence of the Melkite church in Syria and the spread of Roman Catholicism in Bethlehem. In both cases the "breakaway group" had become accustomed to conducting church services in the local vernacular (Arabic)—something that contrasted strongly with the Greek liturgy of the Orthodox Church. As Roman Catholics who were noted for their linguistic versatility, the Bethlehemites might have been expected to attend French Catholic church services in Paris. But the Melkite petition shows that Arabic remained a central part of their identity and that it overrode any official denominational belonging.

The Parisian Periphery of Melkite Authority

There is another dimension to the story of the Parisian Melkite church that sheds further light on how Ottoman Christians forged their own understandings of denomination when the bonds of ecclesiastical control were loosened. In this version of the story, the Bethlehem merchants were not the prime movers behind the campaign to open a Melkite church in Paris; rather, their respectability in the eyes of the French authorities was utilized by a man named Alexis Kateb, the first priest, or *archimandrite*, of the Paris Melkite church. Far from being a faithful enforcer of official Melkite doctrine, Alexis Kateb would run into direct confrontation with his superiors in Syria, demonstrating in the process a looser interpretation of denominational belonging.

Born in Damascus in 1856, Kateb established himself in the Melkite church as secretary to the archbishop of Beirut. In 1886 he was sent, like many promising young Melkite intellectuals from the region, to work in France as an instructor in languages at the Capuchin college of friars in Lyon.[51] It was in this same year that the four Bethlehem merchants submitted their petition for a Melkite church in Paris. When it became clear in August 1888 that a suitable church had been identified at Saint-Julien-le-Pauvre, the Melkite patriarch, Gregory II Yousef, was called upon by the French government to make his nomination. Writing to the French interior minister, he endorsed Kateb as the preferred candidate, describing him as "one of the best subjects of our clergy."[52]

Kateb's position at the Capuchin college in Lyon made him the right man at the right time in the eyes of Patriarch Gregory. But subsequent French intelligence reports tell an intriguing story of how Kateb deviated from the intended script. By the end of August 1888, he had arrived in Paris to pave the way for his appointment. Once established in the capital, he showed an impressive but ultimately destructive ability to ingratiate himself into high-society life. His key contact was a certain "Madame Picard," the wife of one of the Picard merchant jewelers who had risen to prominence in that period.[53] According to the police reports, Picard's clientele in Paris included "the most influential members of the Syrian community," who presumably included the Bethlehem merchants.[54] But the Picard connections extended much further, taking in the Kattan traders in the Russian Empire. The surviving papers of Elias Kattan and Son in Kiev show orders placed in the 1910s with "Picard et Cie" for shipments of "jewellery, rosaries and crosses."[55] Having moved beyond the initial stage of selling Bethlehem-produced religious products, the Kattan enterprise in Kiev found it more profitable in the 1910s to import similar products

from French producers, hinting at the French capital's usurpation of Bethlehem as the trading center of this merchant diaspora.

For Kateb, the Picard connection smoothed his passage to the leadership of the Melkite community in Paris. Not only did Picard give him
access to the most prominent Syrian merchants (presumably including
the Bethlehemites), but the police reports also state it was Madame Picard
who traveled to Syria to obtain authorization from Patriarch Gregory for
the church. But his relations with both Picard and the patriarchate in Syria
quickly broke down once he was installed as the Melkite priest in Paris.
When he began frequenting a certain salon on rue Montaigne run by the
Comtesse de Brimont, Madame Picard and her entourage were said to be
"shocked by the salon's somewhat free manner."[56]

The precise cause of this fallout remains unclear. The Comtesse de
Brimont was certainly renowned for the extravagance of her parties: one
account describes her making an entrance "with live animals disporting
themselves in her gown."[57] Whatever the reasons for Picard's disapproval,
Kateb's association with the comtesse set off a chain of events that led to
his removal as the Melkite priest in Paris by Patriarch Gregory in October
1892, replaced by the altogether more reliable Ignace Homsy.[58] But rather
than submit to Gregory's orders and return to the Ottoman Empire, Kateb
remained in Paris for almost three years before eventually being subjected
to a Foreign Ministry expulsion order in January 1895.[59] During those
years he seems to have occupied a position as unofficial priest to the Syrian
community in Paris, while also pursuing a political career. Despite Kateb's
being ostracized by the church at Saint-Julien-le-Pauvre, the police reports
state he continued to garner support from the Syrian community and particularly among the women who were said to call on him for "spiritual
guidance." When charges of fraud and money laundering were brought
against Kateb, several "prominent members" of the Syrian community
testified in his favor. Likewise, when he was stripped of his earnings, he
relied upon "the generosity of his compatriots and co-religionists" to support himself.[60]

When he was finally forced to leave France in 1895, he traveled to Cairo
to beg the pardon of the Melkite patriarch. Having apparently obtained it,
he was granted a new position in Rome as procurator of the Melkite Order

of St. Basil. Despite being barred by both the patriarchate and the French government from reentering France, Kateb was determined to return to his beloved Paris. In April 1900 he journeyed to the capital, where he celebrated mass at Saint-Julien-le-Pauvre and was even permitted to give a sermon.[61] Greatly angered by this act of defiance, the Melkite patriarch complained to the French authorities, ordering the priest in Paris to summon Kateb immediately. This time, however, Kateb acted swiftly and was already on his way back to Rome by the time the orders arrived.[62]

On January 1, 1889, the ancient church of Saint-Julien-le-Pauvre in the Fifth Arrondissement on the Left Bank of the Seine was formally consecrated as a Melkite church. The establishment of a new "Eastern" parish in Paris attracted a good deal of attention. Joris-Karl Huysmans was among those individuals who voiced their objections, claiming the church represented "an intrusion of the Levant" that was "in absolute disagreement with the surroundings."[63] Generally, however, the reception was favorable. Many of the national newspapers, from *Le Monde* to *La Vérité*, ran stories on the church's opening, emphasizing the Melkites' communion with Roman Catholicism as well as their political ties to France.[64] As *Le Gaulois* later reported on one of the church services: "Numerous prelates, friars and priests of the Latin Church took part in the ceremony, affirming the ever closer union between the two churches."[65]

Seen from this angle, the story of the Parisian Melkite church could be read as another example of the co-option of Ottoman Christians in the interests of European colonial ambition. The church's first priest, Alexis Kateb, seems to be a case in point. He receives brief mention in numerous historical works, but only in the context of his political activities in Paris.[66] During his three years as persona non gratis (1892–95) in Paris, he published a short book titled the *Oeuvre patriotique de propagation de la foi Chretienne et de la penetration Francaise en Syrie et dans tout l'Orient*, apparently in an effort to win back the favor of the French government and thus remain in the city. He even briefly published a weekly newspaper in both Arabic and French named *al-Raja'/l'Esperance* with a similar agenda of promoting French influence in Ottoman Syria.[67]

In this picture Ottoman Christians living in France appear as a French wedge through which wider agendas could be enacted, or as "vectors" of an emergent Arab nationalism. But such characterizations miss the individual agency of the people who helped establish the Melkite church at Saint-Julien-le-Pauvre. Far from being mere pawns in the "great game," they pursued their own interests that often diverged wildly from their political and religious superiors. At times their stories provide glimpses of life beneath the surface of national, imperial, and ecclesiastical politics, revealing a well-established Syrian community in Paris that still maintained strong ties to the Ottoman Empire. Elias and Yaqub Kattan paid little attention to confessional boundaries in their constant search for new markets. Indeed, they often deliberately transgressed these boundaries in the name of commercial expansion. In the case of Alexis Kateb, meanwhile, the manner in which he was supported by the wider Syrian community in Paris after his formal sacking as the priest at Saint-Julien-le-Pauvre demonstrates that church leaders, even when supported by colonial governments, could not guide the religious practices of their subjects so easily. Particularly striking in Kateb's story is the extent to which Syrian women in Paris, a group largely invisible in other sources, seem to have prioritized familiarity and personal acquaintance over official church authority.

Most of all, the microhistories of these individuals reveal a world in which borders, both geographical and denominational, were constantly transgressed. Consequently, we are forced to reassess our image of Ottoman Christians being neatly divided into discrete "minority" communities. Far from the centers of ecclesiastical power in Damascus, Jerusalem, or Istanbul, these wandering merchants and clergymen had more freedom to define their religious affiliations on their own terms. Rather than representing a world completely disconnected from the Ottoman Empire, the migratory communities of Paris and Kiev provide us with opportunities to study the attitudes of relatively low-level Ottoman Christians. As the work of Akram Khater and Sarah Gualtieri has already shown us in other arenas of Arab migration, the frequent movement of these people in and out of the Ottoman Empire meant their experiences abroad can feed back into our understandings of Ottoman society.[68]

Bethlehem was in many ways an exceptional Ottoman town, marked by its unique combination of Roman Catholicism and high levels of migration. But the tendency of its residents to defy denominational categorization was not so unusual. Like Melkites in Aleppo, Maronites in Mount Lebanon, or indeed other religious groups in the empire, their ambitions rarely overlapped neatly with the aspirations of the high clergy or colonial policy makers. Denominational identity was certainly an important factor in these people's lives, but rarely was it conceived in the same rigid terms as the missionaries and imperial officials who sought to control them. The precise ways in which notions of kinship, economic interest, and linguistic affiliation mapped onto these religious practices require much closer historical attention. This project is by no means limited to intra-Christian relations. In Bethlehem the deeply embedded but often uneven relations between a Christian majority and a Muslim minority upset many of the established notions of "minority life" in the Middle East.[69] Likewise, the frequency with which Bethlehem's merchants established trading links with Jews in the Ottoman Empire is further evidence of the fluidity of religious relations in the pre-Zionist period.

When their interests were threatened by an overly dogmatic church clergy, Bethlehem's merchant migrants were not shy of voicing their protest. When Elias Kattan's son Yaqub settled permanently in Kiev, he still insisted his children be schooled back in Palestine. But rather than send his youngest son, Nicola, to a Catholic school, he chose the Anglican St. George's school in Jerusalem—something that was common at the time, not just among non-Anglican Christians, but also among middle-class Muslims.[70] When the Latin priest in Bethlehem threatened to ex-communicate Nicola in 1919, Yaqub was incensed. He wrote to the Latin patriarch of Jerusalem, reminding him of the family's considerable economic standing in Bethlehem and stating that he was "willing to adopt the Orthodox or Protestant rites as a counter-measure."[71]

Not all Ottoman Christians could transgress confessional boundaries with the defiance shown by the Kattan cousins and Alexis Kateb in the late nineteenth and early twentieth centuries. Indeed, the Kattans may be regarded as an unusually mobile and eventually very successful family of migrant merchants. But microhistory, in its truest form, has never aimed to provide explanations of an indiscriminate majority. Rather, its individual case studies are often chosen from outside the mainstream, precisely because they interrogate and challenge the generalized theories posited by macrohistory. The examples raised in this chapter are designed to do just that. They do not provide a comprehensive explanation of the role played by denomination in the lives of Ottoman Christians. Instead, they raise questions about the prevailing methods used by historians of Christians in the Middle East and the conclusions they have drawn. For too long, these people have been discussed through the lens of missionaries, imperialists, and nationalists. When viewed in their own terms, the picture begins to look very different. Perhaps more confusing, but different nonetheless.

3

Becoming a Sectarian Minority

Arab Christians in Twentieth-Century Palestine

LAURA ROBSON

Early-twentieth-century Palestine was home to a remarkably integrated Muslim and Christian Arab middle class: highly literate, primarily urban, interested in emerging conversations about political independence, and, increasingly, vocally anti-Zionist. Arab Christians constituted approximately 10 percent of Palestine's population, but made up a much higher proportion of the urban bourgeoisie who were rapidly emerging as its political and intellectual leaders. Though communal identification impacted political, social, and economic roles in Ottoman Palestine, it did not define or dictate them in an absolute way, and Christians made up an important part of the emerging Palestinian Arab political elite.

When the British entered Jerusalem in 1917, they brought with them a very particular conception of Palestine, viewing it as a biblical "Holy Land" to which Western Christians had a special claim. They also brought a system of colonial governance, devised first in India, which relied heavily on maintaining clear religious and ethnic divisions among their colonial subjects for the purpose of averting the growth of secular nationalism. Furthermore, the new mandate government was charged with the task of promoting a "Jewish National Home" in Palestine for European Zionists, a policy that aroused further hostility from an almost entirely Arab population who viewed the Zionist project as an extension of European imperial ambition in the Middle East. All these considerations led the mandate government toward a mode of governance in Palestine in which the legal and political rights of its inhabitants were tied to their communal identifications, and colonial subjects were clearly categorized into "majorities" and "minorities" whose interests were declared separate and potentially discordant.

This colonial crafting of sectarianized minorities had especially deleterious consequences for Palestine's Arab Christians. The British promotion of sectarian political identities deliberately separated Christians, whose commitment to secularist nationalism, vocal anti-Zionism, and ties to international Christian institutions constituted a potentially serious challenge to the colonial state's mandate, from the rest of Palestinian Arab (Muslim) society, weakening their influence. The colonial creation of legal and political sectarian identities for Palestinian citizens transformed Palestine's Arab Christians from integral members of a multireligious middle class into a legally defined religious minority. Given the subsequent popular portrayal of Christians in Palestine-Israel as a shrinking and struggling "minority," it is worth investigating how it was largely the structures of the British colonial state that moved Arab Christians in Palestine from a position of integration and leadership to one of exclusion and marginalization.

Palestine as the "Holy Land"

The British interest in Palestine, which eventually led to their military occupation of Jerusalem in 1917 and assumption of the mandate in 1920, was rooted in a nineteenth-century imagining of the region as historically and spiritually central to Western Protestantism. This Protestant vision viewed Palestine, and particularly Jerusalem, as naturally belonging, in both a cultural and a political sense, to the "international community" by virtue of its central place in the theological worldviews of Muslims, Christians, and Jews. Protestants in Britain and the United States used this argument to legitimize British imperial control over Palestine and, later, to justify international intervention in the growing conflict between the new state of Israel and the dispossessed Palestinian Arabs.

From the beginning, the presence of indigenous Arab Christian communities in Palestine complicated this Protestant narrative. In order to make a specifically Christian claim over Jerusalem and Palestine more broadly, it was necessary to explain away or delegitimize the Christian community already in place. The British in Palestine during the nineteenth century did so in two ways. First, they drew a distinction between the "degenerate" forms of Orthodox Christianity, which they associated with Catholicism and "papism," and the "pure" Christianity practiced by Western Protestants. This differentiation allowed British Protestants to make the claim that the Christian history of Jerusalem could properly be understood as part of the cultural legacy and heritage of Europe rather than the Middle East, a concept related to the broader realm of Orientalist scholarship situating the ancient history of Mesopotamia and Egypt as a precursor to Greece, Rome, and Europe rather than to the Ottoman Empire and the modern Middle East. Second, they focused on the ancient Jewish history of Palestine, drawing a direct link between the sites of the Old Testament and the contemporary Western Christian experience and pointing toward the ways in which Zionism would come to operate as an entry point for Western Christian claims over Palestine during the twentieth century.

Nineteenth-century British incursions into Palestine primarily took the form of either mission work or archaeological exploration. Early British missions in Palestine were composed mainly of evangelical Protestants who stood some way outside the structures of church and state power in the metropole.[1] The first British missionary group to send representatives to Palestine was the Church Missionary Society, founded in 1799 by a group of evangelical members of the Church of England known as the "Clapham Sect," after the neighborhood where many of its members resided. The members of the CMS, led by the Reverend Josiah Pratt, concerned themselves not only with global evangelization but also with domestic issues of social reform and, crucially, with promoting the abolition of slavery.

The CMS defined itself primarily in opposition to Catholicism. Discussions of CMS missionary activity in the Ottoman Empire during these early years explicitly promoted the idea of a Protestant presence in Palestine as combating the "popish" practices of Catholic missionaries there. In 1812 the CMS report suggested hopefully that "the Romish Church is manifesting gradual dissolution" and that its "scattered members" could be replaced by a "United Church of England and Ireland."[2] The CMS leadership also noted that the Catholics had "set us an example in planting the cross wherever commerce of the sword had led the way, which may put to shame British Protestants."³ Similarly, the CMS saw one of its primary duties as the salvation of Eastern Orthodox Christians by bringing them into an evangelical Protestant fold; its reports called for "assisting in the recovery of [the] long sleep of the ancient Syrian and Greek Churches."⁴ Although there was a vague intention among these early CMS leaders of converting the "heathen," which included the Muslims of the Ottoman Empire, the most clearly imagined targets of their efforts were the other Christians whom the society conceived of as laboring under "popish" beliefs and misconceptions. Islam received very little mention in the CMS's discussion of its projects in the Ottoman provinces.

The other major British mission society to direct its attention toward Palestine was the London Society for Promoting Christianity among the Jews, usually known as the London Jews Society (LJS). This organization emerged as a branch of the London Missionary Society, a collection of evangelical Anglicans and Nonconformists formed in 1795. One of the LJS's first missionaries, a German who had converted from Judaism, founded the LJS in 1809 with the purpose of "relieving the temporal distress of the Jews and the promotion of their welfare," receiving patronage from the Duke of Kent.⁵ Initially, the new organization focused on proselytizing to the Jewish communities of London and its surrounds, but in 1820 it sent a representative to Palestine to investigate the conditions of the Jewish communities there. In 1826 a Danish missionary named John Nicolayson, representing the LJS, arrived in Jerusalem and began to hold Protestant services in Hebrew in the city. Despite tension between Nicolayson and the Egyptian administration, he began to lay the foundations for a mission church in Jerusalem in 1839.

The evangelical Protestant missionaries who worked in Palestine during these early years tended to refrain from comment about Muslim practices, but were openly horrified at the liturgies, educational systems, and institutional practices of the Eastern Christian communities with whom they came into contact. The revulsion that Protestants felt toward Orthodox practice came out especially clearly in their descriptions of the Church of the Holy Sepulchre, which early missionaries and travelers described as "loathsome," a "labyrinth of superstition, quarrels over dogma, stenches and nonsense," and "something between a bazaar and a Chinese temple rather than a church."[6] Ludwig Schellner, a German missionary working with the CMS, went so far as to suggest, "And is not the silent worship of the Muslims across the way, before the mosque, infinitely more dignified?"[7]

Generally, though, neither of these early missions in Palestine was at all concerned with the region's Muslim populations, about which they knew very little. Rather, both the CMS's and the LJS's presence in Palestine was devoted to specifically evangelical Protestant concerns—anti-Catholicism in the case of the CMS and a new interest in worldwide Jewry in the case of the LJS. These early missionaries' ignorance of Islam was almost total, to the point that Islam featured only as a vague evil in their reports and mission statements, against their specific, theologically determined interest in opposing Catholicism and converting the Jews. They drew their converts and made their local connections exclusively with the Christian and Jewish communities and institutions in Palestine and thought of themselves as offering an alternative not to Islam but to the ritualistic, hierarchical practices of Catholicism and Eastern Christianity against which their theology constituted itself.

Following the evangelical Protestant interest in the Jewish presence in the Holy Land, the fund focused its attentions almost exclusively on excavations thought to be related to Old Testament sites and narratives. This was partly because the only known New Testament sites were under Greek Orthodox control, but it also reflected the strong British evangelical interest in the experience of the Jews. The work of the Palestine Exploration Fund was dedicated mainly to identifying sites and artifacts that could be linked to narratives of ancient Israel. Some of the rhetoric that accompanied these projects also suggested a nationalist imperial agenda, positing a philosophical comparison between the "Chosen People" of antiquity and their modern counterparts in the form of the British Empire and its Protestant leaders.

The archbishop of York's comments about Palestine in the opening meeting of the fund in 1865 stand as a remarkable statement of both evangelical and nationalist mission: "This country of Palestine belongs to you and to me. It is essentially ours. It was given to the Father of Israel in the words 'Walk the land in the length of it and in the breadth of it, for I will give it unto thee.' . . . We mean to walk through Palestine in the length and in the breadth of it because that land has been given unto us. . . . [I]t is the land to which we may look with as true a patriotism as we do to this dear old England, which we love so much."[8] This astounding declaration demonstrated the conflation of Protestant evangelical philosophy with the rising rhetoric of political imperialism during the second half of the nineteenth century and suggested some of the ways in which an evangelical Protestant understanding of the significance of the Holy Land could be used to legitimize British political incursions into Palestine. It also suggested that in order to mobilize this theological language to make a political claim, the British would need to promote the idea that sectarian identifications were all that mattered in Palestine.

The fund's history was soon to bear this out, as its members began to undertake archaeological surveys that attempted to prove the veracity of biblical narrative but also functioned as undercover military operations for a government concerned with maintaining a strong presence in Palestine vis-à-vis the other European powers.[9] The conjunction of these two interests in the works of the fund became very clear after 1869, when the institution decided to conduct full-scale surveys of Palestine in order to provide "the most definite and solid aid obtainable for the elucidation of the most prominent of the material features of the Bible," but also to provide accurate and detailed maps of Palestine to the British intelligence services for possible use in the defense of the Suez Canal in the event of Russian threats.[10]

The members of the Palestine Exploration Fund working in Palestine displayed the same lack of interest in Islam and focus on the Jewish and Christian populations that British missionaries showed. Many of them assumed that Islam's reign of power in the Ottoman Empire was on the wane and that Palestine's Jewish and Christian populations would soon be paramount. One archaeologist, writing in a fund-published pamphlet, suggested optimistically, "The Moslem peasantry, whose fanaticism is slowly dying out, coming under such influences [as the Jews and Christians] will gradually become more intelligent and more active, but will cease to be the masters of the country; and as European capital and

European colonists increase in the country, it will come more and more into the circle of those states, which are growing up out of the body of the Turk." Indicating the geopolitical context of such sentiments, he added, "With such a possible future it is hardly credible that western nations will permit the Holy Land to fall under Russian domination."[11] For members of the fund, like the evangelical Protestant missionaries who had preceded them, the Muslim and Ottoman presence in Palestine was little more than a temporary aberration; the true meaning of Palestine lay in its (Protestant) Christian and Jewish inhabitants, its biblical sites, and its importance to Great Power politics. This interpretation of Palestine's history and significance, promoted by both mission groups and archaeological societies, was now beginning to make its way into public rhetoric that sought to legitimize a British political claim to Palestine.

Colonial Rule and the Construction of a Christian Minority

These archaeological and mission approaches to Palestine did a great deal to shape conditions in Palestine under formal British colonial rule. The centrality of the Protestant Christian narrative about Jerusalem became evident at the moment of conquest, when General Edmund Allenby dismounted from his horse upon entering Jerusalem in 1917, to show his Christian respect for the religious history of the city. The colonial officials running Palestine placed this association of theological and political claims over the region at the center of their philosophy from the very beginning of the mandate, privileging religious identities over all others and casting political and economic conflict as essentially theological—an approach that served their imperial agenda and legitimized a Western claim over Palestine.

By 1922 Arab Christians made up about 10 percent of the population of the mandate state of Palestine, probably down from about 13 percent during the war. Three-quarters of them lived in cities, with particular concentrations in the Jerusalem district but present in all the major urban centers of Palestine. The Greek Orthodox community represented the largest denomination of Palestinian Arabs, making up nearly half of the Christian population. These Christians tended to constitute middle-class urbanites, a bit wealthier and better educated than their Muslim compatriots and especially prominent in middle-class fields like teaching, journalism, and medicine. During the last few decades of Ottoman rule in Palestine, the new European commercial, mission, and archaeological presence and a new kind of global consciousness among Palestinian elites contributed to a new interest in secularism and modernity and a desire to move Palestine away from religious identifications and toward domination by a literate, secular middle class.

Palestinian Arab Christian elites were not interested, at this stage, in developing any sort of broad Christian communal consciousness. Rather, they saw themselves as helping build a new secular, middle-class political and social ethos for a post-Ottoman Palestine—through schooling, publishing, and membership in political societies, but also through bourgeois interests like architecture, gardening, music, theater, photography, and sports. Aside from an opposition to Zionism—which was largely shared by their Muslim compatriots—they had a wide range of political ideas and did not think of themselves as constituting any kind of specifically Christian political entity.

When the British took over the mandate, the new administration decided to promote communally organized legal and political structures in Palestine, on the model of imperial policy in India. Under the Ottomans, Christian and Jewish communities in the Arab provinces were categorized as millets, a word indicating a non-Muslim community that had the right to a certain degree of communal autonomy (for example, their own courts for issues of personal law like marriage, divorce, and inheritance). The British decided to take this idea and expand it greatly, so that religious identity would be the basis for all political and civic engagement in mandate Palestine. They introduced new political and legal structures that categorized people by religion and permitted political participation only through religious organizations. Under this new system, Christians became merely a minority religious community rather than, as they had been before the mandate, an integral part of the elite Palestinian Arab political class.

The new system began under Sir Herbert Samuel, Palestine's first high commissioner, appointed in 1920. Samuel was a Jewish Englishman who had never before worked in the colonies, and he arrived in Palestine with the view that it was an essentially sectarian region. "[Palestine] has been notorious among the nations," he wrote, "for the bitterness, and sometimes the violence, of its ecclesiastical disputes, creed contending against creed, and sect against sect."[12] Using this idea that there was something particularly sectarian about Palestine, the new mandate government interpreted any dissent in Palestine as nothing more than primitive religiosity and positioned itself as a modern secular institution above a medieval religious fray. This essentialist understanding of Palestinian religious identity also won some support among Muslims whose main claim to power was through the Islamic religious hierarchy.

In 1922 Samuel put his ideas into practice by founding an elected council that would govern the Muslim community, but only with regard to specifically religious affairs. He chose Hajj Amin al-Husayni, the mufti of Jerusalem and a member of one of Palestine's most prominent political families, to head the new "Supreme Muslim Council." Samuel hoped that this approach would have two benefits for the mandate government: it would allow for the easy inclusion of the European Jewish presence in the mandate state, and it would defuse nationalist tensions by confining Arab political action to the communal sphere.[13] He explained his approach thus: "The establishment of an elected Council . . . concerned with purely religious matters will, I think, meet the desire of the Moslem population for some representative body, and may serve to check any agitation for political autonomy."[14] In 1922, then, the Supreme Muslim Council became the only institution of Palestinian Arab political expression that was sanctioned by the mandate government, and it by definition excluded all Palestinian Christians.

Such colonial policies were explicitly designed to encourage Muslim communal identity. By contrast, the new British government was extremely suspicious of Palestinian Christians, because of their long history of associations with other European powers now regarded by the British as potentially hostile. This was especially true of British attitudes toward the Orthodox community, which had strong historical ties not just to Greece but also to Russia. The British also tended to assume, wrongly, that there was a kind of essential divide between Muslims and Christians that would prevent Christians from being genuinely dedicated to any majority-Muslim movement. This point of view sometimes became extreme, as in a 1921 interview with members of the Palestinian Arab delegation (including the prominent Christian politician Shibli Jamal) and Winston Churchill of the Colonial Office. The final request of the delegation was that in the record of Palestinian Arab objections to British policy, the word "Christian" should be added to the word "Muslim" in describing the Palestinian Arab population. Churchill agreed to this request, but added, "But . . . it is no good pretending that you are more closely united to the Christians than to the Jews. That is not so. A wider gulf separates us from you than separates you from the Jew. I am talking of the Semitic races."[15]

The existence of an indigenous Arab Christian community also, of course, represented a challenge to the Western (and especially the British and American evangelical Protestant) narrative about their stake in Palestine, and especially Jerusalem, owing to its prominence in Christian history and theology. Local indigenous Christian opposition to Zionist immigration undermined the Western Christian claim that there was a natural meeting of interests between Christianity and Zionism. These factors all resulted in a British policy of noninterference in Christian affairs and a general unwillingness to acknowledge the existence of the Arab Christian communities, in marked contrast to the encouragement of communal expression among Palestinian Muslims.

The Arab Christian Response

Arab Orthodox Christians, though, were not willing to let their citizenship in a post-Ottoman Palestine fade quietly away. In this new landscape, where religious identification was now firmly associated with civic and political participation, Palestinian Christian leaders began to imagine new kinds of communal identities and to consider how they might be able to present their community as nationalist, political Christian entities.

The Greek Orthodox patriarchate, which possessed huge amounts of land and money, had long forbidden Arabs from participating in any of the higher reaches of the clergy, being considered for membership in the all-Greek "brotherhood" of monks who ran the church, or being eligible for the office of patriarch. Arab members of the Greek Orthodox community in Palestine—and in other parts of the Ottoman Empire as well—had begun to challenge the traditional Greek claim to ownership and control of the church. They wanted Arab representation in the higher reaches of the clergy, an Arabic liturgy, and a greater degree of Arab control over the church's money and land. During the 1920s and 1930s, in response to the marginalization of Orthodox Christians by the British government, this movement emerged as a central part of Orthodox identity. Orthodox leaders began to present their cause as essentially a nationalist political movement, reflecting a broader opposition to foreign claims over Palestinian Arab institutions and property. Palestinian Orthodox Christian identity was redefined as nationalist, antiforeign, and anti-Zionist. In an attempt to make the Orthodox community central to Palestinian identity, the movement's leaders deliberately conflated religious and political identities.

This conflation was made much easier by the fact that early in the mandate, the patriarchate had issued statements of support for Zionism, and in 1923 the commission in charge of the finances sold substantial tracts of land in Jerusalem and its surrounds to the Zionist Palestine Land Development Company.[16] This decision on the part of the patriarchate would make it much easier for the Orthodox laity to understand and depict the Greek hierarchy as a foreign oppressor along the same lines as the Zionists and the British.

Newspaper editor 'Isa al-'Isa was a particularly important mover in this campaign to redefine the Arab Orthodox movement as a nationalist cause. The language he used in his newspaper, *Filastin*, consistently suggested a relationship between the Arab Orthodox resistance to its Greek oppressors and the Palestinian resistance to Zionist intrusion. *Filastin*'s commentary was focused around the foreignness of the Greek hierarchy and its deliberate efforts to deprive Arab Christians of their political right to participate in the institute of the patriarchate. In 1931, as tension rose after the death of the patriarch, *Filastin* explicitly connected the Greek, British, and Zionist oppression of the Palestinians: "These three mandatories have helped one another in depriving Palestinian Arabs of their rights."[17] Such language represented a careful attempt to recast Arab Orthodox Christianity, against the mandate government's depiction, as not a minority religious community but a political movement concerned with the same issues as the broader Palestinian nationalist cause. This collapsing together of religious and political identities—the definition of sectarianism—represented a new phenomenon in mandate Palestine. It had happened not as the expression of a long-standing sectarian impulse in the region, but as a reaction to the specific circumstances of the mandate state.

The Continuing Uses of Sectarianism

This rhetoric of the essential sectarianism of Palestine, originally deployed to legitimize Britain's project of colonial conquest and imperial absorption, took on a new meaning after 1948. Through the second half of the twentieth century, this discourse of sectarianism was deployed to justify Western "international" claims over Jerusalem and continued Western protection and promotion of Zionism after the end of empire. The excision of indigenous Palestinian Arab Christians from the discussion of Palestine's past, present, and future allowed evangelical Christians in the West to cast themselves as the representatives of Christianity in the global conversations surrounding Palestine-Israel and especially Jerusalem. Just as the construction of sectarianism in the mandate had allowed the British colonial government to present itself as a necessary mediator among warring parties in a Palestine hidebound by primitive religious feeling, the same rhetoric now allowed Zionists and their sympathizers in Israel, Europe, and the United States to present Palestinian objections to the state of Israel as the discontents of a fundamentalist Islam intent on "driving the Jews into the sea" and to portray the Israeli state as a bulwark against a primitive and barbaric Muslim religiosity.

The new Israeli government made the decision early on to treat its Arab citizens as members of minority religious entities rather than as an ethnic minority in a secular state. Yehoshua Palmon, the first adviser on Arab affairs in the new state of Israel, suggested dealing with the remaining Palestinian population through the Ministry of Religions, thus preserving two primary tenets of the British mandate state: the inherent importance of religious distinctions in Arab society and the primacy of sectarian over national identifications for Palestinians.[18] This approach cemented a British-created sectarianism as a basic principle of the new Israeli state's legal and political institutions, tying religious identity to judicial process and political representation.

For the new Israeli state, maintaining this sectarianized legal code offered the same benefit it had provided the British mandate government—the enshrining of divisions within the Arab population, with the idea that religious divisions might help prevent the emergence of a unified Palestinian nationalist movement within Israel. The Israeli attitude toward the remaining Arab Christian population in the earliest years of the state further reflected the desire to erase the indigenous Christian presence as an internal threat, both because of their commitment to Arab and Palestinian political identities and because of the strength of Palestinian Christian religious institutions and their ties to international sympathizers. Nur Mashala has recorded in detail one early Israeli plan to "transfer" a number of Christian Arab families in the upper Galilee region to Argentina.[19] Yosef Weitz, the architect of the plan, noted in his diary, "We have an interest in weakening the power of the churches," as well as a need to expropriate Arab land and shrink Arab numbers in the Galilee. Moshe Sharett, the most prominent voice of moderation with regard to Arab populations in the new Israeli state, responded to Weitz's ideas with enthusiasm. In a letter to Ben-Gurion in 1952, he wrote, "To the extent that the emigrants would be Christians, another claim would be added regarding the undermining of the foundations of Christianity in Israel. It seems to me that we should not be deterred by these accusations, and that achievement resulting from showing the way/guiding for an organised exodus of part of the Arab population outweighs [these accusations]."[20] Israeli leaders clearly regarded these communities as primarily Arab rather than Christian in their loyalties; the legal separation of Christians from Muslims in the early years of Israeli statehood represented a strategy of division, and efforts at "transfer" represented an attempt to weaken not only the Arab Christian presence in Israel but also its institutional support abroad.

The minoritization of Palestinian Arab Christians, begun by the British mandate government and continued under the new Israeli state, effectively and radically diminished their presence in Palestine-Israel. The Arab Christian experience in Israel was characterized primarily by mass emigration. Christians emptied out of Israel en masse after 1948 and now constitute approximately 9 percent of the Arab Israeli population, down from about 21 percent in 1950.[21] A similar exodus took place in the occupied territories following the 1967 war. Between 1967 and 1991, approximately three hundred thousand Palestinian Arabs, 18 percent of the Arab population of the West Bank and the Gaza Strip, emigrated out of the West Bank and Gaza; of this number, approximately eighteen thousand were Christians, 40 percent of the Christian population.[22] A survey conducted in Haifa in 1992 reported that three times as many Arab Christians as Muslims planned to emigrate out of Israel.[23] This mass exodus is a consequence, first, of the harrowing political and economic situation in which all Palestinians found themselves, but also of the deliberate policies of division and discrimination imposed especially on Palestinian Christians, first by the British mandate state and then by the Israeli government. Throughout the twentieth century, the colonial crafting of sectarianism in Palestine has had as one of its primary goals the marginalization of indigenous Arab Christian voices in the debate over the region's political future.

Conclusion

During the first half of the twentieth century, the British mandate state adopted deliberate strategies of sectarianization toward their Palestinian Arab subject population. One of the primary purposes of this crafting of sectarianism was the minoritization of a strong and vocal Palestinian Arab Christian community who had drawn on international connections and their own centrality to Palestinian Arab politics to oppose British mandate rule and Zionist immigration. The presence of an indigenous Arab Christian community committed to Palestinian nationalism and anti-Zionism muddied the waters of the long-standing association between Western Christian and Zionist interests. The colonial production of Arab Christians as a "minority" and their concomitant exclusion from Palestine's political landscape served a dual purpose. First, it allowed for the portrayal of the emerging conflict in Palestine as a religious contest between Muslims and Jews for their shared "Holy Land," an interpretation that replaced the colonial origins of the conflict with a narrative of elemental religious conflict and glossed over Britain's centrality to the making of the struggle. Further, this narrative of inveterate sectarianism legitimized Britain's colonial presence as a necessary mediator between ancient religious enemies and, ironically, as a "protector" of non-Muslim majorities in Palestine.

The crafting of a sectarian political landscape continued under the new Israeli state after 1948. Early Israeli leaders made the decision to treat Arab Muslims and Christians separately, as members of religious minorities, in an effort to prevent the emergence of a Palestinian national movement within Israel and to weaken the power of the indigenous Arab churches in Israel. This Israeli deployment of British-derived sectarian policies has led to two new tropes about sectarianism in Israel-Palestine. One is the dissemination of the idea, especially in the United States, that the Israeli-Palestinian conflict is primarily an ancient theological dispute between Jews and Muslims—an idea reinforced by any number of writings purporting to discuss the Israel-Palestinian conflict that begin with a history of Palestine in biblical times, implying that the roots of the conflict lie in the ancient past. The second is a portrayal of Israel-Palestine, and especially of Jerusalem, as a "crossroads" where the three major monotheistic faiths meet and have conflicting religious and political claims over particular sites. In this vision, Christianity is represented not by the small remaining communities of indigenous Arab Christians but by the Western evangelical Protestants who have flooded into Israel on "Holy Land" tours in the past twenty years.[24]

Sectarianism does not represent a political phenomenon intrinsic to Palestinian Arab politics but a deliberate colonial introduction, deployed to make the business of colonial rule easier and allow for the promotion and incorporation of an autonomous European Zionist community into Palestine. The new Israeli state continued to draw on the rhetoric and discourse of sectarianism for similar purposes, minimizing the voices of a small remaining Arab Christian population whose presence served as an inconvenient reminder of a multireligious Palestinian nationalism. Above all, the colonial crafting of sectarianism and the concomitant minoritization of Arab Christians in Palestine and Israel made it possible to promote the idea that Arab-Zionist conflict in Palestine resulted from an age-old religious hatred between Muslims and Jews rather than issues of access to land, political representation, and economic opportunity. This widespread but radically mistaken notion has continued to inform the discourse of international intervention in the Israeli-Palestinian conflict to the present day.

4

Egypt and Its Jews

The Specter of an Absent Minority

JOEL BEININ

Carmen Weinstein, president of Cairo's Jewish community since 2004, passed away on April 13, 2013, at the age of eighty-two. In a statement announcing her election as Weinstein's successor, sixty-one-year-old Magda Haroun told the press that there were twenty-one Jews in Cairo, all elderly women except for Magda and her recently deceased younger sister, Nadia. There are a similar number of Jews in Alexandria; the only male among them serves as community president.[1]

This tiny Egyptian Jewish community is overburdened and overdetermined by its location at the intersection of several highly contentious historical and contemporary political and cultural issues. By the time Egyptian president Anwar Sadat signed the Egyptian-Israeli peace treaty in 1979, few Egyptians had ever seen a Jew. The treaty generated an upsurge of interest in the community in both Egyptian and Western public discourse that continues today. Its past and current conditions have been repeatedly scrutinized, motivated by a mélange of empathic curiosity, hostile suspicion, sensationalist journalism, scholarly inquiry, and nostalgia.

Opponents of the peace treaty and of "normalization" of relations with Israel commonly regard Egyptian Jews as potential conduits for pernicious Israeli influences. In Israel and the West, their status has often been a gauge of Egypt's commitment to peace and political liberalization. Nationalist Egyptians justifiably resent this neocolonial paternalism and typically regard any allegation of Arab or Muslim anti-Semitism as a Zionist-Western stratagem to divert attention from Israel's oppression of Palestinian Arabs, making it very difficult to discuss the sources and motives of contemporary Egyptian anti-Semitism.

The Dispersion of Egyptian Jewry, my intervention in the post-1979 moment, offers an alternative to the framing of the history of Egyptian Jews in the dominant paradigms—Zionism and Egyptian nationalism.[2] Egyptian English and Arabic editions appeared several years after the original English publication, and Egyptian readers demanded engagement. I would otherwise not have reconsidered the subject, as I am not aware of any available new evidence since the book was first published in 1998. Well before then, journalists, amateur historians, and public intellectuals supersaturated the discourse on Egyptian Jews, mostly recycling the same facts and fictions. In the process, the few Jews living in Egypt sometimes became collateral damage.

The surge of interest in Egyptian Jews following the 1979 peace treaty persisted into the first decade of the twenty-first century, but with a new twist. With some exceptions, such as the writings of Samir Raafat, most Egyptian representations of Jews in the 1980s and 1990s are negative or conspiratorial in tone.[3] Alternatively, Jews are simply absent from Egypt's modern history.[4] Negative representations and historical erasures persist. But a new trend emerged in the early 2000s emphasizing the positive contributions of Jews to modern Egypt, or at least seeking to understand their presence in its historical context. At least three histories, four novels, two films, and dozens of journalistic articles and blog entries in Arabic and English exemplify this development.[5] Among other things, these works continue the project begun by Samir Raafat—implicit opposition to the regime of President Hosni Mubarak expressed by a revalorization of what was considered the relatively more democratic and cosmopolitan era of the monarchy. Positive representations of Jews also suggest concern for Egypt's much larger religious minority, Copts.

Carmen Weinstein's Funeral

Carmen Weinstein's funeral was a marker of the trend toward a more positive representation of Egyptian Jews. It was held in the grand synagogue on 'Adli Street. Marc al-Fassi, a Moroccan-French rabbi who had been engaged with the community for more than a decade, officiated. A substantial crowd was present, as well as a large contingent of security and media personnel. Representatives of the government and al-Azhar, international diplomats, émigré Egyptian Jews who returned for the occasion, North American Jews who had shown an interest in the community, and ordinary Egyptians—mostly young, curious, and supportive—attended. The current and past Israeli ambassadors were present, rendering the event suspect to nationalist and Islamist ultras.

Carmen Weinstein struggled to define the past and present of the Egyptian Jewish community on her own terms in the face of pressures from the disparate currents of thought represented by those individuals who attended her funeral. She and her mother, Esther, who presided over the community before her, were not Zionists and did not think Israel was the center of Jewish life. They considered Egypt their homeland. But they did maintain contact with Israel and Israeli officials after 1979.

They demonstrably differentiated themselves from the New York–based Historical Society of Jews from Egypt, founded by the late Victor Sanua, who left Egypt in 1950. By calling themselves "Jews from Egypt" rather than "Egyptian Jews," HSJE adherents indicated that they did not consider themselves fully Egyptian. In 2002 the HSJE lobbied the US Congress to make future US aid to Egypt contingent on the Egyptian government "transferring our Jewish religious artifacts and copies of our community records to an institution in the United States." They claimed that "Mrs. Esther Weinstein and her daughter, Miss Carmen Weinstein, are unable to run the affairs of a rapidly dwindling and aging community numbering no more than a dozen souls, let alone fulfill requests from abroad. We also do not believe they speak freely[;] they only echo government policy and provide propaganda value."[6]

The Weinsteins rejected these allegations. In a rare interview after becoming president of the community, Carmen said, "There have been Jews in Egypt since Biblical times, the time of Moses, and I don't see why there shouldn't be Jews here until the end of time, sometimes less in number, sometimes more."[7] The Jewish community's buildings, books, and artifacts are part of Egypt's heritage, she told the interviewer. To prevent them from being transferred to the United States, as the HSJE demanded, in 1997 Esther Weinstein asked the Egyptian government to declare these items "antiquities." That is their status today; like pharaonic artifacts, they cannot be sold or exported.

Egypt's president at the time, Mohamed Morsi, did not attend Carmen Weinstein's funeral. But he issued an official statement of condolences, saying that she "was a dedicated Egyptian who worked tirelessly to preserve [the] Egyptian Jewish heritage and valued, above all else, living and dying in her country, Egypt." The statement was not distributed to the press or widely available in Arabic. The Cairo daily *al-Misri al-Yawm* learned of it only through a report in the *New York Times*, one of the few media outlets to receive a copy of the statement.[8] Morsi apparently believed (correctly) that saying anything positive about a Jew for public consumption would damage his domestic and Arab political standing and limited his expression to the minimum required by his official position.

Muhammad Kharrub, a columnist for the Jordanian daily *al-Ra'i*, claimed that Morsi's expression of condolences was suspiciously similar to the words of the US ambassador to Egypt and had the same intent as a letter Morsi had earlier written to Israeli president Shimon Peres congratulating him on Israel's sixty-fifth anniversary of independence. Kharrub reported that Weinstein had visited Israel to see friends and receive medical treatment—an unacceptable breach of the "antinormalization" doctrine that undermined her right to be considered an authentic Egyptian. He accused Morsi of pandering to the Western powers and Jewish and Zionist lobbies and employing a "dual discourse" (*izdiwajiyyat al-khitab*).[9]

The report of the sensationalist weekly *al-Yawm al-Sabi'* was headlined "The Israeli Ambassador Says: We Feel Deep Sadness on the Loss." The article was mostly about the ambassador's words and deeds, a detrimental association for nationalists.[10] The Palestinian-owned, London-based *al-Quds al-'Arabi* framed the story as a report on the condolences offered by the American Embassy in Cairo.[11]

In contrast to the nationalist-populist coverage, Carmen Weinstein's funeral was very sympathetically reported by Zeinobia's *Egyptian Chronicles* blog, featuring live tweets from the event.[12] The main tweeter, Raw'a, encouraged Egyptians to come to the synagogue that evening to offer condolences to Magda Haroun. Zeinobia endorsed Magda Haroun's statement (continuing the policy of Esther and Carmen Weinstein) that the

Egyptian Jewish legacy is a part of Egypt's cultural heritage. She hoped for more extensive media coverage of Magda Haroun and noted with approval her father's outspoken anti-Zionist views.

Zeinobia has been blogging in English since 2004 and was a prominent supporter of the 2011 popular uprising against the Mubarak regime. Her views are characteristic of many younger, left-leaning liberals seeking a more cosmopolitan and less constrained Egypt. A similarly positive account of the history of the 'Adli Street synagogue appeared in *Ahram Online*, featuring interviews with Magda Haroun and Victor Sanua.[13] Such opinions do appear in Arabic, but it is more common to see them in English.

For Zionists, Magda Haroun's election as Carmen Weinstein's successor is a bitter pill to swallow. The Israeli daily *Yedi'ot Aharonot* identified her as "the daughter of Shehata Haroun, who died in 2001 and was known for his anti-Israel views and was even a member of the Tagammu' (The National Progressive Unionist Party) part of the extreme left in Egypt" (not a very accurate characterization of the Tagammu').[14] In the 1940s Shehata joined the current of the communist movement led by Henri Curiel, another anti-Zionist Jew. In 1976 he became a founding member of the Tagammu'—Egypt's only legal left party at that time. As his memoirs reveal, Shehata Haroun was a fervent Egyptian nationalist.[15] His nationalism was even more pronounced than that of his comrades, quite possibly in response to persistent accusations (even within the communist movement) that Jews, and Curiel in particular, were suspect. In 1954 Haroun refused to leave Egypt to seek leukemia treatment for his oldest daughter, Mona, because authorities informed him that if he left, he would not be permitted to return. Mona subsequently died.[16] Haroun was so critical of Israel that upon his death in 2001, his family, rather than secure an Israeli rabbi, invited Marc al-Fassi from Paris to perform the funeral rites, the same rabbi who conducted Carmen Weinstein's funeral. Though perhaps less militant, Magda Haroun's opinions about Israel are essentially the same as her father's.

Muslim Brothers and Jews

In January 2013 President Muhammad Morsi's views about Jews became an explosive story widely reported in the American media. A video of his January 2010 speech to the Doctors Syndicate of Sharqiyya Province, released by the Middle East Media Research Institute, revealed a much more hostile stance than his correct, if reserved, response to Carmen Weinstein's death.[17] Morsi, then a high-ranking member of the Muslim Brothers and a member of its parliamentary delegation, told the assembled physicians, "We must never forget, brothers, to nurse our children and our grandchildren on hatred for them: for Zionists, for Jews. . . . The hatred must go on for God and as a form of worshiping him."[18] In an interview on al-Quds TV a few months later, Morsi described Zionists as "these bloodsuckers who attack the Palestinians, these warmongers, the descendants of apes and pigs" (a common anti-Jewish slur among Muslims, although Morsi's reference here is to "Zionists").[19]

Seven US senators, led by John McCain (R-AZ), visited Cairo on January 16, 2013, a few days after the story broke. At their meeting with President Morsi, they expressed "strong disapproval" of his recorded remarks.[20] According to Senator Chris Coons (D-DE), Morsi complained that his words were taken out of context and, in attempting to explain himself, said, "Well, I think we all know that the media in the United States has made a big deal of this and we know the media of the United States is controlled by certain forces and they don't view me favorably."[21] The senators and many others interpreted this statement as meaning that Morsi believes that Jews control the US media, a common anti-Semitic trope. Morsi's leading positions in the Muslim Brotherhood suggest that his views and sensibilities are shared widely in the organization.

Well beyond the circles of the Muslim Brothers, many Egyptians are, at best, careless about making distinctions between "Jews" and "Zionists." However, I agree with Gilbert Achcar that while anti-Semitism was common among the Muslim Brothers and the quasi-fascist Young Egypt in the 1930s and 1940s, anti-Semitism in Egypt since 1956 has been largely driven by the Arab-Israeli conflict.[22] This is what Morsi clumsily tried to suggest in claiming that his remarks about Jews were reported without consideration of the context of Israel's 2008–9 assault on the Gaza Strip, which he apparently felt justified a scurrilous attack on "Zionists" and "Jews."

Like most Egyptians, Morsi does not understand the multitiered relationship between Israel and the West. Egyptians typically regard the

American and Western support for Israel as unjust and primarily motivated by the influence of the Zionist lobby and the disproportionate
presence of Jews in the mass media. Few understand that the Nazi mass
murder of European Jews made even a hint of anti-Semitism unacceptable
in respectable post–World War II Western political discourse. The Zionist lobby—political money, media spin, the organized Jewish community,
and Christian Zionism—has long been a factor in American perceptions
of Israel, although it has arguably become more important as an independent factor in determining government policy since the end of the Cold
War. But Arab opinion typically disregards Israel's strategic contributions
to US hegemony in the Middle East and beyond, which were very substantial from 1967 to 1991 and have increased as a factor since 2011.

The inability to understand modern Jewish identity and experience
was highlighted by the remarks of vice chair of the Freedom and Justice
Party (FJP) and former member of the Muslim Brothers' Guidance Bureau
'Isam al-'Aryan, in a December 27, 2012, interview on Dream TV. In the
context of criticizing the regime of Gamal Abdel Nasser, for expelling
Egypt's Jews, he said, "I wish our Jews [to] return to our country, so they
can make room for the Palestinians to return, and Jews return to their
homeland in light of the democracy" evolving in Egypt. "Egypt is more
deserving of you. . . . Why stay in a racist entity, an occupation, and be
tainted with war crimes that will be punished."[23]

FJP spokesperson Muhammad Sudan affirmed al-'Aryan's statement.
"Our policy is clear. . . . We call on all occupied people to return to their
lands. . . . [W]e hope, that Palestinian people will return. . . . If you ask for
one group to return, so too must we ask the others." Jews should return to
wherever they may have come from, "Poland, Egypt or anywhere."[24] President Morsi, on the other hand, distanced himself from al-'Aryan's remarks.[25]

Al-'Aryan's comments aroused a storm of protest, most of it on the
grounds that Jews should not be invited to return to Egypt when Palestinians were still refugees. Moreover, they might make financial claims on
property they lost or act as a fifth column for Israel. In early January 2013
al-'Aryan resigned his position as a presidential adviser.

Khaled Fahmy, then chairman of the Department of History at the
American University in Cairo, responded to al-'Aryan in several television

appearances and op-eds in English and Arabic. Although he is a staunch opponent of the Muslim Brothers, he was rhetorically prepared to engage with al-'Aryan. He told ONTV, "I am taking the call seriously. I would like to see it in part as respectable, as addressing morals and high principles." Egyptians should talk about the past "harm to Egyptian Jews" and consider them as retaining Egyptian nationality. "I wish this was put to a public discussion."[26] Fahmy went on to attack al-'Aryan by criticizing the Muslim Brothers' recent political actions: "Do you honestly expect Jews to leave the country they now live in for another that has just passed a Constitution [in December 2012] that does not treat citizens equally, that has allotted a significant role for Egypt's highest Islamic authority Al-Azhar in interpreting the Constitution and that has laid down the first block of a religious state?"[27] Fahmy's positions on Jews are exceptionally principled. But here advocating a national discussion on Egypt's historical treatment of its Jews is intertwined with his critique of the role of Islam in the sharply contested 2012 constitution.

But with fewer than fifty Jews in Egypt, the current question for someone like Fahmy is the status of Copts. The Mubarak regime, the interregnum of the Supreme Council of the Armed Forces, and the Morsi administration all tolerated (and in several cases incited) violence against Copts, to say nothing of systematic discrimination for decades. In response, in 2007 left-leaning liberals established Egyptians against Religious Discrimination whose slogan is "Egypt for all the Egyptians." The movement's button depicts a crescent and a cross, but no Star of David. The urgency of raising consciousness about the precarious status of Christians overrode the political complications of acknowledging the existence of Egyptian Jews and openly supporting their equal rights, even though several movement members are children of Jews and their personal opinions are unimpeachable.

The Politics of Synagogue Restoration

Khaled Fahmy's critique of the 2012 constitution linking it to a rather hypothetical question about Jews but much more substantial question about Copts is emblematic of how the past and present of Egyptian Jews are readily understood as meaning something else. After signing the peace treaty with Israel, Anwar Sadat understood that cultivating good relations with world Jewry could advance his goal of consolidating Egypt's new alliance with the United States. Therefore, he invited Jewish organizations to restore two of the nine synagogues owned by the Cairo Jewish community.

In the 1980s the World Sephardic Federation renovated Cairo's main synagogue, Sha'ar ha-Shamayim (the Gate of Heaven), on 'Adli Street, originally dedicated in 1907.

In 1980 Sadat proposed to Edgar Bronfman, president of the World Jewish Congress, that the congress undertake restoration of the Ben Ezra synagogue in Old Cairo (Fustat). The synagogue was first established on the site where Pharaoh's daughter retrieved the baby Moses from the Nile, according to local tradition in the ninth century. The structure built in the 1890s was in disrepair by the second half of the twentieth century.[28] The work was done from 1987 to 1993 with funding from the Bronfman family under the architectural direction of Phyllis (Bronfman) Lambert.

The original building of the Maimonides Synagogue in Cairo's historic Jewish quarter (*harat al-yahud*) was constructed in the tenth century and renamed for Maimonides sometime after he moved to Cairo in 1168. The structure deteriorated after it was last used for regular prayer around 1960. In 1986 it was designated an Egyptian antiquity. The building was flooded after the 1992 earthquake. In 2009–10 the Egyptian government spent some two million dollars to restore it.

In 2010 Farouk Hosni, the minister of culture, declared that he considered Jewish sites as much a part of Egypt's cultural heritage as mosques and Coptic churches. Therefore, the Egyptian government would bear the costs of renovating them all.[29] Zahi Hawass, general secretary of the Supreme Council of Antiquities, concurred. "If you don't restore the Jewish synagogues, you lose a part of your history," he told *New York Times* correspondent Michael Slackman.[30]

But Hawass and Hosni were also aware of popular anti-Jewish sentiment forthrightly exemplified by Khalid Badr, a neighbor of the Maimonides Synagogue: "We hate [the Jews] for everything they have done to us. . . . We can remove [the synagogue] and build a mosque in its place." Hawass would not consider building a historical museum to house Jewish artifacts, similar to the Coptic Museum in Old Cairo. "If you make a museum like that while Israel is killing Palestinian children, people will kill me," he told Slackman.[31]

Hawass was also unwilling to collaborate openly with international Jewish bodies, as President Sadat had done. Rabbi Andrew Baker, director of international affairs for the American Jewish Committee, confirmed the positive work of the Egyptian authorities. But he seemed perplexed by their attitude: "We are doing these things, but you can't tell anybody about it [they told him]. . . . We accept this as our responsibility to care for our Jewish heritage, so we will do things ourselves. . . . They didn't want to do it in a formal relationship with us."[32]

The Egyptian authorities agreed that the Jewish community of Cairo could organize a ceremony to dedicate the renovated Maimonides Synagogue on March 7, 2010. An official inauguration was planned for later that month. About 150 people attended the Jewish community event, none of them Egyptian officials.

On March 14, 2010, the official inauguration ceremony was suddenly canceled. Hawass explained that the cancellation was due to media reports of Jews "dancing and drinking alcohol in the synagogue" during the private March 7 dedication, actions he characterized as a "provocation to the feelings of hundreds of millions of Muslims in Egypt and around the world."[33] Later he added that the decision to scrap the ceremony was made at "a time when Muslim holy sites in occupied Palestine face assaults from Israeli occupation forces and settlers."[34] Hawass later declared he canceled the ceremony to give "the Zionist enemy a strong slap in the face."[35]

Hawass may not have anticipated that dedicating a synagogue would involve blessings over wine and dancing with the Torah. Muslim neighbors may indeed have been offended by religious practices not witnessed in their neighborhood since the 1960s. Nonetheless, the synagogue dedication had no connection to Israel. Suggesting otherwise pandered to widespread popular sentiment that does not clearly distinguish between Jews and Zionists or Israel and contradicts Hawass's own correct statement that the Maimonides Synagogue is a part of Egypt's heritage; Maimonides was the personal physician of Saladin.

Nostalgia for (and by) Egypt's Jews

In the 2000s nostalgia for the era of the monarchy and positive memories of Egyptian Jews became a vehicle for indirect criticism of the Mubarak regime. This longing was expressed in the many new and reprinted books on the period in bookstores and the strongly positive reception of the Saudi-produced Ramadan 2007 television serial *al-Malik Faruq* (King Faruq). The monarchy era was represented as more democratic because there were sometimes competitive elections, there was a relatively free press, and the rule of law was more rigorous. Most important in relation to Jews, Egypt was a much more cosmopolitan and tolerant place than it had become by the 2000s. Several Egyptian Jewish émigrés writing in English and French engaged in a parallel literary movement.[36]

Muhammad Abu al-Ghar's *The Jews of Egypt: From Prosperity to Diaspora* expresses this new sensibility.[37] Abu al-Ghar is a professor at Cairo University's Faculty of Medicine and has no training in history. Although based largely on reputable works by professional historians, the book contains errors of fact and interpretation.[38] But it does not demonize Jews as a community and acknowledges that many were well integrated into Egypt. Abu al-Ghar became a prominent leader of the Egyptian Social Democratic Party, established soon after the demise of Hosni Mubarak in 2011. Therefore, the book expresses an understanding of Egyptian Jews that is acceptable in left-liberal circles.

In the 1930s and 1940s, the Marxist Left embraced Egyptian Jews. Several were prominent leaders of the movement. However, in 1958, when the three main Marxist trends formed a single party, they adopted a policy of excluding Jews from the central committee. Nonetheless, in the 2000s Communists, former Communists, and children of Communists were prominent promoters of positive representations of Egyptian Jews.

The late Yusuf Darwish was a labor lawyer and one of the founders of Workers' Vanguard (later the Workers and Peasants Communist Party). He won the confidence and respect of thousands of workers and was widely respected for his political tenacity and personal bravery. Although Darwish converted to Islam for convenience in 1947, most Egyptians nonetheless considered him a Jew. He was, therefore, excluded from the leadership of the united Communist Party of Egypt in 1958.

For most of his adult life, Darwish had no special interest in anything Jewish. But by the early 2000s, he was sufficiently distressed by the extent of intolerance in Egypt that he decided to translate the late Jacques Hassoun's *Histoire des Juifs du Nile*.[39] Hassoun had been expelled from Egypt as a Communist in 1954 and taken French citizenship. But he always considered himself an Egyptian.[40] Darwish's translation was published by Dar al-Shuruq, the most prestigious privately owned press in Egypt, which also published the Arabic translation of *The Dispersion of Egyptian Jewry* the same year.

Darwish's death in June 2006 elicited several positive obituaries.[41] But the countertendency to erase the Jewish presence in Egypt persisted, even among his admirers. A memorial photo display at the 2007 Cairo Social Forum failed to mention his Jewish origins. Like Egyptians against Religious Discrimination, affirming Jews' membership in the Egyptian national community was too great a political burden for the organizers.

Two recent documentary films depicting Egyptian Jews—Nadia Kamel's *Salata Baladi* (An Egyptian Salad [2008]) and Amir Ramses's *'An yahud misr* (The Jews of Egypt [2012])—have Communist connections. Dismayed by the religious intolerance her ten-year-old nephew was exposed to, Kamel persuaded her mother, Marie Rosenthal, to participate in a film telling her family history. Rosenthal was born to an Italian Jewish family in Cairo, but they converted to Catholicism because of anti-Semitism in the Italian community in the 1930s. A few years later Marie became a Communist; she married a Muslim comrade and converted to Islam. The family of a cousin she had been close to emigrated to Palestine in 1946. They had not seen each other since then. The film documents family reunions in Italy and Israel—a forthright challenge to the "anti-normalization" taboos of left-nationalist politics. *Salata Baladi* is the first Egyptian production filmed partly in Israel. It features scenes depicting an Egyptian Israeli Jewish family whose older members retained elements of Egyptian culture: Arabic language, food, and enthusiasm for the music of Umm Kulthum. The film could not be commercially shown in Egypt and was subjected to vicious criticism, even in relatively open-minded forums.[42] Nonetheless, it was well received in several private venues and provoked long-suppressed discussions.

Salata Baladi indirectly encouraged the production of Amir Ramses's historical documentary on the Egyptian Jewish community in the first half of the twentieth century, *'An yahud misr.* The film was produced by Haytham al-Khamisi, whose parents, like Nadia Kamel's, were Communists. It received an Egyptian screening license in September 2012 and an export license in December 2012. Its Egyptian theatrical release was scheduled for March 13, 2013. In late 2012 and early 2013, it was screened at several international film festivals.

An intervention by the National Security Apparatus (Jihaz al-Amn al-Watani, formerly Mabahith Amn al-Dawla) delayed its Egyptian premier. The director of the film censorship committee, 'Abd al-Sattar Fathi, who claimed he "supported the film all along," received a note from the National Security Apparatus prohibiting the screening, "because it is a documentary." When he contacted the apparatus for further details, Fathi was told, "The film's title might cause public uproar, particularly after Essam El-Erian's statements on Jews, and in light of the tension on the street."[43] *'An yahud misr* belatedly premiered in two theaters in Cairo and one in Alexandria on March 27, 2013.

'An yahud misr sought to reclaim Egypt's more cosmopolitan past. Ramses asked himself, "How did the Jews of Egypt turn in the eyes of Egyptians from partners in the same country to enemies?"[44] The film's portrayal of Jews was attacked in the predictable circles. In September 2013 it was one of several Egyptian films Muslim Brotherhood supporters protested at the Malmo Arab Film Festival, where it won the "Best Documentary" award.[45] Following the demonstration, Ramses defended the film and its representation of Jews as an integral part of Egypt, declaring, "If sympathy with the Jews of Egypt is an accusation ... then I am guilty."[46]

Michal Goldman, director and producer of the highly regarded documentary *Umm Kulthum: A Voice Like Egypt* (1996), was then in Egypt researching a biopic about Gamal Abdel Nasser. I asked her about public response to *'An Yahud Misr.* She replied, "Egyptians who have watched it don't want to talk about the Jews at all. Instead they want to see the film entirely as a metaphor for 'what is happening now to the Copts.' ... Every

Egyptian I have spoken with—the ones who have seen the film as well as the ones who have only heard or read about it—speaks about the film in this way."[47]

Amir Ramses and Haytham al-Khamisi made a film about Egyptian Jews seeking to valorize cosmopolitanism. Egyptian state authorities saw it as a security threat. At least some of the Egyptian public thought the film was "really" about the current status of Copts. Muslim Brotherhood supporters in Sweden thought screening the film indicated support for the July 3, 2013, military coup (which was, in fact, supported by the great majority of Egypt's artists). Egypt's diminishing Jewish community is caught in the cross-fire as discourse about Jews stands in for discussions of other issues.

PART TWO

Minorities, Nationalism, and Cultural "Authenticity"

THIS SECOND PART analyzes some communal responses to the state-driven processes of minoritization detailed in the first group of chapters. By the interwar period, many non-Muslim and non-Arab communities across the Middle East and North Africa had become aware of their new status as legal, political, and cultural "minorities" within majoritarian nation-states. To deal with this new situation, they developed a wide variety of tactics that they hoped would open paths of inclusion in the new forms of political community that emerged across the Arab world in the colonial and postcolonial periods.

These tactics often involved political commitments to secularist visions of nationalism and internationalism, which allowed "minorities" explicitly to declare involvement in modern projects of state building and a strong identification with nationalist cultural and political identities. For instance, Aline Schlaepfer demonstrates that the substantial and important Jewish community in Baghdad refused to accept marginalization as a British-protected "minority," instead spearheading a specifically nationalist anticolonial movement that also objected to an Iraqi rapprochement with the emerging Axis powers. This approach simultaneously declared Baghdadi Jewish loyalty to Iraqi national identity and maintained a commitment to transnational Jewish interests. Similarly, as Alda Benjamen points out, in the 1940s and 1950s Assyrians in Iraq—far from viewing themselves as a separate polity—often found themselves attracted to the Iraqi Communist Party for its inclusive secularist vision of Iraqi identity as much as for its active program of labor advocacy in and around the oil city of Kirkuk, where many Assyrians worked. For Egypt Hiroko Miyo-kawa investigates how the Coptic community carefully remade a Coptic Christian religious holiday into a national display, thereby declaring Coptic commitment to the Egyptian state and advertising their long-standing participation in Egyptian cultural nationalism. And in North Africa, Samuel Liebhaber argues, the Berber-speaking Touareg made spurious but convenient claims of a Yemenite origin for their non-Arabic languages, thereby claiming a kind of cultural Arabness and rejecting implications of minority or outsider status.

In all these cases, communities newly tagged as "minorities" within these twentieth-century nation-states largely refused to accept their own marginality to a majoritarian political system and national identity. Instead, they declared passionate commitments to broad (and often secular) concepts of Egyptian, Iraqi, and Arab nationalism and worked to ensure their own ongoing participation in political projects of national belonging and cultural "authenticity." In these active declarations by Baghdadi Jews, Iraqi Assyrians, Egyptian Copts, and Tunisian Berbers that they fully belonged to their emerging nation-states, we can see resistance to the imposition of the "minority" label as a marker of outsider status and vigorous attempts to reconfigure the political landscape to allow for full participation in emerging national identities across the modern Arab world.

5

When Anticolonialism Meets Antifascism

Modern Jewish Intellectuals in Baghdad

ALINE SCHLAEPFER

In Youssef Chahine's autobiographical masterpiece, *Iskanderija . . . lih?* (1979), a scene takes place during the battle of El Alamein in 1942. It shows Egyptian and British officials attending a play staged by Yahya, a young Christian who wants to become a movie director, in Alexandria. In this metatheatrical and humorous mise en abyme, one can see British drinking tea and chatting, Germans yelling at each other, and Italians eating pizzas and obeying the Germans. Two bedouins sitting in the desert and fed up with too many comings and goings decide to impose a toll on foreigners who wish to pass through their territories. Two Egyptians pass by and try to bargain over the price. Eventually, the two bedouins agree to sell them a half-price ticket. In this set of footage drawn from both archival material and Chahine's memory as a young man, European powers, whether German, Italian, or British, are openly condemned and equally seen as intruders on Egyptian soil. And as trivial as it may look, it prompts the thought that negative responses to Nazism and fascism were not uncommon in the public sphere and naturally coexisted with anti-British and anticolonial discourses.

Israel Gershoni and Amy Singer have argued that voices emanating from individuals or groups of individuals fighting for pluralism, freedom of expression, and democracy have systematically been silenced by the established historiography about the region.[1] According to the narrative this void has produced, the totalitarian nature of power left no room for a counterdiscourse and, more generally, for an open debate in the public sphere. Accordingly, the radicalization of Arab nationalism that took place in the 1930s was closely associated with Nazi Germany.[2] In a later phase of historiography, however, studies have focused on internal factors leading to the formation of Arab nationalism, such as the conflict in Palestine and the French and British interference into economic and intellectual life.[3] The notion of totalitarianism has consequently been put into perspective and fundamentally challenged. New debates and new preoccupations—in most cases independent of or opposed to Nazi influences—have been unveiled. The new conclusions this historiographical trend has put forward have contributed to the deconstruction of a monolithic vision of political and ideological life in the Middle East and succeeded in showing the complexity of its history. Juan Cole has successfully criticized the "black legend of the Axis in Iraq" by demonstrating the Nazis' overall lack of interest in Arab affairs. Gilbert Achcar has distinguished between Arab actors who were accomplices of Nazism and fascism and those individuals who turned toward Germany and Italy for the sake of an "alliance of convenience." Similarly, Götz Nordbruch has meticulously analyzed the public actors who supported Nazi discourses and those individuals who systematically opposed them, even at times of great turmoil, such as when Syria and Lebanon were ruled by the Vichy regime. While a systematic historical paradigm has not yet been completely defined, Ulrike Freitag and Israel Gershoni have formally expressed the necessity of examining with renewed attention the many and various Arab responses to Nazism and fascism during and after the Second World War, in order to fully restore the intellectual history of the Middle East.[4]

This chapter aims to examine the writings left by Jewish intellectuals in Baghdad with this consideration in mind, for several reasons. First, the Jewish population represented an important part of the urban society. During the late Ottoman period, the Baghdadi Jewish community was the third-biggest community in the empire after Salonika and Istanbul, with a total of 35,000 members in 1882, 35,000 in 1896, and 45,000 to 53,000 between 1908 and 1910. The total population of Baghdad was estimated at 150,000 souls in 1908; the Jews consisted of 35.8 percent of it.[5] A 1910 report sent by the British consul general in Baghdad about the Jewish community stated that a "rich and well-off class, consisting almost entirely of merchants and bankers,"[6] represented 5 percent of the Bagh-dadi Jewish population, while 30 percent composed the middle class, 60 percent were poor, and 5 percent were beggars. The rapid increase of the Jewish population in Baghdad throughout the nineteenth century and the beginning of the twentieth century left its marks on the urban land-scape. While the Jewish population was originally centered around the old Baghdad (Taht al-Takiyya, Qanbar 'Ali), they started to move southeast toward the Christian quarters in the 1900s, to the latter's great annoy-ance.[7] Later (in the late 1920s), the more affluent of the community settled in the new residential quarter of Battawiyyin, outside the Eastern Gate (Bab al-sharqi). As a result of this demographic growth, a substantial Jew-ish middle class quickly developed and flourished in Baghdad, and so did its modern intellectuals (*muthaqqafun*), more politically active and vocal on political issues than their traditional counterparts (*udaba'*).[8]

Second, Jews—as a non-Muslim community under the rule of a Muslim leadership—were particularly keen to express themselves on the importance of pluralism and rejection of totalitarianism. Also, alarmed by the growing threat of anti-Semitism in Europe, Iraqi Jews were deeply concerned by the consequences of a possible rapprochement between Iraq and Germany. They accordingly became very vocal in the public sphere, as we are about to see.

Third, and most decisively, Baghdadi Jewish *muthaqqafun* were fully immersed in local debates on models of society. Geopolitically speak-ing, Iraq was rather distant from European influences compared to the Mediterranean Levant, and so were its Jews. In addition, Jews from Arab lands did not benefit from the same attention paid by the European pow-ers to Christian communities, because they did not share the same reli-gion. When the Ottoman self-governing system of millets collapsed, Iraqi Jews progressively lost their social, financial, political, and religious inner structures, as Peter Sluglett demonstrates in his contribution to this vol-ume. And unlike the Jews in Algeria, for instance, their hope for obtain-ing a European nationality vanished as early as 1918.[9] They did not benefit from the protection of Ashkenazi Jews or local Christians, either, as was the case in Lebanon.[10] And even though some middle-class educated Iraqi Jews knew French or English as a second language, in most cases they mastered Arabic only. In the lower classes, Iraqi Jews who were sent to schools went to governmental ones, where they were taught only Arabic. In other words, notwithstanding their fragile link with Europe and any other protective entity—or rather because of it—Iraqi Jewish intellectuals had to develop strategies in order to define a place of their own in society. The social, political, and professional networks established with Iraqi journalists and writers played a role of major importance in this regard. Many Iraqi Jewish journalists and writers became acquainted with a group of young Iraqis, claiming to be "liberal intellectuals (*muthaqqafun*) and progressive (*taqaddumiyyun*) democrats (*dimuqratiyyun*),"[11] who founded the Ahali Group in 1932. Because Iraqi Jewish intellectuals had similar views on the models of society they wished to live in, they could relate to their ideologies. In addition, the group attracted the interest of Jewish intellectuals because of its "nebulousness" around certain issues in relation to the Iraqi Left.[12] For instance, they did not agree on the idea of revolution leading to a proletariat dictatorship.[13] Though fiercely opposed to "intellectual conformism," notes Hanna Batatu, the Ahali Group wished to keep a certain flexibility regarding its members' political orientation.[14] Similarly, Jama'at al-Ahali represented a coalition of individuals committed to a broadly defined, democratically oriented political platform of what they denoted as *al-sha'biyya*, or popularism.[15] Many Jews did not wish to jeopardize their security by adhering to controversial political views and consequently joined the Ahali Group. It can therefore be said that Iraqi Jews were profoundly imbued with debates on Iraqi and Arab political issues and expressed themselves accordingly in the public sphere.

Like other non-Muslim communities, Iraqi Jews were deeply affected by the process of minoritization undergone in the Arab Middle East after the establishment of the mandate system, which Laura Robson identifies in her introduction to the present volume. However, throughout the mandate period, Jews tended to view themselves not as a minority (*aqalliyya*) but rather as a community (*ta'ifa*)—a concept they inherited from the nineteenth-century Ottoman system, where *millet* and *ta'ifa* were used interchangeably.[16] In the Iraq constitution of 1925, both terms (*aqalliyya* and *ta'ifa*) are used. But in the chapter concerning the judicature—where the remnant of the millet system is clearly identifiable[17]—only *ta'ifa* appears. Similarly, according to the "Law for the Israelite Community No. 77" enacted by the Iraqi government in 1932, Jews are officially referred to as a *ta'ifa (isra'iliyya),* and the word *aqalliyya* is never used.[18] Besides, since the formation of the Kingdom of Iraq in 1921, linguistic nationalism was intensively promoted by the government in general and by the director general of education Sati' al-Husri in particular. The fact that Iraqi Jews— as Arabic speakers—did not constitute a separate ethnolinguistic community in Iraq actually facilitated their self-representation as a natural part of the Iraqi Arab nation. Finally, unlike some ethnolinguistic minorities in Iraq who had been victims of forced displacements and massacres (as was the case of Assyrians), Iraqi Jews developed a strong territorial patriotism throughout the first half of the twentieth century. Unsurprisingly, then, Iraqi Jews strongly opposed the process of minoritization whose target they became under British rule.

As a result of this process, they were often perceived as allies of the British and therefore looked at suspiciously by public opinion, as anti-British sentiment grew rapidly from the late 1920s. In order to counter this direct effect of minoritization, Iraqi Jews needed a place to be visible. In the words of Habermas on the Greek self-interpretation of the polis, "Only in the light of the public sphere did that which existed become revealed, did everything become visible to all."[19] The public sphere consequently became the only "legal-social realm where modern political subjectivities . . . negotiate rights and obligations."[20] In other words, presence meant existence. The press and proliferation of public ceremonies thus became privileged media for Iraqi Jews to express their full loyalty to the country and their absolute indispensability to the survival of Iraqi society.

By scrutinizing Jewish intellectuals' positions on Western powers after independence (1932), I will ask how—in a similar vein to Chahine's young progressive intellectuals who fought against all colonial powers, whether German, Italian, or British—Iraqi Jews condemned European policies in the Middle East. My argument is twofold. First, they naturally adopted an anti-British discourse, in order to dissociate themselves from the colonial enterprise. Second, with regards to the issue of fascism and Nazism, Jews contributed substantially to public arguments against totalitarianism.

In an early phase of their history of public visibility, Iraqi Jews found praise of King Faysal I of Iraq the best way to express their will to belong. They frequently organized shows and plays in honor of the monarch, in the presence of the Jewish community's officials and public figures. These ceremonies organized by the Jewish community found a positive echo in the Iraqi press (Jewish and non-Jewish). For instance, al-'Alam al-'arabi, though well known for its nationalistic and at times anti-Jewish positions, often reported on those ceremonies and wrote in praise of their organizers. These reports were later reproduced by Jewish journals, such as al-Misbah, a weekly founded by Baghdadi Jews in 1924.[21] However, in 1929, Iraq experienced a major crisis in domestic and foreign politics. British high commissioner Sir Gilbert Clayton (1875–1929), initially known to be well disposed toward Iraqis' aspirations for independence, died of a heart attack in September. During the same year, negotiations began between the British and the Iraqis, leading to the signing of the Anglo-Iraqi Treaty in June 1930. Finally, the newly appointed prime minister, 'Abd al-Muhsin al-Sa'dun, committed suicide in November 1929. All three factors led to a feeling of general dissatisfaction among journalists and intellectuals, as hopes of seeing Iraq become an independent member of the League of Nations temporarily seemed to vanish.[22] As a result, toward the end of the 1920s, the heroic Anglo-Hashemite coalition that led to the establishment of the Kingdom of Iraq had known—and lost—its hour of glory in literary and journalistic motifs. Iraqi muthaqqafun started to firmly express themselves against the mandate. The Jews' expression of national attachment also took that direction. Only allusive at its beginnings, the anticolonial discourse soon accused the British of being responsible for al-Sa'dun's death, a rumor that spread like wildfire.[23] Sha'ul Haddad, a Jewish journalist (1910–2010), commented on the prime minister's death in an article entitled "The Motive for the Suicide." The journalist unmistakably accused the British of being responsible for this tragic event, by pointing to the "English rifle."[24]

Until the mid-1930s, Iraqi muthaqqafun's archenemy and the power they considered to be the most serious threat to the country's autonomy remained Great Britain. The words "colonialism" (al-isti'mariyya) and "occupation" (al-ihtilal) were used in the press to refer to the will of the British Empire to maintain its grip on power through the economic and political means provided by the mandate. But from the 1930s onward, other European powers appeared as threats too. Some public opinion and political elites started to express admiration toward the military superiority of Germany and Italy, in which they saw a model of authority and society.[25] Iraqi ultranationalists such as Sami Shawkat, a medical doctor and director general of the Ministry of Education, considered that fighting with Germany was the right political move in order for Iraq to gain economic and military independence from the British. Lost in a biased syllogism on coalition whereby the enemy of one's enemy is one's friend, they hoped the Germans would be a powerful ally against the British. In 1933 Shawkat gave a speech entitled "Profession of Death" in which he exhorted young students and soldiers to be prepared to die for the nation. He took the example of successful national struggles, such as the armies of Mustafa Kemal, the Pahlavis, and Mussolini:

> If Mustafa Kemal did not have 40000 officers well-trained to the profession of death in order to lead the revolution in Anatolia, we would not have seen Turkey restore the glory of Yavuz Sultan in the 20th century. If Pahlavi did not have thousands of officers ready for the sacred profession, we would not have seen him restore the glory of Darius. If Mussolini did not have tens of thousands of Blackshirts well-trained to the profession of death, he would not have been able to restore the crown of Rome's first Caesars, in the name of Victor Emmanuel's Temple.[26]

However, notwithstanding the undeniable sympathy toward Nazi and fascist models of society within certain circles, Shawkat's speech, as well as other political essays published under the title *These Are Our Goals* in 1939, caused a mass controversy among public figures in Iraq. Sati' al-Husri, former director general of education and ideologue of Arab nationalism, fiercely condemned Shawkat's "blind fervor." In his memoirs, he repeatedly expresses his "disappointment," "sincere regret," and deep "embarrassment" vis-à-vis Sami Shawkat, as both the minister of education and an essayist, as early as 1931.[27] More generally, voices emanating from milieus that historians have long portrayed as radical nationalists but who actually opposed pro-Nazi tendencies were not uncommon, as Orit Bashkin has shown.[28]

Indeed, Kamil al-Chadirchi, early follower of the Ahali Group and chief editor of its mouthpiece, *Sawt al-Ahali*, expressed his concern regarding Shawkat's words. For him, Mussolini was the cause of "the biggest catastrophe History has ever known," referring to the Holocaust. Accordingly, he considered any historical narrative in which the Italian leader played the role of an ideal national leader to be very dangerous for his country. In an article titled "The Iraqi Mosley," published in *Sawt al-Ahali* on January 2, 1946, al-Chadirchi explicitly associated Sami Shawkat with fascism. He compared the medical doctor to the founder of the British Union of Fascists in 1932, Sir Oswald Mosley (1896–1980).[29] When Shawkat fought back by accusing the "leftists (*al-yasariyyin*) of being hostile to Arab nationalism" in *al-Zaman* on January 8–9, 1946, al-Chadirchi replied in a series of editorials titled "The Rise of Fascism in Iraq,"[30] published every day in *Sawt al-Ahali* for several weeks. These editorials were eventually compiled and published under the title *Rise of Fascism in Iraq* by the printing house Maktabat Baghdad the same year and advertised in the Ahali Group's mouthpiece.[31] Among the acerbic accusations al-Chadirchi addressed to Sami Shawkat and other sympathizers of fascism were their imperialistic ambitions. As Gershoni and Freitag have pointed out, for those supporting social democracy, the "new aggressive expansionism and oppressive imperialism [of Nazi Germany and fascist Italy] was much worse than the old imperialism of Britain and France."[32] In the first editorial of *Sawt al-Ahali* in July 1942, al-Chadirchi posed the journal's editorial line: "The journal aims to explain to the Iraqi public opinion the damages fascism causes financially, morally and culturally. It aims to clarify why German occupation (*al-ihtilal*) is a threat to Arab countries and to Iraq."[33] *Sawt al-Ahali* also stressed the fact that the Italians glorified imperialism, while the democrats rejected it: "Italian fascism, for instance, glorifies the Roman Empire and thinks that it is possible to restore it. . . . But are the need to control other nations . . . and fascist mentality a sane thinking?" Al-Chadirchi continued on Sami Shawkat's vision of colonialism: "It is clear from [Shawkat's book *The Arab Empire*] that the doctor supports the colonial (*al-isti'mari*) principle, as he demands the Arab countries apply colonialism (*al-isti'mariyya*)." For al-Chadirchi and other members of the editorial board, however, "the Arab nation needs liberation and unification, not hostility toward other peoples and colonialism."[34] Iraq's memory of the struggle against colonial Great Britain was fresh and its citizens' bitterness deep. In such a climate, to openly associate one's ideological enemies with imperialism was the best way to disqualify and dishonor them. In these instances, the two words originally used to refer to colonial Great Britain (*al-ihtilal* and *al-isti'mar*) were applied to the German and Italian cases. By using this semantic shift and associating the fascists or anyone openly sympathizing with them with the inexcusable sin of colonialism, Ahali journalists could more easily rule them out of the political debate in the eyes of public opinion.

In this context, it comes as no surprise that Jewish intellectuals declared themselves against Nazi and fascist models of society in the same terms. The weekly *al-Hasid*, literally "The Harvester," a journal that promoted equality (*al-musawat*), justice (*al-'adala*), democracy (*al-dimuqratiyya*), freedom (*al-hurriyya*), and progress (*al-taqaddum*),[35] was founded in Baghdad in 1929 by a group of young intellectuals of Jewish origin. They openly opposed Nazi and fascist influences on society, and toward the end of the 1930s not a week went by without references to the threats of the Axis powers and political developments related to them: "If the literary press wishes to encourage human principles . . . such as freedom and democracy . . . is it possible to do so without condemning unjust systems like fascism and Nazism?"[36]

In a similar vein to the Ahali Group, Jewish intellectuals perfected a discursive strategy whereby behind the usual anti-British discourse would hide an anti-Nazi or antifascist argument, knowing the readership's support for the anticolonial struggle. The strategy was twofold. First, European policies were systematically deconstructed and equally scrutinized. In a special issue that came out in April 1936, Sati' al-Husri was invited to express his views on the situation in Europe. In the article, he compared the European nations to a caravan lost in the desert and divided into several parts. After a long sleep, the traveler, that is, the embodiment of Iraq and other Middle Eastern nations, does not know where to look, which direction to take, or which part of the caravan to follow. The mission of the "thought leaders" (*qadat al-fikr*), he argued, is to redirect the "Oriental nations" and to make them stop repeating "We should imitate the West."

Here, al-Husri invited the reader to put distance between himself and a Europe that no longer offers reliable support to Iraq. In an article echoing one by al-Husri in the same issue of *al-Hasid*, Anwar Sha'ul, an Iraqi Jewish journalist, poet, and chief editor of *al-Hasid* (1904–84), reasserted the role of the "thought leaders" (*qadat al-fikr*) by examining British and French policies vis-à-vis Germany after the First World War. Without naming them, he accused the British of enhancing German humiliation through endless and useless "post-war conferences, treaties, and agreements": "Certain states have become aggressive, others powerless. Certain states have become richer, others have become poorer. . . . Gradually, oppositions against unjust peace treaties have been voiced. Certain states came out of the war whispering: 'Revenge will come!'"[37] The journalist's barely disguised allusion to Nazi Germany reveals his deep concern. And understandably so, as by the time this issue of *al-Hasid* was published in April 1936, the Nuremberg Laws had been introduced and Hitler had just remilitarized the Rheinland, thus ending the Locarno Agreements signed in 1925. Interestingly, though, while he clearly attempted to raise his readers' awareness to the ever-growing threat of Nazism, he subtly played the English guilt card. In his attempt to warn the people of Iraq against a possible German threat, he assumed that anti-British bait would successfully win his readership's sympathy.

The other facet of the discursive strategy—and likely the most effective one—was to associate German and Italian powers with the colonization project in order to discredit them, as *Sawt al-Ahali* did. Jewish journalists attempted to demonstrate that Germany and Italy were no less colonial than the British or the French and therefore also represented a threat to the country's independence. They took every opportunity to unveil the true intentions of colonial Germany and the state's machinations to nourish hatred. They stressed German colonial revisionism, which began during the Weimar Republic after the Treaty of Versailles, when Germany was deprived of its colonies, but was more generally popularized during the Third Reich. Numerous associations for promoting the "colonial idea," under the aegis of the Koloniale Reichsarbeitsgemeinschaft (Colonial Empire Association), were founded.[38] The famous *Deutsche Afrika Schau* (German Africa Show), for instance, was a traveling exhibition in which

African actors staged scenes from folklore and everyday life while propagandizing for the benefits of German colonization. These discourses were backed up with the concept of *koloniale Schuldlüge* (lies of colonial guilt), which was part of the broader narrative of German humiliation stirred up by the French and the British.[39] On November 4, 1937, *al-Hasid* reported on the following from the German press: "'We want our colonies back.' . . . 'The German will not be satisfied before the Reich gets its colonies back.' . . . 'If the Reich does not get its colonies back, Europe is condemned to a tragic end.' In other words, Europe is menaced by war if it does not give Germany its colonies back."[40]

'Ezra Haddad, a Jewish historian, political analyst, and main contributor to *al-Hasid* (1900–1972), addressed the issue of raw material (*al-mawadd al-awwaliyya*) in the European colonies. He insisted on the role played by Germany: "Europe is divided into two opposing groups: . . . In the first one, Germany, which has been deprived from its small colonies in Asia and Africa and islands in the Indian Ocean . . . , and Italy. . . . We can see that the deprived group fearlessly and clearly threatens the world and denounces an unjust distribution of colonies. This German Goebbels says: 'We are a poor nation. We have been deprived of our colonies and raw material. We declare to the nations of the world that time has come for us to ask for our colonies back.'" In the case of Italian imperialism, the strategy of discredit was similar. But the argument carried more weight, as Italians did have a history of colonialism in the Arab world (Libya) that offered an example to which an Arabic public could relate. They also had a very recent one in Africa, as Italy occupied Abyssinia in 1936. In an article entitled "Fascism" and signed by an anonymous "democrat," the author stated the following: "Mussolini declares that 'fascism considers the colonial expansion (colonialism) as the true expression of imperialism.' . . . So what did fascism bring to the world? It gave the most horrible example of colonisation. It has tortured, exterminated and deprived its people from their freedom. It has expelled and executed its loyal leaders."[41]

Similarly to the Nazis, fascist rhetoric also developed a discourse on the necessity of colonialism in order to fully accomplish the fascist mission. Modernity would offer local populations in Africa the means to overcome backwardness and chaos and bring true civilization to them.[42]

In response, in 1935 Anwar Sha'ul composed the "Maid of Ethiopia," a poem inspired by the French "Maid of Orléans," Joan of Arc. The poem relates the story of a young woman, the granddaughter of King Menelik, famous for her act of resistance against the Italian troops: "They told her: 'We came to you in order to civilize your people and make it happy.' . . . [She told them]: 'Your words are honey but your actions are poison.' . . . She fought for her beloved nation."[43]

On a formal as well as a narrative level, Sha'ul expresses resistance to Western acculturation and colonialism. The use of the literary genre of the *qasida*—rather than composing short stories (*qisas*), a genre he was much more familiar with until the late 1950s[44]—reveals his will to preserve the structure of traditional Arabic poetry. And his linking of the semantic field of civilization, on the one hand, and war, aggression, and violence, on the other, suggests that the colonial power has evil intentions.

'Ezra Haddad analyzed the factors that led to the formation of the Italian Empire in an article entitled "How Did Italy Build Its Empire? Unveiling the Colonial Machination." He lamented the fact that nobody paid attention to Italy's deadly occupation of Abyssinia: "History has buried its past in the darkness of oblivion and indifference." No one should forget, he wrote, that the Italian Empire had devastated the African country on the pretense of bringing civilization, science, and culture to a people who were victims of their own ignorance and backwardness. But these arguments were nothing but lures, he argued, because behind the civilizational facade, the true goal of the Italians was to subdue and oppress the people of Abyssinia: "It is with sub-machine guns and gas bombs that Italy has brought European culture to Abyssinia." After a detailed analysis of the military conquest of Abyssinia by Emilio de Bono (*Anno XIIII: Conquest of an Empire* [1937]), 'Ezra Haddad eventually asked with consternation: "Do you see, dear reader, how clear were [the Duce's intentions]? Do you understand, now, how colonialism has dealt a mortal blow to the weak and unfortunate nation?" These instances show that the Jews' anticolonial rhetoric functioned as a means to disqualify Nazis and fascists in the eyes of a public possibly in favor of an alliance with Germany against the British. According to this discursive strategy, if the German *colonial guilt* was publicly acknowledged as the British had once been, its candidacy as a new ally for Iraq would easily be disqualified.

Jewish intellectuals' voices joined others in an attempt to create an alternative narrative supporting democracy and rejecting fascism, Nazi totalitarianism, and British colonialism. The Jews made sure that their message would be heard and read by Iraqis outside of the community. *Al-Hasid* was a "political journal" above all, with no sign of Jewish affiliation. The chief editor associated his journalistic enterprise with influential political personalities from the Ahali Group such as Hikmat Sulayman, but also with more nationalistic ones, such as Satiʻ al-Husri, Rashid ʻAli al-Gaylani, Bakr Sidqi, and Yasin al-Hashimi. But the *function* of both anticolonialism and antifascism was different when the Jews were involved. The political situation gave Iraqi Jewish journalists and writers a double incentive to express their opposition to British colonial rule. As Iraqis they claimed independence for their country along with other Iraqis. But as Jews they also needed to reject the process of minoritization in which they were involved and to fight against what the British believed to be a natural alliance with the colonial power. The same went for fascism and Nazism: As Iraqi progressive *muthaqqafun*, they believed that the Nazi regime, perceived as totalitarian by nature, could only harm and destroy their country. But as Jews, they also feared that a German occupation of Iraq would put them in great danger and jeopardize their rights and security.

In conclusion, Iraqi Jews took an active part in the process of remodeling historical and political narratives about Germany and Italy through the press. By doing so, they not only contributed substantially to an alternative public debate on both Nazi and fascist totalitarianism and on the general anticolonial debate, but also gave new meaning to this act of resistance.

6

Assyrians and the Iraqi Communist Party

Revolution, Urbanization, and the Quest for Equality

ALDA BENJAMEN

From the 1940s to the early 1960s, Assyrian communities in Iraq found themselves drawn in disproportionate numbers to the Communist Party. This chapter looks at the context of revolution and urbanization that led Assyrians to leftist and Communist activism, focusing especially on the experience of Assyrians in Kirkuk—a multiethnic oil city with a history of workers' strikes and urban violence and where the Iraq Petroleum Company (IPC) employed a significant number of Kirkukis, including Assyrians. In the revolutionary and postrevolutionary periods, ties between the Assyrian community and the Communist Party were further defined through a series of court-martials accusing Assyrians of antigovernment activity.[1]

Kirkuk experienced accelerated economic and urban development following the discovery of an enormous oil field in 1927. Many Assyrians relocated from surrounding rural districts and Mosul to this new urban space in search of employment at the Iraq Petroleum Company, in a process that altered the demographic makeup of the city. Assyrian workers at the IPC became politically engaged, forming workers' unions, going on strike, and joining the Communist Party. Within this new urban space, they were able to mobilize politically, emerging from the peripheries to take a visible and active role in the urban politics of Kirkuk. Their activities disrupted the existing order, igniting overlapping socioeconomic and ethnic tensions.[2] In this context, many Assyrians were drawn to the Iraqi Communist Party (ICP), attracted by the party's emphasis on socioeconomic and ethnosectarian injustice and its promotion of antisectarianism, secularism, and minority rights—"a struggle shared by all religions and ethnicities" in Iraq.[3]

In the second half of the twentieth century, the Assyrian community became urbanized. As they moved to larger city centers, or continued living in towns that became more urbanized such as Kirkuk, Assyrians began working for larger firms—for example, the IPC—and studying in mixed high schools and universities. Alongside injustices they might have suffered as a community, urban centers exposed them to grievances that had an impact on other Iraqis on their socioeconomic level, such as workers in the IPC. Leftist ideology and exposure to a more vibrant Iraqi press during this period helped draw them toward communism. In Kirkuk these influences were supplemented by active workers' unions and a Communist Party growing in strength and influence.

The republican state under 'Abd al-Qasim's leadership, which replaced the monarchy in 1958, did not translate into what Communists might have anticipated, but the toppling of Qasim in 1963 unleashed extreme violence toward Communists and their sympathizers. Alleged Assyrian Communists, members of the Iraqi Women's League, and thousands of other Iraqis were targeted in the campaign of terror that ensued following Qasim's overthrow. Assyrians were imprisoned for a variety of reasons, but primarily because of their membership in the Communist Party or involvement in one of its affiliated organizations.

Although the ICP claimed to be blind to ethnosectarian affiliations of members, and many of its urban cells comprised members of diverse backgrounds, Assyrian Communists generally organized according to their communal affiliations. This sort of organization simply made sense to a newly urbanized community flocking to large cities such as Baghdad and Kirkuk from much smaller towns and villages. In urban centers, new migrant communities relied on communal and regional affiliations to find employment and housing and learn how to navigate a big city. Such communal affiliations within the party and community were strengthened after 1963, when the party's center shifted to the rural north and many Assyrian relatives and townspeople were collectively punished by state forces. The ruling authority came to identify the community, at least in certain areas, with the Communist Party, and punished them accordingly during its corrective revolution. In turn, a certain village or town would have felt obliged to stand in union with the Communists in defending their village, further reinforcing the affiliation between party and community members.

Assyrian Communists, especially following 1963, thus found themselves in an ambiguous position. They had joined the Communist Party to transcend their ethnic and religious associations, yet they found that their party affiliations ultimately tended to reinforce their communal identity—partly as a result of the attacks on their communities by state agencies in the name of anticommunism.

Identity and Urbanization

Most studies of Iraqi Christians depict community members as adhering to one of a handful of Syriac churches that do not share conceptions of ethnic identity with one another.[4] They take divisions between Nestorians and Chaldeans, for instance, to be primordial, pointing to religious denominations as demographically static, governed primarily by rigid religious institutions.[5] Despite the internal sectarian divisions experienced in the nineteenth century and resulting from Western colonial and missionary encroachment into Ottoman territories, members of the Nestorian, Jacobite, and Chaldean Churches understood themselves to be descended from the ancient Assyrians and by the end of the century were claiming to be heirs of early Mesopotamian civilizations. For instance, at the 1919 Paris Peace Conference, an "Assyrian delegation" comprising Nestorians, Chaldeans, and Jacobites attended collectively to petition for an Assyrian national homeland. The delegation defined the Assyrian community in its petition as including all of the Syriac religious communities.[6] In Mosul British sources reveal that the "old Syrians," or Jacobites, responded in January 1919 to a British inquiry on Iraq's independence by introducing their community as "belonging to the Assyrian race."[7]

The genocidal campaigns of the First World War, the creation of new nation-states whose borders divided Assyrians from one another, and the pinning of the blame for those events by government officials on Nestorian Assyrians all disrupted the social process of nationalization, leading to what Aryo Makko calls a "crisis of identity."[8] The Nestorians were the primary targets of the Iraqi army in the village of Simele, but the massacre soon spread to neighboring Chaldean and Jacobite towns thereafter. Tuma Tumas notes in his memoirs that Alqosh was under threat of attack for harboring escaping Nestorians.[9] Although the event seemed to draw the community together in its immediate aftermath, interdenominational divisions began to emerge, as the Chaldeans—like the Jacobites—began to distance themselves from the Nestorians and the Assyrian identity, given the way Nestorians were presented in the Iraqi national press, and linked to the British. During the 1940s and 1950s, the Syriac Orthodox (Jacobite) religious leadership increasingly distanced itself from the Assyrian identity.[10] Not every community member espoused this position, and secular and nationalist movements emerged in opposition to religious ones—the Assyrian Democratic Organization, for example, was founded in Qamishli, Syria, by Jacobites in 1959. Nonetheless, the aftermath of the Simele massacre saw denominational schisms within the larger Assyrian community.

The urbanization of Assyrians in the second half of the twentieth century removed them from the northern Iraqi villages and small towns where they had traditionally lived. In cities like Kirkuk, Assyrians from various religious denominations and geographical origins lived together in new neighborhoods that were constructed mostly by the Iraq Petroleum Company and found themselves adversely affected by the same issues, regardless of their denominations, under the Iraqi republican governments. In Kirkuk, Baghdad, and other urban centers, they revived earlier efforts to standardize the Eastern Aramaic dialects. By associating with their new neighbors and friends, and through interdenominational marriages, they gave rise to a koine dialect. Intermarriage led Assyrians from different denominations to move past institutional religious boundaries and raise children who felt a less intense and exclusive connection with a specific church. Though such marriages were patriarchal, and tradition dictated that the woman follow her future husband's church and celebrate the wedding ceremony in his parish, there was still some room for negotiation; the wife and her children were rarely completely alienated from her own religious tradition.

Moreover, religious institutions did not always espouse sectarian positions. For example, the late patriarchs of the Chaldean Church Mar Raphael I Bidawid (1922–2003) and of the Assyrian Church of the East Mar Dinkha IV (1935–2015) famously championed an international theological dialogue between their two churches in the mid-1990s, leading in 1997 to the ratification of the "Joint Synodal Decree for Promoting Unity," which in turn initiated dialogue between the Assyrian Church of the East and the Roman Catholic Church.[11] In an interview conducted in Lebanon, probably just before Mar Bidawid's death, he answered a question on the ethnic background of the Chaldean Church by insisting, "We have to separate what is ethnicity and what is religion. . . . I myself, my sect is Chaldean, but ethnically, I am Assyrian."[12] This position complicates our view of Assyrian identity and sectarianism in its various denominational manifestations. Although sectarian identities did crystallize in certain communities, especially in the diasporas, throughout the mid- to late twentieth century, Assyrians of various denominations were not rigidly confined to a specific sect.[13]

Kirkuk and the Politics of Oil

The first gusher at Baba Gurgur, an area just northwest of urban Kirkuk, flowed profusely on October 14, 1927, leading to the discovery of an enormous oil field.[14] The discovery of oil in Kirkuk transformed the city. When Baba Gurgur's gusher struck, Kirkuk's urban population was estimated to be around 25,000. Two decades later the population of urban Kirkuk had more than doubled, reaching approximately 68,000, according to the 1947 census. The British government estimated that in 1948, IPC workers and their families numbered 30,000, half of whom were economically dependent on the oil industry. By 1957 Kirkuk's urban population had doubled again, to more than 120,000.[15]

The number of Assyrians also began to increase in Kirkuk from the 1920s onward; by 1957 Assyrians made up 10.5 percent of the urban population.[16] It is difficult to determine exactly how many Assyrians were employed at the IPC, but British sources allow one to speculate. In 1943 approximately 1,300 discharged Assyrian levies were employed at the IPC.[17] In a conversation between Dr. Nazim al-Pachachi, Iraqi director

general of economics, and Mr. Furneaux from the IPC, regarding the formation of an Assyrian Battalion to aid in the war efforts for Palestine,
1,000 Assyrian IPC workers were said to have volunteered.[18] These numbers seem to be mainly of ex-levy soldiers and do not take into account
other Assyrians who moved to Kirkuk in search of employment and were
not interested in participating in the war effort.[19]

Between 1944 and 1946 sixteen labor unions were allowed to form
in Iraq, twelve of which were controlled by the Communist Party. The
most significant unions were formed in the important industrial centers
of Basra Port and the Iraqi Railways—both under British administration.
In both centers, major strikes for increased wages took place in 1945 at the
railways and the late 1940s at the port. In Kirkuk, however, unions were
not licensed. As a result, workers in Kirkuk went on strike in July 1946,[20]
guided by the Communist Party.[21]

The strike was led by Hanna Ilyas, known as Ilyas Guhari, using his
mother's last name (as Alqoshis take their maternal last name if the mother
comes from a well-known family).[22] Ilyas was twenty-three years old and
a previous member of the Supervisory Council of the Railway Workers.
After moving to Kirkuk he was employed as an oil worker and became
a member of the Kirkuk local Communist Party committee.[23] On July 2
Ilyas along with other Communist workers helped organize the workers,
forming committees and striking regularly. Batatu, British sources, and A.
Q. help us in forming a more complete list of workers' demands. Batatu's
list includes the right to form a union, increase of the minimum basic
daily pay rate from 80 fils to 250 fils, to stop arbitrary firing of workers,
and social security.[24] The British reports list some of these points but also
include workers' demands for housing, transportation, and bonuses.[25] A.
Q. offers a vivid account of this turbulent period, describing himself as an
active participant in the strike and a member of the Communist Party who
became instrumental in founding the Oil Workers Union under Qasim.
His list includes demands for a social club for workers and calls for better
meeting the needs of desert workers.[26]

On July 3 about 5,000 workers went on strike,[27] including approximately 700 Assyrians. The workers would meet in the gardens of Gawur
Baghe, and as testament to the diversity of the workers, Arabic, Kurdish,

Turkomen, Syriac, English, Armenian, and even Hindu was used by the various speakers in their address to the workers.[28] Edward Odisho recalls, "As a child, I remember my illiterate father used to sing out those slogans at home before joining the rest of the demonstrators at the field in Gawur Baghe. One of the slogans said: 'What do you want?' . . . The response from the masses came: 'We want our bread and our children's bread.' . . . Another slogan said: 'What do you want?' The response came: 'We want naphtha for our houses.'"[29]

The *mutassarif* of Kirkuk refused to use force against the demonstrators and was consequently replaced by a new one that proceeded to do so. On July 12 mounted policemen began firing at the workers in Gawur Baghe, killing between 10 and 16 workers, and injuring 27.[30] Further, about 10 workers were detained, including Aprim 'Ama, who would become an important mentor for the youth who formed the Assyrian Democratic Movement in 1979. A. Q. remembers participating in a silent demonstration the next day, where the workers demanded the release of the detainees and to bring the police to justice. Both demands were carried out, and the police were tried in courts eventually. The company eventually conceded to some of the demands of the workers, such as higher wages, but refused to allow them to form a union. The workers returned to work on July 16.[31]

It would take another decade for the oil workers to establish a union. A. Q. was instrumental in the formation of this union, which came into being under Qasim's rule in 1959. In honor of the workers killed in Gawur Baghe in 1946, and their efforts in forming a union, a statue of a worker representing those killed was erected near the oil workers' club in Kirkuk, close to Gawur Baghe.[32]

Some Assyrian employees of the IPC and active within this labor movement eventually joined the ranks of the Communist Party. One was Tuma Tumas himself, a Communist leader and an Assyrian nationalist figure, whose statue was placed in a park dedicated to him in the center of Alqosh in July 2011. His memoir reveals the path to membership in the IPC and ICP for this soon-to-be Communist leader began, ironically, with the Iraqi Levies. After not being accepted into high school in 1941, Tumas remained without school or employment until an opportunity presented itself in 1942, when the British began enlisting Assyrians (members

of the Nestorian and Chaldean Churches) and Kurds into the Iraqi Levies. According to Tumas's memoirs, a British colonel came to Alqosh and
enlisted seventeen-year-old Tumas as an officer in the Iraqi Levies. Tumas
remained with the levy forces until 1948. In that year the Iraqi army
decided to form a special brigade composed of Assyrian volunteers to participate in the war efforts for Palestine. Tumas along with hundreds of
Assyrians in the levy joined.[33] The continuation of the Iraqi Levies into the
1940s contradicts the general assertion that they were disbanded in 1932.
In the Iraqi Levies Tumas, along with Kurdish, Armenian, and Assyrian
officers, "accepted democratic principles," and some joined the Communist Party. Reflecting on his reasons for joining the Communist effort, he
stated: "As for me, it was a result of the arrogant stances of British officers,
the rising democratic tide, my communication with martyr Ilyas Hanna
Guhari,[34] and our exposure to Iraqi press, especially the newspaper *al-
Ahali*, the most influential in the progression of my political awareness.
I began to feel the enormity of my error in joining the levy army. This
feeling deepened for me further in my years of employment at the IPC in
Kirkuk. I often collided with British officers who considered themselves
higher than local (native) officers."[35]

In 1950 Tumas began working for the IPC in Kirkuk. He also started
receiving political (Communist) publications and paying membership
fees to the party on a monthly basis.[36] Tumas described a heightened
political awareness among IPC workers as a result of Communist activities. In addition, he believed that the arbitrary politics of the company and
its refusal to accept the "simplest requests of workers" contributed to the
politicization of workers as well. Tumas was further frustrated by the look
of contempt given by the British to Iraqi workers and staff. For instance,
Iraqi employees at the company were required to use the phrase "Yes, sir"
when addressing Englishmen employed at the IPC. The president of the
IPC, according to Tumas, had absolute powers in Kirkuk; even the police
and security officials obeyed his command.

In his memoir Tumas identified various events that led him toward
the Communist Party in his early life, beginning with the Simele massacre and including his inability to continue on to high school given his
socioeconomic background.[37] The labor movement in Kirkuk certainly

heightened his political commitments. Such political activism exacerbated socioeconomic and ethnic tensions among the various Kirkuki communities, reaching a boiling point in 1959.

The 1959 Kirkuk Crisis

The July 1959 crisis in Kirkuk was a watershed event whose lasting repercussions resurfaced in 1963. Though this crisis played a significant role in how Communists and their sympathizers would be treated by nationalists and state authority figures in Kirkuk following Qasim's toppling, the events that transpired in Mosul a few months earlier shed light on the ways in which Assyrians were treated owing to their membership or assumed affiliation with the Communist Party and foreshadowed events in Kirkuk.[38]

On July 14, 1959, violent clashes broke out between Turkomen and Kurds in Kirkuk during a procession celebrating the first anniversary of the revolution. As in the case of Mosul, scholars agree that the conflict in Kirkuk was based on ethnic rather than political tensions—albeit exacerbated by social underpinnings—caused by growing animosity between the more established Turkomen community and the newer Communist-affiliated Kurdish one.[39] The oil industry had attracted more Kurds from surrounding villages, increasing their numbers to one-third of the population in 1959, whereas the numbers of Turkomen had declined to half of the overall population of 120,000. Assyrians accounted for about 10 percent of the population, and Arabs made up the rest.[40] Changing demographics and the appointment of Kurds to many important posts in the city traditionally held by Turkomen contributed to the conflict by causing the Turkomen to feel marginalized.[41] Regardless of the issues underlying the conflict, the Communist Party was held responsible. Furthermore, members of the People's Resistance—a "popular militia" organized by the government in 1958 but heavily influenced by the ICP—also shouldered the blame.[42] Like the Shawwaf massacre in Mosul, the Kirkuk incident highlighted the disgruntlement of traditional nationalists and other established communities in the city of Kirkuk. The emergence of new communities, and in particular their political and economic mobilization, exacerbated ethnosectarian and socioeconomic tensions and led to the eruption of violence. The association of the Communist Party and its affiliate organizations with the 1959 crisis is significant for the courts-martial that were held in Kirkuk in 1963. For the majority population, the crisis evoked the memory of the Qasimite regime; like his presidency, it was referred to by his adversaries as the "chaotic tide," following which the Ba'thists, presenting themselves as the vanguard of the revolution, would proceed to restore order.

In the brief period when Qasim held power (1958–63), the Assyrians enjoyed a relatively beneficial situation. From the 1950s, Assyrians had begun a process of integration into major urban centers, as will be discussed in the following section. During the 1950s, Assyrians moved to cities in large numbers, in search of employment and education. Assyrian refugees from the First World War who were still living in the Habaniyya camp purchased land and began building a new neighborhood on the outskirts of Baghdad.[43] As the city grew, this district was eventually incorporated into Baghdad, attracting more Assyrian families who migrated to the capital from their villages in the northern provinces. In 1959, with their growing presence in Baghdad, Assyrian members of the Nestorian Church opened their first church in the capital since the creation of the republic. In a sign of official support, Qasim and other government officials attended the church's opening ceremony.[44] At the same time, however, Assyrian aspirations to form secular cultural and political organizations were dashed. For instance, April 1961 saw the formation of Khuyada w Kheirutha Athorayta (Assyrian Unity and Freedom), known as Kheith Kheith Allap II. When its application to register was denied by the government, its organizers were prompted to move their activities to the north. Such developments strengthened ties between Assyrian organizations and the Kurdish resistance, especially following Qasim's toppling in 1963. Assyrians within the Communist Party, or sympathetic to it, probably felt ambiguous about Qasim. For instance, A. Q. described how difficult it was to receive a permit for the formation of an oil workers' union even under Qasim's rule. A. Q. and other organizers discovered that Qasim wanted to block their efforts to form a union and instead bestow rights upon workers in a paternal fashion. Qasim eventually allowed the formation of the union, after some skillful maneuvering on the part of its activists—though A. Q., reminiscing about the president, suggested that he had "had a good heart." Regardless of Communists' ambivalent feelings about Qasim, his toppling in 1963—mainly by Arab nationalists and Ba'thists—was catastrophic for their party.

The 1963 Coup and Its Effects

On February 8, 1963, an army coup led by Ba'thists and nationalists toppled the Qasim regime and began a violent campaign against Communists and their sympathizers. On the same day, the new government broadcast Proclamation 13, stating: "In view of the desperate attempts of the agent-communists—the partners in crime of the enemy of God Qasim—to sow confusion in the ranks of the people and their disregard of official orders and instructions, the commanders of the military units, the police, and the National Guard are authorized to annihilate anyone that disturbs the peace. The royal sons of the people are called upon to cooperate with authorities by informing against these criminals and exterminating them." House-to-house arrests of alleged Communists followed, purportedly made possible by lists provided by the US Central Intelligence Agency.[45] During this campaign close to ten thousand people were detained and three to five thousand executed.[46] Those individuals arrested were tortured by "special committees" and by the National Guard, a Ba'thist militia.[47] Ismail posits the campaign of terror resulted from "mixed personal, sectarian, and tribal hatreds," while Batatu emphasizes socioeconomic factors.[48] This campaign against the Communists and their sympathizers continued throughout the upcoming months. In May, as Ba'thists felt more isolated, having had a fallout with the Nasserites and Nasser himself in July and rekindled war with the Kurds, they began to be more violent toward their enemies. This situation was exacerbated in July as Communist-inclined soldiers and officers unsuccessfully attempted to take over the Iraqi military camp of al-Rashid and liberate Communist prisoners there.[49] This violence affected Assyrians as well. In response to an inquiry from the British Foreign Office regarding complaints from Assyrians in the diaspora about discriminatory practices Iraqi Assyrians were facing, the British Embassy in Baghdad confirmed reports that the

National Guard and the army were searching the Assyrian quarter for Assyrian Communists and in the process raping Assyrian women.[50]

The more progressive elements within the Ba'th Party criticized the level of violence used against Iraqi Communists by Ba'th Party members and the National Guard.[51] They were concerned with how these trials reflected on their party internally within Iraq and externally to regional and Western audiences. For instance, Michel 'Aflaq, founder and secretary-general of the party, gave a speech on this subject on February 2, 1964, at the Extraordinary Congress of the Syrian Ba'th.[52] Although this self-criticism was never officially or publicly stated, it could have been the reason for the public trials of Communists that followed.

The Case of Barkhu and His Colleagues

The subsequent trials of Assyrian men affiliated with the ICP focused on ethnic identity and questioned Assyrians' status as Iraqi. Barkhu and his three colleagues were employees at the Iraq Petroleum Company and residents of Kirkuk. They were accused of being members of the Communist Party and its associated militia, the People's Resistance. Barkhu was a twenty-nine-year-old electrician with a leadership role of some kind in his department.[53] Babajan was twenty-one, worked as an electrician in the same department, and was also a bandage dresser at the IPC hospital.[54] The two Sahakians were father and son; the father was a forty-seven-year-old stock clerk at the IPC,[55] while his son was a twenty-seven-year-old employee of the electrical department.[56] Two of the four men were sentenced to five and two years in prison, where one died mysteriously while serving his sentence.

The investigation was initiated on March 4, 1963, with the questioning of seven witnesses, most of whom were employed in the electrical department of the IPC, while some held positions in its hospital. The witnesses accused their colleagues of being members of both the People's Resistance and the Communist Party. Following these reports, the men were arrested according to Article 12/31 Q.'A.B.[57] On March 5, 1963, the four accused men were questioned in turn. All men were asked whether they were members of the Communist Party, whether they owned a firearm, whether they had participated in the 1959 Kirkuk crisis, and whether they had insulted Baʻthists, Nasser, or Turanians. In their responses, the accused men declined being members of the Communist Party, owning firearms, and having insulted the Baʻthists, Nasser, or the Turanians. Each also denied participating in the violent events of 1959, Barkhu claiming he had been in Baghdad vacationing with his family during that week. They were asked whether they had any animosity toward the witnesses or could suggest reasons for such accusations being made against them. The Sahakians were surprised by these accusations, Barkhu believed that the senior position he held in the department was the root cause of the resentment, and Babajan questioned the idea that membership in the People's Resistance was assumed to include membership in the Communist Party: "I joined the People's Resistance without being a Communist. My purpose [in joining] was patriotic (*watani*). I did not know that every Resistor (Muqawim Shaʻbi) becomes [identified as a] communist. No one [asked me] to become a Communist. I did not commit any crimes, and these accusations against me are not true."[58]

The house search did not yield any evidence for prohibited items, whether firearms or illegal press.[59] On March 16, 1963, the Investigation Committee forwarded the cases to the military court of the northern region.[60] The report indicated that there was incriminating evidence against Barkhu, Babajan, and Sahakian Jr. for acts committed during the "chaotic tide." They would continue to be detained, and their case would be forwarded for further investigation. It was determined, however, that not enough evidence was available on Sahakian Sr., and he was released on bail of five hundred dinars.

The three remaining men—Barkhu, Babajan, and Sahakian Jr.—were questioned further, along with the witnesses. Sahakian Jr. still denied being part of the Communist Party or any related organization.[61] Barkhu denied being part of the Communist Party, but admitted to collecting membership funds for the Workers' Syndicate[62] and to being a member of the People's Resistance—though he had carried arms only during practice. He had joined the People's Resistance with a large number of people out of a patriotic commitment to defending the nation. Babajan continued to avow his membership in the People's Resistance, but not the ICP.[63]

Witnesses had testified that he had distributed ICP newspapers to patients at the hospital; Babajan claimed he had distributed only the newspapers given to him by the company.

On July 15, 1963, the fourth court-martial in Kirkuk was formed, issuing a guilty verdict that declared:

> 1. Barkhu was part of People's Resistance and carried an armed gun during the chaotic tide. He insulted the Ba'th party and Jamal 'Abd al-Nasir. He collected memberships for the Worker's Union. He attacked all nationalists, and supported the Kurdish rebellion. He claimed to be a descendant of the Sumerians [or an Assyrian]. [Note: witnesses made this accusation; Barkhu did not provide a clarification.] Therefore article 12/31 from Q 'A B applies to his actions and he will be tried according to it.
>
> 2. It has been proved to the court that Babajan was part of the People's Resistance. He distributed Communist newspapers to the sick at the Iraq Petroleum Company's hospital. Therefore article 12/31 from Q. 'A. B. applies to his actions and he will be tried according to it.
>
> 3. Sahakian Junior used to carry a weapon in his private car [during] night patrols under pressure from the People's Resistance. Due to the lack of evidence against him, the court has decided to release him according to article 155 and [illegible] the bail, which was taken from him.[64]

Barkhu was sentenced to five years of hard labor, plus one year of parole following the completion of his sentence, and Babajan was sentenced to two years of hard labor and one year of parole. The sentences were carried out in Suleiman Prison.

In 1964 and 1965 the Ministry of Justice apparently reinvestigated some Communist Party members and sympathizers. These crimes became known as "crimes of intellect." In Barkhu's case, an appeal initiated by his wife was denied in 1964 by the Investigation Body for the Martial Law Cases, although recommendations to reduce his sentence were advanced by the Ministry of Defense.[65] The appeal appears to have been raised again in 1965, which appears to have triggered further negative consequences, as a new investigation into his citizenship was now requested. The report issued an inquiry into Barkhu's citizenship, specifying that if he had acquired Iraqi citizenship through naturalization instead of birth, he should be sent back to his country of birth upon the completion of his sentence.[66] On April 29, 1965, Barkhu was proclaimed dead in al-Diwaniyya hospital.[67] No cause of death was specified, and the case was closed.

The case of Barkhu brought into question the "Iraqiness" of Assyrians, triggering an inquiry into his citizenship, and tested how the new political elites would deal with the identity of Assyrians, whose claim of descent from ancient Mesopotamians was included as incriminating evidence by the fourth court-martial. As members of an ethnoreligious minority, some of these Assyrian men and women had benefited from the new political and economic opportunities available to them. Some, such as Barkhu, held positions of leadership within the IPC, while others joined the Communists or affiliated organizations. Members of these organizations were visible in the Kirkuki public sphere and, together with the Communist Party, were held responsible for the 1959 incident in the city. These men and women had contributed to the "chaotic tide" by crossing ethnic and confessional boundaries and claiming a degree of citizenship not available to members of their community. In addition to their political mobilization, some were accused of highlighting their Assyrian identity in a way that exacerbated Arab nationalist fears of being sidelined by the Qasimite regime.[68] These cases were by no means isolated; according to A. Q., who was also imprisoned in 1963, many Assyrians were interrogated and temporarily imprisoned. Out of five hundred convicted Kirkukis, one hundred were Assyrian. If the Kurdish farmers from beyond Kirkuk are included, the number of prisoners in Kirkuk increases to fifteen hundred.[69]

Conclusion

These trials and convictions had severe consequences for the Assyrian community. In cities the families of the arrested were devastated; Barkhu's wife appealed the case of her husband years after his conviction and imprisonment. Moreover, although Assyrians were arrested for a variety of reasons, the fact that some cases involved personal conflicts and identity issues would have caused the community to feel targeted. This impression is reinforced by complaints from the Assyrian community in England to British officials about the treatment of Iraqi Assyrians in 1963.

Although the British investigation focused mainly on Baghdad, the court cases, ICP publications, and oral interviews indicate that Assyrians in Kirkuk and other areas also felt threatened. For instance, on June 30, 1963, the army and the Juhush forces—Kurdish militia affiliated with the state—advanced toward Alqosh, threatening to attack it. The residents escaped to Alqosh's mountain and were saved by Communist forces, some of whom were probably Alqoshis and Assyrians from neighboring villages.[70] The National Guard planned a second attack in Alqosh on July 9—this time equipped with artillery and tanks. The intention appears to have been the arrest of Communists and their families—but Alqoshi residents were attacked and injured and two elderly men killed. During the battle a number of Communist Alqoshis died as well. Some of these men were eventually transported to the martyrs' cemetery in Saint Hormizd Monastery, a seventh-century religious and cultural site that is of significance to both Alqoshis and Assyrians. This interment location indicates that the townspeople did not think of these slaughtered men only as politically motivated individuals who were members of the Communist Party but also took pride in them as Alqoshi community members, commemorating their deaths by burying them in one of the community's most sacred places.[71]

Whether such attacks on Assyrian villages were isolated incidents or a common practice affecting other communities as well, given that they were combined with the arrests of Assyrians in urban centers and attacks on some Assyrian quarters, it is reasonable to assume that the community would have felt threatened. It seems that, in certain cases, when the attacks extended to majority Assyrian villages, the Assyrians were being targeted as a community, whereas in others they were tried narrowly on the basis on their activism within the Communist Party and its affiliated organizations. Regardless of the aftermath of the 1963 coup, membership of Assyrians within the Communist Party should not be limited to communal interpretations only, although it was an indication of their interest in being better integrated within Iraq. Ironically, because of their association with the Communists, many Assyrians instead felt isolated and targeted after the 1963 coup.

1

The Struggle over Egyptianness

A Case Study of the Nayruz Festival

HIROKO MIYOKAWA

In the latter half of the nineteenth century, new notions of nationalism, ethnicity, and "minority" were introduced to the Middle East under European colonial influence. In Egypt the Coptic Christians were positioned as Egyptian citizens and categorized as a "minority" group at the same time. This ambiguity stemmed from two different visions—liberal and ethnoreligious—of the Egyptian nation-state.

During this period, Copts emerged as strong supporters of a liberalism that confined religion to the private sphere and therefore secured them a position as Egyptian citizens equal to their Muslim compatriots. At the same time, they were enthusiastic about positioning themselves as *authentic* Egyptians, presenting ancient cultural practices as proof of belonging. Either way, Copts refused the label of minority and tried to demonstrate that they were full and committed members of the newly born Egyptian nation-state.

In previous studies concerning the Copts in the early twentieth century, equality, national unity, and Coptic participation in national politics emerged as primary themes.[1] Much of this literature assumed that Copts identify themselves as Egyptians simply because they are indigenous people who have lived in Egypt from ancient times. In this chapter, I focus instead on the *creation* of Coptic Christians' ethnoreligious identity as "authentic" Egyptians around the turn of the twentieth century. The revival movement of the Nayruz festival in the early twentieth century, and its second revival very recently, can serve as a lens through which to observe this construction of Egyptian cultural "authenticity" and clarify how modern transformations forced the Copts to construct a new kind of ethnicity and deal with their "minority" status.

Egyptian Nationalism and Pharaonism

Around the turn of the twentieth century, two strands of a nascent Egyptian nationalism were emerging: a broadly liberal understanding of national identity and a more specifically "ethnic" vision of national belonging. Coptic activists, writers, and thinkers drew from both philosophical strands to promote a new vision for Coptic participation in an emerging Egyptian national movement, but placed particular importance on an ethnic understanding of Egyptian identity that privileged ancient Egyptian history and geography as the primary marker of modern Egyptian national identity.

Liberal Egyptian nationalism in this period defined Egyptians as people who live in Egypt, have no other homeland, and are loyal to their homeland, irrespective of their ethnic or religious affiliations.[2] This trend of Egyptian nationalism was based on Western-style liberalism; it supported the idea that racial, ethnic, and religious affiliations should be ignored in the public sphere, and those individuals who had different backgrounds should be equally treated because these affiliations belonged to the private sphere. The main promoter of this liberal trend of Egyptian nationalism in the early twentieth century was Ahmad Lutfi al-Sayyid (1872–1963), known as *ustadh al-jil*, the "professor of the generation," who was particularly influential in the development of Egyptian nationalist thought.[3] Wendell cites Lutfi's opinion in his newspaper, *al-Jarida*, dated October 21, 1911, that "the Egyptians must not, in the interests of the country, make religion—under these circumstances—the basis for their political acts." Carter also points out that "Lutfi al-Sayyid was one of the first to help lay a foundation for a polity in which Muslims and Copts could participate on an equal basis."[4]

This trend not only aimed to introduce the new concept of the Egyptian nation-state but also tried to create an Egyptian nation loyal to the Egyptian nation-state by integrating different religious and ethnic groups. Coptic Christians were positioned as Egyptian citizens under this type of nationalism.[5] In addition to indigenous Egyptians, ethnic minorities who lived in Egypt at that time—encompassing Syrians, Greeks, and Armenians who had immigrated to Egypt earlier in the nineteenth century—were also positioned as Egyptian citizens.

A competing vision of "ethnic" Egyptian nationalism developed almost simultaneously, especially in the 1920s and 1930s, focusing on the construction of an ethnically Egyptian national history and the establishment of a national literature. As is widely known, ethnic Egyptian nationalism attached importance to the physical environment, particularly the Nile Valley, which was viewed as a primary shaper of the Egyptian personality. Citing civics textbooks published in the 1920s, Gershoni and Jankowski point out that "the natural environment was thus made into the primary element forging the unity of the nation." This ethnic trend of Egyptian nationalism overlapped to some degree with the liberal nationalism in defining the Egyptian nation, but also contained some fundamental differences, aiming to nurture an Egyptian ethnic identity among the people who had lived along the Nile Valley generation after generation. Muhammad Husayn Haykal (1888–1956), an Egyptian nationalist thinker, asserted that when people from neighboring areas such as Greeks and Turks settled in Egypt, the natural environment Egyptianized them over generations so that eventually they became homogeneous Egyptians.[6]

Pharaonism, a branch of this "ethnic" Egyptian nationalist thought, promoted the concept of ancient Egyptian civilization as a foundation for a modern cultural and ethnic Egyptian identity. Unlike the ethnic Egyptian nationalism mentioned above, Pharaonism mooted a blood relationship between ancient and modern Egyptians that created both physical and mental similarities between them.[7] Egyptology, which developed dramatically and rapidly after the decipherment of hieroglyphs by Jean-François Champollion (1790–1832) and excavations conducted by European archaeologists in the nineteenth century, contributed to the birth of this type of Egyptian nationalism. In nineteenth-century Egypt, knowledge about and interest in ancient Egypt were rather limited, and Egyptians did not generally share Europeans' fascination with ancient Egypt. It was through contact with Europe that Egyptian intellectuals of the day like

Rifaʻa al-Tahtawi (1801–73) and ʻAli Mubarak (1823–93) became acquainted with ancient Egyptian civilization. The situation changed when the tomb of Tut Ankh Amen was discovered in 1922, when Egypt gained nominal independence from Britain after a fierce nationalist struggle against colonialism. The discovery of ancient treasures in the year of independence sparked the Pharaonic boom among Egyptian intellectuals in the 1920s and 1930s, although new Arab-Islamic tendencies rapidly overtook Pharaonism in the popular imagination after the 1930s.

For the Coptic Christians, however, Pharaonism had special significance in fortifying their position in the framework of Egyptian nationalism. Because Copts are an indigenous religious minority and are considered to be descendants of ancient Egyptians who later embraced the Christian faith and maintained it after the arrival of Islam, the emphasis on their indigenousness and pure-bloodedness seemed a potentially viable basis for positioning the Copts as *authentic* Egyptians. Indeed, after the Copts took a growing interest in ancient Egypt, influenced by European Egyptomania, they began to argue that many of their religious traditions had their origin in ancient Egypt. The Coptic language, for instance, had long been abandoned as a spoken language by the nineteenth century but was still in use in psalms and liturgy of the Coptic Church.[8] After the decipherment of hieroglyphs, the relation between the Egyptian language and Coptic became clearer, and Coptic was considered to be in the fifth stage of the evolution of the Egyptian language.[9] Based on this new knowledge, Iqlawdiyus Labib (1868–1918), a Coptic lecturer at the Coptic seminary, tried to revive Coptic as a daily spoken language and promoted it as a "true Egyptian language" to both Copts and Muslims in his magazine, *ʻAyn Shams*. He asserted, "In order to be called an Egyptian, not nominally but actually, one has to learn this Egyptian language, its literature, its wisdom, and its traces."[10] Ancient Egyptian cultural heritages such as the Coptic language and the Coptic calendar, it was argued, had been passed down among Copts in Christianized forms.

This reinterpretation of ancient Egypt as the ethnic origin of the Egyptians provided the Copts with a solid footing for positioning themselves as full-fledged Egyptians and compensated for their weak position as non-Muslims. In addition, the reinterpretation of ancient Egypt as the origin of their religious traditions provided them with grounds for positioning Coptic Christianity as a cultural heritage from the great past and thus a part of Egyptian national culture. Unlike liberalism, which promoted equality by ignoring the religious affiliation of the Copts, Pharaonism linked Coptic religious traditions to the great ancient past, thereby enshrining Coptic identity as fundamentally and "authentically" Egyptian.

The Nayruz Festival

Today, the Egyptian Nayruz festival is widely known as the Martyrs' Festival. It is celebrated inside the Coptic Orthodox Church on September 11, which falls on New Year's Day by the Coptic calendar. The Nayruz festival is a Christian festival that commemorates the Coptic martyrs persecuted by the Roman emperor Diocletian in the third century. The Coptic calendar, which employs basically the same system for calculating the year and has the same month names as the ancient Egyptian calendar, came to be called by this name when the Coptic Church set the year 284 CE, the first year of Diocletian's reign, as the first year of the Coptic calendar to commemorate the persecution.[11] Therefore, the Coptic calendar is also known as the Martyrs' Calendar (Taqwim al-Shuhada'), and the celebration of its New Year's Day is the Martyrs' Festival. However, the Egyptian Nayruz, or the celebration of Egyptian New Year's Day, has its roots in ancient Egypt, having been previously celebrated as one of the major Nile festivals. New Year's Day in ancient Egypt was called Wept Renpet (the beginning of the year), and it is considered to be one of the oldest festivals in ancient Egypt.[12] It was a celebration for the advent of the Nile inundation and the manifestation of Isis.

It is not clear whether the New Year's Day festival continued to be celebrated in the Greco-Roman or Coptic eras, although remarks about the celebration of New Year's Day in the Coptic calendar appear in medieval chronicles dated as early as the tenth century.[13] By this time, the festival's name had been changed to the Nayruz or the Nawruz. It is not clear when this name was adopted or where it came from; some argue that it was taken from the Persian "Nawruz," and others argue that Nayruz is a corrupt form of its original Coptic name.[14] However, 'Awad points out that the name of the Nayruz in Coptic is "the beginning of the year."[15]

Therefore, it seems more likely that the appellation "Nayruz" came from the Persian "Nawruz."

In the fifteenth century, al-Maqrizi reported that the Nayruz was celebrated as a Nile festival and that its celebration included popular rituals of revelry, including violence. Its highlight was the procession of the Prince of Nayruz, who acted as a collector of a fabulous debt of dignitaries. Even though the festival was generally regarded as Coptic, both Muslims and Copts celebrated it. Because of the revelries, which included transvestism, masquerade, and violence, the Nayruz in medieval Egypt was banned in 1385 when Sultan Barquq ordered the celebrations to be abolished. Accordingly, the festival had disappeared in Cairo by the fifteenth century.

The Nayruz as a Nile festival was forgotten in the capital, though it survived in the provinces. According to Shoshan, the celebration of the Nayruz as a Nile festival continued in rural areas, and there are at least four cases reported by European travelers and scholars between the nineteenth and early twentieth centuries.[16]

The Revival of the Nayruz Festival

The revival of the Nayruz festival in modern Egypt was inaugurated by Tadrus Shenuda al-Manqabbadi (1857–1932), a Coptic notable from the city of Asyut. He was known as a nationalist activist, and during the 'Urabi Revolt in 1881 he sent food aid to support the 'Urabi camp. Inside the Coptic community, he was one of the reformists who opposed the clergy's control over church estates.[17]

He founded the Society for the Preservation of the Coptic Calendar in 1884. Prior to the foundation of this society, the Coptic calendar was abolished as the official calendar of the government in 1875, and the Gregorian calendar took its place. The objective of the society was to preserve the Coptic calendar, record it, and put it to use, as in the past.[18] The society was the first to promote the revival of the Nayruz in modern Egypt, and the first celebration was conducted in Asyut in 1885.

There were other associations that promoted the revival of the Nayruz. One such association was the Tawfiq Society, which was based in Cairo and had several branches in other cities. Its first Nayruz was celebrated in

1893, two years after its establishment. The Coptic Association of Growth, also based in Cairo, printed the Coptic calendar for the first time in 1897, citing its importance as an agricultural and ecclesiastical calendar.[19]

The abolition of the Coptic calendar gave rise to its revalorization among the Copts, and the revival of the celebration of its New Year's Day, the Nayruz, came to be promoted as a means to emphasize its cultural importance. The Coptic calendar has long been used as an agricultural calendar in Egypt among the peasants of both faiths. Because the Hijri calendar is a lunar calendar, it was not suitable for agriculture, and the Coptic calendar had been used to know the periods for agricultural events such as the Nile flooding, sowing, and harvesting. Each month of the Coptic calendar has a phrase to highlight the quality of the month. For example, the month of Amshir, which falls on February to March by the Gregorian calendar and is known as the month of sandstorms, has the phrase "Amshir abu al-zaʿabib al-kathir, yukhabbat yulabbat fih min rawaʾih al-sayf," meaning "The month of Amshir has numerous storms, but gives the feeling of summer."[20] In addition, each month has its delicacies, such as milk of Baramhat (March to April) and fig of Abib (July to August). The Coptic calendar was closely related to the daily lives of Egyptians and had meteorological significance. At the same time, the Coptic calendar was the ecclesiastical calendar of the Coptic Orthodox Church, so Christian festivals were calculated according to it; the whole month of Kiyahk is consecrated to the praise of the Virgin Mary, for its twenty-ninth day is the Nativity of Christ.[21] Therefore, the Coptic calendar was considered to represent ethnic Egyptian indigenous culture, Coptic Christianity, and ancient Egypt at the same time. These intertwined characters of the Coptic calendar had a significant meaning for the Copts. It served as a means to demand an acknowledgment of their specificity and Egyptianness at the same time; the revival of the Nayruz festival by al-Manqabbadi was one such attempt to construct Egyptianness.

Al-Manqabbadi moved to Cairo in 1895 to begin a newspaper titled *Misr*, at Butrus Pasha Ghali's invitation. *Misr* was the chief Coptic publication in the first half of the twentieth century, along with *al-Watan* and *al-Manara al-Misriyya*, and it later became one of the major official newspapers of the Wafd Party.[22] Al-Manqabbadi continued the revival of the

Nayruz in Cairo and publicized the Nayruz as the Coptic New Year's Day in his newspaper every year. He also issued a yearly magazine titled *al-Hadiyya al-Tutiyya*, which denoted the gift of the Coptic New Year, on Coptic New Year's Day and distributed it in the venues of the Nayruz festival.

Celebrations of the Revived Nayruz

According to the articles about the revived Nayruz in *Misr*, it was celebrated under the initiative of lay Coptic associations like the one al-Manqabbadi established in Asyut or the Tawfiq Society, which was one of the main promoters of the Nayruz. The major fields that these associations were engaged in were social welfare and education, and the leaders of such groups were among a growing contingent focused on the progression and modernization of Egypt.[23]

At the festival, religious leaders and notables including Muslims were invited, intellectuals gave speeches, and schoolchildren put on plays and sang songs. The revived Nayruz, then, was not celebrated with revelry similar to the medieval Nayruz. The great majority of the participants were Copts, and the festival was organized with the loose cooperation of the Coptic Church. The venues included the headquarters of Coptic associations, Coptic schools, and Coptic churches. The revived Nayruz was not celebrated only in Cairo; *Misr* on September 13, 1899, reported that the Nayruz festival was celebrated in Alexandria, Zaqaziq, Qaliyub, and Suez, among others, all of which were located on the Delta. On the following day, *Misr* reported the Nayruz festival in al-Minya and on September 19 of the same year in Qina in Upper Egypt.

According to *Misr* on September 12, 13, 14, and 19, 1899, at the Nayruz festival in 1899, Iqlawdiyus Labib, the reviver of the Coptic language, delivered a speech in Coptic, and another speech was delivered by Archdeacon Habib Girgis (1876–1951), the leader of the Sunday school movement. Until the 1910s, the guests were mainly Coptic figures who played active roles as members of the Coptic community. However, with the rise of nationalist movement and the 1919 Revolution, the Nayruz festival played the role of providing an occasion to confirm the national unity between Muslims and Copts. Beginning in the 1920s, then, high-ranking political and religious leaders came to be invited to the festival. In 1920 and 1923, Sa'd Zaghlul (1859–1927), the leader of the 1919 Revolution, was invited to deliver a speech at the Nayruz festival organized by the Tawfiq Society. His speech in 1923 was about the role of the Copts in the 1919 Revolution, their fight against colonialism, and the importance of national unity. In 1942 Prime Minister Mustafa al-Nahhas and Patriarch Yusab the Second were invited to the festival, and in 1952 Muhammad Nagib, the first president of Egypt, and Patriarch Yusab the Second were also invited.

The Nayruz Festival and Egyptianness

Since the 1910s, al-Manqabbadi began making comments on the revived Nayruz from the nationalist point of view. In *Misr* on September 14, 1916, he placed the manuscript of his speech delivered on the occasion of the Nayruz at a Coptic association called the General Reform Society, entitled "The Oldest Festival for the Oldest People." In this speech he asserted that the Nayruz was

> the oldest festival known in Egypt, nay, in the whole world. However, after it continued to be celebrated as a public festival for long centuries, regarding it as the festival of whole Egyptian people (*al-'umma al-misriyya*), . . . these days, the Nayruz is regarded as a festival unique to Copts as if it is a solely religious festival even though there is no relation to religion by itself. . . .
>
> The Nayruz is the beginning of the Egyptian agricultural year, the year of irrigation and inundation. Ancient Egyptians set its beginning and the months of current Coptic year in the reign of King Menes I. They applied days and months of this year for cultivation of the soil, planting, irrigation, and all that is related to agriculture. To this time, an Egyptian farmer (*fallah*) and the common people do not know except Coptic months and days in all of their works.

In *Misr* on September 15, 1916, he published the rest of his speech:

> This old festival has been observed in Egypt in all past generations. Even Persians, Romans and Arabs also, all of them in their period had to celebrate the Nayruz in conformity with Egyptian people. The Fatimid and the Abbasid Caliphs and Arab Amirs who took over this country from

them participated in the celebration of this festival by themselves and absorbed the cost of large celebrations and many ceremonies from the budget of the government.

In *Misr* on September 10, 1918, al-Manqabbadi placed an announcement to inform the readers that the Nayruz would be the following day. He announced, "Tomorrow is the biggest festival of Egypt, the festival of irrigation, agriculture, and all that is special to Egypt and her Nile and all of its specialties." After pointing out that the rulers of Egypt throughout the ages hosted and sponsored the Nayruz celebrations, he noted, "But today, only some Coptic associations are interested in its revival even though it is every Egyptian's duty to remember and celebrate it for its historical, national, and agricultural importance."

In *Misr* on September 10, 1924, in an article titled "Holiday of the Employees on the Nayruz Day," al-Manqabbadi noted:

> It was permitted for the Egyptian Christian "Copt" civil servants to conduct liturgy in their churches on the Nayruz day until ten o'clock in the morning just like every Sunday. However, many of them demanded that the Nayruz of every year should be made a holiday for them in honor of one of the oldest Egyptian national festivals. Then the Ministry of Finance fulfilled its employees' demand and decided the exemption from work for them on the Nayruz day tomorrow.
>
> We hope that the holiday of the civil servants in the Ministry of Finance become generalized in all of the ministries and offices, or at least among the Coptic civil servants just like their brothers in the Ministry of Finance, if it was not set as a holiday of the ministries for its being a national festival (*'id watani*) that all the nation (*umma*) participate in its Egyptian appearance and ceremonies.
>
> The Nayruz festival is not a religious festival but it is a general national (*qawmi*) festival. It is the beginning of the Egyptian agricultural year that I hope to be the beginning of our freedom and independence and our power of unity and our strong solidarity.

From these articles, we can see that al-Manqabbadi deployed the Coptic calendar and the Nayruz festival as representations of ancient Egypt,

Egyptian indigenous culture, and Coptic Christianity. Copts needed to prove their authenticity in the context of nationalism and minoritization; therefore, though the Nayruz was generally known as a Christian Martyrs' Festival and thus a religious occasion, al-Manqabbadi repeatedly rejected its religious character and demanded that the revived Nayruz be recognized as a national holiday. His objective was to receive an acknowledgment of Coptic culture as a part of a national culture by de-Christianizing it. In other words, he tried to embed Coptic culture in Egyptianness.

He promoted other markers of Coptic cultural identity as authentically Egyptian as well, suggesting that cultural traits attributed to Copts, such as the Coptic language and the Coptic calendar, were not necessarily Christian, and in a sense they were shared with Muslims as well. On September 9, 1913, al-Manqabbadi noted in *Misr*: "Today, we sent a letter to respectable *al-Mu'ayyad* newspaper for this occasion (the Nayruz), asking them to use this calendar (the Coptic calendar) again in their paper like other newspapers because it ceased to use it recently, probably because of negligence or obliviousness. We also asked the same request to respectable *al-Ahali* newspaper, and we hope that they respond to it because it is a shame that Egyptian newspapers disregard the Egyptian calendar that has all these ancient and important virtues and it is still a calendar of irrigation, agriculture, weather, and production until today." On September 12 of the same year, al-Manqabbadi reported that he received a reply from *al-Mu'ayyad* newspaper that "we will use the Coptic calendar again in *al-Mu'ayyad* from tomorrow, responding to the request from our excellent colleague and for the merit of farmers." As for *al-Ahali* newspaper, he reported, "It began putting the Coptic calendar on the front page from the beginning of this Coptic year." Thus, al-Manqabbadi was trying to embed Coptic culture, which was represented by the Coptic calendar and the revived Nayruz festival, in an Egyptianness that was still being constructed.

However, Coptic culture was very much intertwined with ancient Egyptian cultural heritages and indigenous Egyptian culture, and it was not necessarily easy to separate these Coptic Christian aspects. Al-Manqabbadi may have theoretically succeeded in de-Christianizing the Nayruz by presenting it as a revived ancient festival, but attempts to de-Christianize the celebration itself were largely unsuccessful. As he admitted, the organizers were Coptic associations, the venues were facilities owned by Copts, and the turnout was overwhelmingly Coptic, though Muslims were invited to attend the celebrations. The Muslim guests at the Nayruz celebrations took the opportunity to express their support for national unity and delivered speeches concerning the importance of the solidarity between Muslims and Copts, as seen in the case of Sa'd Zaghlul in 1923. For Muslim guests, the Nayruz festival represented the occasion not to confirm their Pharaonic roots shared with the Copts, but to confirm the importance of national unity by attending a celebration organized by the Copts. Therefore, it could not attract Muslims in any significant number, nor was their participation widespread. The revived Nayruz was regarded as a Coptic festival celebrated on a limited scale and never achieved recognition as a national holiday.

In the 1930s, the Pharaonic boom passed, and Arab nationalism rose as a sweeping trend. The new regime established after the July Revolution in 1952 was based on Arab nationalism and socialism. On the other hand, the Coptic notables who led the revival of the Nayruz festival were supporters of Egyptian nationalism and from the upper and upper-middle classes. They were deprived of arenas for their activities after the July Revolution—they lost their political base such as the Wafd Party and were negatively affected by the agrarian land reforms. With the decline in the influence of the lay Coptic notables, the leadership of the Coptic community shifted to the Coptic clergy. The fall of lay Coptic notables also meant the decline of the revived secular Nayruz because the Coptic Orthodox Church preferred to celebrate it as the conventional Christian festival of the martyrs, rather than the nonreligious Nile festival.

As mentioned earlier, the Nayruz was celebrated in 1942 and 1952, inviting the prime minister, president, and patriarch of the Coptic Orthodox Church. The Tawfiq Society was the main promoter of the Nayruz festival since the early twentieth century and even after the decline in enthusiasm among other Coptic associations in the mid-twentieth century. In 1962 the Tawfiq Society celebrated the Nayruz under the auspices of Pope Kyrilus the Sixth.[24] In 1973 the society also celebrated the Nayruz, inviting Pope Shenuda the Third, Cardinal Estefanos the First of the Coptic

Catholic Church, and 'Aziz Yusuf Sa'd, the minister of irrigation. Pope Shenuda noted, "As a matter of fact—oh my brothers—when I attended this gathering, I thought it would be just a simple gathering that a Coptic association had organized, and I was not expecting that it would change into a national (*watani wa qawmi*) conference in this manifest way."[25] Thus, the revived Nayruz that aimed for the unity of Muslims and Copts under Pharaonism was still celebrated in a limited scale in the 1970s.

The Nayruz Festival in the Twenty-First Century

Although the revived Nayruz has lost its popularity even among the Copts themselves, Pharaonism did not follow the same pattern. Pharaonism took root among the Copts and was often used as a ground for claiming that they were *authentic* Egyptians, especially in the context of protests against inequality and injustice. This kind of Pharaonism appeared almost simultaneously with al-Manqabbadi's Nayruz revival. As we have seen, Pharaonism of al-Manqabbadi was supportive of the national unity between Muslims and Copts who were considered to have the same roots. Meanwhile, as Bayly illustrates by an example of Kyriakos Mikhail, who made an appeal to the British around 1910 that the Copts were discriminated against in employment in civil services, Pharaonism among the Copts sometimes had a separatist tendency, especially when it was used to protest anti-Coptic discrimination.[26] This tendency could be observed in a number of different contexts, such as the Coptic Nation (*al-'umma al-qibtiyya*) in the early 1950s and among some expatriate Copts since the 1970s.

The Nayruz reviver in the early twenty-first century, Father Matiyas Nasr of Saint Mary's Church in 'Azbat al-Nakhl District in Cairo, is one such Coptic activist who promotes Pharaonic and Coptic identity through the newspaper *al-Katiba al-Tibiyya* (Theban Legion). According to Iskander, the newspaper is published under the supervision of Father Matiyas, and its editor B. Awad explained that the paper was "aimed at Copts as a separate and defined section of society with problems and needs that require their own media to serve them." The title of the newspaper was taken from a hagiography of Coptic martyrs in the third century who were called to Gaul to assist the Roman emperor Maximian but were executed for their refusal to harm local Christians.[27]

Even though Pharaonism that aimed for national unity under the common Pharaonic past did not vanish, Pharaonism with a separatist tendency became more vocal after the decline of liberal nationalism in the late 1930s as the situation surrounding Copts changed dramatically. During the 1919 Revolution and the following decade, the national sentiment was supportive of the national unity between Muslims and Copts to fight against the British to obtain independence. But in the 1930s, with the socioeconomic crisis triggered by the Great Depression, new religious and semireligious groupings like the Muslim Brotherhood that called for a social and economic order based on Islam attracted more middle-class youth. In the 1940s, sectarian tension spread and there were several attacks on Coptic churches in Cairo, as well as election obstruction that included physical attacks.[28]

These changes accelerated following the rise of Islamist movements and a general rise in religiosity in Egypt from the 1970s onward. President Sadat (1970–81) utilized Islam and Islamists to fortify his legitimacy, which was disadvantageous to Copts. Because President Gamal Abdel Nasser (1956–70) weakened the Christian secular elite, which had included Coptic representatives in Parliament, and liberal institutions like Parliament itself, the Coptic Church came to be involved in politics, representing specifically Coptic interests. As is well known, President Sadat and Pope Shenouda the Third of the Coptic Orthodox Church had a severe conflict in the 1970s, which resulted in the abolishment of the presidential decree that nominated Pope Shenouda the Third as pope and his house arrest in a desert monastery. Since the 1970s a number of Islamist attacks against Copts have been reported. The assassination of President Sadat by an Islamist group changed the regime's attitude toward Islamists, and they became the common enemy for both the Mubarak regime and Copts. Even so, the general situation did not change; Islamists attacked Copts especially in Upper Egypt in the 1990s; common troubles in local communities turned into sectarian strife, as is shown by the incident of the village al-Kushih in 2000; and the Egyptian government did not change its discriminatory treatment against Copts—for example, restricting the construction or restoration of church buildings.[29]

In such surroundings, Coptic clergymen have come to play an important role not only as spiritual leaders of the Coptic community but also as political opinion leaders. They often engage in politics in order to represent Coptic interests and Coptic voices. Father Matiyas Nasr, who celebrated the Nayruz with a sense of Pharaonism, is one such priest who is highly politicized and therefore considered to be a radical. In the current tense situation, the political activities to protect Coptic collective rights have emerged as increasingly militant.

The Martyrs' Nayruz in Pharaonic Style

The daily newspaper *al-Yawm al-Sabi'* reported on September 12, 2009, that the celebration of the Nayruz festival as a Martyrs' Festival occurred under the initiative of Father Matiyas in the 'Azbat al-Nakhl district of Cairo. The prayer of the Christian Nayruz was held, followed by a demonstration demanding a uniform legal framework for building churches and protesting against the abduction of minors. The celebration was both a Christian festival to commemorate the Coptic martyrs of the third century and a political assembly. The priests attending the festival were wearing *'Ankh*, or the "key of life," which is considered to have influenced some of the shapes of the Coptic Cross, and some participants were wearing Pharaonic costumes and others T-shirts emblazoned with the *'Ankh* emblem.[30]

The Nayruz was again celebrated in 2010. *Aqbat Muttahidun*, an expatriate Coptic newspaper, reported on September 26, 2010, that the *Theban Legion* newspaper, which Father Matiyas supervises, had organized the celebration of the Nayruz, beginning with the old national anthem of Egypt (1923–36) in both Arabic and Coptic. Father Matiyas delivered a speech in which he emphasized that the Coptic Church was the church of martyrs, a typical and classic self-definition of the Coptic Church, and praised the martyrs' courage and strong faith. He also mentioned the contemporary "martyrs" of the sectarian incidents that occurred in the villages of al-Kushih and Nag' Hammadi and criticized the subsequent action taken by the government.

The celebration of the Nayruz in 2011 was different. *Al-Yawm al-Sabi'* reported on September 11, 2011, that the Nayruz had been celebrated in the Church of Saint Mary the Virgin and Saint Mina in the Zarayib District in the northern part of Greater Cairo under the initiative of Father Matiyas. Because the festival was conducted after the January 25 Revolution that revitalized nationalist sentiment, Muslim politicians and thinkers and different political groups participated. The celebration was given the title "We Are Egyptians." Father Matiyas delivered a speech and said, "We will send a message that Egypt is for Egyptians and therefore a lot of Muslims participated in this celebration."[31] Bearing in mind that there were radical Islamists who called for the abolishment of the Shamm al-Nasim festival, another festival of ancient Egyptian origin,[32] and the demolition of ancient statues, Father Matiyas also expressed his wish that the Nayruz festival would be a national holiday for all Egyptians, regardless of their religious affiliations, because it represented the origin of Egyptian history and corresponded to the beginning of the agricultural season. In this celebration, again, priests were wearing the *'Ankh* emblem along with the usual Coptic cross, and some participants again had Pharaonic costumes and T-shirts emblazoned with the *'Ankh* emblem.

Pharaonism and the Struggle over Egyptianness

The three occurrences of the Nayruz festival in the twenty-first century show intertwined Coptic Christian and revived Pharaonist traits. All of the instances clearly show that it was celebrated as a Christian Martyrs' Festival, but also exhibited varying degrees of Pharaonism. In the case of the Nayruz festival in 2009, Pharaonism was not utilized for uniting Muslims and Copts. Rather, it was a tool to claim "authentic" Egyptianness for Copts. In contrast, Pharaonist claims made in the Nayruz festival in 2011 were similar to al-Manqabbadi's, promoting the idea of the national unity between Muslims and Copts under Pharaonism. The basic idea of the definition of Egyptians in these two Pharaonisms is the same, which is that they are the descendants of ancient Egyptians and heirs to their great cultural heritages, but the difference lies in the position of Coptic Christianity. In the former type of Pharaonism, Coptic Christianity is not excluded from the definition of Egyptians or Egyptianness but is integrated into it.[33] It aims to reconfirm Copts' Egyptianness among themselves, which is often shaken by discriminatory policies of the government and violent attacks against Copts in the name of Islam. On the basis of this sense of Egyptianness, Father Matiyas and the participants of his Nayruz festivals demanded equal treatment for Copts. Radical Copts tend to advocate this type of Pharaonism, and it is therefore associated with Coptic separatism. However, its actual aim is to confirm the Egyptianness of Copts and ideologically support their struggle to gain a position of equality *within* Egyptian society.

The 2011 Nayruz, in light of the rise of radical Islamist attacks, was also a struggle over Egyptianness. Pharaonic identity was used to confirm Coptic Egyptianness in the Nayruz in 2011 as in the previous years; however, it was also a protest against the claims of radical Islamists who reject ancient Egyptian cultural heritages on the grounds that they are un-Islamic. Even though these claims to reject ancient Egyptian traits in Egyptian culture are largely considered unacceptable among Egyptians in general, their existence poses a serious threat to the position of Copts because they deny the Copts' last mode of claiming their "authentic" Egyptianness.

Conclusion

The discovery of ancient Egyptian civilization and its reinterpretation as the common past for all Egyptians, regardless of their religious affiliations, gave birth to Pharaonism in the late nineteenth and early twentieth centuries. It was widely accepted by Egyptians of both faiths, but had special meaning for Copts. It played an important role in ensuring their Egyptianness; Copts were positioned as descendants of ancient Egyptians and heirs to ancient Egyptian cultural heritages, which were represented by the Coptic calendar and the Coptic language, among other cultural markers.

The revival of the Nayruz festival in the early twentieth century was based on this Pharaonic identity, and it aimed to promote acknowledgment of Coptic culture by the larger Egyptian society as a part of the Egyptian national culture. It needed to be de-Christianized in order to be shared by all Egyptians. In the end, the attempt to make the revived

Nayruz a national holiday failed, but a concept of Pharaonic identity took hold among Copts that remains today.

The revival of the Nayruz festival in the twenty-first century, in contrast, was an opportunity for the Copts to confirm their Egyptianness, which had been shaken by recent sectarian conflict. As in the earlier period, the repositioning of the festival was intended to obtain acknowledgment of Copts from the larger Egyptian society and the government as full-fledged "authentic" Egyptians and thus to promote equal treatment for Coptic communities facing an uncertain political future.

8

From Minority to Majority

Inscribing the Mahra and Touareg into the Arab Nation

SAMUEL LIEBHABER

As developed by Laura Robson in the introduction to this volume, the primary direction of non-Arab and non-Muslim identity formation in the modern Arab world has been toward minoritization, that is, a movement away from polyvalent conceptualizations of self and community toward more rigidly defined codifications of religious, ethnic, and linguistic identity. The interlocking case of the Mahra of southern Arabia and the Touareg of North Africa offers a counterpoint to the prevailing pattern. These two linguistic minority groups have been subject to a process of majoritization thanks to the transposition of their origins onto the legendary Qahtanite lineage, an affiliation that betokens unadulterated "Arabness."[1] This leap is achieved through semantic gerrymandering: by activating the historical label of *himyari* (Himyarite), a term redolent of both Arabian authenticity and linguistic uncanniness, the Mahra and the Touareg gain majority status even though the non-Arabic, maternal language of both communities seemingly disqualifies them from it. In this way, we can discern the creativity—coupled with historical logic—of indigenous discourses concerning communal belonging or not belonging, as well as the multidirectional pathways to and from majority to minority status in the Arab world.

The Mahra of Yemen and Oman (estimated population 135,000) challenge the common conceptualization of Arab identity, stated by one of the foundational theorists of modern Arab nationalism, Sati' al-Husri, thus: "Every Arabic-speaking people is an Arab people. . . . Every individual belonging to one of these Arabic-speaking peoples is an Arab."[2] On the one hand, the Mahra fulfill the primordial ethnic and cultural conditions of being "Arab" (*'arabi*) since they are migratory bedouin (*'a'rab*) who range across the steppe and deserts of the southern Arabian Peninsula. Despite a modest history of education in the Qur'an and the Islamic sciences, the Mahra claim an untarnished pedigree as Muslims born and raised within the strictly Islamic milieu of the Arabian heartland. On the other hand, the native language of the Mahra is not Arabic (*al-'arabiyya*), but Mahri (or Mehri, ISO 639-3: GDQ), an endangered remnant of a once unbroken swath of non-Arabic, Semitic languages that extended across the South Arabian littoral into the Yemeni highlands.

The Mahra have been consistently overlooked in sociolinguistic studies of the Middle East and North Africa (MENA). This oversight is surprising since the past half century has witnessed a surge of interest in the sociolinguistics and linguistic anthropology of the Arab world.[3] For instance, Yasir Suleiman does not address the unique status of the Mahri language in his multiple works on language and national identity, language and conflict, and language ideology in the Middle East.[4] Reem Bassiouney includes the Mahri language in a list of languages spoken in the Middle East, yet provides no further elaboration in her comprehensive study of Arabic sociolinguistics.[5] Even in her excellent study of the ethnolinguistic minorities of the Middle East, Catherine Miller describes Yemen and Oman as "countries with a mainly homogeneous Arabic-speaking population" and does not specify Mahri or any of the other Modern South Arabian languages spoken in Yemen and Oman.[6]

The geographical isolation of the Mahra in eastern Yemen and western Oman is insufficient to explain the absence of the Mahri language from the linguistic and sociolinguistic record of the Middle East. The silence of the scholarly record confirms Enam al-Wer's conclusion that perceptions of language variation in the Arab world are subject to ideological forces alongside empirical analysis.[7] For instance, Ahmad Abdussalam offers a legal argument based on Islamic jurisprudence for circumscribing minority languages within the Islamic community, even as he argues that language diversity outside of it is an essential human right.[8]

The lack of attention to indigenous linguistic diversity within the MENA area, and particularly the Arabian Peninsula, has led to the misconception that language diversity in the Middle East lies either within Arabic (oratorical, standard Arabic versus its colloquial dialects) or within the binary of Arabic and foreign colonial languages such as French, English, or Hebrew.[9] In Arabic scholarly and popular discourses, the non-Arabic, indigenous languages of the MENA are generally relegated to the far margins of social relevance and archived in the public imagination as moribund artifacts, or ignored altogether.[10]

The exceptions are the Berber languages of North Africa, which have provided a rich vein for scholarship in the disciplines of sociolinguistics and linguistic anthropology. Unlike the Mahra of South Arabia, the Berber languages are widely recognized across the Middle East as distinct linguistic entities, and historical encounters between Arabic- and Berber-speaking communities are well documented in Arabic scholarship and in the popular imagination. During the colonial and postcolonial eras in particular, the relationship of the Berber languages to the Arabic superstratum is characterized by political and social anxiety, and the resultant frisson has generated substantial scholarly attention.[11] In recent years, governments in North Africa have relaxed postindependence Arabization policies and demonstrated a willingness to lend financial, moral, and legal support to the Berber languages. For instance, King Hassan II of Morocco proclaimed in 1994 that "Berber is an intrinsic part of the linguistic and cultural heritage of Morocco and should be preserved by speaking it and teaching it in schools,"[12] and the Tamazight language has been recognized as the second national language of Algeria through a recent (2002) constitutional amendment.[13] Since the January 14 Revolution in 2011, Tunisian Tamazight speakers have emerged from their republican-era dormancy to proclaim their presence as a small, yet vital, bilingual population.[14] Although neither the Amazigh identity nor the Tamazight language is mentioned in the postrevolutionary Tunisian constitution, the fact that both appeared in public debates on the nature of Tunisian identity reverses a half century of official silence.[15]

Even though the Berber languages are rightly regarded as indigenous to North Africa by reputable scholarship, an alternative strand of thinking endeavors to ascribe an Arabian lineage to the Berber languages in order to justify some of the more extreme claims of Arab nationalism (*'uruba*). This school of thinking has revitalized one of the longest-lived themes of language ideology in the Arab world: the purported prehistoric connection between the Tamashek-speaking Touareg of North Africa and the pre-Islamic indigenous peoples of southern Arabia, most notably the Himyarites of the Yemeni highlands.[16] As early as the ninth century CE, genealogist Ibn Kalbi (d. ~819 CE) proposed that certain Berber tribal confederacies—the Kutama and the Senhaja, to whom the Touareg appertain—were of Yemeni descent. Echoing Ibn Kalbi, the tenth-century belletrist al-Mas'udi (d. 956 CE) proposed that the Berbers descend from Arabian tribes dispersed by the "flood of 'Arim," a legendary event associated with Ma'rib and the pre-Islamic states of the Yemeni highlands.[17] Even the skeptic Ibn Khaldun allows a "Himyari" lineage for the Berber Senhaja (that is, Touareg) tribes. Sixteenth-century Sudanese historian 'Abd al-Rahman al-Sa'di suggests a historical narrative: The Touareg descend from the loyal followers of a Himyari king who adopted monotheism but was killed by his pagan subjects. Those individuals who maintained his faith fled Yemen by covering their faces and eventually settled in the farthest Maghreb. In this way, to quote al-Sa'di, "Their veil became an honored and indispensable garment [and] their was speech was corrupted through contact and intermarriage with their neighbors."[18]

In recent years, the affiliation of the Berber with South Arabian Arabs has been advocated in a number of monographs, of which the following are a sample: al-'Arbawi's *Al-Barbar: 'Arab qudama* (The Berber: Ancient Arabs), Madun's *'Urubat al-barbar: al-Haqiqa al-maghmura* (The Arabness of the Berber: The Hidden Truth), and al-Bayd's *Al-'Aqalliya al-barbariyya fi Tunis* (The Berber Minority of Tunis).[19] The central argument of all three monographs is that the Berber languages descend from a common "ancient Arabic" ancestor; evidence is adduced through later borrowings from the Arabic language and a reliance on scriptural and folk genealogies. The fact that these three monographs were the sole resources on Berber origins and identity in the holdings of the Bibliothèque Nationale in Tunis speaks to the weight that this theory holds in contemporary discourse in the MENA area. On a popular level, the "Himyarite" origin of the Berber is still the official version of history taught in the Tunisian secondary school curriculum.[20]

The crux of this theory is the Himyarites, a general term in Arabic historiography for the native inhabitants of the Yemeni highlands who established a series of tribal states that flourished in the pre-Islamic era. In Arabic historiography and lexicography, Himyar is associated with "linguistic uncanniness" that emanates from southern Arabia. Although *himyari* ultimately refers to any non-Arabic language substrate indigenous to the Yemeni highlands, by the first centuries of the Islamic era the label *himyari* had come to signify a distinct cluster of Arabic dialects spoken by their Arabicized descendants.[21] Although *himyari* Arabic in the early Islamic era was influenced by a non-Arabic substrate, it was still intelligible to other Arabic speakers—albeit with difficulty.[22] For this reason, anecdotes abound regarding communication mishaps between normative Arabic speakers and persons who spoke *himyari* Arabic.[23] Despite their uncanny linguistic heritage, the Himyarites and their descendants still lie within classical and modern conceptions of "Arabness," since their ancestors were natives of the Arabian Peninsula whose mythological genealogy embedded them within the Arab lineage of Qahtan. In light of the fact that the Himyarites straddle the boundary between genealogical "Arabness" and linguistic "otherness," I suggest that the designation of "Himyari" has been used to integrate non-Arabic-speaking peoples who *ought* to be Arab—either because they maintain a bedouin pastoralist lifestyle that evokes Arabian authenticity (Arabic *'asala*) or because of their commitment to Islam—into the sociopolitical fabric of the Arab world.

In the modern era, the same language and ideological processes brought to bear on the Berber languages—and specifically the Berber-speaking Touareg—have been used to integrate the non-Arabic Mahri language into the Arabic dialectal continuum. This motif is not a diachronic constant by any means. Al-Hamdani (d. ~956 CE), al-Idrisi (d. 1166 CE), al-Istakhri (d. 957 CE), al-Mas'udi (d. 957 CE), Ibn al-Mujawir (d. 1204 CE), and al-Muqaddasi (d. ~1000 CE) felt no reservations against referring to the Mahri language as fundamentally different from Arabic, using terminology such as *ghutm* (gibberish) and *'ajami* or *musta'jima* (foreign) to describe it. Recognition of the Mahri language as a sui generis entity fades from the scholarly record from the thirteenth century onward, as the center of scholarly gravity in the Arab world shifted north and west away from the Arabian Peninsula and Iraq. However, Mahri was still heard by Arabic monolinguals who would have resorted to the label "Himyari" to account for its South Arabian provenance and linguistic uncanniness. The same misidentification can be found in a statement attributed to Abu 'Amr ibn al-'Ala' (d. 770 CE): "The speech (*lisan*) of Himyar and the furthest reaches of Yemen (*'aqasi al-yaman*) is not our speech and their Arabic (*'arabiyyatuhum*) is not our Arabic."[24] "The furthest reaches of Yemen" likely refers to the steppe and desert east of Hadramawt—the core territory of the Mahra—since it is the easternmost region of most historical conceptions of Yemen and is bounded farther to the east by the politically, linguistically, and ecologically distinct regions of Dhofar and the Jibal al-Qamar.

As a distinct linguistic entity, the Mahri language remained absent from historical and philological reckoning in the Arabic world until the 1980s, when scholars and interested amateurs from the People's Democratic Republic of Yemen began to turn their attention to the linguistic "anomalies" in their own backyard: Mahri and the closely related Soqotri language. The rediscovery of the Mahri language in Arabic-language scholarship over the past twenty years has led to a scholarly and popular campaign to embed the Mahra into popular narratives of "Arabness." Identical to the processes I have outlined for Berber-speaking Touareg, two scholarly tactics are used toward this end: the first is to argue that the Mahri language descends from "Ancient Arabic" (understood to be "proto-Semitic"), and the second is to affiliate the Mahra with Himyar.[25] Of the four Arabic monographs devoted to the topic of the Mahri language (including one on the closely related S'hçri language of Dhofar), none deviates from this narrative. They are al-Ways's *Fiqh al-'arabiyya wa-sirr al-lugha al-mahriyya* (Comprehension of Arabic and the Secret of the Mahri Language), Marikh's *Al-'Arabiyya al-qadima wa-lahajatuha* (Ancient Arabic and Its Dialects), al-Shahri's *Lughat 'Ad* (The Language of 'Ad), and al-Hafiz's *Min lajahat "Mahra" wa-adabiha* (Concerning the "Mahri" Dialect and Its Literature).[26]

Al-Ways's book stands as the most comprehensive attempt to embed the Mahri language into the Arabic-language dialectal continuum. Al-Ways not only demonstrates the political and religious bona fides of the

Mahra, but also endeavors to demonstrate that the Mahri language is a modern iteration of "Ancient Arabic" and therefore ought to be classified as an "Arabic" language or dialect, not as a separate entity. Further, al-Ways rejects the idea that the "Himyari" dialects of Arabic may have stemmed from a non-Arabic linguistic substrate. In doing so, al-Ways relates the distinction between the Arabic, Mahri, and Himyari languages to a foreign—and perfidious—attempt to sunder the unity of the Arab world.

The similarity in language and ideological treatment between Mahri and the Berber languages suggests their equivalent status in Arabic sociolinguistic thinking. Unlike the other minority languages of the MENA region such as Hebrew, Aramaic, and Coptic, the language boundaries between the Mahra, the Touareg, and Arabic monolinguals are not coterminous with religious or sectarian boundaries. Moreover, the Touareg and the Mahra possess social currency as nonurban camel pastoralists, and the quality of cultural authenticity (Arabic 'asala) accrues to them.[27] On this basis, the similarity of tactics used to integrate both communities into narratives of "Arabness" stems from a consistent reasoning. In fact, the common treatment of the Touareg and the Mahra in language-ideological thinking has been taken a step further in the past decade: the two distinct language communities are merged into a single entity through the argument that the Berber languages descend from Mahri or one of the closely related Modern South Arabian languages.[28] This theory has been advanced in a number of different forums and is popularly circulated in al-Mahra and elsewhere in Yemen.[29]

Even if the South Arabian—Himyari, Mahri, or otherwise—origin of the Touareg is insupportable on linguistic grounds, a vexing question remains: why are the Touareg—and the Berber in general—associated in the popular imagination with Yemen rather than Egypt, Iraq, or the Levant? Because the linguistic exceptionalism of the Mahri language has only recently been rediscovered in Arabic scholarship, these other regions could have provided more plausible origination mythologies. In the face of such a broadly felt conviction, we ought to consider whether a historical intersection between the Mahri and the Touareg may have given rise to the claim of a common Himyarite origin.

This line of questioning leads to one of the mainstays of traditional Touareg society and economy: the mahri (pl. mahari) riding camel. Small, hardy, and fleet-footed, the mahri camel is held in particularly totemic regard by the Touareg.[30] To quote Ibrahim al-Kuni, a Touareg-Libyan novelist writing in Arabic: "We always say that the Mahri is the mirror of his rider. If you want to stare into the rider and see what lies hidden within, look to his Mahri."[31] In addition to the almost certain derivation of the gentilic "mahri" from the proper noun "al-Mahra," the Touareg mahri shares the characteristics of the riding camels bred by the Mahra of southern Arabia: small size, speed, and endurance.[32] In fact, the Mahra are more widely known outside of their core territory in southern Arabia for their camel stock—whose agility and speed have been amply vindicated in camel races held in the Gulf states—than for their unique language. Similarity, the mahri camel of North Africa is regularly celebrated at the annual "Festival of the Sahara" in Douz, Tunisia, which evolved out of a series of mahri camel races organized by the French military authorities in the early twentieth century to display the prowess of their "*meihariste*" camel cavalry.

The consensus among North African specialists in the mahri riding camel is that it is not native to North Africa and likely originated from the Arabian Peninsula. In *Rihla fi 'alim al-'ibl* (A Journey through the World of the Camel), Tunisian scholar Salim al-Tariqi writes that the mahri camel of the Touareg descends from Mahra bin Haydan, the eponymous ancestor of the Mahri tribes.[33] Beyond this statement, I have not found any written sources that suggest how and when the mahri camel came to North Africa. In an oral communication, 'Abd al-Latif Belgacem, director of the Douz Sahara Museum, suggested that the mahri camel was introduced to North Africa by the Bani Hilal tribes in the eleventh century CE.[34] However, the Mahra played no verifiable role in the Hilalian migration, a fact that undermines the merit of this suggestion.

A more probable point of intersection between the Touareg and the Mahra may have occurred during the Islamic conquest of North Africa in the seventh century CE. In his historical treatise *Futuh Misr wa-'akhbaruha* (Conquest of Egypt and Its Accounts), Ibn 'Abd al-Hakam (d.

871 CE) indicates that Mahri troops played a significant role during the Islamic conquest of Egypt and North Africa, despite their small population overall. For instance, the Mahra received special commendation from military commander of the Muslims 'Amr ibn al-'As for the central role they played in breaching the defenses of Alexandria. After Mahri soldiers led the Muslim vanguard over its walls, 'Amr ibn al-'As is reported to have said of them: "As for the Mahra, they are a people who slay, but are not slain" (*'Amma mahra fa-qawm yaqtuluna wa-la yuqtaluna*). The Mahra settled al-Fustat in sufficient numbers that they had their own district named after them: *khittat mahra*. More significantly, Ibn 'Abd al-Hakam notes that six hundred Mahri troops (out of a combined force of twenty thousand troops) were sent to "Ifriqiyya" (roughly speaking, modern-day Tunisia) under the command of 'Abdullah bin Sa'd ibn Sarh.[35] The six hundred Mahri troops would have provided the most plausible point of contact between the sociolinguistic uncanniness of southern Arabia and the linguistic "otherness" of Tamashek-speaking Touareg camel pastoralists. If Mahri troops maintained their own camel stock—as suggested by the fact that the Mahra were granted their own camel-grazing pastures west of the Nile[36]—it would provide the mechanism by which the mahri camel was introduced to Touareg camel pastoralists.

According to this scenario—speculative as it is—the South Arabian genealogy of the mahri camel was transferred to the Touareg, who, among the diverse peoples of North Africa, adopted the mahri camel with particular ardor and interbred them with their own indigenous stock. Furthermore, the Touareg, as non-Arabic-speaking Islamicized camel pastoralists, may have taken their cue from the six hundred Mahri troops who passed their way. In the Mahra, the Touareg would have met a similarly nomadic-pastoralist people who did not speak Arabic yet were firmly integrated into the Arab Muslim community. Through their own agency and with historical and genealogical justification provided by classical and medieval Arab scholarship, the Touareg could have followed the route of the Mahri into the fold of "Arabness" (*'uruba*). With the passage of time, the memory of the Mahra as a distinct linguistic community faded from common circulation outside of Yemen and Oman. However, an echo of al-Mahra's ancient Arabian—yet non-Arabic—linguistic cadences lived in

the Touareg's mythological origins from "Himyar," a byword for genealogical prestige tempered by linguistic uncanniness.

In this way, a brief historical intersection was buttressed by centuries
of language ideology to turn the Touareg into Himyarite Arabs who speak
Berber, in the same way that the Mahra are perceived to be Himyarite
Arabs who speak Mahri. Spanning the premodern and modern eras, the
historical and language ideological label of "Himyari" thus offers a side
entrance into the edifice of "Arabness" (*'uruba*) for those persons lacking
the linguistic key. Importantly, the label "Himyari" is applied to the Mahra
and Touareg as much from outside their communities as it is claimed from
within them, suggesting that the process of minority and majority identification in the Middle East may be governed less by majority fiat than by
mutual agreement.

PART THREE

Minorities in the Transnational Sphere

THE CREATION OF "MINORITY" IDENTITIES has been a global as well as a regional process. In this final part, we see the many ways that the concept of minority has developed not only in response to the emergence of new forms of statehood and national identity in the Arab world itself, but also through engagement with diaspora communities, international institutions, and transnational concepts of political identity.

This process has sometimes involved dramatic redefinitions of the terms "minority" and "majority." In Tunisia, for instance, David Bond demonstrates that the political rhetoric surrounding minorities has been built partly in conversation with the idea of an idealized pluralistic Mediterranean past—a concept with both romantic appeal and economic benefit in the form of the tourist economy. To support this vision, the pre-revolution Tunisian government of Ben 'Ali applied the label of "minority" not only to non-Arab indigenous groups but also to communities of foreigners living in Tunisia, thus emphasizing Tunisia's historical participation in the community of Mediterranean states and its long-standing links with Europe. Liora R. Halperin argues that in Palestine, European Jewish settlers wishing to avoid the international label of "minority" advocated for the recognition of Hebrew as a majority language against all the demographic evidence, in an effort to reframe both their position within Palestine and the literary status of their newly reinvented language as essentially majoritarian in a global context. Such dramatic reformulations of "minority" and "majority" demonstrate the fragility and novelty of the concepts and indicate how their meanings were (and are) being worked out in transnational as well as local contexts.

Diaspora communities have also attempted to solidify and sometimes dramatically reinvent minority identities to serve the purposes of immigrant communities trying to carve out new political, economic, and cultural roles in a host country. As Yasmeen Hanoosh suggests, the immigrant reinvention of Chaldean Christian identity in the United States as simultaneously ethnic, national, religious, and social does not necessarily reflect the nature of Chaldean identity in the homeland; rather, it derives primarily from an immigrant desire to create a functional transnational network for social and economic support in a challenging new environment. Similarly, Lucia Volk shows that the discourse of "minority" disenfranchisement (alongside flexible and sometimes disingenuous claims of particular national identities) among Muslim immigrants in Germany has almost nothing to do with the communal loyalties or historical experiences of these individuals and everything to do with the particularities of the international regime surrounding refugees, asylum, and citizenship. In other words, transnational interests have been every bit as important as local and regional developments in structuring and institutionalizing concepts of Middle Eastern "minority" identities in the modern era.

9

Tunisia's Minority Mosaic

Constructing a National Narrative

DAVID BOND

The sober neo-Moorish facade of the British Embassy in Tunis was for generations a landmark at Bab al-Bahr, generally taken as the frontier between the modern city constructed during the French protectorate (1881–1956) and the precolonial medina. On an April morning in 2004, a Scottish bagpiper stood on a balcony of the embassy playing "Flowers of the Forest" as the Union Jack was lowered. This ceremony marked the closure of the British Embassy at Bab al-Bahr and its move to the new Berges du Lac development outside Tunis. Staff from the adjoining restaurant Le Pacha looked on curiously from the pillared balconies of what had once been the Raffo Palace. Giuseppe Raffo, of Genoese descent and born in Tunis in 1795, held high office in Tunis and was ennobled by the king of Sardinia in 1851.[1]

The short ceremony concluded in the British Council library. On a small pedestal was a portrait of Richard Wood, British consul in Tunis from 1851 to 1879.[2] The key of the embassy was returned on a cushion to the Tunisian authorities, while a plaque commemorating the British presence in the building was unveiled. Meanwhile, not far from the embassy, work was under way on the Mediterranean Centre for Applied Arts in the former Église Sainte-Croix.[3] This church, closed in 1964, was constructed in 1837 on the site of a hospital for European captives of Tunisian corsairs.[4] The Sainte-Croix project would, according to the Association du Sauvegarde de la Médina, link the medina to the modern city of Tunis:

153

The building is an architectural entity capable of assuming a cultural role of great significance as a cultural hub linking the central Medina to what is termed "the European city" via the *Quartier Franc* with its history of conviviality among people from different Mediterranean countries. In the *Quartier Franc* are situated the former British embassy and Italian consulate, the French *fondouk*, and the Garibaldi house. The conversion of the Église Sainte-Croix into a Mediterranean centre of Applied Arts will reinforce the values of tolerance which has characterised the history of the Medina and highlight the Mediterranean identity of the city of Tunis.[5]

The embassy ceremony itself and the Sainte-Croix restoration project encapsulated "Tunisianness," an openness to the "Other" as part of national specificity.[6] It was also a demonstration of the public bonhomie marking relations between the Ben 'Ali regime and its foreign interlocutors. This chapter, partly based on research carried out in Tunisia between 2006 and 2010 prior to the ousting of Zine el 'Abidine Ben 'Ali in early 2011, will first study the reworking of official Tunisian narratives of the country's history under the Ben 'Ali regime between 1987 and 2011. In this context academic historians and chroniclers reconstructed the history of Tunisia's "mosaic" of minority communities as they existed prior to independence in 1956, a "mosaic" that could be seen as implicitly evoking a "plural" Tunisia in contrast to the authoritarian Ben 'Ali regime. The chapter shall also be attentive to the ways that the city of Tunis has sought to valorize its built heritage as a reflection of the presence of transnational Mediterranean communities.

Tunisia as a harmonious mosaic of communities is one of the myths propagated by the regime between 1987 and 2011, alongside myths of economic achievement, democratic gradualism, and *laïcité* (secularism).[7] These myths are part of a wider national narrative that attributes to "Tunisia" the continuity of a subject and allows public figures to speak as if such a continuous subject exists, one that can be understood by analogy with the *persona ficta*, or fabrication, in the sense of an institutional effect.[8] For its part, "the myth distorts, producing instead a blend of meaning and form. . . . [M]yth is the loss of historical quality of things, of their memory that they once were made."[9] Béatrice Hibou has shown how in Tunisia prior to the 2011 revolution, both the regime and independent thinkers adhered to these myths, available for appropriation by all in different ways. The smoothing over of conflict and untidiness and the appropriation of diverse community histories into national history recall Partha Chatterjee's discussion of how the Bengali middle-class nationalist elite of Calcutta incorporated diverse identities into a classical "Indian tradition," a process that Chatterjee terms the "vertical appropriation of sanitized popular tradition."[10] How did this inclusive narrative take shape in the case of Tunisia?

Historical Context, 1956–87

In Tunisia, as elsewhere in North Africa, decolonization saw the departure of most of the country's Italian and French minority communities together with a large proportion of the indigenous Jewish community.[11] Meanwhile, historians displaced the colonizers from the center of the colonial universe and inserted in their place the colonized peoples themselves. The Africanizing of African history, as Frederick Cooper noted, was the central item on the agenda of the 1960s.[12] Tunisian history was, however, seen as marked by openness to other cultures. In 1974 Bechir Ben Slama's *Al-shakhsiyya al-tunisiyya: Khasaisuha wa muqawwimatuha* (The Tunisian Personality: Specificities and Components) identified among the components of the Tunisian "personality" a capacity for unity and cooperation that had enabled Tunisians to assimilate the successive civilizations that since antiquity had existed on the national territory.[13] This notion contrasted with the view of colonial historian Arthur Pellegrin that "the decisive events in Tunisia's history are the result of outside forces. Its history is that of a territory much coveted and often invaded, rather than that of a people conscious of its historical continuity."[14] Habib Bourguiba personified respect for French culture while seeking from the early 1930s onward to preserve Tunisian identity.[15] Tunisian school secondary school history manuals, while underlining the violence of colonial repression in Algeria, did not foreground the violence of the French colonial occupation.[16]

In 1987 the Revue de l'Institut des Belles-Lettres Arabes in Tunis published a collection of articles entitled "La Tunisie scrute son histoire." Mohamed Hédi Cherif, examining Tunisian historiography, noted that out of the ten *doctorats d'état* presented up until 1987 by Tunisian scholars, only two concerned the twentieth century. The postindependence period had seen the publication of numerous books, articles, and memoirs, although, published during what Cherif termed the "sensitive period of decolonisation," they tended to highlight the tensions and violence of the colonial experience and the resistance of the local population. Cherif mentions as an exception Bechir Tlili's 1984 study of French socialists in North Africa and the development of indigenous trade union and political movements.[17]

In the latter years of Habib Bourguiba's presidency, a narrower narrative developed. By 1979 the fifteen-volume *Histoire du mouvement national Tunisien* had been published, highlighting the role of Habib Bourguiba in the independence struggle. The history of the Tunisian national movement was presented as the history of Bourguiba himself, starting with the founding of the Arabic-language newspaper *al-Amal al-Tunisi* (*L'Action Tunisienne*) in 1932.[18]

The personality of the nation evolved over the centuries in a halting fashion and was now guided by the nationalist movement: "Over the centuries, this country has known many periods of prosperity, yet has subsequently fallen into decline. . . . [T]he movement of progress has not been followed by all the population. Entire regions and collectivities have remained isolated. . . . [A]ll our effort is directed towards the integration of the nation, first psychologically, then economically, fusing together all the social classes in a single crucible: the homeland."[19]

The Tunisian people would be delivered from obscurantism and division: "The people have suffered too much from the plurality of factions and now have to align themselves with the only party (the Neo-Destour of Bourguiba) united around one man and a single ideology."[20] The publication in Paris of the Franco-Tunisian author Hélé Béji's *Le désenchantement national: Essai sur la décolonisation* in 1982 was a somber assessment of the evolution of Tunisia since 1956.[21] In Bejis's words, "The absence of freedom characterising independence today must be questioned, as it contains a terrible contradiction: the entity which liberated us is the one that today dominates us, and while dominating also reassures, by protecting our new sense of national belonging against the crushing weight of neo-colonialism."[22]

Ben 'Ali's Mediterranean

In November 1987 Zine el 'Abidine Ben 'Ali succeeded the ailing Habib Bourguiba and, unable to draw on the historical legitimacy of Bourguiba as "supreme combatant," recentered the national narrative on the multicultural past of Tunisia.[23] This new focus was reflected in Tunisian school curricula after 1987:

> Our country is situated on the shores of the Mediterranean. Since the dawn of history Tunisia has been a place of encounter and exchange between civilisations. . . . [A] civilisation of Afro-Roman origin developed in our country, a Roman branch springing from a Carthaginian trunk. Without Carthage and the role of its maritime commerce which facilitated the movement and diffusion of civilisational influence, without Magon and the manuals which caused agricultural sciences to progress, without Hannibal's genius, the mosaics of the African provinces, the thought of Tertullian and Saint Augustin, Mediterranean culture and Christian culture in Europe would not be what they are today.[24]

The term "heritage" (*patrimoine*) acquired a new prominence, with the promulgation of a Heritage Code in 1994 and the elaboration of a historical narrative composed of successive layers of civilization: Carthage was destroyed by Rome, but the Roman city of Carthage succeeded it; ruptures and conflict are succeeded by continuity. Tunisians would be reconciled with their past, one in which openness to other cultures and civilizations was a constant theme.[25] In 1988 the Institut National d'Archéologie et d'Art was renamed the Institut National du Patrimoine. The Arabic adjective *wataniyya* (patriotic) replaced *qawmiyya* (national) to designate the national identity card.[26] "*Watan*" is a term in Arabic designating, among other meanings, a sense of rootedness in a place.[27] A place implies ancestors who have lived there in the past and who have handed down the place and its associated culture. These ancestors represented the successive cultures in Tunisian history: one of the rare corridors with a non-Arab name in the 9 Avril Faculty of Human and Social Sciences in Tunis was named after the third-century patristic scholar Cyprian of Carthage.[28] While Tunisian banknotes in the Bourguiba era generally carried a portrait of Bourguiba himself, from 1993 onward figures such as Hannibal, Elissa (founder of Carthage), Kheireddine Pasha, and Abu'l-Qasim Chabbi all appeared on banknotes. Carthaginian antiquity, the nineteenth-century reforming statesman, and Arabic romantic poetry of Chabbi converge.

This "patrimonializing" of a history as an unfolding tableau took place in the wider context of construction by the regime of political consensus. In a speech in early 1989, President Ben 'Ali spoke of "confronting together our difficulties as if we were a single person" and "uniting citizens around their patriotism and spirit of sacrifice."[29] The National Pact of 1988, a statement of political philosophy to which a variety of political parties adhered, including the Islamist Mouvement de la Tendance Islamique, acknowledged the centrality of Tunisia's Arab-Islamic heritage while evoking modernizers such as statesman Kheireddine Pasha, suggesting that this latter figure was a native of Tunisia and not an Ottoman mamluk from the Caucasus. Tunisia's foreign partners often underlined the stability and modernity of the country, echoing regime discourse. Tunisia was the first North African country to sign a Euro-Mediterranean Association Agreement in July 1995.[30] The Mediterranean became an area of convergence with Tunisia's European partners: in 2008 Nicolas Sarkozy would visit Tunis and declare that "Tunisia is at the heart of the Mediterranean, where East and West converge. Tunis is as close to Nice as Nice is to Dunkirk." His Tunisian counterparts reiterated that Tunisia unfailingly supports "every initiative aimed at building solid bridges of communication, dialogue and understanding between civilisations and religions, in a context of tolerance, moderation and mutual respect."[31]

Tunisia's Minority Communities

It was in this context that Tunisian historians in the mid-1990s began to study the communities composed of nineteenth-century migrants to Tunisia from the northern shores of the Mediterranean, although the Tunisian Jewish community was generally included among these "communities."

This attention coincided with the formalization of relations between Tunisia and Israel. In April 1996 Tunisia and Israel established interest sections in each other's countries.[32] Despite the controversies generated in the Arab world at this time by "normalization" of relations with Israel, Israeli and Tunisian Jewish historians were invited by their Tunisian colleagues to participate in renewed study of Tunisia's Mediterranean communities: "Convinced that the history we are writing should be the synthesis and expression of diverse sensibilities we are favourable to the idea that Israeli university colleagues should join us in our research. Many Jews originally from Tunisia are now in Israel: around 20,000 Jews left Tunisia for Israel between 1948 and 1955."[33] In 1998 the "History and Memory" research unit based at the Faculty of Letters, Arts, and Humanities of the University of Manouba organized an academic colloquium to study relations between Jews and Muslims in Tunisia. In February 1998 Habib Kazdaghli, one of the historians involved, presented the research unit Histoire et Mémoire in these terms: "The independence of Tunisia (in 1956), the reaffirmation of the rights of the Arab and Muslim majority together with the conception of national unity which prevailed after 1956, meant that it was inopportune to highlight the presence or the numerical strength of other communities or groups living in the country."[34] The minister of higher education, Dali Jazi, quoted a 1992 speech made by Zine el 'Abidine Ben 'Ali that evoked "a national history and a collective memory resplendent in the richness of all its dimensions and specificities through the centuries."[35] The "Tunisianness" of the Bourguiba years is perpetuated: ambivalence between understanding the other and withdrawal into self.[36]

Dali Jazi went on to say that members of the Tunisian Jewish community had the right to serve their *patrie* (Tunisia), even though in reality the majority of the Tunisian Jewish population had left Tunisia between 1956 and 1970.[37] It is also striking that while this colloquium was centered on the Tunisian Jewish community, Tunisian historians would go on to study "communities" with very different historical trajectories, such as the Sicilians, the French settlers of the protectorate period, together with the White Russians and the Spanish Republicans of the interwar period.

We noted the international context in which Tunisia's "mosaic" of communities became an object of study. With regard to the wider scholarly landscape, since the 1980s historians have come to recognize that multi-cultural colonial societies defy simple description or heavy abstraction. Conflict and coexistence between various groups in colonial societies are beginning to be more clearly delineated.[38] Following the publication in 1996 of Robert Ilbert's magnum opus on Alexandria between 1830 and 1930, the cosmopolitan port cities of the Middle East became objects of scholarly study and also nostalgic celebration.[39] In a sense, the study of Tunisia's minority communities is also directed toward an "international gallery" that hankers for a more tolerant past and laments the present-day state of the Middle East.[40] Will Hanley, in an article published in 2008, highlights the "anti-nationalist teleology, grieving nostalgia, and bour-geois fantasies" underlying descriptions of cosmopolitan urban societies in the Middle East. Hanley mentions in particular the Tunisian director Férid Boughedir's 1996 film *Un été à La Goulette/A Summer in La Gou-lette*, cited in the context of an article on Middle Eastern cosmopolitan-ism by sociologist Sami Zubaida in *Conceiving Cosmopolitanism* (2003).[41] Zubaida sees *A Summer in La Goulette* as an example of memory as pro-test against puritanical nationalism. The old cosmopolitan milieus have been overwhelmed by "recently urbanized masses" and the homogeneous globalized culture of international capital. In the present day, the opposite of cosmopolitanism is "nationalist and religious xenophobia." The film's political message opposes narrow nationalism, but "the medium of cri-tique—a fiction of sunny beaches, sleep and food, female adolescent beauty under male gaze, and of course schematic sectarian conviviality—is of no practical or ideological value."[42] *A Summer in La Goulette*, in common with other films of the "new Tunisian cinema," is an allegorical portrayal of Tunisia. We shall see that some historians sought to make a political point through the study of Tunisia's minority communities.

In his discussion of the term "cosmopolitanism," Will Hanley sug-gests that it functions as a kind of "tag" or shorthand that promises to draw together scholarly introductions when in reality it serves to cam-ouflage differences, privileging labels over content.[43] It therefore func-tions as a myth, which, as we noted earlier, produces a blend of meaning and form.[44] One can critically evaluate the terms "Mediterranean" and "community" as used in the Tunisian context through Hanley's lens. The term "community" becomes a convenient label for non-Muslim Tunisians whatever the length of their presence in the country, be it Spanish Republican exiles or Tunisia's indigenous Jewish communities. The term "communities" is sometimes used in conjunction with "Mediterranean," creating an impression of comity on the basis of Mediterranean belonging.[45] For some French commentators of the colonial period, the Italians were effectively "Latin sisters," for others the "Sicilian peril," for yet others the Sicilian immigrants to Tunisia and the Maltese were classed in a derogatory fashion as the "Sicilo-Maltais," a term hardly redolent of Mediterranean fellow feeling.[46]

Gaston Loth, a Tunis-based French scholar, suggested in 1905 a policy of assimilation of the Italian population through education and military service. This policy, he claimed, would hasten the fusion in Tunisia (and in Algeria) of the three "Latin peoples" (French, Spanish, and Italians) into a new French nation. North Africa would be a gigantic melting pot rather than a juxtaposition of rival groups of settlers of different origins. Loth claimed that Italians resident in Tunisia shed their national identity and saw themselves as "Tunisians." The assimilation of these "Tunisians" into the French population would be hastened by the fact that they were the descendants of the Normans who occupied Sicily in the eleventh century. Loth also indulged in some craniological speculation, suggesting that dark-haired individuals with smaller than average cranial width in proportion to length were found in large numbers in Italy and in France.[47]

A community-centered approach (French, Italians, Sicilians, Greeks, and so forth) by contemporary researchers of the study of Tunisia's population obscures shifting and reimagined identities. Partha Chatterjee notes that one of the changes of the colonial period was "the impoverishment of the earlier 'fuzzy' sense of community sense and an insistence on the identification of community in the 'enumerable' sense." Reified terms such as "the French" and "the Italians" risk running along "channels excavated by colonial discourse," to use Chatterjee's term. At the same time, we can note a curious convergence between the inclusive "Tunisianity" of the historiography of the 1990s with the desire on the part of some colonial commentators to extend the meaning of "Tunisian." In 1937 General Paul Azan criticized a tendency among what he termed "narrow-minded (French) bureaucrats" and "indigenous xenophobes" to limit the term "Tunisian" to what was indigenous and Muslim; according to Azan, "Tunisian means everything which develops in Tunisia under French protection, both people and their intellectual and artistic achievements."[48]

While the regime of Ben 'Ali sought to impose consensus on all fronts, including historiography, some of the scholars involved in the history of the country's Mediterranean communities sought to mobilize memory in the cause of political pluralism. Writing in *Attariq aljadid*, the weekly journal of the Ettajdid Party, founded in 1993 after the demise of the Tunisian Communist Party, Habib Kazdaghli (of the Manouba Histoire et Mémoire research unit) commented, "By assembling the scattered fragments of their memory the Italians contribute not only to the writing of the history of their own collectivity, but also the history of Tunisia, for this memory is also that of plural Tunisia."[49]

Under Ben 'Ali the term "plural Tunisia" functioned as a rallying cry for the legal opposition. This evocation of a pluralistic social reality that existed in the past is prospective in nature, an appeal for a better future.[50] The conciliatory role of the "elites" in Tunisian history in the nineteenth century was mentioned at an international forum on the theme of religious coexistence in the Mediterranean organized by the weekly newsmagazine *Réalités* in November 2009 in Tunis. Today's "elites" could play a similar role, reconstructing the "cosmopolitan identity of Tunisia," an identity of which the majority of the population are unaware.[51] Today's "elites" are not those individuals who controlled the municipalities of Tunis or Alexandria in the late nineteenth century in societies structured around national and religious communities with a strong degree of autonomy.[52] As Frederick Cooper has pointed out, an attempt to illuminate present issues may be worthy motivation for exploring the past, but it risks a confusion of categories. Here the term "elite" is used by Kazdaghli as a term to express his vision of what the role of the "elite" in the Tunisia of the early twenty-first century might be, skirting the historical context in which Mediterranean urban elites were formed. "Trying to illuminate present issues is a fine motivation for exploring the past," as Cooper comments, "but as one looks backward one risks anachronism."[53] This "presentist" evocation of past golden ages is one common to champions of cosmopolitan

Mediterranean societies and also those individuals who recall an Islamic golden age. Commenting on the situation of post-Mubarak Egypt in early 2011, Hazem Kandil stated:

> In the past five or six years, a sort of fixation on the Egypt of the twenties, thirties and forties has developed, an idealization of the period as a liberal utopia that has become very widespread in novels and movies. Alaa Al-Aswany is a prime example. One of the advantages the Islamists possessed lay in the captivating image of the Prophet and his life in Medina—another kind of utopia to return to. Now it is the golden age of the 1920s that has taken hold of the Egyptian imagination. All the Presidential candidates are evoking this image of a better, more open and cosmopolitan past.[54]

A "plural" Tunisia and the liberal Egypt of the first half of the twentieth century were thus ways of critically framing a present dominated by autocratic regimes.

Italiani, Brava Gente?

Hitherto we have examined how Tunisian scholars have revisited the multicultural past of Tunisia of the nineteenth and twentieth centuries. We have also noted multiple interpretations from official consensus to discreet contestation in the pre-2011 period. In this section we shall turn our attention to the Italian contribution to the reconstruction of the country's multicultural history. The Italians involved include former members of the Italian settler community in Tunisia, Italian academics, and present-day residents of Tunisia of Italian origin, such as the Finzi family, who piloted from 1997 onward the Progetto della Memoria, a series of publications that sought to reconstruct the memory of the Italian collectivity of Tunisia.[55]

When British traveler Captain Charles Kennedy visited Tunis in the middle of the 1840s, there were between 4,000 and 5,000 Sicilians, Sardinians, and mainland Italians in Tunisia. At the time the population of Tunis was estimated at 120,000. The modernization projects of Ahmad Bey had attracted workers and artisans. A considerably smaller number of Jewish immigrants had arrived in Tunis from Leghorn in the eighteenth and early nineteenth centuries and were active in commerce and the professions. When Kennedy met Ahmad Bey, the ruler of Tunis, the conversation took place in Arabic and Italian, and the interpreter was Giuseppe Raffo, the bey's secretary, whom we encountered at the beginning of this thesis. Of Sardinian descent, though born in Tunis in 1795, Raffo held, as Kennedy notes, one of the highest and most confidential posts in the regency from the 1820s until 1862.[56] At the other end of the social scale, Kennedy's Maltese servant Angelo spoke "execrable Italian," while his mamluk escort, Baba Jebb, spoke "very indifferent Italian."[57]

After the French occupation of Tunisia in 1881, a Franco-Italian agreement in 1896 had secured Italian recognition of the French protectorate in Tunisia in return for a series of conventions guaranteeing a large measure of autonomy to Italian institutions. There were at this time 55,000 Italians in the country, outnumbering the French by 5 to 1.[58] Italians and other immigrants were recruited in preference to Tunisians on infrastructure projects. The resulting animosity exploded into violence in 1911 when Tunisians clashed with residents of a nearby Italian area. *Le Colon Français* attributed the blame for the disturbance to Turkish agents-provocateurs stirring up Tunisian opposition to the Italian offensive in neighboring Tripolitania, which had begun on October 5, 1911.[59] The same issue of *Le Colon Français* also criticized the "insolence of the Italian lower classes" who were involved in daily scuffles in front of the offices in central Tunis of *Le Colon Français*'s rival publication, *La Dépêche Tunisienne*, which posted news of Italian victories in Tripolitania.

After the First World War, the French authorities sought to facilitate the naturalization of Italians, who outnumbered the French by 2 to 1. French literature on Tunisia tended to relegate the Italian population to the background even in areas such as Beja or Grombalia, where the Italian population was numerous.[60] A British military handbook on Tunisia dating from the Second World War described the Italians as lacking, in the eyes of Tunisians, the "prestige of the French," who formed "the aristocracy of the population."[61] After the defeat of Axis forces in 1943 in Tunisia, Italian institutions were abolished, and the French authorities sought to assimilate Italians into the French community. As nationalist activity in Tunisia increased in the 1950s, the majority of the Italians seem to have

tacitly supported the French presence, although a minority did sympathize with the nationalist movement. After independence in 1956, most of
the Italians departed, and by 2000 only 800 Italians from the preindependence period remained.[62]

Italian scholars began to document Italy's settlement attempts in
French-controlled Tunisia, producing a well-crafted narrative of benev-
olent Italians struggling for opportunity in a land controlled by the
French.[63] The collected monographs of the Progetto della Memoria of the
mid-1990s are built on a number of assumptions, including a "neglect" of
emigration history (such as the Italian emigration to Tunisia in the nineteenth century) by conventional historians and a postmodernist challenge
to the objectivity of history, which becomes merely one narrative strategy
among others.[64]

The website Euromedcafe of the Naples-based Fondazione Mediterra-
neo, which favors "the mutual understanding through images and music,"
has included in its program the short film *Suk al Grana/Italiani di Tunisia*,
made in 2008 by Federico Ferrone and Akram Adoini. "Mediterranean
intellectuals" like Italian Tunisian novelist Marinette Pendola believe that
the experience of Italian migrants in Tunisia is anchored in a tradition of
Mediterranean openness and tolerance.[65] The experience of the Italians
of Tunisia is studied as microhistory by the omnivorous Progetto della
Memoria, which incorporates fragments such as monographs on literature, art, recipes, and architecture, while detaching them from their original context, which involved, as we have seen, rivalry and violence between
Tunisians and Italians as well as conviviality.[66] The Progetto della Memoria echoes Lyotard's criticism of "grand narratives" while participating in
the construction of the Tunisian national narrative of which the Italian
experience is part.[67] We noted earlier the tendency to study individual
communities as part of the Tunisian mosaic: as Daniela Melfa has recently
noted, the term "Italian" has been adopted uncritically, with a category of
practice used for self-understanding ("Italians") adopted as a category of
analysis.[68] This tendency has been accentuated by the dominance of scholars who are both analysts and protagonists of Italian identity and history
in Tunisia, often with personal or family connections to the collectivity
whose history they are reconstructing.[69]

Despite the Progetto della Memoria's interest in social microhistory, in some ways it recalls older Italian historiography in other parts of the Mediterranean, such as Egypt. Anthony Santilli has recently studied how Italian historians, notably Neapolitan Angelo Sammarco (1883–1948) in works such as *Gli Italiani in Egitto: Il contributo italiano alla formazione dell'Egitto moderno*, published in 1937, sought to highlight the participation of Italians in the development of Egypt. Sammarco belonged to the officially sponsored school of "royalist scholarship" in the Egypt of the 1920s. He highlights, for example, the often-overlooked Italian contribution to the building of the Suez Canal.[70] The Progetto della Memoria tends to emphasize the contribution of Italians to the development of Tunisian infrastructure, notably in the architectural domain.[71]

Both Sammarco and the Progetto della Memoria see the contribution of the Italians as part of the modernization of Egypt (in the case of Sammarco) and Tunisia (in the case of the Progetto della Memoria). Although the Progetto della Memoria's shift of focus away from elite-centered "grand narratives" has enabled new ground to be broken, in other ways the Progetto remains confined within the traditional paradigm of Western-driven modernization and progress espoused by earlier scholars such as Sammarco.

The "royalist" school of historiography in Egypt also stressed Egypt's capacity to integrate the "foreign colonies," which, according to Henein Bey Henein, writing in 1926, lived in perfect harmony with Egyptians. The Italians in particular were in contact with "all classes of the indigenous population."[72] We find traces of this approach in the celebratory tone of some elements of the Progetto della Memoria: the "Week of Intercultural Dialogue" held in Tunis in 2008 with the participation of Tunisian scholars and Italian artists, diplomats, and politicians explored themes such as "Italian emigration in Tunisia: its role as a vector in Tuniso-Italian encounter."[73] In a preface written in 2000 by the Italian ambassador in Tunis for one of the Progetto della Memoria's publications, the tone is somewhat smug: "The promoters of the Progetto della Memoria see the past as providing a model of co-existence between different peoples. The Italian community showed a constant capacity to engage with the

Tunisians in an atmosphere of openness and fruitful conviviality, which was not always the case of other communities at the time."[74]

As Albert Memmi showed, the Italians occupied a position in Tunisia between colonizers and colonized. They were much less removed from the Tunisians than the French, whose relationship with the Tunisians was "stilted and formal." Italians spoke Arabic, formed friendships with Tunisians, and sometimes married Tunisians. Nevertheless, continues Memmi, "the same European origin . . . and a majority of identical customs bring them sentimentally closer to the colonizer. . . . It will be understood that as much as they may be outcasts in an absolute sense their behaviour vis-à-vis the colonized has much in common with the colonizer."[75] The Progetto della Memoria could also be examined in light of the work of Italian historians such as Angelo Del Boca who have interrogated the narrative of *Italiani, brava gente*, according to which Italians were somehow more tolerant in colonial settings than other Europeans, owing to a national aptitude for empathy and understanding.[76] As well as promoting a generally positive vision of Italian colonial legacies in North Africa, then, this Italian historiography did much to develop the narrative of multifarious Tunisian "Mediterraneanness" that would be deemed useful by the Ben 'Ali regime.

A Mediterranean City

We began this chapter at Bab al-Bahr in central Tunis, with the departure of the British Embassy from its site between the medina and the colonial city. We return now to the built heritage of Tunis, to explore how the "Mediterraneanizing" of national history affected the country's capital, how it was depicted, and how it was remodeled.

Writing in 1988, one year after the coming to power of Ben 'Ali, Michel Péraldi described the colonial city as resembling a down-at-the-heels provincial French town whose clocks had all stopped about 1965. The juxtaposition of the two cities—the medina and post-1881 Tunis constructed under the protectorate—conveyed the unresolved tension of the colonial experience: "This city resembles a sea too vast for the few craft who navigate it, seemingly deserted by a part of its life whose trace cannot be effaced. It is a town from a French province whose clocks seem to have stopped toward the 1960s right in the middle of the city center. Not a void, but a sort of spatial rigidity. This city waits its turn to be reappropriated and revisited. Medina and colonial city seem to thrive on their mutual opposition."[77]

After 1956 scholars had placed Tunis in the category of "villes d'économie sous-développée" and highlighted the problems of integration between the European city, the slums constructed by rural migrants (*bidonvilles*), and the old city or medina.[78] This perception of the city persisted until the 1980s.[79] By the early twenty-first century, legislation governing the protection of architectural heritage sites in Tunis and elsewhere in the country was extended to cover buildings dating from the mid-nineteenth century onward. Additions to the national heritage list in 2001 included Jean Resplandy's Art Nouveau Municipal Theatre on avenue Bourguiba, the Moorish-style Trésorerie Générale designed by Raphael Guy on avenue Habib Thameur (formerly avenue Roustan), and the Banque d'Algérie (rue de Rome), all dating from the early twentieth century.[80] The railway station at Tozeur in southern Tunisia, a miniature masterpiece of *Arabisance*, with its blue wooden *tindas* shading the windows, was also listed as part of national architectural heritage. The first listed building from the protectorate period had been the Erlanger Palace "En-Nejma ez-Zahra" at Sidi Bou Said. Between 1956 and 1985 the only building given listed status had been the Ribat of Monastir.[81]

Between 2000 and 2001 major work was undertaken to improve the avenue Bourguiba, from the Bab al-Bahr on the eastern edge of the medina to the end of the avenue Bourguiba on the bank of the lake separating Tunis from the Mediterranean. A fountain system was installed after months of muddy disruption to the Place de la Victoire at Bab al-Bahr in front of the British Embassy. On avenue de France pavements were widened, and café terraces spilled across the widened pavements, effectively reducing the space available for pedestrians. Facades of nineteenth-century buildings were cleared of trailing wires and garish plastic signs. On the avenue Bourguiba workmen labored around the clock, removing some of the ficus trees (and all the florists) from the central Ramblas-like esplanade. The facades of buildings such as the former

Maltese Club on rue de Grèce and the former Politeama Rossini were restored, while next to the Municipal Theatre a commercial center was constructed in a pastiche art nouveau style on the site of the demolished Tunisia Palace Hotel. Street furniture on period models recalling Haussmannian Paris was installed.[82] The Roman Catholic Cathedral of Saint Vincent and Saint Paul had already been extensively renovated in the mid-1990s, while the smaller Greek Orthodox Cathedral and Russian Orthodox churches were also refurbished. Small plaques outside these latter buildings now describe them as centers of the Greek and Russian "communities" of Tunisia.

The untidy juxtaposition of a crumbling medina and a half-finished modern city was now presented by urban historians in 2004 working on a project funded by Euromed Heritage II as "two forms of closely linked urban fabric."[83] In the same way that facades became sleek and smooth, the asperities of history were smoothed over; conservationists and urban scholars avoided terms evocative of past conflict such as the "colonial city" and designated central Tunis outside the medina as "the twentieth-century city," the product of a period of urban growth around the Mediterranean from Tangiers to Latakia, via Marseille and Alexandria.[84] *Tunis: The Orient of Modernity* (2010), one of the last coffee-table architectural works of the Ben 'Ali period, describes the modern city of Tunis as a "dense and coherent form, a harmonious balance between the Medina and the European city. . . . [A] convergence was possible only under the tolerant skies of Tunisia."[85] In 2013 the Association de Sauvegarde de la Médina produced a weighty tome entitled *Tunis patrimoine vivant: Conservation et créativité Association de Sauvegarde de la Médina, 1980–2012.*[86] This work, published in French, with an English translation in preparation but no Arabic version, has on its cover a picture of the ochre facade of the Palais Cardoso at the entrance to the medina, reinforcing the image of Tunis as a Mediterranean city, as the Cardoso family was part of the Tunisian Jewish community descended from emigrants from Leghorn. Such discourse is part of a wider revival of the cosmopolitan component of the hybrid cities, such as Saigon, Shanghai, Zanzibar, and Istanbul, whose growth accompanied the increase in world trade, European imperial expansion, and the decline of older inland cities.[87]

Officially obliterated for decades, their cosmopolitan component, long associated with an abhorred colonialism, is experiencing an unprecedented revival. Today, nostalgia for a transnational culture and its expressions in provincial cosmopolitanism is becoming a powerful political tool in an increasing number of cities.[88]

The nostalgia here is not the bittersweet longing of loss ("reflective nostalgia") but rather a "restorative nostalgia" that patches up the past and restores it in the form of architectural projects and financial investments.[89] In the case of Tunis, the early 1990s saw a series of initiatives—exhibitions and publications as well as the ambitious renovation of the avenue Bourguiba in the heart of the colonial city—in order to reinforce the image of Tunis as a Mediterranean city at the crossroads of various civilizations.[90] This process was controlled by urbanists and architects working within official structures such as the Association de Sauvegarde de la Médina. Recent years have nevertheless seen not only measures of protection and restoration of existing buildings but also conversions that purport to retain a particular "spirit of place": the Tunis architectural review *Archibat* praised the successful conversion of a former bank on the avenue de France into a hotel.[91] The term "spirit of place" suggests that a visionary reconnection can be enacted to a past otherwise unreachable, recalling Byron's musings before the Acropolis or Lawrence Durrell's "spirit of place."[92] In Byron's words: "The sense aches with gazing to behold / the earliest scenes our dreams have dwelt upon."[93] Unnoticed by *Archibat*, however, the names of the architects and contractors (Fourneron Bey and Allar-Clemens) as well as the one-hundred-year-old plaque bearing the name of the adjoining street (rue de l'Ancienne Poste) have all vanished from the smooth, sleek facade of what has become the Tunisia Palace hotel with its wood-paneled "Bar 1900."[94] As Svetlana Boym has observed in her study of the "restoration" of the frescoes of the Sistine Chapel in the 1980s, restorative nostalgia has no use for the signs of historical time. The past is a value for the present; it is not a duration, but a perfect snapshot of a prelapsarian moment. David Lowenthal notes, however, "We expect most artefacts to show signs of wear and age. . . . Because we feel that old things should look old, we may forget that they originally looked new. . . . An element of mystery and uncertainty distinguishes past from present.

We expect the past not to be precise or specific, but rather to be vague and incomplete, waiting to be filled in by our own imaginations."[95]

Sometimes amid the restoration work in the early twenty-first century, one encountered former members of preindependence elites who lamented the way that Tunis had been occupied by uncouth rustics (*afaqis*, a person "from the horizons") from the rural hinterland and listed the names of now-closed bars: Les Ambassadeurs, Tic-Tac, Bar de l'Air, Chez les Nègres, Bar Paul, echoing the drunken commentary of Zaki Bey al Dassouki in Alaa al-Aswany's *Yacoubian Building*: "There used to be a lovely bar here with a Greek owner. Next to it there was a hairdresser's and a restaurant, and here was the leather shop La Bursa Nova. The stores were all fantastically clean and had goods from London and Paris on display. . . . See the wonderful architecture! This building was copied to the last detail from a building I saw in the Quartier Latin in Paris."[96]

The Tunisian state and conservationists have sought to remake avenue de France and other colonial streetscapes as places of consumption. This remodeling is, however, a reconstruction, smoothing over facades and consuming history while doing so. Individual *Yacoubian Building*–style nostalgia is a disruptive commentary on such efforts of conservationists, as the restorative nostalgia of the developers and the Tunisian state spurs counternostalgias among former elites, marginalized from the period of Habib Bourguiba onward.

While the initial protests against the Ben 'Ali regime began in peripheral regions, starting in Sidi Bouzid in mid-January 2011, decisive public demonstrations took place on avenue Bourguiba, renovated ten years previously. These rural hinterlands of the "interior" had been marginalized by colonial economic development that, in Tunisia as elsewhere in the Maghreb, had been concentrated on the coasts.[97] Tunis and Tunisia would thenceforth have to reckon with the "*afaqis*" from the distant rural hinterlands where the spark of resistance had been kindled.

A Postrevolutionary Conclusion

After 2011 the debate on national identity was rekindled, notably during the election campaign of autumn 2011, at the expense, according to some observers, of the country's economic challenges. The Ennahda electoral program for the elections of autumn 2011 noted (in terms similar to the words of the Ben 'Ali regime) Tunisia's Arabic, Islamic, African, and Mediterranean links and its historical relationships with various countries along the shores of the Mediterranean.[98]

Tunisia's new leaders were careful to project an image of tolerance, notably with regard to the country's Jewish community. Ten years after the terrorist bombing of the Ghriba synagogue on the island of Djerba in 2002, Tunisian prime minister Hamadi Jebali, speaking at a World Tourism Organisation meeting in Djerba in April 2012, welcomed Jewish pilgrims to the Ghriba. The synagogue is reputedly built on the site of a tomb of a Jewish virgin who brought scrolls from Palestine, and around six thousand pilgrims visit each year thirty-three days after Passover. Jebali spoke of a "tolerant and welcoming" Tunisia, while Tunisian president Mouncef Marzouki welcomed Tunisian Jewish children from Djerba to the presidential palace in Carthage on April 15, 2012. These initiatives came shortly after incidents in central Tunis on March 25, 2012, when calls were made at an Islamist demonstration to prepare for "combat against the Jews." On January 5, 2012, a visiting Hamas leader was acclaimed at Tunis-Carthage airport with "cries of death to the Jews."[99] Even if the term "Mediterranean" may occupy a less prominent place in public discourse than has hitherto been the case, "Tunisianness" as a capability to embrace diversity remains therefore potent. While the "Other" (in this case the Tunisian Jews) has largely left the country, what is important is the integrity of "Tunisianity," endangered by chanting "Salafists" at the Carthage airport. Ironically, the University of Manouba, where the "cosmopolitan" school of historians developed in the 1990s, became the scene of confrontation in late 2011 and early 2012 between university teachers who saw themselves as defending secular and scientific values and "Salafist" students who sought to give Islamic values visibility on the university campus and invoked their right to wear the *niqab*.

Other minority communities are coming to the fore in novel ways as well. Black Tunisians, for long marginalized, are organizing associations to promote equality and overcome racist practices that belie the "tolerant crossroads of cultures" image of Tunisia projected by the Ben 'Ali regime.[100] Some commentators suggest that the proliferation of minority groupings is a reaction against the stifling ambiance of the Ben ʿAli years that saw the cultivation of a *fantasme* of tolerance, with Ben ʿAli as ringmaster in a circus of assembled diversities.[101] A parallel could be drawn with the situation in Algeria in the 1990s when political parties, as Hugh Roberts has shown, were preoccupied with issues of culture and identity and nonclass solidarities, while also playing to the Western "international gallery." One can recall here the international mobilization on behalf of Habib Kazdaghli, one of the pioneering scholars of Tunisia's Jewish community, during his confrontation with students demanding the right to wear the *niqab* during examinations at the University of Manouba. Kazdagli was recently awarded the "Courage to Think" award by the Scholars at Risk organization.[102]

This chapter has, in Pierre Nora's words, been less interested in events themselves than in the way in which these events are constructed over time.[103] The Ben ʿAli regime sought to instrumentalize the history of Tunisia's Mediterranean communities, and the embattled scholars specializing in this area countered by using the past to critically frame Tunisia's present and future. Both, as noted at the beginning of this article, ostensibly adhered to the founding myths of "Tunisianity." As Tunisia continues on its postrevolutionary path, the country's Mediterranean communities may become less of an allegory of what Tunisia should be and more of an area of objective historical research. One might recall in conclusion Herbert Butterfield's observation that "history is all things to all men. She is at the service of good causes and bad. In other words she is a harlot and a hireling, and for this reason she best serves those who suspect her most."[104]

10

Majority and Minority Languages in the Middle East

The Case of Hebrew in Mandate Palestine

LIORA R. HALPERIN

In terms of relative numbers of speakers, the most basic grounds for defining a majority or minority language, Hebrew in Palestine-Israel underwent a complete transformation from minority language in the Ottoman and British mandate years to a majority language and language of power following Israeli statehood in 1948.[1] This transformation, a result of the twin forces of mass Ashkenazi Jewish immigration and Israel's mass displacement of Palestinians, symbolizes for both Jews and Palestinians the realization of the Zionist vision of Jewish sovereignty, the achievement of a Jewish majority in what would become Israel, and the crushing of Palestinian visions of statehood. Arabic in Palestine is "the rare case in which a major language, once spread by conquest," has become, "without a doubt, a minority language."[2] However, this binary understanding of interlingual and interethnic relations in which Jews and Palestinians trade places as minority and majority, though of great significance in the post-1948 period, obscures more complex considerations of prestige, relative power, and perceived status that sociolinguists have argued are also significant in discussion of majority and minority languages.[3] In our particular case, it ignores the layered frameworks of influence and global connectivity in which Zionist Jewish promoters of Hebrew were located before 1948: a mandated territory in which the British yielded both political and cultural influence, such that both the Jewish and the Arab communities, whatever their configurations of power, felt themselves to be minority populations who had reason to learn the language of the majority—in this case English—so as to have access to Anglo-European politics and culture.

This chapter looks at Jewish educators' discourses about Hebrew- and English-language instruction to explore two propositions that stood in tension with one another: First, the Jewish community of Palestine (the "Yishuv") aimed to construct a hegemonic Hebrew space that would create the (fictive) impression that Hebrew was a majority language dealing with the typically Western difficulty of receiving (Jewish) immigrants. I suggest that in the perception and presentation of many Zionists, Hebrew was functioning—or seemed to function—as a majority language well before it became numerically so, even while the majority of Palestine's Jews were not speaking Hebrew as a first language. Second, and in contrast, the chapter suggests that the self-declared Hebrew majority community was subject to reminders of that community's perpetual minority status—not only vis-à-vis the Arab community of Palestine, whose influence Zionist leaders believed they could displace through economic separation and continued Jewish immigration, but also relative to global currents of influence and power, currents that persisted as statehood approached. If the leaders of a minority community could construct its language as a majority hegemonic language through discursive maneuvers and relative prestige and political power, this community could not evade its relative lack of power and nonhegemonic status relative to structures larger than the nation-state. Palestine, like the rest of the Middle East and much of the world, navigated (and in certain ways benefited from) a colonial context in which and through which English was growing in status as an international language.[4] This broader context suggests that the new minority statuses, which emerged as a by-product of anti-imperial nationalist movements (of which Zionism, somewhat counterintuitively, was one), were constructed as much discursively as through hard statistical fact. We must move beyond the numerical fluctuations of Jewish and Arab populations in Palestine toward global and colonial configurations of power and influence when determining who is and is not a minority in the Middle East and, more important, when and for whom the analytical category of "minority" is useful.

Dominance of Hebrew

The Zionist vision, writ large, was to create a self-sufficient Hebrew culture that would not merely be dominant within a small elite community but also construct itself both as a majority host society that could receive and absorb immigrant populations and as a hegemonic language in Gramsci's sense, that is, capable of convincing the masses that "the existing social hierarchy," in this case of Hebrew dominance, "was natural, desirable, and inevitable."[5] This move toward linguistic dominance would signal the end of dependence on surrounding cultures. Only this way, said leading voices in the Hebrew revival project, would the Jewish people sever their relations both with the Jewish diaspora and with the subservient mindset that, they believed, characterized diasporic existence. This project to create a "majority language" within a self-evidently minority population has been most extensively discussed in the realm of literary studies, following the work on major and minor literatures by Gilles Deleuze and Felix Guattari. Despite the small number of Hebrew speakers and writers, writes Hannan Hever, "the mode of Jewish experience in the early twentieth century, as a national minority in the Diaspora, was formulated [by canonical Hebrew writers] in standard utopian terms of a national majority." The project to "present a minority as a national majority," according to Hever, was aimed at rejecting the iconic diasporic status that Jews had so long held (and which most other Jews had long embraced).[6] Writers constructed a "majority" Hebrew literature through celebrating universalist typologies and aesthetics and creating characters that functioned as free-willed national subjects.

This initially fictive promotion of Hebrew as a majority language also occurred in Palestine, where educators, politicians, and party leaders attempted to sideline other languages by framing them as dangerous foreign imports into a hegemonic cultural center rather than the majority tongues of a host society. A late 1930s flyer from the Jewish National Council proclaimed: "Every Jew in Palestine, whether he has just come or whether he is a longstanding resident, must speak, and conduct all of his business in the old-new language of the Jewish people: Hebrew. Our education, our press, and our theater are Hebrew. Just as in public life, likewise also in private and family life, Hebrew is heard among us!"[7] This assertion of hegemony was counterfactual—many languages other than Hebrew were heard on the Jewish street and in Jewish homes—but it nonetheless pervaded discourse on Hebrew study. The presumption that Hebrew was a majority language emerged from a tendency to focus on the New Yishuv, the Zionist-oriented Jewish community of Palestine, not as one of multiple populations in Palestine, and a minority among them, but as the hegemonic center of a diverse Jewish community increasingly bent toward Zionist ideology. In this view, the Ottomans or British rulers were essentially external to the landscape, while the majority Palestinian Arabs were quite literally part of the landscape, natural features, perhaps a wild population to be tamed or convinced, but not a culture that exerted hegemonic power: "The Jews were, of course, aware of the Arab communities, but these towns, villages, and neighborhoods had no place in the Jews' perception of the homeland's landscape. They were just a formless, random collection of three-dimensional entities, totally isolated from the Jewish landscape and viewed as if through an impenetrable glass wall."[8] As such, Hebrew speakers were a self-imagined majority encountering minority Jewish populations who needed, they thought, to be brought in line. Given the highly successful Hebrew educational system, these various Jewish populations—speaking Yiddish, Polish, Russian, German, or other languages—were indeed minorities relative to Hebrew.

Schools were at the forefront of Hebrew promotion and foreign-language exclusion and the most visible facade in the claim that Hebrew was indeed a majority language. They were places where Hebrew seemed to truly dominate even when it did not permeate settings like the home, the streets, or the coffee shops. The Hebrew pedagogical sanctum, a hegemonic space within a society increasingly claiming its own hegemony, had been built specifically through the exclusion of other languages that could be viewed as alternative bearers of culture—for example, German and French.[9] New immigrant students often remember arriving, finding, in the words of a student writer, an "all Hebrew space," not knowing if they could master it but eventually being pleased that they could transition to being Hebrew speakers.[10] In the analysis of Benjamin Harshav, through the establishment of "cells in a social desert," bastions of Hebrew in a space without other claimants to dominance, Hebrew became the "base language" of society.[11]

The sense that Hebrew could and would function as a majority language led to widespread apathy about and opposition toward learning foreign languages. At times this sentiment was directed at lower-level or rural students and based on an assumption that the "nationalist farmer"—the paradigmatic Zionist figure—ought to be monolingual. In 1892, when the first groups of Zionist teachers attempted to organize themselves, teacher and pioneer of Hebrew education Israel Belkind stated that foreign-language study had no place in the schooling of children in agricultural settlements and that it would be relevant only for those who went abroad: "While children in the cities need to learn other languages, too, like for example Arabic and French . . . because who knows where they will go when they finish their schooling, teachers in the agricultural settlements need to . . . teach children the love of labor at home and the love of the soil in the field and in the garden. Thus it is unnecessary to learn foreign languages in the agricultural colonies."[12] Palestine in this construction was an isolated space, the majority of whose population was imagined to be Hebrew speaking and whose interests did not extend beyond the land itself. Though such dictates sound patronizing, some workers appear to have shared them because they privileged practical education and real-world experience over book learning. Tzvi Elpeleg, the son of a carpenter and a homemaker who had immigrated in 1934 from Poland, recalls that he went to school only until the age of fourteen, because "in the eyes of my parents and other parents—not everyone, but the majority of the neighborhood—[up to age fourteen] was the maximum level of education that a person needed to have."[13] Succeeding within a self-enclosed Hebrew-dominant Jewish community was the highest ideal, in this view; the status of the community as a minority population in its environment, more broadly conceived, was immaterial.

Engagement even with the proximate rulers—after 1917, the British—was necessarily assumed. While it was self-evident that some elites elsewhere in the British Empire would need English, it was not so clear in Palestine, where the Yishuv (the Jewish community of pre-1948 Palestine) was largely autonomous, where Hebrew had been recognized as an official language, and where, therefore, elites imagined that they could theoretically manage in Hebrew as though Hebrew were indeed the majority and dominant language. As Oz Almog has noted, the labor movement had a deeply suspicious view of higher education in general and foreign-language study in particular, as such study appeared to have no connection to the quotidian needs of farm labor. Kibbutz schools did not prepare students for university entrance exams.[14] But the sentiment was far more widespread than the labor movement alone. Menahem Ussishkin, head of the Jewish National Fund, once said, "Regarding a foreign language, I don't think we need it at all. We should learn just one language: Hebrew and specifically Hebrew. The multiplicity of languages is unnatural."[15] The proposition that no segment of the Jewish population needed to be educated in multiple languages affirmed a counterfactual discourse about Hebrew's dominance and Jews' self-sufficiency.

The sense that Hebrew would function as a hegemonic majority language, with little space for other language use or instruction, drove educational choices at all levels. Izhac Epstein, known for his writings on the teaching of "Hebrew in Hebrew" (informed by the western European Berlitz method), wrote extensively on the danger of multilingual education. "One of the widespread errors among the public regarding education," he wrote, "is the belief that increasing the number of languages increases knowledge." Noting that many parents were demanding foreign-language study for their children, he proceeded to outline the main psychological danger of combining languages. Cultivating expressive abilities in multiple languages means, in practice, teaching multiple words for the same concepts, words that ultimately become confused with one another in the mind: "The languages that we learn weaken one another."[16]

The imperative for monolingualism came from the perception that Jews were, and could manifestly be, an autonomous nation in the European model, the sort of nation in which they had themselves long lived as minorities. Though many Middle Eastern nationalist movements spoke on behalf of existing majority populations, the Zionist project envisioned the transformation of a minority into a hegemonic majority. This counterfactual insistence on national hegemony reflected a bipolar view of the world as divided into hegemonic nations and minority non-nations. To deny Jews' capacity for nationhood or the self-sufficiency of their language was, symbolically, to acquiesce to diasporic minority status. For Epstein, foreign-language instruction in the schools would therefore reflect and exacerbate the typical Jewish condition of multilingualism, against which the schools were enjoined to fight. "Members of oppressed peoples have to divide their language abilities into two languages from early childhood," he wrote.[17] The antidote to oppression, by this logic, was monolingualism. Unfortunately, Epstein observed, characteristically diasporic conditions did not appear to be dissipating in Palestine, where he observed that individuals regularly switched between languages in their conversations. He called this "hal'azat ha-'Ivrit" (the "foreignizing" of Hebrew, from La'az, a rabbinic catchall term for European languages). Epstein, in setting up an equation between oppression and multilingualism, asserts that monolingualism codes to cultural hegemony.

Epstein was aware that foreign languages could not be eliminated completely—"we are enslaved to our environment and its demands"—but he was insistent that languages should be studied no more than necessary and not unless it was deemed absolutely necessary for one's studies. A student learning a language for commercial purposes should focus on commercial language. A language course focused on reading, likewise, should not include speaking exercises or essay assignments.[18] Epstein's words, written just before the British came to power in Palestine, were held up as a model by the Teachers' Federation, which called his research "broad, full, and comprehensive" and repeated his arguments in their assessments of the important work done by early Hebrew educators.[19]

The psychological harm of language multiplicity, which so concerned Epstein in the years before World War I, was a central plank in educators' opposition to foreign-language study. If multilingualism, historically speaking, accompanied oppression, it also, in this logic, actively led to oppression as a minority group. Fishel Shneurson, a psychologist and pedagogue, conducted a study for a seminar on bilingualism convened by the Tel Aviv branch of the Hebrew Teachers' Federation. Influenced in his work by the large variety of European studies of bilingualism over the past several decades (including a 1928 conference in Geneva on the problem of bilingualism), Shneurson began with the premise that "bilingualism is a problem even when it comes during childhood, during the period of the development of language."[20] His concern for the deep psychological harm caused by bilingualism was indicative of a generation of educators who could not allow foreign-language study ever to become serious, out of a fear that it might begin to impede Hebrew fluency.

The hope for a situation of monolingualism in which the national tongue would be the language for all purposes bespoke what might only be called chutzpah. In practice, I show elsewhere, this premise was regularly questioned and undermined in a society that understood that it had to interact—in other languages—with various other populations, whether the British, with their abundance of global power; the Palestinian Arabs, with their numerical majority; or the Jewish diaspora, which still constituted a majority of the world Jewish population.[21] The construction of the nation as a majority one, however, is central to the self-imagining of the Zionist movement in this period; the Zionist movement's rhetoric and choices are not intelligible without understanding this promajority, antiminority framework shaped by the philosophy known as "the negation of Diaspora."

■ ■ ■

Hebrew, a minority language by all numerical accountings, was constructed nonetheless and for particular ideological reasons as a majority tongue. But the presumption that Arabic was thus the most relevant majority language is not a foregone conclusion. Hebrew's claims to majority status were contested not only by the demographics of Palestine but also by the reality of power relations. In 1924 journalist Mordecai Ben-Hillel Ha-Cohen reflected on the linguistic situation of the Yishuv under British rule, noting the parallel threats posed by English and Arabic but suggesting that English—the language of power—was perhaps more damaging that Arabic, the majority language:

> Threats are bursting forth [against our language] from two sides, fighting with all their might. English has come to our country, the language of the authorities, which has not only political value but also—and this is perhaps even more important—a very rich literature, literature in all

fields, inestimably rich and more imaginative than our poor Hebrew literature.... And from the other side our Arab neighbors are attacking our language with great exertion. Their literature isn't vast and from this perspective our literature might be able to compete with it and it doesn't have the power to subdue our language. But Arabic is supported by a great mass of people who speak it, by the daily life lived in that language, and by the Arab reality.[22]

What is significant here is that while Arabic had the force of numbers behind it (a reality that Zionists actively contested through continued immigration), English was coded to global values that would remain powerful *even if* Hebrew became numerically dominant. Concerns about English tended to evoke both the power of the British government and the historical tendency of Jews to slavishly mimic the cultures of the West. The principle of the Hebrew Gymnasium in Jerusalem warned of a "flood of Anglicization" if the British were to have too much influence on the Jewish schools. Joseph Klausner, alluding to English, warned that Hebrew culture could not "stand up to stronger elements."[23] The Jewish National Council's words to the 'Atid School of Commerce lend insight into this particular combination of insecurity and inferiority vis-à-vis the West: "You surely know the looming danger of assimilation and Levantinism, which is undermining the education of this generation and the styling of its character. How much the more so, then, is it necessary to warn of any move that opens a door to imposing of a non-Hebrew culture in the Hebrew schools."[24] In this fascinating paragraph, Hebrew culture faces two threats: "assimilation" and "Levantinism." Levantinism, which would subsequently be used to refer to Arab-like qualities, was most often defined in the Yishuv as a diasporic form of low culture characterized particularly by the mixing of the national language with higher-status European languages (the term derived from a perception that Arab communities, particularly in Lebanon, were characterized by impure cultural mixing with French). This context, however, suggests an alternative meaning of Levantinism: excessive obeisance to the West shown by a people possessing a deficient culture, that is, a minority not primarily in terms of local numbers, but in terms of global hierarchies of power.

These views—alarmist and dismissive—might easily fit into a historical narrative of Hebrew's tireless fight against linguistic rivals. But they are clearly not the sentiments of a majority language pushing out the rabble competition of immigrant diversity but rather a society recognizing that a specific category of language—languages of power—might have a special and threatening place. As Reichel notes, the overt Zionist rejection of any educational undertaking not directly tied to Jewish national aims coexisted with a "covert model" of a student who would in fact have a wide general education.[25] As she explores with respect to "general studies" more broadly, a widespread discomfort with multilingualism coexisted with a real sense, at least among some Zionist educators, that Hebrew existed as a minority language not only locally but also globally.

Learning a Global Language

Teachers spoke bombastically about the creation of a Hebrew school system and presented Hebrew as a newly dominant language. Nonetheless, their enthusiasm about Hebrew's victory—shared by scholars of Zionist education in later generations—has meant that the existence of foreign-language instruction in the prestate period and real awareness about Hebrew's functional weakness have tended to be obscured.[26] Zionist schools in the mandate period did not exclude all other tongues: they nearly all taught English as well as Arabic. Moreover, justifications for language study were not concerned only with the practical necessity of language knowledge; they also reflected a level of awareness that Hebrew would achieve dominance not only by overtaking Jewish immigrant tongues and displacing Arabic, but also by rivaling global languages like English. This latter ambition, of course, was unrealizable by a small national group, and anxiety about this fact is palpable in discussions about the place of English in school curricula. Set against a notion of diaspora marked by Jewish rootlessness, alienation, and economic and civic underdevelopment, English seemed to offer an antidote: the removal of provincial (or "Levantine") tendencies—it was a powerful language not despite the fact that Hebrew was dominant, but precisely because Hebrew was a minority language and because its promoters were aware that they were embedded in global power structures.

Beyond the Practical: The Stakes of Being a Global Minority

To the extent that English was viewed as simply "technically helpful,"[27] study could be utilitarian and locally focused, nothing more than a technique to manage a foreign pressure on an otherwise hegemonic Jewish community where Hebrew effectively functioned as a hegemonic language. For some who found themselves in Palestine as refugees before and during World War II, English was indeed occasionally a conduit for physically leaving Palestine and getting employment in Europe. But the fact that Jews went from being the quintessential minority to a hegemonic society, and eventually a numerical majority, overlooks real continuities between the diasporic Jewish experience and the experience in Palestine. The Jewish community, even as it gained strength and as more of its number in fact became Hebrew speakers, continued to exist in the shadow of and in relationship to foreign—and especially European—languages.

Teachers' discussions about English instruction reflected a persistent anxiety about Zionists' inability to be fully Western. A teacher who signed his or her name Y. S., writing in the educational journal *Hed hahinukh* (Education Echo) disagreed with a fellow teacher who had recommended getting nearer to the Orient through studying Arabic. The truth, Y. S. wrote, is that the Arabs should turn to the Jews "and learn something from Westerners."[28] For all the emphasis on the authentic Semitic character of the Jews, members of the Zionist movement by and large wished to act and appear European. But the appeal for Zionists to act as Western moderns—in their relations with Arabs or otherwise—was not straightforward. Zionist anxiety over their lack of Semitic authenticity and lack of claim to Palestine was matched only by their concern about lack of sufficient modernity and development, and in this state of anxiety English could be presumed to be a way out, an antidote against the corrosive influences of the East and a means toward ensuring the European quality of the Yishuv. English, wrote Ben-Zion Dinaburg (historian and head of the Jewish Teachers Training College in Jerusalem), was "the chief conduit of European influence" in the Yishuv, and learning it might help Jews escape the degenerative effects of the East and establish a functioning European society.[29]

Two impulses were characteristic of Zionist educators, who were concerned that the Yishuv was only tenuously Western, despite the fact that their European origins and imperial benefactors would eventually help them gain independence. First, from the beginning of the British presence in Palestine, some expressed the hope that the study of English literature might serve as a model for the still incomplete Hebrew literary tradition. Second, many felt that an introduction to the modern culture, nature, and political system of the English (seen as a beacon of democracy particularly in the Nazi era) might serve as a model for the emerging Hebrew society. In both of these discussions, the relative weakness of Hebrew was a touchstone.

A great strength of English was its rich literature, and familiarity with English literature could serve as a model for its still lacking literary tradition. English, Mordecai Ben-Hillel Ha-Cohen noted in 1923, has "a very rich literature, literature in all fields, inestimably rich and more imaginative than our poor Hebrew literature."[30] When the Education Department of the Va'ad Ha-Le'umi published a 1941 report on the teaching of English in Hebrew secondary schools, it asserted that the gymnasiums in particular needed to move beyond language itself to broader cultural concerns. The report cited a 1918 British document that recommended "modern studies," including the study of modern European languages, as "an instrument of culture" that could help "develop the higher faculties, the imagination, the sense of beauty, and the intellectual comprehension." Applying that document's conclusions to the Palestine context, the report recommended that "a similar cultural aim should pervade the study of English in our schools." Exposure to English in Palestine was even more important than the study of other European languages in England, for "Hebrew literature is poorer than English both in content and form."[31]

Literature was not the only exemplary creation of the English; their culture, society, and civic structures, too, could serve as models for an emerging Zionist polity. At root, the recommendation to study foreign languages was premised on the idea that, like its literature, Zionist civic culture itself was stunted in its development and needed an infusion of Western sensibilities. The Safra School of Commerce in Tel Aviv, which taught English largely for professional reasons, noted in its promotional material that through foreign language study, "every educated person can probe the international world of cultures and recognize their achievements."[32] English was at the core of this proposition. The Va'ad Ha-Le'umi report on English insisted that the curriculum focus not only on English literature, but also on English life: "Pupils who have been fed only belles letters remain often with only a poor understanding of the English people." Moreover, a connection with modern people would transmit a set of modern values to the Yishuv, for "the study of modern English thought and institutions can provoke useful discussion and help to correct provincial tendencies."[33] The use of language here is revealing. The word "provincial," used here, evokes the parallel term "Levantine/*levantini*," a word used at this time to describe failed or incomplete Europeanization, ill-formed institutions, and illogical cultural mixtures, if also a sort of exotic allure (it would later be used to refer mainly to Jews of Arab descent).[34] The main feature of cultural provincialism was multilingualism, and its main antidote was adherence to Hebrew only (which was precisely the diasporic impulse against which Hebrew writers militated). But in this case, ironically, one path away from provincialism was the study of a foreign language understood to embody an opposite tendency.

No doubt, it was England itself that first promoted that country as a model society with model values, in Palestine as well as in the rest of the empire. British publishers offered accessible texts about the greatness of the empire in simple English texts, distributed in multiple countries overseas. In a small book called *Here and There in the British Empire*, published in 1902 and transported to the Yishuv, students read that "Greater Britain" had become "a power to which Rome in the height of her glory was not be compared," and it goes on to suggest that this stunning success could be attributed, "in no small measure, to the fact that the British are a hardy, determined, persevering, maritime race" who love adventure, order and justice, and the spirit of law.[35] Tendentious as they may seem to today's reader, these texts by and large confirmed beliefs that Zionists held already. The West's embodiment of modern values was broadly assumed; its epistemic privilege was unquestioned and unquestionable.[36]

Britain was an evident, though complicated, model for a society looking to establish its Western bona fides and, thus, its claims to hegemonic rule while also asserting its distance and independence from Europe. We can see an explicit attempt to negotiate these poles of attraction and distancing in the writings of Professor Hayim Yehuda (Leon) Roth, an Anglo-Jewish professor of philosophy at the Hebrew University. In his 1943 article "The Desired Direction in the Teaching of English," Roth rationalizes the instruction of English in a way that showcases the multiple, often conflicting, sentiments bound up in the decision to teach English in the Zionist schools.

Roth's first question, one that follows him through the essay, is the following: to what extent do we (Jews, Zionists, or the Yishuv) want to be English or be like the English? He begins by stressing unequivocally, "We are not engaging in these studies in order to be English." Immediately, however, he allows himself a bit of wistful musing—"It is true that if we did want to change our skin we would prefer them over any other nation"—and then cuts himself off abruptly: "This isn't a choice we can make because we have already chosen—or been chosen by—another choice. We are Jewish and we have returned to the land of our fathers in order to rebuild Jewish life. And a principal part of this life is Hebrew language and culture." At the end of these serpentine musings, he attempts to distance himself from the language entirely. "English for us is a secondary language, a foreign language."[37] Roth, a native English speaker, makes this point as one who has chosen to leave English behind and cast his lot with the Hebrew project in Palestine. His uncertainty, however, appears to run deeper than a personal crisis of identity: speaking in the name of the Jewish collectivity in Palestine, he admits that the Yishuv experiences the conflicting desires to be a society much like England and to be a society whose uniqueness is marked by and bound up in its commitment to Hebrew.

Why should a society principally committed to Hebrew devote time to English as a foreign language? He proceeds first to discount the older generation's attraction to "great world literature," calling this attraction a characteristic of the "transitional generation" (*dor ha-ma'avar*) that the younger generation might be able to overcome. In fact, echoing voices cited earlier, the need for English derives from a set of practical demands: "commercial needs, recreational needs, and social needs." English is necessary, he writes, first for understanding the words present on road signs, packaging, and advertisements; second, for reading textbooks and manuals in fields from agriculture to commerce; and third for comprehending the many English words that have made their way into Hebrew newspapers and radio broadcasts.[38]

But English for Roth is not merely a means of satisfying day-to-day needs that derive from unavoidable local contacts between the Yishuv and the British. Like Arabic, English study could also be an important means of strengthening the otherwise deficient Hebrew culture: "Hebrew is important and it will remain important, but it needs completion. This completion must come from outside, from a secondary language, an assisting language [lashon-'ezer], a foreign language." While some may ask why this additional language has to be English and cannot be French, Russian, or German, history, he says, has shown that English must be the language. "To whom are we connected through family, literary, commercial, political, and diplomatic ties?" he asks, and answers, "With English speaking countries." Indeed, English is to be "the center of gravity of our future."[39]

■ ■ ■

What do the Yishuv's deliberations about the place of foreign language in its Hebrew curriculum tell us about its status, whether majority or minority, within Palestine and the Middle East? On the one hand, the Yishuv, over the course of the early twentieth century, positioned itself as a hegemonic language vis-à-vis the numerous Jewish immigrant languages whose speakers were flowing into the country; vis-à-vis the Arabic-speaking majority, which it eventually dispossessed in order to become the numerical majority in Palestine; and, at least outwardly, vis-à-vis European languages that might be deemed influential. As such, the Yishuv might be positioned as either an immigrant-receiving country in the European or American mold or a settler colonial society that eventually displaced the native population to become the majority. In neither of these senses was the Yishuv a minority population. But neither of these perspectives, though each relevant in understanding the cultural formation of the Yishuv, explains its vexed attitudes toward English, attitudes that more closely resemble the beliefs of smaller national groups, whether in Europe or in the postcolonial sphere.

English was not simply another modern language, but rather the language of the sovereign and the language of global power, which both Jews and Palestinians in subsequent generations would come to study as global English and what Braj Kachru would call "the other tongue," the highly symbolic additional language that stood for often ruthless power but also facilitated international trade and political engagement.[40] Increasingly, globalization meant that whatever their nationalist commitments, nations considered the merits of foreign-language proficiency and came to understand that their relative hegemony in local settings was largely immaterial in light of the global lingua franca. Like postcolonial states in Africa and Asia, the Yishuv and then Israel created an educational system that cultivated knowledge of the national language (in this case, not unlike the situation with Kiswahili in East Africa and Hausa in West Africa, a national language not spoken natively by all members of the nation).[41] Nonetheless, like those communities, it was forced to acknowledge the benefits of English-language knowledge for administration, commerce, and politics—the local hegemony of elites took on a different cast when held up against a global tongue, against which they were a small national group, comparable in certain ways to a national minority within a hegemonic state.

And like in those settings, English was by no means a neutral code, a tool to deploy in a simple or uncomplicated way: "A view that holds that the spread of English is natural, neutral and beneficial needs to be investigated as a particular discursive construct."[42] As in these other emerging national societies, educators in the Yishuv expressed anxieties that their emerging national language could be swept away by the language of the occupier, which was also the global lingua franca. At the same time, they felt that British society could offer models for development—indeed, that there existed no models for modernity outside the ones offered by the West. If mastery of Arabic meant the mastery of the East for a movement that was, quite evidently, not Eastern, mastery of English meant the appropriation of the West by a society that, though its majority was European in origin, did not consider itself reliably, deeply Western.

This discussion has suggested that while Arabic, the majority language, reminded Zionists of their relative weakness in Palestine, it was

English that provoked more fundamental concerns about the sophistication and maturity of the Zionist project. While Hebrew signaled internally the process of cultural consolidation and Arabic knowledge provided concrete tools for propaganda and intelligence work, Jewish control over Palestine would not have been possible without proficiency in English, for it was the relative sophistication of the Zionist project and its international ambitions that earned it international respect through ongoing negotiations with both Britain and, later, the United States that solidified its political rule. As scholars of global English have noted, "Mastery of global English generates a significant amount of linguistic capital. . . . [G]lobal English capital becomes critical for attaining elite status."[43] To the extent that Britain enabled the creation of a Jewish state and the United States has heavily funded it, it is the hegemony of English, a global language of power not only of Hebrew, the language of the current numerical majority among Israeli citizens, that explains the relative strength of the Zionist project and Israel. If anything, over time and since 1948, skepticism about English as the language of the foreigner imperial power has given way to a sense that speakers of Hebrew can thrive only if they learn English as a second language.

The circumstances surrounding the creation of Israel are unique in the Middle Eastern context and often are excluded from regional discussions. Certainly, the project of positing a minority language as a majority language was neither feasible nor necessary in most other Middle Eastern nationalist contexts, where the national tongue was also the spoken language of the numerical majority. But the looming force of English touched the Middle East as a whole: where there has been active resistance to it, it has in part been resistance to those local elites who wield the linguistic capital of English to their own benefit.[44] In light of this observation, we might expand the scope of our discussion about minorities from the proximate demographic relations in any given country to the global hierarchies of power that hovered over more local political developments.

11

The Chaldean Church between Iraq and America

A Transnational Social Field Perspective

YASMEEN HANOOSH

In September 2006, at the height of sectarian violence that followed the invasion of Iraq in 2003, Pope Benedict XVI made controversial remarks about Islam in Regensburg, Germany, that provoked an outrage in parts of the Muslim world.[1] Almost immediately following that incident, a Chaldean Catholic priest, Father Basel Yaldo, thirty-six, received death threats and was kidnapped from his home in Baghdad for three days. The situation seemed so dismal that he was transferred from Baghdad to a parish in Michigan, where his victimization received ample coverage from local and international media. A year later, in November 2007, the same pope elevated Chaldean patriarch Emmanuel-Karim III Delly to the rank of cardinal bishop, a status that placed him among the most prestigious prelates of the Catholic Church. In Pope Benedict's own words, this gesture was made by way of "concretely expressing my spiritual closeness and my affection" for Iraq's Christian minorities.[2] This "closeness" and "affection" are not a newfound, top-down compassion from a powerful institution for the weak and plighted Christians of Iraq. It has a long and spirited history that is not only hierarchical but, notably, also reciprocal and transnational.

The connection between the Roman Catholic Church and the Chaldean Church as we know it today dates back at least to 1445 CE, when the first official union between the Church of the East and the Catholic Church in Rome took place during the Council of Florence. Ever since, the appellation "Chaldean," revived then by Pope Eugene IV, has come to refer to the Eastern Christians who entered the communion with Rome. Four centuries later, the remainder of the followers of the Church of the East, the smaller segments who did not convert to Catholicism, were to receive the equally antiquated appellation "Assyrian." This time it came from the Anglican Church.[3]

The West-activated transformation of these two churches, which also forged enduring associations between their followers and ancient Mesopotamian symbolism, is part of an important modern transnational history that is substantially abbreviated here. Its importance lies in locating the intermediary position of the Christian churches of Mesopotamia within the Orientalist conceptual divide between "East" and "West."

Traditionally, through its liaisons with the Roman Catholic Church, but also the Russian Orthodox Church, the Anglican Church, and the various groups of missionaries that frequented the Christian communities in northern Mesopotamia, the Chaldean Church has acted not only as a formal site for collecting, organizing, preserving, and transmitting information and aid among its members in multiple locations, but also as a mediator between its Western protectors and the local Ottoman authorities. In recent decades it has also been an active political mouthpiece on behalf of the endangered Chaldean community in Iraq and a trusted source of data for international aid organizations interested in helping Iraq's religious minorities. Today it continues to extend a multifaceted influence from its American stronghold, coordinating efforts with other nonreligious community organizations and with its religious branches in other parts of the world.

The Chaldean Church currently consists of eight dioceses in Iraq, although the number of its followers there has dwindled to fewer than four hundred thousand, with more than a million having been displaced in the wake of the 2003 US occupation of Iraq and the 2014 infiltration of its northern region by the Islamic State in Iraq and Syria, or ISIS. There are several additional dioceses and eparchies outside of Iraq (India, Lebanon, Australia, the United States, Egypt, Turkey, and Iran) and a continuously expanding diasporic population whose spokespersons estimate its size to be more than twice the size of the Chaldean population remaining in Iraq.[4]

Despite the transnational networks upon whose dynamism and durability religious institutions—certainly the Chaldean Church among them—have consistently relied, scholars have only recently begun to explore the relationship between religion and transnational migration.[5] The salience of religious institutions as a set of doctrines, practices, and cohort of personnel lies particularly in that they are not coincident with the borders of the nation-states that contain their followers. Yet it is precisely because of this absence of physical fixity, which allows for delineating a sending nation and a receiving one, that migration theory has in part ignored the social impact and power of migrants' religion.

Immigrants are often expected to develop religious institutions in the host country as part of the process of incorporation—which the Chaldeans did as early as 1947 in Detroit, Michigan—but these institutions are also expected to lose their force over time with the assimilation of subsequent migrant generations.[6] This prediction does not coincide with the development of Chaldean religious institutions in America, mainly, I argue, because the Chaldean Church operated from the outset within a transnational social field suitable for replenishing its force, namely, within a human network that is organized through the decisions that transnationally circulate between diaspora bishops, ancestral land archbishops and prelates, and the Rome-based pope.

There are a number of histories of the Chaldean Catholic Church that describe it as a locale with specific events that fall along the linear line of its evolution and transformation. In this chapter I argue that the modern Chaldean Church, especially since the mass exit or internal displacement of the majority of its Iraq-based followers since 2003, is predominantly a dynamic process that is more effectively understood if explored as an arena for expressing membership in multiple polities—hence a transnational conceptual social field. Although it is not coincident with the borders of the nation-states where its followers reside, the church may coexist with them or create new spaces for belonging within these nation-states. As such, the religious Chaldean social field transcends the territorial and political boundaries of Iraq and the United States, among other nation-states, and forges in the process an alternative, region-flexible site for the expression of loyalties and a substantive global network of social and economic support.

There are several terms that recur frequently in this chapter. Because some share slightly overlapping historical or conceptual developments or are complex and have been used to denote multiple meanings in previous scholarship and in other chapters of this book, I will introduce these terms along with the working definitions that I develop through the arguments in this paper.

By "Chaldeans" I refer to the individuals or groups who choose this designation for themselves, situationally or essentially, or for whom this designation has been chosen by another authority, such as the Roman Catholic Church, the influential demographics definers such as the US Census Bureau, or the public discourses of modern diasporic Chaldean institutions. Unless I refer to individuals as Chaldean by descent to refer to their origins in modern-day Iraq and to the set of conditions that make them socially perceived as Chaldeans (language, race, religious affiliation), I treat the ingredients of the term "Chaldean" as fluid and changeable. When an internal or external agency tries to dictate the Chaldean identity by fixing and stabilizing the term's contours, I use the word "Chaldean-ness," to signal the essentialization to which fluid identities are subjected in certain representational modes. I also use the term in a collective reference to certain variables when they appear as essentialized and stylized components to constitute a symbolic reference to a putative collective Chaldean identity. These variables are most commonly Mesopotamian antiquities, the Aramaic language, and the Chaldean village of Telkeif, among others.

My use of the term "identity" as it pertains to the Chaldeans is inspired by Stuart Hall's understanding of the term as a "process of identification," and as a "structure that is split" between contesting affiliations, and therefore one that "always has ambivalence within it."[7] As such, I employ the term "identity" to refer to the products of historical, religious, and social events or processes that get assigned the identification Chaldean in a number of intersections, diachronically and synchronically.

My approach to the term "ethnicity" resembles my approach to "identity" in that I treat it as an open-ended construct capable of encompassing multiple and changeable definitions of individuals and collectives. The term "ethnicity" becomes particularly important in my text as I discuss Chaldean identity in representations of the collective that take place in the United States. My understanding of Chaldean ethnicity is heavily colored by Warner Sollor's definition of "American ethnicity" as "a matter not of content but of the importance that individuals ascribe to it."[8]

The term "minority" denotes something analogous to "ethnicity" in my work. Using the term "ethnicity" in reference to the Chaldeans of Iraq would prove problematic when the group was not permitted to express its difference from the majority as an ethnic or racial minority, but rather only as a religious minority (*'aqalliyya diniyya*) during the greater part of the twentieth century. Moreover, ethnicity (as opposed to race, *'irq*, or nationality, *qawmiyya*) in the Arabic language is still a fairly recent coinage (*ithniyya*) that has yet to become integral to the modes of self-articulation in Iraqi societies. Therefore, uniform use of the term "ethnicity" in reference to the Chaldeans of multiple locales would not result in an accurate representation of the Chaldeans who have not adopted American modes of identification.

My reference to the "Chaldean community" traces the use of the expression by Chaldean individuals and groups who posit the presence and stability of such a collective delineation of their group. I use "community" when I examine the imagined site where Chaldeans view themselves as sharing and reproducing the same cultural values for a group larger than their immediate family and kinship networks, where they view themselves as being pressured to belong by a collective agency larger than their face-to-face Chaldean network, or where they see themselves as agents in charge of raking up, standardizing, and certifying the collective for the recognition of those who stand outside it. The latter group I call "Chaldean culture makers," to signal their active role in dictating the ingredients of Chaldean identity not only for themselves but also for the entire imagined community. My usage of the term "community" is then strongly influenced by Benedict Anderson's understanding of the imagined quality of communities, which, according to him, "are to be distinguished, not by their falsity/genuineness, but by the style in which they are imagined."[9] Accordingly, I examine the Chaldean community as a conceptual site in which identification becomes a practice and in which values are produced and enacted through the coming together of resistance and agency to form the multiple tensions that yield various inflections of Chaldeanness.

To examine the current transnational relations maintained by the Chaldean Catholic Church and its key members, it is important to review the politics of church-state relations in Iraq during the second half of the twentieth century and their consequences that led to the formation of a transnational religious social field. Two religious figures dominate this context, Patriarch Paul Cheikho and Patriarch Raphael I Bidawid.

Transnational Foundations: The Chaldean Patriarchate during the Twentieth Century

Far from being geographically tied to one place, as its name suggests, the Chaldean Patriarchate—dubbed "Patriarchate of Babylon" after its Catholic conversion—moved the seat of its patriarch in multiple directions within and outside of Asia over the centuries. It did not establish a measure of stability in modern times until the settlement in Mosul in 1830. During this century, members of the church engaged in a sustained multicultural exchange with the West through contacts with religious and archaeological missions. This exchange happened at home, just as the originary land of the newly fashioned "Chaldeans" (formerly known as Nestorians or followers of the Church of the East) was transforming from Mesopotamia and Anatolia into the modern states of Iraq and Turkey, respectively. During that era, American and European missions also enabled several Chaldean individuals to engage in a multiregional lifestyle through which they served as importers and exporters of cultural perceptions between "East" and "West."

After settling in Mosul, it took 120 years for the need to relocate to present itself again. In 1950 the patriarchate's transfer to Baghdad coincided with large waves of migration of Chaldeans from the northern villages to the capital city. By 1958 the church elected its new Alqosh-born patriarch, Paul Cheikho, and transferred him to Baghdad from his post as a bishop in Aleppo,[10] hence beginning a new phase of transnational relations and inflecting the Chaldean Church with a renewed awareness of its diasporic character.

We cannot fully grasp the current profile of the Chaldeans as a social group without first understanding the foundations of the church's modern transnational networks. As a set of new circumstances evolved in the twentieth century, the role of the clergy was transformed, changing the ways the community identified itself both at home and in diaspora.

Paul Cheikho: Iraq-Vatican Conduit

The political milieu of Paul Cheikho's tenure as patriarch in Iraq (1958–89) provides a crucial context for the transnational profile of the Chaldean Church during that period. While in office for more than thirty years, Cheikho navigated the Chaldean Church and its followers through a rapidly transforming Iraq, where many were taking up a new ideology of Arabism that was later to conflict with their ethnic filiations. At the time also, an oil-driven economy was emerging, three different regimes usurped power (Monarchic, Communist, Ba'thist), three national revolutions took place (1958, 1963, 1968), and an eight-year war with Iran (1980–88) transformed the socioeconomic infrastructure of the country. By the late 1960s and early 1970s, most of the Western missions had to relinquish their posts in the socialist Iraqi state, which coincided with the emergence of stable forms of Chaldean settlement in America.[11]

A critical event transformed the lives of the Chaldeans present in Iraq during that century, an event that also highlights the transnational political environment in which Cheikho fulfilled his leadership role: the 1974 nationalization of the school system. This initiative had a direct impact on the provisions for Catholic education, which came predominantly from foreign missionary establishments in the country.[12] The private schools—mostly established and operated by Christian missions—were closed down, and their foreign priest educators were deported.[13] Moreover, for a period, the Iraqi government attempted to impose the study of the Qur'an on all schools, including those institutions where Christian students were the majority. These developments were fairly rapid, taking place less than two years after a 1972 decree had granted the Syriac-speaking churches—Chaldean, Assyrian, and Syrian—the right to teach

Syriac in schools with classrooms of a Christian attendance of 25 percent or more.[14]

The 1972 religious education decree was rarely implemented, and official measures to place restrictions on religious activities in Iraq after 1974 were enacted through educational reforms as well as other political tactics. Established Chaldean and Assyrian civil society organizations and media venues either were closed down or came under the direct scrutiny of the state.[15] The Ba'thist regime ostensibly professed secularism and the constitution endorsed religious freedom, but legal procedures shaping political life, mixed marriages, inheritance, and property ownership remained highly influenced by shari'a law. For example, while Muslims could inherit property from Christians, the reverse was prohibited; children of Muslim-Christian marriages had to become Muslim; and Christian men marrying Muslim women had to convert to Islam. The same went for the social, literary, and pastoral activities of the Chaldean Church, all of which were closely watched and required prior authorization. In 1981, for instance, the Iraqi government wanted to nationalize all Christian places of worship through the Ministry of Waqfs (religious properties and endowments) and to control all the churches' functions, transforming church dignitaries, including the bishops, into state employees. Although this plan did not formally materialize, the religious leaders at the top had to secure political authorization before the assignment of any new posts.[16] Also in that same decade, the National Assembly included four Christian representatives when parliament membership was 250 individuals. Eight would have been the number proportionate with their population.[17]

These unfavorable transformations in minority status and religious liberty in Iraq were occasionally criticized by Chaldean clergy in diaspora who were encouraged to take a stance by the Vatican and other advocates of Christianity in the West. To situate Iraq's Chaldeans within the context of that political era, it must be stressed that in Ba'thist Iraq, the livelihood of the Chaldean communities and their church depended on the right interplay between religion and politics, with Chaldeanness as an ethnicity falling outside of the confines of legally recognized affiliations. The 1970 constitution recognized "the legitimate rights of all minorities in the context of Iraqi unity," a statement that enacted the legal recognition of the existence of five Christian communities (Chaldeans, Assyrians, Syrian Orthodox, Armenians, and Latins) as religious minorities, while the various ethnicities these groups professed elsewhere (in diaspora or during other historical periods) were subsumed under the new unifying identity of "Iraqi citizen."[18] These restrictions on collective identifications significantly affected the ways in which Chaldeans related to their homeland and revived their conceptual affinity with the Christian West.

In this political atmosphere of tightening religious freedoms, transnational religious ties with the West manifested themselves as a source of power. While maintaining a formal loyalty to the local government, a patriarch like Cheikho could carry his actions on behalf of the Chaldean community to an international audience, the only audience, in his estimation, who could lend an ear to the collective concerns of Christian minorities. In 1984, for example, he led an ecumenical and interfaith delegation to the Vatican as witness to the suffering of the Christian communities in Iraq from the consequences of the war with Iran.

Cheikho diplomatically navigated his way between the dictates of the central government of Iraq and the circuitous protection of Vatican networks. But the patriarch did not work single-handedly to check and stabilize the conditions of Chaldean minorities in Iraq through his connections with the powerful transnational religious networks of the Vatican. During the second half of the twentieth century, which was dominated by the traumatic internal displacement of Iraq's Christians and their southward migration into the major cities of Baghdad, Kirkuk, and Basra,[19] Raphael I Bidawid, subsequent patriarch of Babylon (1989–2003), had also activated certain transnational ties on behalf of the Chaldean community in Iraq. He represented the Chaldean community in transnational contexts, advanced ecumenical bonds, launched a literary heritage–saving campaign in diaspora, and established Chaldean dioceses in the United States.

Raphael I Bidawid: Away from Home and into Diaspora

Bidawid's earliest exposure to transnational circles dates back to the 1940s, to his time in the junior Chaldean seminary in Mosul, which was administered by the Dominican mission. However, his tenure in Lebanon (1965–89) serves as a useful example of how the current formulation of the Chaldean "minority" cannot be understood without reference to transnational processes and the changing political environment in the Middle East.

Bidawid continued his education in Rome, which, coupled with his subsequent exposure to the West, allowed him to obtain a position as the chaplain in service of the Christians working in the Iraq Petroleum Company. This company extended from Tripoli in Lebanon to Kirkuk in Iraq, ethnically diverse regions with sizable Christian expatriate communities.[20] In 1958, at a time when the Iraqi government engaged in a tumultuous conflict with the Kurds, Bidawid was serving as the bishop of one of the largest Chaldean dioceses that spread through a large section of Kurdistan, a region that would become the center of the conflict between the fighting Arab and Kurdish factions. While Bidawid had to employ a great deal of political tact in order to maintain good relations with the fighting Kurdish factions and the government of Iraq, he was aware that transnational political relations were as essential as transnational religious ties for extending protection to the politically marginalized Chaldean minority in the turbulent post–World War II Iraq.

From 1958 until his transfer to Lebanon in 1965, Bidawid's challenging task was to maintain good relations with both factions, without compromising the position of the Chaldean Patriarchate in Baghdad or the livelihood of the Chaldean villages caught in the maelstrom. Moreover, witnessing the fragmentation of the Chaldean communities in the Nineveh Plains region and their mass migration to major cities in Iraq or abroad, Bidawid foresaw the beginning of a heritage-saving campaign that was to extend its roots internationally wherever Chaldean families congregated.

Starting in the early 1960s, Bidawid began supervising the cataloging and transferring of the rich holdings of books and manuscripts from his bishopric to the patriarchal library in Mosul. He also published several articles on the Chaldean Church's relations with the Christian West, a topic about which he was exceptionally passionate.[21]

Since 1965, when Bidawid's tenure in Lebanon began, until his death in 2003, he did not confine his career to literary and theological pursuits. While residing in Beirut, Bidawid focused his efforts on representing the

Chaldean community in multiple transnational contexts. In addition to presiding over the religious life of the Chaldean community that numbered approximately twenty thousand individuals in Lebanon, the Chaldean Church he headed there provided a social nucleus for Iraqi exiles, tourists, and businessmen of various religious affiliations. He represented the Catholic Church in the Fourth Assembly of the Council of Churches of the Middle East in Cyprus (2003) and advocated the church's membership in the council as well as participating and heading several religious committees that advocated ecumenical bonds. Moreover, deploying his Lebanese connections, Bidawid acted on behalf of the Iraqi Chaldeans when the Iraqi Ba'thist regime was attempting to strike friendly relations with the Maronite community in Lebanon.

Finally, during the 1990s, after the first Gulf War, Bidawid utilized his status as a patriarch to formulate multiple new responses to the growing number of displaced Chaldeans, internally in Iraq and externally in various parts of the world. In 1995, for instance, he created Akhawiyyat al-Mahabba (or Confrérie de la Charité, or Caritas Iraq), which became a full member of Caritas Internationalis, a confederation of 162 Catholic relief organizations, and gained the support of all four Catholic Churches.[22] During the years of the sanctions, the Akhawiyya was the only private local aid agency that could distribute humanitarian aid to all regions of Iraq.

In addition to acting in person as a transnational player on behalf of the Chaldeans, Bidawid also encouraged more important senior Catholic figures to employ their transnational powers to publicize the effects of the embargo worldwide. He facilitated the visit of Cardinal Silverstrini, prefect of the Congregation of the Oriental Churches, to Iraq in 1993 as well as the visit of the Catholic patriarchs of the Oriental and Latin Churches the following year. Although Bidawid's attempt to clear the path for Pope John Paul II's "biblical pilgrimage" to Iraq in 2000 was aborted by US diplomatic interventions and other embargo-related factors, the work of the Chaldean Patriarchate eventually prompted papal contacts with UN, American, European, and Ba'th authorities in an effort to bring about the end of the sanctions on Iraq. Indeed, as O'Mahony writes, "apart from Tariq Aziz, Bidawid was one of the few Christian personalities who had any real [political] profile during this [1990s] period."[23]

Between 1982 and his death in Lebanon in 2003, Bidawid was also involved in establishing Chaldean dioceses in Detroit, Chicago, and California to accommodate the arrival of the new Chaldean immigrants to the United States. Serving the Chaldeans in transit during that period also, he appointed a patriarchal vicar to attend to more than sixty thousand Chaldean refugees living under harsh circumstances in Jordan.[24]

In summary, like Cheikho, the transnational career of Bidawid made strong strides toward ecumenism that worked politically in favor of the survival and westward mobility of the Chaldean communities. Together the two patriarchs acted to define papal policy toward Iraq and to take on the roles of intermediaries between Rome and Baghdad. They established mutual bonds between the Chaldean Church and the more influential Church of the East, subsequently dubbed "sister Churches," which also had their favorable resonance abroad, where the Chaldean immigrant communities settled near other Eastern Christian diasporas, such as the Assyrian communities in Illinois and California. The ambivalent relations the Chaldean Patriarchates of Cheikho and Bidawid kept with the Ba'thist regime since its coming to power in 1963 also served, though erratically, to enhance the position of the Chaldean communities in and outside of Iraq for a while. The contacts between Saddam Husayn's government and the Chaldean Church and communities need to be viewed within the context of other transnational relations that were charted in diaspora since the establishment in 1947 of the first Chaldean-American Church in Michigan.

The Chaldean Church in the United States: From Lay to Religious Social Field

In the fall of 2014, a few months after the Islamic State (known as Daesh in Iraq) infiltrated the Nineveh Plains in northern Iraq and began a reign of terror against the religious minorities in the region, Louis Raphael I Sako, the current Chaldean patriarch of Baghdad, ordered several Chaldean priests in the US diaspora to return to Iraq to help preserve the church or face excommunication.[25] The priests, who were mostly US citizens, demurred, as did their lay-community leaders in California and elsewhere. The latter group loudly protested that their priests are not "cattle for the slaughter." Backed by their diasporic communities, the priests appealed to Pope Francis of Rome, who told them they need not cede to Sako's orders.

The fact that the pope has supported the priests' appeal to stay safe in diaspora and overturn the patriarch's orders is noteworthy, since the Chaldean Church is not strictly under the jurisdiction of Rome, but not out of the ordinary given the historical precedence of this power hierarchy. What is unusual and reflective of a critical shift in circumstance is the patriarch's response: Sako went against the will of the pope in insisting on his ultimatum of excommunicating the priests if they do not return to Iraq.

This incident, which has not been resolved yet as I write this chapter, sheds new light on a significant tipping or fragmentation of power within the internal structure of the church hierarchy. Most critically, it testifies to the power of the US-based section of the Chaldean Church and its cumulative autonomy and increasingly independent dealings with the Vatican. Additionally, it points us to a fascinating codependency between church personnel in the US diaspora and their affluent lay supporters there. How did the Chaldean Church in the United States become so powerful as to maintain its legitimacy in the eyes of its followers despite threats of excommunication by the two-thousand-year-old stronghold in Iraq? This consolidation of power, as we shall see, was a gradual process that spanned a full century.

The first Chaldean parish to exist in the United States was Saint Ephrem Church, which was organized in Chicago in 1913.[26] However, the most conspicuous formation of an autonomous Chaldean religious body in the American diaspora, the Mother of God Parish in Detroit, Michigan, took place only after a somewhat unified Chaldean collective had already been organizing itself in the social, nonreligious sphere. The anonymous author(s) of "The History," an article written in celebration of the fiftieth anniversary of the Mother of God Parish, do not exaggerate when they state, "The history of Mother of God Parish is the history of Chaldeans in the United States."

In the early 1920s, when the Chaldean community in Detroit numbered fewer than thirty families who had settled near the older and larger Lebanese Maronite community, Chaldeans combined their religious practices with the practices of the Maronite Church. As the community grew larger and more autonomous in the 1930s, socially active members founded the Chaldean-Iraqi Association—later the Chaldean-Iraqi Association of Michigan—to represent their particular common interests. In less than a decade, the size of the community grew to approximately seventy-five families, whose social needs and activities were marshaled through CIAM. The principal goal of CIAM's founders was to "unite the community, to retain a Chaldean priest and to later acquire a church of their own."[27] To this end, the Chaldean Church was initiated into the diasporic life of its community of followers via an association delegate who was the first to coordinate between the Chaldean Patriarchate in Iraq and the Catholic Archdiocese of Detroit in an effort to import a Chaldean priest from Iraq to serve the growing Chaldean community in the United States.

After obtaining their first priest, Detroit Chaldeans enthusiastically sought to acquire their independent Chaldean church through the financial assistance of the Archdiocese of Detroit. The Chaldean religious institution continued to expand and to be transformed in the US diaspora, with the transfer of the first Detroit pastor, Toma Bidawid (not to be confused with Raphael Bidawid, former patriarch in Iraq), to a new Chaldean parish in Chicago and the arrival of a second priest from Iraq, Toma Reis, to serve the Detroit community in his place, and so on. In subsequent decades, the growth of the Chaldean-American Church paralleled the growth of the Chaldean American community. By 1951 the community grew to about 125 families, who could offer more help with the functions and financing of the church through volunteer work and donations. A communal effort between Chaldean immigrant families helped the Chaldean Church achieve more independence by paying its debt to the Archdiocese in Detroit. While the Chaldean community and its churches grew correspondingly, the mobility pattern of Chaldean families triggered a parallel mobility of their places of worship. As families began to move from the city of Detroit to its residential suburbs in the 1960s, so did the Mother of God Parish, which was relocated in the city of Southfield in 1964.

The westward Chaldean migration that was initially facilitated by the transnational connections of the Chaldean Church in Iraq continued to have mixed effects on the demographics of the Christian communities remaining in Iraq, which began to shrink steadily since the 1960s.

At the same time, migration and transnational networking served as a vital expression of the identity of Eastern Christianity in the United States. While its establishment and maintenance depended heavily on the diaspora community's contributions, at the leadership level the institution of the Chaldean Church in the United States for a long time exhibited more autonomy from its lay followers and more dependence on the decisions of the patriarchate in Iraq.

The diaspora church was predominantly operated by functionaries who had previously lived and received their religious training in Iraq, the Middle East, or Rome. By 1952 the Chaldean Church in Detroit was able to organize and administer its own variety of religious activities while drawing on financial assistance from the first Parish Council, which was composed of influential lay members from the Michigan-based community. Visits from Patriarch Cheikho during the 1960s and 1970s also implemented, through his assessments, changes and additions in the allocation of religious posts in various areas in southeastern Michigan where Chaldean families were rapidly multiplying.

Church functionaries also enjoyed a high level of mobility between Iraq and Detroit, which enabled them to chart one of the earliest religious and political transnational networks within the Chaldean American social field.[28] After serving as a pastor of Mother of God Parish, for instance, Toma Reis was appointed bishop of the Diocese of Zakho, Iraq, while Gorial Koda was transferred from Iraq to his post as the third pastor of the Mother of God Parish. After serving a three-year term, Koda was transferred back to Iraq, and a fourth pastor exchanged countries with him to serve in the same Detroit parish.

This cyclical mobility pattern brought the attention of the Iraqi political authorities of the time to the Chaldean community in diaspora. As early as 1953, when the Detroit Chaldean community had almost doubled in size to number three hundred families, King Faysal II of Iraq was to pay them a friendly visit. Ostensibly friendly transnational relations between the Iraqi authorities and the Chaldean diaspora continued to exist until the first Gulf War through the conduit of the church.

Saddam Husayn's bond with Chaldean Detroit reportedly started during his first year as the president of Iraq, in 1979, when he donated

$250,000 to the Reverend Jacob Yasso's Chaldean Sacred Heart Church in Detroit. The money is said to have helped build the Chaldean Center of America, located on Seven Mile Road next to the Sacred Heart Church, in the district that is dubbed today "Chaldean Town." In an effort to network strategically with these proponents, and their US government backers, in Detroit alone it was estimated that the Iraqi government doled out $1.7 million to Chaldean churches and organizations in 1980.[29] These generous "donations" earned Saddam Husayn a "key to Detroit" from Mayor Coleman Young, a symbolic gesture that, according to a broadcast report on the local Channel 4 at the time, officially granted Iraq's president the status of an honorary citizen of the city.[30] This citation, of course, was at a time when the Ba'thist regime was still an ally of America and had entered the first phase of the eight-year war with Iran, America's fierce enemy. Nonetheless, not long after this exchange of courtesies, Federal Bureau of Investigation (FBI) agents, together with Assyrians and Chaldeans from Detroit's diasporic communities, alleged that the Iraqi regime was paying certain Chaldean and Assyrian immigrants on a regular basis to provide reports on the activities of coethnics in the United States.[31]

According to several reports by Chaldean, Assyrian, and American media, the Ba'thist regime made numerous attempts to improve its image, placate Chaldean Americans, or *Arabizanate* (Arabize) them by either threat or bribery through church liaisons.[32] US State Department officials, for instance, asserted that, while donating money to US-based Chaldeans and Assyrians, the Iraqi government was also establishing an elaborate network of spies that infiltrated the US-based Iraqi Christian diaspora. It is not clear now what the specific goal behind these monetary gifts was intended to be. In all likelihood, Husayn, who had become Iraq's president only months prior, was expressing gratitude for the loyalty and political support he received from Iraqi expatriates in the United States that had in recent years critiqued the school nationalization and church reforms implemented by the Ba'th Party.

The Chaldean community in its US diaspora, however, never fully trusted the intentions of the Ba'th government. In 1981 Monsignor Ablahat Najor, pastor of Chaldean Assyrian Saint Thomas Parish in Turlock, California, was murdered. Najor was one of many expatriate Christian Iraqi religious figures to have received monetary gifts from Saddam Husayn. In his case, the $250,000 gift that he had received that year was used to construct a social hall for the church. The FBI was involved in investigations. Although the identity of the assailants was not determined, "beatings, arson, and even homicide" in the Iraqi Christian immigrant communities were ascribed by the FBI to agents hired by the Iraqi government. Despite the absence of conclusive evidence, the violent event reinforced these communities' conviction that the Ba'thist government of Iraq was committing "acts of terrorism" against its diasporic members when they did not comply with its expectations of espionage.[33]

Transnational politics of this sort did not always infiltrate the everyday activities of the church in its diasporic stronghold. To the majority of the lay Chaldean migrant population, new church personnel simply introduced new ways of involving the diaspora community in religious life. During the 1960s, the same decade when Monsignor Najor was assigned pastor in California, the fourth arrival from Iraq to Michigan, Pastor George Garmo (later elevated to the rank of monsignor by the patriarch), established youth activities at Mother of God Parish, obtained a section of the Holy Sepulcher Cemetery in Detroit for the burial of members of the Chaldean community, and opened a Mission House for the Chaldean Sisters. Also at Garmo's behest, the Chaldean American Ladies of Charity was established in 1961 for the purpose of providing social services and financial assistance to new immigrants. In a couple of decades the twenty-three active women members of CALC initiated additional networks of community services for coethnics through their fund-raising efforts for the construction of a senior citizens center under the auspices of the Chaldean Church.

Since its inception and to the present, the transnationally oriented Chaldean Church of Michigan continues to be grounded within a lucrative network of local lay organizations. In the 1970s CIAM was searching for a site to build a Chaldean social club. This goal materialized in 1975 through the purchase of three acres from the site of the Mother of God Parish in a mutually beneficial agreement between the parish and CIAM, resulting in the creation of the "Chaldean Heritage Association."

In addition to striving to become a "community-wide venue for activities" through working locally with lay organizations and transnationally with the patriarchate in Baghdad, the Michigan-based church slowly forged nationwide connections with other Chaldean churches. In 1982 a milestone was achieved through the appointment of Pastor Ibrahim Ibrahim of the Saint Paul Chaldean Assyrian Church of Los Angeles, as the first "bishop of the St. Thomas Chaldean Catholic Diocese of the United States of America." Through the event, the Mother of God Parish became his see (diocese) and was proclaimed "Our Lady of Chaldeans Cathedral." During that time, too, English was introduced to mass services at the Michigan-based Cathedral (originally Arabic and Aramaic only). By 1990 English masses were added permanently to the schedule of Sunday and holiday church services, allowing second-generation Chaldeans more access to the religious life of the community. This feature facilitated the maintenance of social interaction between Arabic- or Aramaic-speaking new immigrants and English-speaking second-generation Chaldeans through the opportunity to sustain a common faith while sharing the physical space of the same ethnic church.[34]

Second-generation English-speaking Chaldeans have been claiming membership in the life of their ethnic church. This fact has endowed the religious institution in its American diaspora with a special symbolic authority over the affairs of the community in spite, or because, of owing its material existence and financial robustness to their initiative and unremitting aid.

Symbolic authority refers here to the power of the verbal or textual endorsements offered by the church in the context of formal or informal secular undertakings, such as a "Chaldean Household Survey" that was sent to every identifiable potential "Chaldean" household in southeastern Michigan in the spring of 2007. The research for this survey was conducted by the Walsh College of Business and United Way for Southeastern Michigan, commissioned by the Chaldean American Chamber of Commerce, and funded by as diverse a set of corporations as DTE Energy, Charter One Bank, and Country Fresh Dairy.

That a two-line letter of support by Father Manuel Boji, rector of Our Lady of Chaldeans Cathedral, should preface the bundle of papers making up the application materials of a socioeconomic study might seem irrelevant in other contexts. But Boji's succinct statement, "I support this project hoping that this survey will benefit the whole Chaldean community. I would like to thank the Chaldean Chamber of Commerce for its effort in this matter," suggests that the church holds a prominent role in legitimizing and legalizing community projects.[35] From the perspective of the members of the Chaldean community in diaspora whose input the survey seeks to elicit, no other lay institution, no matter how prestigious or popular, is able to vie with the symbolic authority and assurance of the church.

The *Chaldean News*, an English-language monthly community publication designed predominantly to draw a second-generation Chaldean readership, reserves a permanent column titled "Religion," in addition to regularly featuring full-length articles, special issues, and cover illustrations about the pope, the Chaldean bishops, and other religious dignitaries in Iraq and elsewhere—another compelling indication of the active role the church continues to play in the life of the diaspora community and in turning its attention to transnational matters.

As a transnational player with strong symbolic power over the Chaldean American community and protective influence on behalf of the Chaldeans in Iraq, the Chaldean Church functions as a conduit between its communities of followers in the two countries, creating a conceptual social field of belonging where the two geographically separated communities can engage in transnational activities on familiar terms. Not only do US-based Chaldeans readily fund their religious institutions in the diaspora, but they also trust the branches of this institution as the legitimate disseminators of financial aid to the Chaldean communities in the homeland and elsewhere. The program "Adopt-a-Refugee-Family," first piloted in 2007, is now one of the most community-trusted programs in which monetary contributions made by US-based Chaldeans are collected and sent to Chaldean refugees overseas. The funds are collected by the Chaldean Federation in Michigan and regularly wired to religious personnel (Father Joseph Burby in Amman and Bishop Antoine Audo in Aleppo) to be disseminated among Chaldean refugees in Syria, Jordan, and elsewhere. Another example is Patriarch Emmanuel Delly, who in 2005 and beyond worked with funds raised and donated by CALC to make significant contributions for a prestigious Chaldean seminary in Iraq.[36]

Contrary to public appearances, it is important to note that financial remittances transmitted through transnational institutional media within Chaldean sociopolitical networks are often offered with expectations. In fact, they turn the process of giving and receiving into a cycle of mutual transnational profit. CALC members made their donation of ten thousand dollars with the knowledge that six young men had recently joined the seminary in Iraq and were on their way to becoming Chaldean priests. Within the past decade or so, CALC and other community members have been critically concerned with the problem of a shortage in the number of priests in the quickly expanding Chaldean American parishes.[37] By financially contributing to the fostering and ordination of new priests in the country of origin, the US-based community secures the continuation of its "authentic" church in the diaspora.

CALC's monetary contribution to the Iraqi seminary is one of the examples that point out the junctions where secular Chaldean transnational activities redound to the maintenance of a Chaldean religious transnational social field and vice versa. Within the transnational context, this example offers an opportunity to conceptualize the migrant Chaldean community as a site where multiple transnational social fields, such as the church and lay institutions,[38] exist within and intersect across the borders of nation-states. It is also worth emphasizing that the early institutionalization of the Chaldean religion in diaspora depended on community-oriented efforts of Chaldeans as an ethnic minority, a role reversal from the historical precedence at the homeland, where the institution of the church had continually acted on behalf of its lay followers to ensure their survival and protection as a religious minority that had no right to express its identity in terms of ethnicity.

For at least two decades now, US-based Chaldeans, together with other diasporic Iraqi Christian groups, most conspicuously the Assyrians, have been pushing for practical as well as symbolic forms of American involvement. Samuel G. Freedman rightly points out the diasporic efforts made for the "creation of a protected zone and safe-passage corridors for Christians still in Iraq; an increased number of refugee visas and streamlined approval by State Department and Homeland Security screeners for Christians trying to reach America."[39] Claims of entitlement for these special provisions from the US government are essentially based on the Christian identity of these groups. For this reason, applying a transnational framework to study the modern Chaldean Church—or other Eastern churches with diasporic lives—clarifies existing misperceptions about the institutional life, economy, and politics not only inside the church but also among members of the minority communities that affiliate with it. The transnational paradigm requires capturing participant migrants' simultaneous engagements in political processes occurring in the United States, the originary country, or host countries other than the United States. This framework demands methodological shifts from ethnic, migration, minority, and diaspora studies to the transnational dimensions of the social phenomena they examine, shifts that focus on empirical illustrations of the intersections between social networks of Chaldeans in diaspora and Chaldeans remaining in the ancestral homeland and also on instances in which a "transnational imaginary," in which certain transnational ties are imagined rather than enacted, is at work among members of the migrant generations.

12

Permanent Temporariness in Berlin

The Case of an Arab Muslim Minority in Germany

LUCIA VOLK

Applying the premise that the category of "minority" is the result of a variety of historical, political, and social processes of minoritization, this chapter seeks to demonstrate that Arab Muslim war refugees who came to reside in Germany are a unique Muslim minority group, separate from the larger, predominantly "Muslim minorities" from Turkey that are the focus of much of the scholarly literature.[1] One of the most important tools nation-states employ to create identity categories of inclusion and exclusion, of citizen and noncitizen, are immigration laws that assign each noncitizen to a specific category marked by its own set of rights and restrictions. These legal differences are often misrepresented or misunderstood by the mainstream media, which tend to discuss Muslims in Germany as if they were a homogeneous group or "Turks," neither of which is accurate. The argument here is that particular legal categories of immigration create not only minorities but also minorities within minorities. In other words, the legal processes of inclusion and exclusion shape experiences of Muslim immigrants in Germany differently, as they create different kinds of "Muslim minorities."

Over the past decade and a half, public debates about the role and fit of Muslim minorities in German society have been particularly lively. Before the 1960s, the number of Muslims in Germany was "fairly negligible," but by the early 2000s their number had reached approximately 3.5 million in a total population of around 80 million.[2] The increase in numbers is tied to a post–World War II "guest worker" program that aimed to solve, temporarily, existing labor shortages in Germany. Yet many of the recruited foreign workers did not return to their countries of origin, as politicians had envisioned, and after the labor recruitment stopped in 1973, migration to Germany continued, and even accelerated, under the umbrella of family unification.[3] In the late 1970s and through the 1990s, Muslim war refugees from conflict zones across the Middle East and the former Yugoslavia entered Germany under temporary humanitarian visas. Civil war refugees from Lebanon were among them, and what made their case unique among the other humanitarian refugees is that they could not be sent back home after the hostilities ended. Instead, they entered a legal and social space of "permanent temporariness," which gave them limited rights in Germany and pushed them to the margins of the existing and growing Muslim minority communities.

This marginalized Arab Muslim minority group was singled out in former Berlin finance minister Thilo Sarrazin's 2010 book, *Germany Is Doing Away with Itself.* Sarrazin predicted the demographic and cultural demise of Germany because of the threat of a fertile, welfare-dependent, "education-resistant" (*bildungsfremd*), and largely urban segment of Muslim immigrants. Comparing educational achievement data of immigrants from Africa, Asia, and southern Europe, Sarrazin states that immigrants from the former Yugoslavia, Turkey, and Arab countries—that is, Muslim minorities—constitute "the core" of Germany's immigration problem.[4] Compared with the 34 members of the Organization for Economic Cooperation and Development countries, Germany's aggregate student scores ranked somewhere in the middle rather than on the top of the list. Germany's urban schools especially stood out in the rankings, with high dropout rates and low student achievement, as well as a large percentage of immigrant students. Sarrazin is a card-carrying member of the center-left Social Democratic Party, whose platform promotes better integration of foreigners into German society. The party tried to expel Sarrazin from its ranks, but party statutes guarantee each member the right to his or her own public opinion, even if it diverges from party dogma. The fact that Sarrazin lives and works in Berlin, a city known for its progressive immigration policies, guaranteed that the book would find a stormy reception.

It is easy to locate Arab Berlin in the neighborhood of northern Neu-kölln: Sonnenallee is a wide boulevard lined with Arabic signs and adver-tisements. In Sonnenallee's small stores you will find olive oil and the aromatic *zaatar* herb mix, Arab fast food, coffee and smoke shops, halal butchers, as well as international phone-card and cell-phone stores. The language on the street is Arabic. Women wearing head scarves push their strollers; middle-aged men sporting big mustaches or full beards sit with their small coffee cups, smoking cigarettes and exchanging news. Young people in trendy jeans and colorful, yet modest, outfits congregate on the sidewalks outside movie theaters and cafés, texting, joking, and check-ing out passersby. Many storefront windows sport the Lebanese flag or pictures of the mountains or coastline of Lebanon. A shop owner, who had come to Berlin from his native Sidon in South Lebanon twenty years earlier, gave me the tour of Sonnenallee one day, naming each store by the owner's family name.

Another Berlin neighborhood with significant Muslim, and majority Turkish, populations is Kreuzberg. Yet whereas Kreuzberg is considered "a hip, young, multicultural neighborhood that attracts students and art-ists," Neukölln makes headlines as a neighborhood of drug dealers and violence in its schools.[5] Newspapers have called youth violence in Ger-many a "Lebanese problem."[6] A separate article in the same issue of the paper points out that the vast majority of so-called repeat perpetrators are descendants of immigrant families from the Middle East. "Repeat per-petrators," or *Intensivtäter* in German, are defined as persons who have committed more than ten armed robberies or assaults in a year. A dispro-portional number of youths within that category of criminal offenses are said to come from Lebanon.[7] These Arab problem youths are described as resistant to integration into German society, prone to joining criminal gangs, and inclined to clash with German authorities.

According to German immigration statistics, 64,000 Arab individu-als—the majority of whom are from Lebanon—currently live in Ber-lin.[8] National estimates of Lebanese who reside in Germany as refugees or descendants of refugees are as high as 180,000.[9] After the Muslims from Turkey and Southeast Europe (especially the former Yugoslavia), Arabs constitute the third-largest segment of Muslims in Germany.[10] The majority of them arrived as refugees from Lebanon during recurring episodes of violence in the 1970s and 1980s, but most of them are not actually Lebanese citizens. Instead, they are of Kurdish or Palestinian origin, with a history of prior displacement.[11] They came to Germany alongside displaced Lebanese citizens, and, like them, they were granted temporary residency during the ongoing war. Yet after hostilities ceased, they remained in Germany under the legal injunction of *Duldung*.

Historical Background: How the Lebanese Arrived in Berlin

West Berlin became a safe haven for refugees from Lebanon during the country's 1975–90 civil war, owing to Berlin's then unique legal status as a divided city with unusually porous borders. For more than forty years, West Berlin, a walled-in city in the middle of East Germany, led a symbolically important yet economically marginal existence as part of larger Cold War politics. The city was almost entirely dependent on financial aid from West Germany and its then capital, Bonn. At the post–World War II conference in Potsdam, the French, British, US, and Soviet occupying powers had decided that Berlin would not have any state borders in the traditional sense. Thus, during the period of a divided Berlin, travelers who managed to get a transit visa to East Berlin's Schönefeld Airport could enter the Western sector of Berlin at Checkpoint Charlie with relative ease. During the German unification transition period between 1989 and 1991, there was not even a checkpoint to cross. The visa application to East Germany in Lebanon was relatively simple, and the flights from Beirut to Berlin were affordable.[12] Families also traveled by car through Eastern European states that would grant them visas until they arrived in East Berlin, where they crossed to the West.

It is thus through a legal loophole that many Lebanese found their way first into East and then West Berlin and, with the tide of history, into Germany's newly unified capital of Berlin. Lebanese were not the only residents from conflict zones who made Berlin their destination. As a result, the resident profile in Berlin today differs significantly from profiles in other German cities. Fewer than 50 percent of the city's current residents were born in Berlin, and 25 percent of Berlin's approximately 3.4 million residents are migrants or descendants of migrants.[13] Once in West

Germany, the refugees applied for asylum, which was typically denied, since German asylum is reserved for individuals persecuted for political reasons (Asylum Law §16). As long as conflict raged in the country of origin, the refugees remained in Berlin on humanitarian grounds. Yet within a decade of the end of the Lebanese civil war, more than 10,000 of Lebanon's war refugees had been sent back home.[14] Two "Lebanese" refugee groups remained in the newly unified Germany, because they could not be extradited: Arabic-speaking Kurds and Palestinians, who had been born and grown up in urban slums and refugee camps on the margins of Lebanon's society and who lacked Lebanese citizenship or work permits.

Most of the Arab Kurds originally arrived in Lebanon via Syria, as refugees from the Mhallami region in southeastern Turkey. Mhallami Kurds speak an Arabic dialect and are thus a minority within the majority Kurdish-speaking communities in Syria, Iran, Iraq, and Turkey (although there are many variations of Kurdish spoken among members of these communities). Some Kirmanci-speaking Kurds do not consider Mhallami Kurds coethnics but call them "Arabs."[15] For most of modern Turkish history, Kurds were forbidden from speaking their native language and practicing their cultural heritage. Repeated violence between the Turkish army and Kurdish "rebels" in the 1920s and 1930s turned many residents in southeastern Turkey into refugees. In Lebanon the predominantly Muslim Mhallami Kurds could not obtain citizenship (with the exception of some refugees who had settled in predominantly Sunni Muslim Tripoli) and instead obtained so-called *Laisser passer* papers.[16] They entered the unskilled labor force and the informal sector, which perpetuated widespread poverty and illiteracy. It was not until after the end of Lebanon's 1975–90 civil war that Kurdish residents who had remained in Lebanon were offered citizenship. A study done in 1995 found that 85 percent of Lebanon's Kurds lived at or below the poverty line, and 60 percent were virtually illiterate.[17] Many of the Kurds lived in poor neighborhoods that came into the cross-fire during Lebanon's civil war, which is why they fled to Western Europe, many of them to Berlin.

The Palestinians arrived in Lebanon in large numbers after the wars of 1948 and 1967. The majority moved into refugee camps, supported by the United Nations Relief and Works Agency, a UN institution that was specifically created after 1948 to look after Palestinian refugees. Some Christian Palestinians were able to obtain Lebanese citizenship papers. The Lebanese state did not want to extend residency or citizenship rights to the majority Muslim Palestinian population, as it tried to preserve a presumed Christian-Muslim population balance in Lebanon.[18] Many of the Palestinian camps were built in marginal areas, next to Lebanon's other historically disenfranchised population, the Shi'a. Many of Lebanon's Shi'a would later take up arms in defense of the Palestinian right of return to their own country, especially those Shi'a who live in Lebanon's southern region, close to the border with Israel. During Lebanon's 1975–90 civil war, Palestinian refugee camps and neighborhoods became repeated targets of right-wing Lebanese militias that opposed the Palestinian presence in Lebanon. Particular tragic moments of the civil war were the massacres of camp residents at Tell al-Zaater in 1976 and Sabra and Shatila in 1982. Many of the survivors of those massacres used their Lebanon-issued travel documents (DDV, for *documents de voyage* in French) and sought safety and better opportunities in northern Europe, especially in Germany and Scandinavian countries that offered asylum processes, refugee status, and some financial support.[19]

"Stateless" under international law, both Lebanon's Kurds and Palestinians—including a group of Shi'a from villages in the border zone, who considered themselves Lebanese but were turned into Palestinians after a contested border adjustment of European mandate powers in 1924[20]—do not possess valid passports, and therefore they cannot not travel internationally. Both groups come with a history of dispossession as well as experiences of discrimination and violence. When their temporary residency permits based on humanitarian grounds expired in Germany, these Palestinian and Kurdish civil war refugees obtained their summons to leave Germany immediately, as did all the Lebanese citizens. Yet without valid passports, they could not leave, and they ended up in Germany's temporary legal category of *Duldung*, which suspends the existing deportation order.

On *Duldung* the person has no legal rights to reside in Germany—that is, the person has no *Aufenthaltstitel*—yet at the same time he or she will not be punished for not leaving. It makes *Duldung* a de facto residency permit yet without any of the rights that come with an actual residency permit. *Duldung* can be renewed repeatedly, and every so often Germany will implement an amnesty law for those individuals who can prove long-term residency with some income and without a criminal record, a law called *Altfallregelung* (literally, "old case resolution"). The beneficiaries of the *Altfallregelung* who were able to obtain legal residency and work authorization then become the points of entry for further refugees from the same village, camp, or neighborhood in Lebanon, providing the newcomers with necessary cultural and legal knowledge to navigate Germany's immigration processes. They also provide them with job opportunities, often illegally, in restaurants, grocery stores, or car-repair workshops.[21]

Duldung and German Immigration Law

Duldung translates awkwardly to the English word "toleration." It is better understood as a legal state of suspension that entails a temporary stay on deportation without granting the person any political or social rights; in fact, under *Duldung* the person is considered illegal, as deportation remains the ultimate goal. Foreigner Law (*Ausländergesetz*) §56.1 defines *Duldung* as follows: "Toleration only grants stay on deportation. It does not grant residency rights to the foreigner. His [*sic*] residence in Germany remains illegal; his duty to leave Germany untouched." Initially, *Duldung* is granted for three and then six months, but if the reasons that prevent deportation cannot be surmounted—that is, if no legal travel documents are forthcoming or if the person is too sick to travel—the time can be extended repeatedly, resulting in so-called *Kettenduldung* (literally, "chain toleration"). *Duldung* requires that the person remain ready to be extradited at a moment's notice. Some Palestinians I spoke to in Berlin in the summer of 2011 had been thus permitted to stay in legal limbo for two decades.

According to a report in *Die Süddeutsche Zeitung*, 202,000 persons lived on *Duldung* in Germany at the end of 2004, and of that number 65,000 had been living on *Duldung* for a variety of reasons for more than ten years.[22] While *Kettenduldung* can turn into a temporary residency status with rights to work and some social welfare benefits, the reality is that few people on *Duldung* obtain the right to remain in Germany legally, because immigration officials have the primary political mandate to deport individuals whose applications for asylum have been denied.

As discussed by legal scholar Phillip-Asmus Riecken, *Duldung* represents a conundrum for Germany's constitutional law experts: The persons in this immigrant category have no legal status to remain in Germany. They are tolerated only for the purpose and duration of finding ways to overcome the obstacles that prevent them from leaving German territory. Yet at the same time, they are inside German territory, and because of their physical presence they are entitled to constitutional rights and freedoms. As persons whose status is illegal, they are under several restrictions: they may not work, their mobility is restricted, and they have to remain in regular contact with—that is, under the surveillance of—the authorities. Yet because they legally cannot leave for reasons that are ultimately beyond their control, they are also not breaking any laws and therefore should not be subject to restrictions of their basic freedoms. It is a catch-22 situation: people on *Duldung* are simultaneously illegal (*unrechtmäßig*) for not having a right to reside in Germany, but also legal in Germany, because there are specific paragraphs of German immigration law that allow the stay on deportation. As Riecken pointedly asks at the end of his first chapter: on the basis of the German constitution, should a legal category such as *Duldung* even exist?[23]

The peculiarities of *Duldung* are part of the larger system of German immigration law that seeks, on the one hand, to extend legal residency and work options to educated foreigners while, on the other hand, barring entry to Germany to those foreigners who would become a burden on its welfare system.[24] The urgent demands for more skilled labor—Germany's population is expected to decline from about 80 million to about 58 million in 2050[25]—and the concern over rising welfare costs in a country with a rapidly aging population have created a legal landscape that affords the resident immigrant population in Germany varying rights and sources of financial support. Foreigners from any of the European Union (EU) countries are given temporary residency status (*befristete Aufenthaltserlaubnis*) that allows them to work, according to European immigration laws, which are laws that, first and foremost, guarantee rights. Foreigners from so-called third nations (*Drittländer*), by contrast, are considered foreigners who need to be contained or kept out. Third-nation citizens, many of whom arrive in Germany seeking asylum or humanitarian or refugee status, are subject to a wide array of restrictions on their movement, eligibility and access to work, educational opportunities, and social benefits. Moreover, TNCs who arrived in Germany via a "safe third country" are denied the right to the asylum process in Germany. German authorities send them back to the country whose border they first crossed to enter the European Union, unless those countries, as happened in 2015 in the cases of Hungary and Greece, cannot cope with the number of newly arriving refugees.[26]

In 1990 a new Foreigner Law (*Ausländerrecht*) in Germany opened, for the first time, the possibility of turning time-limited residency permits into permanent residency permits, in light of those Turkish and South European guest workers who had been holding steady jobs for decades and thus had been paying into the German welfare system. In other words, a particular category of non-EU guest workers obtained the right to ask for permanent residency, if they met uninterrupted financial self-support conditions and spoke German at a certain level of competency.[27] At the same time that one group of TNCs obtained more rights, the law curtailed them for others who had not been working and instead subsisted on welfare payments or in the informal sector, creating a deep rift between status and work-seeking TNCs in Germany. So in addition to a division between European and non-European migrants in Germany, there is a deep divide between Turkish and Arab migrants as well, despite the fact that they share certain cultural and religious beliefs and practices.

Moreover, until yet another new law was passed in 1999, German citizenship was tied to the requirement of being a descendant of German parents, the so-called right of blood (*ius sanguinis*), which meant that certain civic rights, such as the right to a passport or the right to vote, were restricted to those individuals who could prove German ancestry, no matter how far back in history. Since 1999 children born of non-German-ancestry immigrants who have been in Germany as legal residents for at least eight years can now opt for German citizenship based on that residency, or "right of the soil" (*ius soli*). This process requires giving up the parents' nationality, as Germany permits dual citizenship only in rare cases. The new law aims to grant citizenship status to second- and third-generation Turkish migrants, many of whom speak limited Turkish.

To recall the Turkish story briefly: Post–World War II, Germany was in need of labor to run steel factories, coal mines, as well as agricultural operations, and they turned to the Turkish, Spanish, Greek, Italian, Portuguese, and Yugoslav governments to recruit their un- or underemployed laborers. The German government signed "recruitment treaties" with the respective heads of state between 1960 and 1968. As the only two Arab countries, Morocco and Tunisia signed work contracts in 1961, but the number of North Africans who chose to migrate to Germany rather than to France—the country with historical ties to North Africa—remained relatively small. These so-called guest workers were "invited" to come to Germany to do their jobs and expected to return home after a period of time, taking their savings with them to start a new career and family there. Labor migrants in this category faced extradition if they became welfare recipients for any reason. In other words, the "guest workers'" legal status lasted only for as long as the person had employment and was financially self-supporting.

In the aftermath of the oil crisis of 1973 and the subsequent economic depression, the German government passed a law that discontinued the recruitment of foreign laborers (*Anwerbestopp*) and thereby closed the legal pathway into Germany via work migration—coincidentally about the time when fighting erupted between Palestinians and Lebanese that would eventually lead to the Lebanese civil war in 1975. So the Lebanese arrived in Germany as war refugees, subject to humanitarian immigration procedures, at a time when work-migration pathways had closed. Because they arrived as asylum seekers, which requires a lengthy review process during which the applicants were not allowed to work, the "Lebanese" became German welfare recipients. Because more recent pathways to "legal residency" require evidence of holding a job for eight years, German immigrant law discriminates between what we may call the "hard-working, deserving (and mostly Turkish) migrants" and the "undeserving (majority Arab) migrants" whose legal options remain limited.

Even if refugees from Lebanon had been able to obtain some form of work permit when they initially arrived in Berlin, it would have been unclear if unskilled jobs would have been available for them—by the late 1970s and early 1980s, Germany's low-skilled industrial jobs in steel or mining were beginning to decline in response to low-wage competition from abroad. For the duration of the asylum-review process, the refugees had to remain in special, often substandard, housing, intentionally chosen to discourage the refugees from extending their stay in Germany. While the children of parents on *Duldung* or unaccompanied minors had the right to go to school, they did not have the right to practical training or jobs after they graduated. The legal category of *Duldung* thereby created its own minority population within the larger Muslim minority communities in Germany.

Life as "de Facto Refugees" in Germany

Social psychologist Von Bethlenfalvy coined the term "migrants in an irregular situation" for refugees from Lebanon in the late 1970s and early 1980s, based on their escape from a conflict zone, their statelessness, the peculiar legal status of the city of Berlin, and Germany's constitutional guarantee to the right of an asylum *process* (not to be confused with the right to asylum). As a matter of fact, German courts reject the vast majority of asylum petitions, which usually leads to a lengthy appeal process and subsequent extradition. At this point, the applicants are no longer in the legal category of refugees. Yet political scientist and Islamic studies scholar Ralph Ghadban calls them "*de facto* refugees," in reference to their stay on extradition that keeps them in Germany.[28]

By the mid-1980s, about twenty thousand Arabs lived in West Berlin, five thousand of whom were minors, with an estimated two thousand unaccompanied minors.[29] Lebanese parents preferred to send their teenage sons alone to Europe rather than have them become part of a militia. By the end of the 1980s, "Lebanese" refugees were the largest single "de facto refugee" group in Germany. In light of the ongoing civil war in Lebanon, and reports of atrocities and massacres, left-leaning German parties, churches, and charitable organizations lobbied that refugees from Lebanon should be allowed to remain in Germany. As a result, Berlin's senator of the interior Heinrich Lummer passed a special law in 1983 that put a stay on all deportation orders for Palestinians from Lebanon. Moreover, in 1987 and 1990 the government of Berlin passed amnesty laws—the so-called *Altfallregelung*—that granted residency for some of the "Lebanese" refugees in Berlin.[30]

Ralph Ghadban, himself a migrant of Lebanese origin who came to Germany as a university student, wrote the only extended study of "Lebanese" refugees to date, titled *Die Libanon-Flüchtlinge in Berlin*.[31] Based on interviews and surveys conducted with refugees from Lebanon, Ghadban described the devastating effect of German immigrant laws that prevented war refugees from working in Germany and made no attempts at their integration. As a consequence, the immigrants came to rely on family and ethnic networks, and they shunned German society, which they considered not only unwelcoming and biased against Muslims but also morally suspect. Unlike Turkish "guest workers," refugees from Lebanon had no German coworkers, and they had little incentive to learn German. The Germans they encountered were mostly immigration officials or police officers. Of course, many of the refugees were more than reluctant to return to their lives in the camps or urban slums in Lebanon, and they tended to miss their embassy appointments or forget or lose important documents, which did not help to expedite extradition. This practice of noncooperation led to German accusations of "subterfuge of the law," which then allowed German authorities to deny their requests to move them from *Duldung* to a more permanent residency status.

Over time, the "Lebanese" refugees, who had been relying on close-kin networks in Lebanon for matters of pragmatism and survival, began to arrange marriages of family members in Germany and Lebanon, and the continued influx of Arabic-speaking, often culturally conservative family members solidified "ethnic enclaves," or so-called *Parallelgesellschaften*. German church-affiliated charitable organizations, such as the Protestant Diakonisches Werk, began to hire Arabic-speaking staff to reach out to the Lebanese. Moreover, after the immigration reforms of 1990, the left-of-center Berlin city government gave grants to ethnic Arab organizations, in the hopes of creating more effective community support from within. For instance, in Berlin in 2011, a variety of Arab community organizations—Deutsch-Arabische Unabhängige Gemeinde, Deutsch-Arabisches Zentrum, Arabische Eltern Union, al-Karameh, al-Dar, al-Beit, al-Nadi,

and others—were in operation, with limited coordination among themselves and some competition for state and federal funding. While these
efforts at multicultural outreach to Arab residents were generally welcomed among Berlin's left-leaning politicians, they were also criticized by
migration experts, as the community organizations perpetuated the isolation of the Arabic-speaking refugees who could now obtain legal help and
social services without learning German.[32]

Only in 2005 the German government decided to place a time limit on
Duldung: §25 in the Foreigner Law stipulates that after eighteen months,
any person in that particular immigrant category has *the right to remain
and work* in Germany for humanitarian reasons. Additionally, in 2009,
§18a gave temporary residency with work permits to persons on *Duldung*,
if they possessed skills that made them employable.[33] The cynics will argue
that labor needs made the government change their laws to become more
inclusive of de facto refugees; church and charitable organizations claim
that it was their steady lobbying efforts in the Berlin senate and with federal legislators that made these legal changes possible. Discussions continue, however, both in the media and on municipal, state, and federal
levels, and the main concern remains the employability of the refugees: if
they work, they may stay; if they require welfare payments, they should go.

Opposing Muslim Minority Discourses in Germany

Two opposed camps exist that advocate for and against Muslim minority
communities as part of the larger German national community. The pro-
integration and reform camp associated with the political Left demands
more rights for Muslims in Germany and assigns blame for the failure
to integrate certain groups on inconsistent or discriminatory federal and
state policies. Among proponents of this group are German academics
and members of left-leaning political parties, such as Frank Gesemann,
Klaus Bade, Werner Schiffauer, and Günter Piesing. The opponents, allied
with, but not necessarily members of, the political Right, blame Muslim
minorities for their withdrawal into ethnic enclaves or "parallel societies"
and their refusal to learn the German language or accept German ideas
and values, in particular the value of gender equality rather than gender
complementarity. Using the metaphor "The boat is full," they urge for

more restrictive laws to stem the influx of new migrants. Prominent in this group, aside from Thilo Sarrazin, mentioned in the introduction, are academics Bassam Tibi, Necla Kelek, and author Güner Yasemin Balci, who are of Arab, Turkish, and Kurdish descent, respectively. In other words, those individuals who defend the rights of Muslim minorities are predominantly native German citizens, while it is Middle Eastern migrants who attended university in Germany and have come to call Germany their home who call for more stringent conditions on coethnics in order to promote their full integration into German society. The class aspect of the debate should not surprise us: university-educated Muslims are welcome in Germany; the "Muslim proletariat," as Sarrazin calls it, is not.[34]

Syrian-born international relations professor Bassam Tibi has published several studies that purport to show the incompatibility of Islamic and European values.[35] He points out that Islam rejects true pluralism and acceptance of other religions and cultures, since Judaism and Christianity are protected beliefs, but of *lesser status*. Christian communities in Turkey or Egypt, for instance, do not obtain the same protections from the government to practice their religion as Muslims do. He adds that little tolerance is shown by Muslims to Muslims in competing denominations—that is, Sunnis vis-à-vis Shi'a, 'Alawites, Druze, and so on. Tibi proposes the formulation of a new kind of "Euro-Islam," one that emphasizes pluralism, equality, individual freedoms, and the adaptation of Islamic texts to modern life.

Political scientist Frank Gesemann's survey of existing Muslim minorities in Germany points to overall positive integration trends, as evidenced by increasing social interactions between Germans and immigrants.[36] He warns of singling out specific ethnic groups as problematic based on their cultural traits and instead urges policy makers to focus the conversation on socioeconomic factors, such as the laws that limit educational and job opportunities for certain groups of Muslim minorities. Citing Klaus Bade, Gesemann claims that the government has missed a lot of opportunities via misguided immigration policies in the past and that migrants as a group have much "unused potential."[37] In an earlier study of the status of Muslim migrants in Berlin specifically, Gesemann similarly argued that Islamic religious organizations, once fully recognized by the state and placed on similar footing with Christian and Jewish organizations, would help to integrate Muslim residents into German society.[38]

Gesemann, similar to Sarrazin, cites survey responses, while Tibi constructs his Euro-Islam based on his experience of Muslim practices. Bade argues that "Muslim minorities" have much untapped potential, while Tibi emphasizes ongoing conflicts within "Muslim communities." In other words, these studies trade in aggregates. Within this debate, Muslims in Germany are either "victims" of German rejection and racism or "deviants" who undermine the very fabric of German society. Debates cast within this oppositional framework have mostly served politicians who want to score points with various voting publics. Immigrants have become caricatures rather than persons with a specific migration trajectory. Very little attention is paid to the historical contexts that produced Muslim migrants and the role that Germany's legal categories play in the creation of minority communities with vastly different opportunities. The media have an easier time deploring the existence of "criminal Lebanese youths" than they have examining the minutiae of immigrant law. It is also easier to accuse Germans of racism than it is to look at the ways different German actors interpret and implement specific laws that were created for a reason but do not always operate as intended. *Duldung* is a temporary injunction governing a migrant's delayed departure, not a migration status category in itself.

Germany's Palestinian and Kurdish Refugees in International Perspective

Stigmatized as refugees in Lebanon, and stigmatized as criminals or welfare recipients in Berlin, many of the Palestinian and Kurdish refugees from Lebanon have few legal options or political recourse. They also have few strong public advocates in the German government. Already in a legal state of exclusion as noncitizens in Lebanon before they fled to Germany, they imported a problem that the international community has been unwilling or unable to solve.[39]

Both Palestinians and Kurds make claims on territories they consider homelands that challenge the sovereignty of existing states. Being stateless, some of the refugees in Germany are tied to their own national identity politics and political movements that oppose attempts to assimilate them into the states where they reside. From their perspective, the refugees have a state, but they currently do not have the right to go there. Living in diaspora in marginalized conditions helps some community leaders to keep national identity claims, and the desire to return, alive among their coethnics. From the perspective of international law, the Geneva Convention of Refugees stipulates that "stateless peoples" should be given a passport by countries that receive them. But Germany, similar to other European states, is quite reluctant to grant the "stateless" label to refugees it wishes to extradite. Unwilling to give a "grand amnesty," which, it is feared, might draw Palestinians from many of the remaining camps across the Arab world, the German government has decided to keep working with the problematic legal status of *Duldung*, extending temporary residency and some social welfare payments on a case-by-case basis.

Germany's special relations with Israel and Turkey do not permit a serious discussion of the "tolerated" refugees' return to the villages and towns of their families' origin. While high on the list of humanitarian-aid donors to the Palestinians, Germany is muted in its demands that Israel change its refusal to let Palestinian refugees return. Israeli politicians have claimed that the Jewish state needs to preserve the majority status of its Jewish citizens; some politicians go so far as equating the return of Palestinian refugees with the destruction of the state of Israel. Palestinian refugees have been excluded from peace and final-status talks between Israeli and Palestinian delegations, leaving them as permanent charges of the United Nations Relief and Works Agency for Palestine Refugees in the Near East or as holders of a wide array of refugee permits and visas in the countries that harbor them.[40] Turkey has long refused to recognize the existence of Kurds within its borders, and it has had laws that make the mention of Kurdish culture and identity, or the use of the Kurdish language, a criminal offense. Arabic-speaking Kurdish refugees in Lebanon have been granted citizenship papers, which allow them to travel freely and exercise their rights in Lebanon. They remain, nevertheless, a very marginalized and stigmatized community, both inside Lebanon as well as within the larger Kurdish-speaking communities around the world.

The government of Lebanon has been following an active strategy of neglect of Palestinian and Kurdish Muslims who reside inside the country, because it wants to preserve a population status quo that favors Lebanese Christians. Lebanon's political system is precariously built on a quota system that allots each religious community in the country a certain number of seats, based on a population census carried out in 1932 by French mandate forces. A government that has historically favored the country's Christian communities has actively worked to prevent the naturalization of Muslim populations, while granting, for instance, citizenship to Armenian Christians who fled the genocide in Turkey during World War I. Moreover, many Lebanese citizens blame Palestinians who came to reside in their country in the aftermath of the 1948 and 1967 wars with Israel for having caused Lebanon's civil war.[41] It is, of course, ironic that it is precisely this war (they allegedly caused) that turned these persons into repeat refugees. The Lebanese authorities were happy to pass these unwanted ethnic minorities on to the German government—or any other government, for that matter.[42]

As (bad) timing would have it, the efforts of these "Lebanese" refugees to obtain a more permanent status after their humanitarian visas expired coincided with German unification. The cost of unification to the German taxpayer hardened German attitudes toward foreigners who received welfare payments. Additionally, after the fall of the Soviet Union, Germany absorbed large numbers of refugees who could prove German descent (so-called *Aussiedler*), which led to the impression—fed by a sensationalist media—that Germany was overrun by people from the East seeking to take advantage of social safety and financial support afforded by its constitution. Moreover, the 1991–95 civil war in Yugoslavia created a massive refugee stream, especially after the massacres of ethnic Bosnians by Serbian militias. Approximately four hundred thousand mostly Muslim refugees arrived in Germany in 1996 alone. The spike in asylum applications led to a breakdown of the entire asylum application process. The political solution was to create a new legal category for "war refugees," which granted temporary residency and immediate rights to work. This new law in turn helped some of the "Lebanese" refugees who were able, temporarily, to obtain "war refugee" status that afforded more rights than the restricted category of *Duldung*. But after the civil war in Yugoslavia ended and the country dissolved, the majority of Bosnian war refugees were sent back, their special rights rescinded.

The status of the "Lebanese" Muslim community within the larger Muslim minority in Germany may be simultaneously too big and too small to solve effectively. On the one hand, as Von Bethlenfalvy argued in the early 1980s, the "complex problem" of "irregular migrants" such as Palestinians and Kurds needs an international resolution.[43] The international actors that have a stake in resolving the final-status question of these refugees are many: the Palestinian leadership, Israel, Turkey, the United Nations, the European Union, and all those states that harbor refugees or migrants who are descendants from territories now under Israeli and Turkish control. That the Lebanese government does not want Palestinian and Kurdish refugee populations returned to Lebanon, that the German government has no leverage to argue for stateless Palestinian or Kurdish communities to return to the places they consider "home," and that some of these migrants prefer to remain in Europe together create a political, social, and legal predicament that is difficult to resolve on the domestic level in Germany alone. Courageous leadership is required, across ethnicities and nationalities, to recognize the rights of "irregular" migrants. Those debates need to be carried out separately from the debates about work migrants, both within and without Europe, in order to break out of the generic narratives of "troublesome minorities" in an undifferentiated German or European context.

Conclusion

After its experiences with different Muslim minorities—Turkish, Arab, and Bosnian—in the twentieth century, Germany in the early twenty-first century changed its laws to promote integration of its resident Muslim minorities and their descendants. These changes facilitated the reception of Syrian refugees who began fleeing civil war after 2011, although the sheer number of arrivals posed tremendous logistical and political challenges.

With their much longer history in Germany and their much larger numbers, Muslim "minorities" from Turkey have been able to obtain more and more rights and recognition within German society. Turkish organizations in Germany have instituted Islam classes in Germany's kindergarten through high school curricula, German universities now offer the option to study for the position of an imam, and persons of Turkish background have been active in local and state politics. Since 2005 children of Turkish migrants can opt for German citizenship, and many of them have done so. It has taken decades for the German legal system to change and create new residency and citizenship categories and to change the discourse of foreigners who temporarily reside in Germany to one of migrants who are there to stay.[44] But consistent efforts of migrant advocacy groups, as well as binding changes in migration policy on the European Union level, have made new definitions of who is a German possible.

The question of whether repeated extensions of *Duldung*, and similar temporary and restricted immigrant laws, are constitutionally defensible needs to be answered, and scholars like Riecken have started the debate. In July 2015, Chancellor Angela Merkel was confronted with a fourteen-year-old Palestinian girl, Reem Sahwil, during a televised town hall–style meeting with a group of students. In fluent German that suggested she had been in the country for a long time, Reem explained how hard it was for her to live in a situation of perpetual uncertainty, and when Merkel told her that Germany was not able to take in all the migrants who wanted to stay, Reem broke into tears. The subsequent media storm unfortunately focused on Merkel's awkward attempt to console the girl rather than the dilemmas created by temporary residency categories for families like the Sahwils. Since July many more war refugees from Syria, Iraq, and Afghanistan have reached Germany, many obtaining humanitarian visas that allow them to stay for three years. What will happen to them when the time comes to renew their papers? Will they be asked to leave or become residents who form their own Muslim minority groups within the growing Muslim community in Germany? The legal, political, and social contexts for immigrants and minorities in Germany have changed profoundly in the past decade, proving that the process of minoritization is itself ongoing. Further studies in this area are undoubtedly needed, alongside political wisdom and acts of courage.

Notes

Bibliography

Contributors

Index

Notes

Introduction

1. Albert Hourani, *Minorities in the Arab World*, 1.

2. Gabriel Ben-Dor, "Minorities in the Middle East: Theory and Practice," 6.

3. Hourani, *Minorities in the Arab World*, 2.

4. See, for instance, Laure Guirguis, *Les copts d'Egypte: Violences communautaires*, which makes use of this concept of minoritization.

5. Aron Rodrigue interview with Nancy Reynolds, "Difference and Tolerance in the Ottoman Empire." Benjamin Thomas White makes a very similar point, noting that "in a religiously-legitimated monarchy, whether or not the ruler shares the language or 'ethnicity' of the ruled is irrelevant." See White, *The Emergence of Minorities in the Middle East: The Politics of Community in French Mandate Syria*, 31.

6. For an overview of these forced migrations, see Dawn Chatty, *Displacement and Dispossession in the Modern Middle East*, chap. 2.

7. White, *Emergence of Minorities in the Middle East*, 32–33.

8. On this development, see especially Joshua Schreier, *Arabs of the Jewish Faith: The Civilizing Mission in Colonial Algeria*.

9. The best guide to the mandates system in the interwar Middle East remains Peter Sluglett and Nadine Meouchy, eds., *The British and French Mandates in Comparative Perspective*. See also Susan Pedersen, "The Meaning of the Mandates System: An Argument."

10. On this point, see especially Laura Robson, *Colonialism and Christianity in Mandate Palestine*; Nicholas Roberts, "Dividing Jerusalem: British Urban Planning in the Holy City"; and Rashid Khalidi, *The Iron Cage: The Palestinian Struggle for Statehood*.

11. Peter Sluglett and Marion Farouk-Sluglett, "Some Reflections on the Sunni/Shi'i Question in Iraq."

12. On the construction of mandate Lebanon, see especially Kais Firro, *Inventing Lebanon: Nationalism and the State under the Mandate*.

13. Elizabeth Thompson, *Colonial Citizens: Republican Rights, Paternal Privilege, and Gender in French Syria and Lebanon*.

14. See Paul Sedra, "Writing the History of the Modern Copts: From Victims and Symbols to Actors"; and Guirguis, *Les copts d'Egypte*.

15. On the revolt, see especially Michael Provence, *The Great Syrian Revolt and the Rise of Syrian Nationalism*.

16. On this episode and its reverberations, see especially D. M. Hart, "The Berber Dahir of 1930 in Colonial Morocco: Then and Now (1930–1996)"; Bruce Maddy-Weitzman, *The Berber Identity Movement and the Challenge to North African States*; and Patricia Lorcin, *Imperial Identities: Stereotyping, Prejudice, and Race in Colonial Algeria*.

17. For examples, see Sarah Gualtieri, *Between Arab and White: Race and Ethnicity in the Early Syrian Diaspora*; Madawi al-Rasheed, *Iraqi Assyrian Christians in London: The Construction of an Ethnicity*; and Pieternella van Doorn-Harder and Kari Vogt, *Between Desert and City: The Coptic Orthodox Church Today*.

1. From Millet to Minority

1. See Seteny Shami, "'Aqalliya/Minority in Modern Egyptian Discourse," for a discussion of the Copts.

2. "Although since 1980 the Shi'is have constituted more than 30 percent of the total population of Lebanon . . . they still behave as a minority. Neither their demographic size not their political power can bring about a radical change in the confessional political system of the country." Kais Firro, "Nationalism and Confessionalism: Shi'is, Druzes and Alawis in Syria and Lebanon," 251.

3. This topic became a matter of considerable contention between French administrators in Syria and Syrian nationalists after the admission of Iraq to the League of Nations in 1932. See Benjamin Thomas White, *The Emergence of Minorities in the Middle East: The Politics of Community in French Mandate Syria*, 131–61. See also http://en.wikipedia.org/wiki/Anglo-Iraqi_Treaty_(1930) for the full text of the Anglo-Iraqi Treaty of 1930. The word "community" (rather than "minority") appears in the text of the French mandate for Syria (see the discussion of White's work below).

4. This discussion does not seem to have gone any further, and the topic evinced considerable misgivings in Coptic circles. See Shami, "'Aqalliya/Minority in Modern Egyptian Discourse," 164–65.

5. Broadly speaking, that the subjects of a ruler should follow his religious confession.

6. Another important provision of the treaty was that of state sovereignty, the notion that states did not have the right to intervene in each other's domestic affairs.

7. Peter Sluglett, "An Improvement on Colonialism? The 'A' Mandates and Their Legacy in the Middle East," 420. "The two great minorities of 1918, the Germans and the Jews, have in different ways been eliminated; minorities form a smaller proportion of national populations in Central and Eastern Europe today than before the war." Mark Mazower, "Minorities and the League of Nations in Interwar Europe," 60.

8. See Carole Fink, "Minority Rights as an International Question."

9. See Pertti Ahonen, "Domestic Constraints on West German Ostpolitik: The Role of the Expellee Organizations in the Adenauer Era."

10. In most of these regions, communal conflict was sporadic rather than endemic, and when it did occur it was frequently connected with (often overzealous) Ottoman efforts to bring such areas under "regular" administrative rule. For evidence of the effects of this process in eastern Anatolia, see Brad R. Dennis, "Explaining Coexistence and Conflict in Eastern Anatolia, 1870–1878."

11. See J. F. Coakley, *The Church of the East and the Church of England: A History of the Archbishop of Canterbury's Assyrian Mission*. The mission was active between 1886 and 1914.

12. At this stage confined to Evvoia, Livadia, the Peloponnese, and the Cyclades islands. See Paul Robert Magocsi, *Historical Atlas of Central Europe*, map 26a.

13. Kemal H. Karpat, *Ottoman Population, 1830–1914: Demographic and Social Characteristics*, 55.

14. Except for the Dodecanese islands (including Kalymnos, Karpathos, Kos, Leros, Patmos, and Rhodes), which were occupied by Italy from 1915 until 1947, when they became part of Greece.

15. Karpat, *Ottoman Population*, 55.

16. Ibid., 49. Recent research has revealed more details of these terrible events. See M. Hakan Yavuz, "Warfare and Nationalism: The Balkan Wars as a Catalyst for Homogenization."

17. Anna Mirkova, "Citizenship Formation in Bulgaria: Protected Minority or National Citizens?," 472.

18. See Anna Mirkova, "Landownership and Modernization in the Transition from Ottoman Imperial to Bulgarian National Rule (1877/78–1908)." As with other religions, the practice of Islam under the Communist regime (1946–89) was considerably restricted. There are only about a half-million Muslims in Bulgaria today, some 8 percent of the population.

19. "For the historian, the exchange of often Turkish-speaking Greek Orthodox Christians for sometimes Greek-speaking Muslims is a warning not to assume that 'national' groups exist as self-evident and discrete units: it took Greece and Turkey enormous effort to forge these populations into 'Greeks' and 'Turks.'" White, *Emergence of Minorities*, 23–24.

20. Both topics have been the subjects of an immense body of literature. For recent research on the Armenian genocide, see Taner Akçam, *The Young Turks' Crime against Humanity: The Armenian Genocide and Ethnic Cleansing in the Ottoman Empire*; and Donald Bloxham, *The Great Game of Genocide: Imperialism, Nationalism, and the Destruction of the Ottoman Armenians*. For the Greek-Turkish population exchange, see Bruce Clark, *Twice a Stranger: How Mass Expulsion Forged Modern Greece and Turkey*; and the older work of Renée Hirschon, *Heirs of the Greek Catastrophe: The Social Life of Asia Minor Refugees in Piraeus*.

21. Bruce Masters, *Christians and Jews in the Ottoman Arab World: The Roots of Sectarianism*, 61.

22. Karen Barkey, *Empire of Difference: The Ottomans in Comparative Perspective*, 130–32.

23. Benjamin Braude, "The Strange History of the Millet System"; see also his better-known article "Foundation Myths of the Millet System."

24. See Najwa al-Qattan, "The Damascene Jewish Community in the Latter Decades of the Eighteenth Century: Aspects of Socio-economic Life Based on the Registers of the Shari'a Courts" and her "Dhimmis in the Muslim Court: Legal Autonomy and Religious Discrimination."

25. See Maurits van den Boogert, "Millets Past and Present."

26. For example, if a Greek Orthodox man appeared in the *mahkama* shari'a in Aleppo in the latter part of the nineteenth century, the clerk would note that he was "min ta'ifa Rum Orthodoks."

27. Hidemitsu Kuroki, "The Orthodox-Catholic Clash in Aleppo in 1818."

28. See Hidemitsu Kuroki, "Zimmis in Mid-Nineteenth-Century Aleppo: An Analysis of Cizye Defteris." The *jizya* assessment apparently doubled in the province of Tripoli between 1814 and 1815; see Farouk Hoblos, "Public Services and Tax Revenues in Ottoman Tripoli (1516–1918)," 122.

29. Hidemitsu Kuroki, "Mobility of Non-Muslims in Nineteenth Century Aleppo."

30. Bruce Masters, "The Establishment of the Melkite Catholic Millet in 1848 and the Politics of Identity in Tanzimat Syria."

31. Unlike the Venetians, who dominated the trade of the eastern Mediterranean until the beginning of the sixteenth century, the French were unequivocal in associating themselves closely with the activities of the Catholic Church, especially after the establishment of the Propaganda Fide in 1622. See Molly Greene, *Catholic Pirates and Greek Merchants: A Maritime History of the Mediterranean*, 100–108.

32. See Masters, *Christians and Jews*.

33. As described by Laura Robson in *Colonialism and Christianity in Mandate Palestine*.

34. See Braude, "Millets Past and Present."

35. The Sublime Porte seems to have been quite wary of these arrangements. In 1806 it ordered the authorities in Aleppo to investigate the status of the dragomans accredited to the city's twelve foreign consulates. As a result, officials confiscated illegal licenses from 352 [sic] non-Muslims. Kuroki, "Mobility of Non-Muslims," 134.

36. Charles Issawi, "The Transformation of the Economic Position of the Millets in the Nineteenth Century."

37. Peter Sluglett, "Aspects of Economy and Society in the Syrian Provinces: Aleppo in Transition, 1880–1925."

38. The inability of the Lebanese religious communities to "change themselves" is well illustrated in a blistering critique by Ahmad Beydoun, *La dégénérescence du Liban ou la réforme orpheline*.

39. Including the Land Law of 1858; the Law of Vilayets of 1864, which defined provincial administrative units and regulated provincial administration; and the *mecelle*, or civil law code, of 1877.

40. David McDowall, *A Modern History of the Kurds*, 87–88.

41. There are two points to bear in mind here: first, the specter of the unratified Treaty of Sèvres of 1920 (which decreed the partitioning of Anatolia into, inter alia, an independent Kurdistan and an independent Armenia) long haunted the politics of the infant Turkish Republic, and in some ways still does; and second, Atatürk considered that the republic represented the entire Turkish people, including the Kurds, whom he "declared to be Turks."

42. These wars ended with the Treaty of Zuhab in 1639; both the Alevis of eastern Anatolia and the Twelver Shi'a were regarded with suspicion for their potentially pro-Iranian leanings.

43. Stefan Winter, *The Shi'is of Lebanon under Ottoman Rule, 1516–1788*, 5.

44. See Heinz Halm, *Shi'ism*.

45. To some extent, the Sublime Porte "accepted the legitimacy of the Twelver Shi'ites, whom they called Caferiyye. . . . Ilber Ortayli notes how Twelver Shi'is were never subjected to anything as harsh as certain Ottoman policies that were directed against other heterodox Muslim communities, such as Yezidis, Druze, Nusayris or Alawis." Max Weiss, *In the Shadow of Sectarianism: Law, Shi'ism and the Making of Modern Lebanon*, 66–67.

46. But see Stefan Winter, "The Nusayris before the Tanzimat in the Eyes of Ottoman Provincial Administrators, 1804–1834."

47. Firro, "Nationalism and Confessionalism," 259.

48. Quoted in the US *Bureau of Democracy, Human Rights and Labor, International Religious Freedom Report for 2012 (Syria)*, http://www.state.gov/j/drl/rls/irf/religious freedom/index. Membership in the Druze and Isma'ili communities is generally determined by birth.

49. See Arnon Soffer, "Lebanon: Where Demography Is the Core of Politics and Life."

50. That is, the notion that Shi'ism formed an "acceptable" or "canonical" school of Islamic law alongside the four more traditional Sunni legal schools, Hanafi, Hanbali, Maliki, and Shafi'i.

51. See Weiss, *In the Shadow of Sectarianism*. For the earlier period, see Tamara Chalabi, *The Shi'is of Jabal 'Amil and the New Lebanon: Community and Nation State, 1918–1943*.

52. See note 3.

53. Engin Akarli, *The Long Peace: Ottoman Lebanon, 1861–1920*.

54. White, *Emergence of Minorities*, 43, 88, 51–52.

55. Both areas were transferred to the control of the Syrian government in 1942. Philip S. Khoury, *Syria and the French Mandate: The Politics of Arab Nationalism, 1920–1945*, 595–96.

56. For the history of the concept of "minority" in "European social science," see White, *Emergence of Minorities*, 21–42.

57. For an account of these events, see Sami Zubaida, "Contested Nations: Iraq and the Assyrians."

58. White, *Emergence of Minorities*, 89–90, 146–48, 150–51.

59. Ibid., 162–208, 209.

60. For Iraq, see Tom Nieuwenhuis, *Politics and Society in Early Modern Iraq: Mamluk Pashas, Tribal Shayks and Local Rule between 1802 and 1831*; and Dina Khoury, *State and Provincial Society in the Ottoman Empire: Mosul, 1540–1834*.

61. See Yitzhak Nakash, *The Shi'is of Iraq*.

62. Especially after the Revolution of 1920, most Shi'i tribal leaders took advantage of the fiscal and other benefits that "came along with" support for the mandatory regime.

63. See Werner Ende, "Iraq in World War I: The Turks, the Germans and the Shi'ite Mujtahids' Call for Jihad." It is also significant that many Iraqi Shi'i 'ulama' had been involved in the Iranian constitutional movement in the first decade of the twentieth century.

64. See Peter Sluglett, "The British, the Sunnis and the Shi'is: Social Hierarchies of Interaction under the British Mandate."

65. This seems to have been equally true for Iraqi Jews, many of whom were profoundly engaged in (opposition) politics before their expulsion (mostly to Israel) in the early 1950s: see Orit Bashkin, *New Babylonians: A History of Jews in Modern Iraq*.

66. But see "A Note on Shi'i Politics," in *Britain in Iraq: Contriving King and Country*, by Peter Sluglett, 219–32, which shows the range and nature of Shi'i discontent under the British mandate.

2. Across Confessional Borders

1. Edmund Burke and Nejde Yaghoubian, eds., *Struggle and Survival in the Modern Middle East*. The most recent microhistory set in the Middle East is Dana Sajdi, *The Barber of Damascus: Nouveau Literacy in the Eighteenth-Century Ottoman Levant*. Another work particularly relevant to this study is Nelly Hanna, *Making Big Money in 1600: The Life and Times of Isma'il Abu Taqiyya, Egyptian Merchant*.

2. Among the classic texts that employ this approach are Derek Hopwood, *The Russian Presence in Syria and Palestine, 1843–1914: Church and Politics in the Near East*; and John Joseph, *Muslim-Christian Relations and Inter-Christian Rivalries in the Middle East: The Case of the Jacobites in an Age of Transition*.

3. See Laura Robson, *Colonialism and Christianity in Mandate Palestine*, and Noah Haiduc-Dale, *Arab Christians in British Mandate Palestine: Communalism and Nationalism, 1917–1948*.

4. Most relevant to this essay is the scholarship on Christians in late Ottoman Palestine. For recent examples that treat denominational groups as distinct, separate entities,

see Konstantinos Papastathis and Ruth Kark, "Orthodox Communal Politics in Palestine after the Young Turk Revolution (1908–1910)"; various chapters in Anthony O'Mahony, ed., *The Christian Communities of Jerusalem and the Holy Land: Studies in History, Religion and Politics*; and Hanna Kildani, *Modern Christianity in the Holy Land*.

5. The violence that occurred in Mount Lebanon and Damascus in 1860 is held to be a marker of the entrenchment of sectarian identity. Recent works on this subject have shown the complex interaction of factors, both local and international, in these events. See Ussama Makdisi, *The Culture of Sectarianism: Community, History, and Violence in Nineteenth-Century Ottoman Lebanon*; and Leila Tarazi Fawaz, *An Occasion for War: Civil Conflict in Lebanon and Damascus in 1860*.

6. Akram Fouad Khater, *Embracing the Divine: Passion and Politics in the Christian Middle East*.

7. Carlo Ginzburg, *The Cheese and the Worms*, 68–69.

8. For the reimagining of Bethlehem in Western culture, see Jacob Norris, "Bethlehem: The Global Story of a Little Town"; and Eitan Bar-Yosef, "Bethlehem."

9. My thanks to Megan Armstrong for sharing with me her research on the role of the Counter-Reformation and its impact on the Holy Land. Her forthcoming book is provisionally titled "De-centring the Reformation: Franciscans and Catholic Expansionism, 1500–1700." See also Bernard Heyberger, *Les Chrétiens du Proche-Orient au temps de la Réforme Catholique*, 274–75.

10. See Jacob Norris, "Exporting the Holy Land: Artisans and Merchant Migrants in Ottoman-Era Bethlehem," 16–18.

11. Latin Parish Records, Kattan family.

12. Norris, "Exporting the Holy Land," 17–18.

13. The emergence of the Melkite Church is widely discussed in the historical literature. A good account is given in Bruce Masters, *Christians and Jews in the Ottoman Arab World: The Roots of Sectarianism*, 80–88.

14. J. B. Barron, ed., *Palestine: Report and General Abstracts of the Census of 1922*, 45.

15. Letter written by Father Pietro Marino Sormanni da Milano from Jerusalem, Oct. 30, 1678, Archives of the Sacred Congregation of the Propaganda Fide (SCPF), Scritture Riferite nei Congressi, Terra Santa e Cipro, 2:113.

16. For example, see ibid. and 3:207.

17. Letter signed by around fifty Arab Catholics from Jerusalem and Bethlehem, May 8, 1681, SCPF, Scritture, 2:383–84.

18. Masters, *Christians and Jews*, 87. See also Heyberger, *Chrétiens du Proche-Orient*, 219–20.

19. As discussed in George Sammur, *Bayt Lahm 'Abr al-Tarikh*, 45–53.

20. As an example, the brothers Bulus and Murqus, sons of Butrus, appear in the Ottoman tax survey of 1691 as Greek Orthodox. See Başbakanlýk Arşivi, Istanbul, Maliyeden Midevver Defterleri, 3643 (14). But the same brothers also feature in

correspondence with the Propaganda Fide the previous year, stressing their allegiance to the Roman Catholic Church. See letter written by "Marco figlio di Pietro," Aug. 1690, SCPF, Scritture, 3:158–59.

21. As discussed in Thomas Philipp, *Acre: The Rise and Fall of a Palestinian City, 1731–1830*, 94–135.

22. See Norris, "Exporting the Holy Land," 19–20, 24–25.

23. This information and most of that which follows on Elias Kattan was kindly provided by Jack Kattan, great-grandson of Elias. I would like to thank him and the Kattan family for generously sharing their family records with me.

24. Kattan and Son business records, private collection of Jack Kattan, Amman.

25. The contracts are recorded in Omar al-Saqqaf (Alsagoff) to Yaqub Kattan, Aug. 10 1921, Jack Kattan private collection. The standard history of the Alsagoff family in Southeast Asia is Syed Mohsen Alsagoff, *The Alsagoff Family in Malaysia: A.H. 1240 (A.D. 1824) to A.H. 1382 (A.D. 1962)*. The family also features prominently in Ulrike Freitag, *Indian Ocean Migrants and State Formation in Hadhramaut: Reforming the Homeland*.

26. For Bethlehem merchants in Southeast Asia, see William Gervase Clarence-Smith, "Middle Eastern Migrants in the Philippines: Entrepreneurs and Cultural Brokers."

27. For examples, see Derek Hopwood, *The Russian Presence in Syria and Palestine, 1843–1914: Church and Politics in the Near East*; A. L. Tibawi, "Russian Cultural Penetration of Syria: Palestine in the Nineteenth Century"; and T. G. Stavrou, *Russian Interests in Palestine, 1882–1914*.

28. Bertha Spafford Vester, *Our Jerusalem: An American Family in the Holy City, 1881–1949*, 92.

29. Letter dated 1905, Jack Kattan private collection.

30. Business log, 1896, ibid.

31. Ministère de l'Instruction Publique to Prefecture de Police, May 15, 1886, Archives Nationales (AN), Pierrefitte-sur-Seine, F/19/5590.

32. Ibid.

33. For the settlement of a wider community of Bethlehemites in Kiev, see Kathy Kenny, "The Power of Place: Katrina in Five Worlds."

34. As recorded in Latin Parish Records, Kattan family.

35. See Harvey Levenstein, *Seductive Journey: American Tourists in France from Jefferson to the Jazz Age*, 128–30.

36. Charles Offrey, *Cette grande dame que fut la Transat*, 20.

37. As recorded in Adnan Musallam, *Folded Pages from Local Palestinian History in the 20th Century: Developments in Politics, Society, Press and Thought in Bethlehem in the British Era, 1917–1948*, 44.

38. For a recent collection of essays on Palestinian migration to Latin America, see Viola Raheb, ed., *Latin Americans with Palestinian Roots*.

39. Ministère de l'Instruction Publique to Prefecture de Police, May 15, 1886, AN F/19/5590.

40. Ibid.

41. René Goblet to Président du Conseil du Ministre de l'Interieur, Aug. 11, 1888, ibid.

42. See Philipp, *Acre*, 109–16; and Ian Coller, *Arab France: Islam and the Making of Modern Europe, 1798–1831*, 36–38.

43. Ministre de l'Interieur to Ministre de la Justice et des Cultes, Aug. 26, 1888, AN F/19/5590.

44. Coller, *Arab France*, 36–38.

45. Thomas Philipp, *The Syrians in Egypt, 1725–1975*, 41–42.

46. This gap is typified by Asher Kaufman, who writes that the political activity of the 1910s "was characterised not by the mass presence of a Syrian community, but through the activity of a few individuals." See Kaufman, *Reviving Phoenicia: The Search for Identity in Lebanon*, 79.

47. Prefecture de Police to Ministre de l'Instruction Publique, June 24, 1886, AN F/19/5590.

48. My thanks to George al-A'ma for this information as well as in the private collection of Jack Kattan.

49. Prefecture de Police to Ministre de l'Instruction Publique, June 24, 1886, AN F/19/5590.

50. Petition included in Ministère de l'Instruction Publique to Prefecture de Police, May 15, 1886, AN F/19/5590.

51. Sub-directeur de la Sureté Générale to Direction Générale des Cultes, May 26, 1900, ibid.

52. Gregoire Yussif to Ministre de l'Interieur, July 6, 1888, AN F/19/5590.

53. See Jacqueline Viruega, *La bijouterie parisienne, 1860–1914*, 126, 132, 178.

54. Sub-directeur de la Sureté Générale to Direction Générale des Cultes, May 26, 1900, AN F/19/5590.

55. Jack Kattan private collection.

56. Sub-directeur de la Sureté Générale to Direction Générale des Cultes, May 26, 1900, AN F/19/5590.

57. Christina Vella, *Intimate Enemies: The Two Worlds of the Baroness de Pontalba*, 321.

58. Ministre des Affaires Étrangères to Ministre de la Justice, Oct. 5, 1892, AN F/19/5590.

59. Note submitted to the Sureté Générale, Jan. 1, 1895, ibid.

60. Sub-directeur de la Sureté Générale to Direction Générale des Cultes, May 26, 1900, AN F/19/5590.

61. Flyer for a service at Saint-Julien-le-Pauvre, Apr. 25, 1900, AN F/19/5590.

62. Archevêché de Paris to Ministre de l'Interieur et des Cultes, May 28, 1900, ibid.

63. Joris-Karl Huysmans cited in Robert Ziegler, "The Containment and Diffusion of History in Huysmans' Saint-Séverin," 255.

64. See newspaper clippings included in AN F/19/5590.

65. *Le Gaulois*, Mar. 28, 1898, included in ibid.

66. For example, see M. Şükrü Hanioğlu, "The Young Turks and the Arabs before the Revolution of 1908"; and Mohammed Telhine, *L'Islam et les musulmans en France: Une histoire de mosques*, 96.

67. Copies of the newspaper are held in AN F/19/5590. For Kateb's attempts to win back the favor of French government officials, see Kateb to Directeur Général des Cultes, Sept. 30, 1898, ibid.

68. See Akram Fouad Khater, *Inventing Home: Emigration, Gender, and the Middle Class in Lebanon, 1870–1920*; and Sarah Gualtieri, *Between Arab and White: Race and Ethnicity in the Early Syrian American Diaspora*.

69. For a study of the emergence of the category of "minorities" in the twentieth century and its subsequent anachronistic use to refer to the Ottoman period, see Benjamin Thomas White, *The Emergence of Minorities in the Middle East: The Politics of Community in French Mandate Syria*.

70. As discussed in Ela Greenberg, *Preparing the Mothers of Tomorrow: Education and Islam in Mandate Palestine*, 103–5.

71. J. E. Kattan to Latin Patriarch of Jerusalem, Oct. 27, 1919, Jack Kattan private collection.

3. Becoming a Sectarian Minority

1. Scholars have disputed the extent to which evangelical Protestant missionaries in Palestine represented the cultural arm of a British imperial project. A. L. Tibawi, in his still-important study *British Interests in Palestine, 1800–1901: A Study of Religious and Educational Enterprise*, makes the argument that although these evangelical religious movements aligned themselves with lower-class interests against the dominant aristocracy in the metropole, when they "embarked on ambitious schemes in the colonies and even in dominions of foreign sovereign states such as the Ottoman Empire, they openly joined in the expansion of Europe. The missions were the cultural aspect . . . which followed the territorial, commercial, and political expansion" (5). Andrew Porter mounts a broad challenge to this point of view in *Religious versus Empire? British Protestant Missionaries and Overseas Expansion, 1700–1914*, and Eitan Bar-Yosef suggests with specific regard to Palestine that the Protestant evangelical interest in the "return of the Jews" was "continuously associated with charges of religious enthusiasm, eccentricity, sometimes even madness . . . beyond the cultural consensus." Bar-Yosef, *The Holy Land in English Culture, 1799–1917: Palestine and the Question of Orientalism*, 184.

2. See Thomas Stransky, "Origins of Western Christian Missions in Jerusalem and the Holy Land," 142.

3. Cited in Tibawi, *British Interests in Palestine*, 22.

4. Stransky, "Origins of Western Christian Missions," 142.

5. Tibawi, *British Interests in Palestine*, 6.

6. This last feeling was expressed by Kaiser Frederick William IV himself, who was so put off by his experience of visiting the church that he decided it could not possibly be the site of Christ's grave. See Martin Tamcke, "Johann Worrlein's Travels in Palestine," 244.

7. Ludwig Schellner, *Reisebriefe aus heiligen Landan*, 38.

8. John James Moscrop, *Measuring Jerusalem: The Palestine Exploration Fund and British Interests in the Holy Land*, 70–71.

9. For an extensive investigation of the connections between the Palestine Exploration Fund and British military intelligence, see ibid.

10. See Neil Asher Silberman, *Digging for God and Country: Exploration, Archeology, and the Secret Struggle for the Holy Land, 1799–1917*, 113–27, for a discussion of the intertwining of the Palestine Exploration Fund and the British intelligence services during the 1870s, when the British feared that Russia might threaten their control over Suez. Silberman points out that many of the maps and surveys the fund produced during this period were eventually used in the British occupation of Palestine during the final stages of the First World War.

11. C. R. Conder, *The Future of Palestine: A Lecture Delivered for the Palestine Exploration Fund*, 34.

12. Herbert Samuel, *Report of the High Commissioner on the Administration of Palestine, 1920–1925*, 50.

13. The election of Hajj Amin al-Husayni and the foundation of the Supreme Muslim Council have been discussed extensively by scholars, many of whom have accepted Yehoshua Porath's argument that British policy on the creation of the SMC resulted primarily from Samuel's desire to recognize a Yishuv-elected assembly as representative of the Jewish community in Palestine, which could not be done without some kind of Arab equivalent. Since a representative Arab body would never consent to work within the mandate framework, as the Jewish assembly had done, the only other option was to appoint an institution like the SMC to act as a Muslim representative body. (See Porath, *The Emergence of the Palestinian Arab National Movement*, 199ff.) It was certainly one aspect of the decision, and one that Samuel himself discussed in his memoirs. However, it represents an incomplete analysis of British motives.

14. Samuel to Curzon, Nov. 29, 1920, Foreign Office 141/442/4.

15. Record of Palestinian Arab Delegation meeting at Colonial Office, Aug 22 1921, Israel State Archives, RG 65/P/984/10.

16. I. Katz and R. Kark, "The Greek Orthodox Patriarchate of Jerusalem and Its Congregation: Dissent over Real Estate." Sales of land to the Palestine Land Development

Company were being discussed as early as 1921; see agreement between the PLDC and Orthodox Financial Commission, July 16, 1928, Central Zionist Archives, L18/861.

17. *Filastin*, Oct. 16, 1931.

18. See As'ad Ganim, *The Palestinian-Arab Minority in Israel, 1948–2000: A Political Study*, 20. For an investigation of the many legal and political sectarian institutions carried over from the British into the Israeli state structures, see Robert H. Eisenman, *Islamic Law in Palestine and Israel: A History of the Survival of Tanzimat and Shar'ia in the British Mandate and the Jewish State.*

19. Nur Mashala, "A Galilee without Christians? Yosef Weitz and 'Operation Yohanan.'" For further discussion of expulsion and "transfer" in the early years of Israeli statehood, see especially Shira Robinson, *Citizen Strangers: Palestinians and the Birth of Israel's Liberal Settler State.* For a personal account of individual expulsions of Arab Christians, see Elias Shoufani, *Rihla F'il Rahil: Fusul Min al-Dhakira . . . Lam Taktamul.*

20. Cited in Mashala, "Galilee without Christians?," 219.

21. Nurit Yaffe, *The Arab Population of Israel, 2003.* The Palestinian Arab population of Israel constitutes approximately 20 percent of the population (about 1.3 million people). Most of the Palestinian Christian population is now concentrated in the Galilee region.

22. Bernard Sabella, "Palestinian Christian Emigration from the Holy Land," 75.

23. Ibid., 83.

24. Evangelical Christian tourism now constitutes as much as a third of the American tourist trade in Israel; both Israeli and American tour companies offer Christian pilgrimage tours of Israel aimed at American evangelicals, emphasizing the return of the Jews to the Holy Land in biblical terms. "1/3 of US Tourists Evangelicals," *Jerusalem Post*, Oct. 9 2006. For an examination of the rise of pro-Israeli American evangelical Christianity, see Stephen Spector, *Evangelicals and Israel: The Story of American Christian Zionism.*

4. Egypt and Its Jews

1. David Kirkpatrick, "Carmen Weinstein, Who Led the Jews of Cairo, Dies at 82," *New York Times*, Apr. 14, 2013.

2. Joel Beinin, *The Dispersion of Egyptian Jewry: Culture, Politics and the Formation of a Modern Diaspora* (Berkeley: University of California Press, 1998); paperback edition (Cairo: American University in Cairo Press, 2005); Arabic translation by Muhammad Shukr, *Shatat yahud misr* (Cairo: Dar al-Shuruq, 2007).

3. Samir W. Raafat, *Maadi, 1904–1962: Society & History in a Cairo Suburb*, notes the positive contributions of Jews to the development of Ma'adi. He also wrote positively about Jews in articles for the *Egyptian Gazette* and served as webmaster for the Cairo Jewish community.

4. The history of cinematic adaptations of Nagib al-Rihani's 1941 play, *Hasan-wa-Murqus wa-Kohin*, exemplifies erasure of the Jewish presence. The names of the characters

in the play and the 1954 film version express the coexistence of Muslims, Christians, and Jews, as does the 1949 version, transposed to the feminine, *Fatma wa-Marika wa-Rashil*. Rami Imam's 2008 remake, *Hasan wa-Murqus*, has no Jewish character.

5. The novels—Kamal Ruhayyim, *Qulub munhaka* (Cairo: Sphinx, 2004) and *Ayam al-shatat* (Cairo: Sphinx, 2008); Muʻtazz Fatiha, *Akhir yahud al-iskandariyya* (Cairo: Dar Uktub, 2009); Fatima al-ʻUrayyid, *Safar al-tarhil* (Cairo: Dar al-Tinani, 2013)—are not discussed here.

6. Azza Khattab, "How the President of the Jewish Community of Cairo Is Keeping the Memory of Her Forefathers Alive as She Struggles to Preserve the Nation's Jewish Heritage Sites," *Egypt Today*, May 2005, http://archive.is/ouyUe.

7. Ibid.

8. Muhammad al-Buhayri, "Mursi yanʻi raʼisat al-taʼifa al-yahudiyya sirran," *al-Misri al-Yawm*, Apr. 16, 2013; Kirkpatrick, "Carmen Weinstein."

9. Muhammad Kharrub, "Carmen ʻal-mukhlisaʼ . . . kama wasafaha Muhammad Mursi," *al-Raʼi*, Apr. 17, 2013.

10. Al-Yawm al-Sabiʻ, Apr. 18, 2013, http://www.youm7.com/News.asp?NewsID=10 24811#.Usd5l2RDv_4.

11. *Al-Quds al-ʻArabi*, Apr. 14, 2013, http://www.alquds.co.uk/?p=33682.

12. Zeinobia, *Egyptian Chronicles*, Apr. 18, 2013, http://egyptianchronicles.blogspot .fr/2013/04/carmen-weinsteins-funeral-dying.html.

13. Farah Montasser, "A Closer Look at Cairo's Shaar Hashomayim Synagogue," *Ahram Online*, Apr. 24, 2013, http://english.ahram.org.eg/NewsContent/32/97/70013/Folk /Street-Smart/A-closer-look-at-Cairos-Shaar-Hashomayim-Synagogue.aspx.

14. Roʼi Kis, "Kehilat ha-nashim," *Yediʻot Aharonot*, Apr. 10, 2013, http://www .ynet.co.il/articles/0,7340,L-4369610,00.html. Ahmed Belal gives a harsher translation of the Hebrew in "Interview: Magda Haroun, Head of Egypt's Jewish Community," *Egypt Independent*, July 16, 2013, http://www.egyptindependent.com/news/interview-magda-haroun-head-egypt-s-jewish-community. I have not been able to find a Hebrew text corresponding to his translation.

15. Shihata Harun, *Yahudi fi al-qahira*.

16. Khaled Dawoud, "Humanist against the odds, Shehata Haroun (1920–2001)," *al-Ahram Weekly Online*, Mar. 22–28, 2001, http://weekly.ahram.org.eg/2001/526/eg6.htm.

17. MEMRI is a right-wing think tank whose translations must be used cautiously, but the Arabic videos appear to be genuine.

18. Original Arabic video: http://www.policymic.com/articles/21984/new-video -shows-egyptian-president-morsi-calling-jews-descendants-of-apes-and-pigs.

19. Original Arabic video: http://www.youtube.com/watch?v=Q3NCiaozL0k; see also David Kirkpatrick, "Morsi's Slurs against Jews Stir Concern," *New York Times*, Jan. 14, 2013.

20. John McCain, press conference in Cairo, Jan. 16, 2013, http://www.youtube.com /watch?v=SqQp3EM7vS0.

21. Josh Rogin, "Exclusive: Morsy Implies Jews Control the American Media," *Cable*, Jan. 23, 2013, http://thecable.foreignpolicy.com/posts/2013/01/23/exclusive_morsy_implies _jews_control_the_american_media#sthash.Sg7iZM4F.dpbs.

22. Gilbert Achcar, *The Arabs and the Holocaust: The Arab-Israeli War of Narratives*.

23. Sarah El Deeb, "Brotherhood Official Urges Egypt's Jews to Return," Associated Press, Jan. 3, 2013.

24. *Daily News Egypt*, Dec. 29, 2012, http://www.dailynewsegypt.com/2012/12/29/fjp -backs-el-erians-call-for-egyptian-jews-right-of-return/.

25. *Daily News Egypt*, Jan. 6, 2013, http://www.dailynewsegypt.com/2013/01/06 /complaint-filed-against-essam-el-erian/.

26. El Deeb, "Brotherhood Official."

27. Khaled Fahmy, "The Muslim Brotherhood and Egyptian Jewry," *Ahram Online*, Jan. 6, 2013, http://english.ahram.org.eg/NewsContentPrint/4/0/61868/Opinion/0/The -Muslim-Brotherhood-and-Egyptian-Jewry.aspx.

28. ICOMOS, "Restoration of the Ben Ezra Synagogue, Cairo," http://www.icomos .org/~fleblanc/publications/pub_1986_icomos-canada_esc_nl_vol07_no01_ben-ezra .pdf.

29. Associated Press, "Egypt to Pay for Restoration of All Its Jewish Synagogues," Mar. 9, 2013, http://usatoday30.usatoday.com/news/religion/2010-03-09-egypt-jewish_N.htm.

30. Michael Slackman, *New York Times*, Sept. 6, 2009, http://www.nytimes.com /2009/09/07/world/middleeast/07cairo.html?_r=0.

31. Ibid.

32. Ibid.

33. Alaa Shahine, "Egypt Scraps Synagogue Ceremony after Dancing and Drinking," *Bloomberg News*, Mar. 14, 2010, http://www.bloomberg.com/apps/news?sid=axvXX7lLzX Hk&pid=newsarchive.

34. Agence France Press, "Egypt Scraps Synagogue Ceremony after 'Provocative' Acts," Mar. 14, 2010, http://www.google.com/hostednews/afp/article/ALeqM5hGeLjTB 4LWNTcXyG9CLg9VCPOsGQ.

35. "Egypt Antiquities Chief: I Gave the Zionist Enemy a Slap in the Face," *Haaretz*, Mar. 28, 2010, http://www.haaretz.com/news/egypt-antiquities-chief-i-gave-the-zionist -enemy-a-slap-in-the-face-1.265426.

36. As the context and politics of memory for these works are somewhat differ-ent, they are not considered here. The best-known example of this genre of the 2000s is Lucette Lagnado, *The Man in the White Sharkskin Suit: A Jewish Family's Exodus from Old Cairo to the New World*.

37. Muhammad Abu al-Ghar, *Yahud misr: Min al-izdihar ila al-shatat*.

38. The main sources are Gudrun Krämer, *The Jews in Modern Egypt, 1914–1952*; Michael Laskier, *The Jews of Egypt, 1920–1970: In the Midst of Zionism, Anti-Semitism, and the Middle East Conflict*; and Beinin, *Dispersion of Egyptian Jewry*.

39. Jacques Hassoun, ed., *Histoire des Juifs du Nile*; translation, Yusuf Darwish, *Tarikh yahud al-nil* (Cairo: Dar al-Shuruq, 2007).

40. Beinin, *Dispersion of Egyptian Jewry*, 269–74.

41. Joel Beinin, "Lives of Struggle and Commitment of Social Justice"; Faiza Radi, "The Struggle for Justice: Youssef Darwish (1910–2006)," *al-Ahram Weekly Online*, June 15–21, 2006, http://weekly.ahram.org.eg/2006/799/eg43.htm. See also *al-Masri al-Yawm*, June 17, 2006, http://today.almasryalyoum.com/article2.aspx?ArticleID=20301.

42. Joseph Massad, "Salata Baladi or Afrangi?," *al-Ahram Weekly Online*, Feb. 28–Mar. 5, 2008, http://weekly.ahram.org.eg/2008/886/cu1.htm.

43. Sara Elkamel, "Egypt Security Apparatus Delays 'Jews of Egypt' Premiere," *Ahram Online*, Mar. 12, 2013, http://english.ahram.org.eg/News/66742.aspx.

44. Ben Child, "Egypt Bans Film about Jewish Community," *Guardian*, Mar. 13, 2013, http://www.theguardian.com/film/2013/mar/13/egypt-blocks-film-jewish-community.

45. "Egyptian Delegation at Swedish Arab Film Festival Harassed by Pro-Brotherhood Protestors," *Ahram Online*, Sept. 5, 2013, http://english.ahram.org.eg/NewsContent/5/32/80872/Arts-Culture/Film/Egyptian-delegation-at-Swedish-Arab-film-festival-.aspx.

46. Vicki Habib, interview with Amir Ramsis, *al-Hayat*, Sept. 30, 2013.

47. Email exchange, Apr. 28, 2013.

5. When Anticolonialism Meets Antifascism

1. Israel Gershoni and Amy Singer, "Introduction," 385.

2. Israel Gershoni, "Rethinking the Formation of Arab Nationalism in the Middle East, 1920–1945."

3. Peter Wien, *Iraqi Arab Nationalism: Authoritarian, Totalitarian and Pro-Fascist Inclinations, 1932–1941*; Orit Bashkin, *The Other Iraq: Pluralism and Culture in Hashemite Iraq*.

4. Juan Cole, "Iraq in 1939: British Alliance or Nationalist Neutrality toward the Axis?"; Gilbert Achcar, *Les Arabes et la Shoah*, 59–273; Götz Nordbruch, "Bread, Freedom, Independence: Opposition to Nazi Germany in Lebanon and Syria and the Struggle for a Just Order"; Ulrike Freitag and Israel Gershoni, "The Politics of Memory: The Necessity for Historical Investigation into Arab Responses to Fascism and Nazism."

5. *Bulletin de l'Alliance Israélite Universelle*, 1881–82, 1896, 1910, 1913; Hanna Batatu, *The Old Social Classes and the Revolutionary Movements of Iraq: A Study of Iraq's Old Landed and Commercial Classes and of Its Communists, Ba'thists and Free Officers*, 248; and H. D. S., "Account of the Jewish Community at Baghdad," *Baghdad*, Feb. 17, 1910, reprinted in Elie Kedourie, "The Jews of Baghdad in 1910." It should be noted that numbers and proportions of Baghdadi Jews are sometimes contradictory and overall approximate, owing to the lack of census.

6. Kedourie, "Jews of Baghdad in 1910," 357–58.

7. Ibid., 360–61.

8. Anne-Laure Dupont and Catherine Mayeur-Jaouen, "Monde nouveau, voix nou-velles: États, sociétés, islam dans l'entre-deux-guerres," 10.

9. A petition for obtaining British citizenship addressed to London in 1918 was rejected. "The Jews of Baghdad Petition for British Citizenship at the End of World War I," president of the Jewish Lay Council, Baghdad, Nov. 18, 1918, reprinted in Norman A. Stillman, *The Jews of Arab Lands in Modern Times*, 256–57.

10. Tomer Levi, *The Jews of Beirut: The Rise of a Levantine Community*, 123–48; Laura Zittrain Eisenberg, *My Enemy's Enemy: Lebanon in the Early Zionist Imagination, 1900–1948*.

11. *Sawt al-Ahali* (Baghdad), Jan. 20, 1946.

12. Batatu, *Old Social Classes*, 302.

13. Bashkin, *Other Iraq*, 289.

14. Batatu, *Old Social Classes*, 302.

15. Muzaffar A. Amin, *Jama'at al-Ahali: Its Origin, Ideology and Role in Iraqi Politics, 1932–1946*, 1.

16. For a discussion of the transition from millet to minority, see Peter Sluglett's contribution to the present volume.

17. For instance, the constitutional concept of "spiritual council of the communities" (*al-majalis al-ruhaniyya al-ta'ifiyya*) was competent to deal with matters relating to family and personal status. This judicial autonomy for non-Muslim communities was actually an adaptation of the Ottoman "General Regulations of the Rabbinate" (Hahamhane Nizamnamesi) of 1865. See Zvi Yehuda, "Haham Başı (Chief Rabbi)."

18. "Law for the Israelite Community No. 77," Baghdad, 1932, Article 3.

19. Jürgen Habermas, *The Structural Transformation of the Public Sphere: An Inquiry into a Category of Bourgeois Society*, 3–4.

20. Dyala Hamzah, introduction to *The Making of the Arab Intellectual: Empire, Public Sphere and the Colonial Coordinates of Selfhood*, 1.

21. For instance, *al-Misbah* (Baghdad), July 17, 1924, June 24, 1926.

22. Charles Tripp, *A History of Iraq*, 62–63.

23. "Death of Sir Abdul Muhsin, 14 November 1929–9 January 1930," Colonial Office, 730/150/5.

24. *Al-Burhan* (Baghdad), Nov. 19, 1929. For more on the anti-British discourse in Jewish writings, see Aline Schlaepfer, *Les intellectuels juifs de Bagdad: Discours et allégeances (1908–1951)*.

25. Wien, *Iraqi Arab Nationalism*, 56–68.

26. Sami Shawkat, *Hadhihi ahdafuna* [These Are Our Goals], 2.

27. Sati' al-Husri, *Mudhakkirati fi al-'Iraq (1927–1924)*, 2:116–21, 160–61.

28. Orit Bashkin, *New Babylonians: A History of Jews in Modern Iraq*, 105–11.

29. *Sawt al-Ahali* (Baghdad), Jan. 2, 1946.

30. Al-Chadirchi uses the Arabic word *ba'th* for "rise." By doing so, he conveys a double meaning, as it means either "the Fascist Ba'th" or "the rise of Fascism."

31. *Sawt al-Ahali* (Baghdad), June 2, 1946.

32. Freitag and Gershoni, "Politics of Memory," 320.

33. *Sawt al-Ahali* (Baghdad), July 10, 1942.

34. *Sawt al-Ahali* (Baghdad), Jan. 16, 1946.

35. Salih Twayq, *Dhikrayat wa khawatir* [Memories and Thoughts], 16.

36. *Al-Hasid* (Baghdad), Dec. 17, 1936.

37. *Al-Hasid* (Baghdad), Apr. 30, 1936.

38. Shelley Baranowski, *Nazi Empire: German Colonialism and Imperialism from Bismarck to Hitler*, 147–48.

39. Woodruff D. Smith, *The Ideological Origins of Nazi Imperialism*, 249.

40. *Al-Hasid* (Baghdad), Nov. 4, 1937, 5.

41. *Al-Hasid* (Baghdad), Apr. 29, 1937, 62–63.

42. Ruth Ben-Ghiat, *Fascist Modernities, Italy, 1922–1945*, 126.

43. Anwar Sha'ul, "'Adhra' Ithiubia" [The Maid of Ethiopia] (1935), transcribed in *Qissat hayati fi wadi al-rafidayn* [History of My Life in Mesopotamia], 218–19.

44. Until the late 1950s, he mainly published collections of short stories and started to publish poetry only in 1956.

6. Assyrians and the Iraqi Communist Party

1. The chapter draws on British and Iraqi archival sources, personal memoirs, and oral histories pertaining to members of the Assyrian community, as well as publications of the Iraqi Communist Party. The British colonial sources provide background on communist activity within the Assyrian community from the 1930s to the 1950s. Through its relations with certain members of the Assyrian community during the mandate period, the British Foreign Office (FO) received inquiries from a number of Assyrian figures who either had been exiled by the Iraqi regime following the events of the Simele massacre—perpetuated by the nascent Iraqi army against the Assyrians in 1933—or had immigrated to Britain and its commonwealth nations. Iraqi archival sources pertain to the period following Qasim's toppling in 1963 and comprise a collection of court-martial records of Communists and their sympathizers. Memoirs and oral interviews with Assyrians affiliated with the Communist Party enable a close analysis of individuals and community members, revealing their level of organization and reasons for attraction to the ICP. Their accounts contribute to the construction of the historical memory of the community, which runs alongside, but is often in tension with, the account of the ruling authority—whether it was the British colonial administration or the Iraqi Republican regime. Similarly, publications of the ICP illustrate the party's own narrative of its history, providing a place to commemorate its persecuted members, which it identifies as martyrs. Using a

variety of complementary sources, this chapter provides a unique analysis of an underexamined period in Iraqi history.

2. For cases involving the gendered dimension, see Alda Benjamen, "Negotiating the Place of Assyrians in Modern Iraq, 1960–1988," chap. 2.

3. Orit Bashkin, *New Babylonians: A History of Jews in Modern Iraq*, 143.

4. Sa'ad Salloum's recent edited volume on Iraqi minorities includes a chapter dedicated to the Christians of Iraq, in which Ara Bedlian claims that "the identity of Iraqi Christians can be categorized on a nationalist basis (Assyrians, Chaldeans, Armenians, Syriacs)." Here Bedlian identifies Christians as belonging to four distinct nations in which the Assyrians, Chaldeans, and Syriacs occupied no linguistic, cultural, or religious commonalities. Bedlian, "Christians in Iraq: Decreased Numbers and Immigration Challenges," 60.

5. Fanar Haddad studies the effects of sectarianism within the Iraqi context, arguing that Sunnis and Shi'a "are not monolithic groups; rather they are themselves dissected by various social, economic and political categories that in themselves may unite 'Sunnis' and 'Shi'as' on the basis of, for example, class or political ideology." Haddad, *Sectarianism in Iraq: Antagonistic Visions of Unity*, 8.

6. Sargon Donabed, "Iraq and the Assyrian Unimagining: Illuminating Scaled Suffering and a Hierarchy of Genocide from Simele to Anfal," 3.

7. "Self Determination in Iraq," FO 608/96/11, Feb. 20, 1919, 26–27.

8. Aryo Makko, "The Historical Roots of Contemporary Controversies: National Revival and the Assyrian 'Concept of Unity.'"

9. Tuma Tumas, "Awraq Tuma Tumas (1)." Tumas wrote his memoir between the years 1990 and 1996. It was first published by http://www.al-nass.com in 2006.

10. Sargon Donabed, "Rethinking Nationalism and an Appellative Conundrum: Historiography and Politics in Iraq"; and Sargon Donabed and Shamiran Mako, "Ethnocultural and Religious Identity of Syrian Orthodox Christians."

11. Catholic Near East Welfare Association, "The Assyrian Church of the East."

12. Interview in Lebanon: https://www.youtube.com/watch?v=qQxnpI_nI4Q. See also Mar Bidawid's talk on unity between the Assyrian Church of the East and the Chaldean Church, probably given when the two churches convened for the international theological dialogue, either in November 1996 in Southfield, Michigan, or in August 1997 in Roselle, Illinois: https://www.youtube.com/watch?v=Y8qVJh437OA.

13. Yasmeen Hanoosh, "The Politics of Minority: Chaldeans between Iraq and America."

14. Arbella Bet-Shlimon, "Kirkuk, 1918–1968: Oil and the Politics of Identity in an Iraqi City," 144.

15. Ibid., 161.

16. Ministry of Interior, General Census Administration, Census Summary for 1957, Iraq and Iraqi Expatriates (IIE), table 6, 40–45. For information on al-Diwaniyya and

al-Nasiryyaa Provinces, see table 15A, "Residents specified according to gender, religion, and place of birth in Kirkuk city," 236–37.

17. "Assyrians: Recruitment Palestine," from the Air Vice-Marshal A. Gary, Air Headquarters, Royal Air Force, to Mr. Richmond, British Embassy in Baghdad, FO 624/144, Aug. 18, 1948, no. 720.

18. "Minutes," FO 624/144, Aug. 18, 1948, 720/4/48.

19. P. Garran, "Minutes," FO 371/52456, Aug. 1, 1946, No. E3860.

20. Marion Sluglett-Farouk and Peter Sluglett, *Iraq since 1958: From Revolution to Dictatorship*, 38–39.

21. Hanna Batatu, *The Old Social Classes and the Revolutionary Movements of Iraq: A Study of Iraq's Old Landed and Commercial Classes and of Its Communists, Ba'thists and Free Officers*, 622; A. Q., interview by the author, Toronto, July 10, 2013.

22. Tuma Tumas uses this last name in reference to Ilyas in his memoir, "Awraq Tuma Tumas (1)."

23. Ibid.

24. Batatu, *Old Social Classes*, 623–24.

25. "My dear Doctor Jamali," from British Embassy Baghdad, to Dr. Muhammad Fadhil al-Jamali, Minister for Foreign Affairs, FO 371/52456, July 20, 1946, No. 456.

26. A. Q. interview.

27. Batatu, *Old Social Classes*, 624.

28. A. Q. interview.

29. Edward Y. Odisho, "City of Kirkuk: No Historical Authenticity without Multiethnicity."

30. Batatu, *Old Social Classes*, 264. A. Q. estimates the number of killed workers at sixteen.

31. A. Q. interview.

32. Ibid.

33. Tumas, "Awraq Tuma Tumas (1)." See also "Assyrians: Recruitment Palestine," from the Air Vice-Marshal A. Gary, Air Headquarters, Royal Air Force, to Mr. Richmond, British Embassy in Baghdad, FO 624/144, Aug. 18, 1948.

34. Ilyas Hanna Guhari, who has been discussed earlier, was Tuma Tumas's paternal cousin. In a footnote Tumas reveals that Ilyas Hanna was killed following the 1963 coup after being horrendously tortured. Tumas, "Awraq Tuma Tumas (1)."

35. Ibid.

36. Ibid.

37. Ibid.

38. A rally organized by supporters of the ICP in Mosul led to a rebellion under the command of Colonel Shawwaf and involved Arab nationalist officers and conservative Arab tribes. Sluglett-Farouk and Sluglett, *Iraq since 1958*, 66–68. Farouk-Sluglett and Sluglett state that much of the violence was based on "long standing ethnic and inter-tribal

rivalries between Arabs and Kurds and between different Arab tribal factions and with the hatred of peasants for their landlords than with strictly party political patters." Ibid., 68. According to Communist leader Abu Baz, Assyrians were attacked in Mosul and the neighboring village of Telkaif, where out of six hundred Communists killed, two hundred were Assyrians. Furthermore, five hundred Assyrian families escaped Mosul and the surrounding area for other parts of the country. Abu Baz, interview by the author, Alqosh, Iraq, Dec. 18, 2011. Abu Baz's account is supported by an entry, "Martyrs of Telkaif," in an ICP publication on its martyrs Hizb al-Shuyu'i al-'Iraqi. Lajnat Matbu' Shuhada' al-Hizb, *Shuhada' al-Hizb, Shuhada' al-Watan: Shuhada' al-Hizb al-Shuyu'i al-'Iraqi, 1934–1963*, 300. The effects of the Shawwaf massacre on the Assyrian community, both in the city of Mosul and in Telkaif, confirmed the fragile position of the community and the consequences of the increased political engagement of its members and their affiliation with communism. The attacks were a result of ethnosectarian and socioeconomic factors and underlined the sense of disenfranchisement felt by Arab nationalists and traditionalists that came with the political mobilization of a newer segment of their society. This form of violence was to be repeated a few months later in Kirkuk.

39. Batatu, *Old Social Classes*, 912; Farouk-Sluglett and Sluglett, *Iraq since 1958*, 71.

40. IIE, table 6, 40–45; table 15A, "Residents specified according to gender, religion, and place of birth in Kirkuk city," 236–37.

41. Batatu, *Old Social Classes*, 914; Farouk-Sluglett and Sluglett, *Iraq since 1958*, 71.

42. Farouk-Sluglett and Sluglett, *Iraq since 1958*, 62–63.

43. P.S. to S. of S., signed K. C. MacDonald, "Confidential," AIR 19/764, May 29, 1958, No. A123817/52/Pr. III, 1–2, National Archives, Kew.

44. "Opening of an Assyrian Church in Baghdad," FO 371/141092, Apr. 27, 1959.

45. Batatu, *Old Social Classes*, 982, 985; Tareq Y. Ismael, *The Rise and Fall of the Communist Party of Iraq*, 107.

46. Batatu, *Old Social Classes*, 985–88; Ismael, *Rise and Fall*, 107.

47. Ismael, *Rise and Fall*, 108.

48. Batatu, *Old Social Classes*, 983–85; Ismael, *Rise and Fall*, 108.

49. Batatu, *Old Social Classes*, 985–88.

50. "Dear Goodchild," from R. W. Munro, British Embassy Baghdad, to D. L. N. Goodchild, Eastern Department, Foreign Office, FO 371/170509, July 11, 1963.

51. Batatu, *Old Social Classes*, 990–91; Ismael, *Rise and Fall*, 109.

52. Batatu, *Old Social Classes*, 991.

53. Iraqi National Library and Archive (INLA), 79/122.

54. "Testimony of the Accused Gharib Babajan," INLA, 79/122, Apr. 16, 1963; INLA, 72/107.

55. "Testimony of the Accused John Sahakian," INLA, 79/124, Mar. 5, 1963.

56. Ibid., 79/123.

57. Ministry of Defense, Fourth Military Court-Martial, No. 963/196, "To the Honorable Investigation Judge of Kirkuk," INLA, 78/119, Mar. 4, 1963.

58. "Testimony of the Accused Gharib Babajan," INLA, 79/121, Mar. 5, 1963.

59. "Record of Release," INLA, 79/120, Mar. 5, 1963.

60. "Case Transfers," from Muhammad 'Ali Bandar, head of the Investigation Committee in Kirkuk, to the Honorable General Military Judge for the Northern Region, INLA, 74/111, Mar. 3, 1963.

61. "Testimony of the Accused Farish John Sahakian," INLA, 72/106, Apr. 4, 1963.

62. "Testimony of the Accused Aprim Barkhu," INLA, 72/108, Apr. 16, 1963.

63. Ibid., 72/107.

64. "Criminalization Decision," issued by members of the Fourth Military Court-Martial, headed by Colonel Ahmed al-Khawja, INLA, 15/17, July 15, 1963.

65. "Auditing Body for Martial Law Cases," issued by members of the Auditing Body for Martial Law Cases, headed by Judge Ibrahim Wasfi Rafiq, INLA, 21/23, June 12, 1965.

66. "File Number: 63/196," from the General Military Judge Muhammad Nafi' Ahmed, Ministry of Defense, to the Fourth Military Court-Martial, INLA, 28/31, Dec. 12, 1964.

67. "Wireless Telegram," from Selman Prison to General Prisons, INLA, 2/2, May 2, 1965.

68. Ministry of Defense, Fourth Military Court-Martial, No. 963/196, "To the Honorable Investigation Judge of Kirkuk," INLA, 78/119, Mar. 4, 1963; "Criminalization Decision," issued by members of the Fourth Military Court-Martial, headed by Colonel Ahmed al-Khawja, INLA, 15/17, July 15, 1963.

69. A. Q. interview.

70. Al-Hizb, *Shuhada' al-Hizb, Shuhada' al-Watan*, 344.

71. Ibid., 344–46; Tumas, "Awraq Tuma Tumas (1)," 4.

7. The Struggle over Egyptianness

1. Barbara Carter, *The Copts in Egyptian Politics, 1918–1952*; Samira Bahr, *Al-Aqbat fi al-Hayat al-Siyasiyya al-Misriyya*.

2. Charles Wendell, *The Evolution of the Egyptian National Image: From Its Origins to Ahmad Lutfi al-Sayyid*, 233, 242–43, 259.

3. Israel Gershoni and James P. Jankowski, *Egypt, Islam, and the Arabs: The Search for Egyptian Nationhood, 1900–1930*, 15. He was also known for his stance against the pan-Islamism of Mustafa Kamil (1874–1908) and Arab nationalist currents (14, 18, 97).

4. Wendell, *Evolution of the Egyptian National Image*, 233; Carter, *Copts in Egyptian Politics*, 94.

5. Gershoni and Jankowski, *Egypt, Islam, and the Arabs*, 8.

6. Ibid., 131, 137 (quote), 148.

7. Ibid., 165.

8. The language fell into disuse around the eleventh century in the Delta and the fourteenth to seventeenth in Upper Egypt. The last Coptic speakers were reported from Naqada and Ziniyya villages in the eighteenth century. See Emile Ishaq, "Coptic Language, Spoken," 606a.

9. Rodolophe Kasser, "Language(s), Coptic," 148b.

10. *'Ayn Shams* 1618 AM/1901 CE: 44.

11. As for the use of the persecution by Diocletian for constructing the founding myth of the Coptic Orthodox Church, see Arietta Papaconstantinou, "Historiography, Hagiography, and the Making of the Coptic 'Church of the Martyrs' in Early Islamic Egypt." The Coptic calendar came to be called the Martyrs' Calendar around the latter half of the eighth century.

12. New Year's Day is in the festival list of the Fifth Dynasty (2494–2345 BC). See A. Spalinger, "The Limitations of Formal Ancient Egyptian Religion," 253–54.

13. Boaz Shoshan, *Popular Culture in Medieval Cairo*, 42–43.

14. Subhi 'Abd al-Malak and Nabil 'Adli, eds., *Al-Nayruz . . . 'Id Misri Qadim*, 55; Rufa'il Sami, "'Id al-Nayruz: Tarikh wa Wataniyya wa 'Aqida," 91.

15. Girgis Filuthaws 'Awad, *Al-Nayruz: Al-Khutba alqaha Girgis Filuthaws fi ihtifal jam'iyat al-tawfiq al-fara'iya fi al-Iskandariya bi-ra's sana 1612 lil-shuhada'*, 29.

16. Shoshan, *Popular Culture in Medieval Cairo*, 50–51.

17. Lama'i al-Mati'i, *Mawsu'a 100 Shakhsiyya Misriyya*, 156.

18. Nagib Kirlus al-Manqabbadi, "'Id li-Kull al-Misriyyin: 'Id al-Nayruz Ta'kid li-Huwiyyat-na wa Wahdat-na al-Wataniyya," 79–80.

19. 'Abd al-Malak and 'Adli, *Al-Nayruz*, 128.

20. Ahmad Abdel-Hamid Youssef, *From Pharaoh's Lips: Ancient Egyptian Language in the Arabic of Today*, 68–73.

21. Youhanna Nessim Youssef, "The Coptic Calendar," 451.

22. Carter, *Copts in Egyptian Politics*, 44–45.

23. Vivian Ibrahim, *The Copts of Egypt: The Challenges of Modernisation and Identity*, 101, 112.

24. Mustafa al-Barada'i and 'Adli Sharabi, "Al-Ihtifal bi-'Id al-Nayruz fi Jam'iyyat al-Tawfiq," 33.

25. Subhi Shukri, "Fi al-Ihtifal al-Kabir bi-'Id al-Nayruz," 41.

26. C. A. Bayly, "Representing Copts and Muhammadans: Empire, Nation, and Community in Egypt and India, 1880–1914."

27. Elizabeth Iskander, *Sectarian Conflict in Egypt: Coptic Media, Identity and Representation*, 32.

28. Sana S. Hasan, *Christians versus Muslims in Modern Egypt: The Century-Long Struggle for Coptic Equality*, 48, 52–53.

29. Ibid., 103–4, 209–10.

30. The website article is accompanied with some pictures of the participants. See *al-Yawm al-Sabi'* (2009).

31. *Al-Yawm al-Sabi'* (2011).

32. This festival celebrates the advent of spring, is celebrated on Monday following the Coptic Easter, and is established as a national holiday.

33. The Coptic Orthodox Church has tried to construct the ties between Coptic Christianity and Egyptianness by merging the church history to the Egyptian national history. See Sebastian Elsasser, *The Coptic Question in the Mubarak Era*, 113–21.

8. From Minority to Majority

1. A. Fischer and A. K. Irvine, "Kahtan."

2. Quoted in Mohamed Benrabah, "The Language Planning Situation in Algeria: Historical Development and Current Issues," 413.

3. Niloofar Haeri, "Form and Ideology: Arabic Sociolinguistics and Beyond."

4. Yasir Suleiman, *A War of Words: Language and Conflict in the Middle East.*

5. Reem Bassiouney, *Arabic Sociolinguistics: Topics in Diglossia, Gender, Identity, and Politics*, 211.

6. Catherine Miller, "Linguistic Policies and the Issue of Ethno-linguistic Minorities in the Middle East."

7. Enam al-Wer, "Arabic between Reality and Ideology."

8. Ahmad Abdussalam, "Human Language Rights: An Islamic Perspective."

9. Bassiouney, *Arabic Sociolinguistics*; Zeinab Ibrahim et al., eds., *Diversity in Language: Contrastive Studies in Arabic and English Theoretical Linguistics*; Aleya Rouchdy, ed., *Language Contact and Language Conflict in Arabic: Variations on a Sociolinguistic Theme*; Suleiman, *War of Words* and "Language and Political Conflict in the Middle East: A Study in Symbolic Sociolinguistics."

10. This treatment of indigenous language diversity in the MENA area confirms the language-ideological process of "erasure" proposed by Susan Gal and Judith Irvine in their seminal work on language ideology, "Language Ideology and Linguistic Differentiation."

11. Elabbas Benmamoun, "Language Identities in Morocco: A Historical Overview"; Mohamed Benrabah, "The Language Planning Situation in Algeria: Historical Development and Current Issues"; Ahmed Boukous, "La langue berbère: Maintien et changement" and "Situation sociolinguistique de l'Amazighe"; Moha Ennaji, "Language Contact, Arabization Policy and Education in Morocco," *Multilingualism, Cultural Identity, and Education in Morocco*, and "The Sociology of Berber: Change and Continuity"; and Miller, "Linguistic Policies."

12. Miller, "Linguistic Policies," 8.

13. Benrabah, "Language Planning Situation in Algeria," 430.

14. The founding of the Tunisian Society for Amazigh Culture in Matmata in April 2011 attests to the resurgence of Tunisian Amazigh identity in postrevolutionary Tunisia.

At present this organization is focused on raising awareness of the Amazigh culture—rather than the Amazigh language—in Tunisia since its membership is largely Arabic-monolingual. However, under the tutelage of Moroccan Amazigh teachers based in Zuwara in Libya, Tunisian and Libyan Amazigh speakers are being trained in Amazigh-language instruction in the hope of restoring the Amazigh language to Amazigh-identified populations in Tunisia and Libya (Khadija ben Saidane, president of the Tunisian Society for Amazigh Culture, personal communication, Nov. 2011). In this clip, Khadija ben Saidane speaks about the goals of the Tunisian Society for Amazigh Culture: http://www.youtube.com/watch?v=D6yMN6v0Va0. Prior to the January 14 Revolution, the sole exception to the scholarly neglect of the Tunisian Berber language is an excellent PhD dissertation written by Belgacem Hamza, "Berber Ethnicity and Language Shift in Tunisia."

15. Explicit recognition of Tunisia's Amazigh heritage was briefly mooted in the deliberations of the Preamble and General Principles Committee of the Tunisian Constituent Assembly. However, the idea received no traction among the members of the Preamble Committee and was never seriously pursued thereafter. Most Tunisian Amazigh speakers I spoke with do not believe that there is any contradiction between their Amazigh and Arab identities and are proud of both. The polyvalence of the Tunisian identity with respect to its Amazigh heritage is expressed by Moncef Marzouki in this interview recorded prior to his assumption of the Tunisian presidency in October 2011: http://www.youtube.com/watch?v=krxvV4zxvz8.

16. H. T. Norris, "Yemenis in the Western Sahara"; Maya Shatzmiller, "Le mythe d'origine Berbère: Aspects historiographiques et sociaux."

17. Cited in Shatzmiller, "Mythe d'origine Berbère," 147.

18. Cited in Norris, "Yemenis in the Western Sahara," 318, 320. The Touareg claim of a "Himyari" lineage would have served an important political purpose. Following Ibn Hazm (d. 1064 CE), Shatzmiller links this claim to the efforts of medieval Berber dynasties to embellish their ancestry in the context of Arab chauvinism, notably in Andalusia. See Shatzmiller, "Mythe d'origine Berbère," 149.

19. The list of scholarly works that argue for the Arab origins of the Berber is much longer; I have listed only a sample of the most recent monographs to do so.

20. Hayet ben Zayed, secondary school history teacher and Tunisian Tamazight speaker, personal communication, Nov. 2011.

21. The semantic shift in "himyari" from linguistic unintelligibility to dialectal variety within the Arabic language is mirrored by a similar shift for the Arabic term "nabati." Initially, "nabati" referred to Aramaic-speaking populations in northern Arabia (the "Nabateans") and Aramaic-speaking agriculturalists from the Iraqi Sawad; see Andrew Rippen, "Syriac in the Qur'an: Classical Muslim Theories," 253–56. However, commencing in the thirteenth century CE, "nabati" comes to be applied to the practice of colloquial Arabic poetry from the Najd (Sowayan, al-Shi'r al-nabati [London: Saqi, 2000]: 68, cited in Clive Holes and Said Abu Athera, Poetry and Politics in Contemporary

Bedouin Society, 44). Although the relationship between *"nabati"* and Aramaic has faded from common usage, an echo of its linguistic uncanniness remains in its application to colloquial Arabic "folk" poetry, held to be grammatically "incorrect" according to literary standards (ibid., 2).

22. Al-Hamdani (d. ~956 CE), who was personally familiar with spoken "himyari," viewed "himyari" as lying within the dialectal spectrum of Arabic. In his view, "himyari" indicated a suite of characteristics that influenced to various degrees the Arabic of those individuals who spoke it. See Abu Muhammad al-Hamdani, *Sifat jazirat al-ʿarab*, 277.

23. For instance, al-'Asmaʿi (d. 831 CE) reports the anecdote of a bedouin (*rajul min al-ʿarab*) who visits the court of a Himyari king. The king calls for the visitor to have a seat, using the Himyari imperative of the verb to sit: "thib!" The bedouin understands it to be an order to jump ("thib!"), from Arabic *wathaba*. The bedouin does so and hurls himself to his death. See Abu Yusuf Yaʿqub Ibn al-Sakkit, *Islah al-mantiq*, 162.

24. Ibn Sallam al-Jumahi, *Tabaqat fuhul al-shuʿara'*, 11.

25. From a linguistic standpoint, the Mahri language is not descended from the Himyari language or from any attested Old South Arabian epigraphic languages. While a number of the Old South Arabian languages clearly possessed South Semitic features, there is no evidence that Mahri is a linear descendant of any of them (Aaron Rubin, *The Mehri Language of Oman*, 8). Instead, the common South Semitic features shared by a number of the Old South Arabian languages and the Modern South Arabian languages (including Mahri) are owing to the fact that these languages retained a number of Semitic archaisms that were lost in the more innovative Central and Northern Semitic languages.

26. There are other monographs that deal with the history of the Mahra and gazetteers devoted to the geography, economy, and society of al-Mahra, yet none of them deal with the Mahri language in any systematic fashion.

27. For more on the "Arabian authenticity" of the nomadic Mahra, see http://www.youtube.com/watch?v=MQcuw08dRmM.

28. There is no historical linguistic relation whatsoever between the Berber languages and the Modern South Arabian languages beyond the fact that they all stem from the Afro-Asiatic linguistic macrofamily. Thus, the Berber languages are no more closely related to Mahri than they are to the other Semitic languages or even non-Semitic Afro-Asiatic languages such as Ancient Egyptian, Somali, or Hausa.

29. I do not possess the sole monograph dedicated to this theory: Saʿid al-Darudi's *Concerning the Arabness of the Berber* specifically addresses the Modern South Arabian origins of the Berber languages based on superficial resemblances between the Tifinagh script and characters used in epigraphic graffiti from Dhofar (http://www.alislah.org/component/k2/item/23900.html).

30. Non-Touareg often refer to the mahri camel as "the Touareg mahri" (*al-mahri al-tariqi*). ʿAbd al-Latif Belgacem, director of the Douz Sahara Museum, personal communication, Dec. 2011.

31. Ibrahim al-Kuni, *Al-Tibr*, 16 (cited in 'Ahmad Sa'd Sa'id 'Ali Muqaddam, *Safahat min tarikh al-mahra*, 238. The French term *"meìhariste"* is derived from Arabic *"mahari"* (the plural of "mahri") and was initially used to designate a member of the camel cavalry units organized by the French colonial authorities in North Africa. Nowadays, French *"meìhariste"* is used more broadly as a label for a camel rider or camel devotee. Between 1968 and 1988, the French car company Citroën manufactured an off-road utility car called "the Meìhari," named after the famed mahri camels of North Africa.

32. The only obvious difference by the mahri riding camel and the Touareg mahri is its color: the Mahra breed dark-colored riding camels, whereas the Touareg prefer light-colored mahari. However, color is quickly and easily bred into or out of a strain of camels. In fact, certain regions of southern Algeria breed dark-colored mahari. 'Abd al-Latif Belgacem, personal communication, Dec. 2011.

33. Salim al-Tariqi, *Rihla fi 'alim al-'ibl*, 181.

34. Personal communication, Dec. 2011.

35. *Al-Hakam* (1920): 76–77, 184.

36. Rajab Muhammad 'Abd al-Halim, *Al-'Azd wa-l-Mahra fi Misr* (cited in Muqaddam, *Safahat min tarikh al-mahra*, 93).

9. Tunisia's Minority Mosaic

1. Giuseppe Raffo was the eleventh child of a Genoese watchmaker. In 1825 he became *bash-kasak* (master of the Wardrobe) and was responsible for correspondence with European consuls. The king of Sardinia ennobled him in 1851, and he carried out a number of diplomatic missions in Europe. Raffo, promoted to the rank of general, was appointed in 1860 member of the Tunisian *majlis al-akbar* and died in Paris in 1862. See Ahmad ibn Abi l-Diyaf, *Ithaf ahl al zaman bi akhbar Tunis wa'Ahd al aman*, chaps. 4–5, 160.

2. Wood's eldest daughter, Farida, married into the Raffo family in 1874. Julia Clancy-Smith, *Mediterraneans: North Africa and Europe in an Age of Migration*, 361.

3. Daniela Melfa kindly photographed this sign for me in June 2012.

4. Paul Sebag, *Tunis: Histoire d'une ville*, 224, 279.

5. http://www.asmtunis.com/detail-projet2.php?projet=187.

6. Béatrice Hibou, *The Force of Obedience: The Political Economy of Repression in Tunisia*, 228–29.

7. Francesco Cavatorta and Rikke Hostrup Haugbølle, "The End of Authoritarian Rule and the Mythology of Tunisia under Ben Ali."

8. Etienne Balibar and Emmanuel Wallerstein, *Race, Nation, Class: Ambiguous Identities*, 87, 96.

9. Roland Barthes, *Mythologies*, 142.

10. Hibou, *Force of Obedience*, 220–23; Partha Chatterjee, *The Nation and Its Fragments: Colonial and Postcolonial Histories*, 73.

11. By 1970, fourteen years after independence, 90 percent of the French and Italian communities had departed from Tunis. Paul Sebag gives a total of ninety-five hundred French residents and forty-eight hundred Italian residents of Tunis. In 1970 the Tunisian Jewish population of Tunis was sixty-seven hundred, compared with nearly forty thousand in 1956. See Sebag, *Tunis: Histoire d'une ville*, 611–13.

12. Frederick Cooper, *Colonialism in Question: Theory, Knowledge, Practice*, 18.

13. See Adnen Mansar, "La personnalité nationale chez l'élite nationaliste en Tunisie et en Égypte (1956–1970)," 209.

14. Arthur Pellegrin, *Histoire de la Tunisie depuis les origines jusqu'à nos jours*, 27.

15. Mansar, "La personnalité nationale," 209.

16. Driss Abbassi, *Quand la Tunisie s'invente: Entre Orient et Occident des imaginaires politiques*, 69.

17. *Revue de l'Institut des Belles-Lettres Arabes* 159 (1987): 91–114, 98.

18. Abbassi, *Quand la Tunisie s'invente*, 64.

19. Habib Bourguiba, "Une nation homogène," *Discours*, 10, quoted in Helé Béji, *Le désenchantement national*, 43.

20. Habib Bourguiba, "Dimensions du sous-développement," *Discours* (1963), quoted in ibid., 52.

21. Béji was born in 1948 in Tunis. Her mother was French, and her father, Mundher Ben Ammar, was brother of the second wife of Habib Bourguiba. Her husband, Khaled Béji, from a family of notables in Le Kef (northwestern Tunisia), is a Paris-based lawyer and uncle of the husband of Cyrine, one of former president Ben 'Ali's daughters. (I am grateful to Ezzedine Riahi for providing these background details.) Following the publication of *Le désenchantement national: Essai sur la décolonisation* in 1982, Hélé Béji left her teaching post at the University of Tunis and worked for UNESCO. In 1998 she founded the Collège international de Tunis in her house situated in the Bab Menara quarter of Tunis, as a setting for informed and free debate.

22. Béji, *Le désenchantement national*, 15.

23. Kenneth Perkins, *A History of Modern Tunisia*, 185.

24. Ibid., 89.

25. Abdelhamid Larguèche, "L'histoire à l'épreuve du patrimoine."

26. Abbassi, *Quand la Tunisie s'invente*, 77

27. U. Haarmann, "Watan."

28. Personal observation of the author, 1995.

29. Hibou, *Force of Obedience*, 205.

30. Abbassi, *Quand la Tunisie s'invente*, 94.

31. Sarkozy affirmed on the same occasion that the Union pour la Méditerranée was "a dream which for centuries had waited for a generation capable of its realization." His Tunisian counterparts reiterated that Tunisia unfailingly supports "every initiative aimed at building solid bridges of communication, dialogue and understanding between

civilisations and religions, in a context of tolerance, moderation and mutual respect." See *Tunisie Plus* 1 (2008): 6.

32. The government of Tunisia operated an Interests Section in Israel from April 1996 until the outbreak of the Second Intifada in 2000. http://www.state.gov/r/pa/ei/bgn /5439.htm/. On the subject of relations between Tunisia and Israel, see Giovanni Sciolto, "Tunisi—Tel Aviv tra normalizzazione e antisemitismo."

33. Habib Kazdaghli, presentation of the research unit Histoire et Mémoire, Faculté des Lettres de Manouba (Université de Tunis I), Feb. 1998, http.//www.harissa.com/D _Histoire/histoireetmemoire.htm.

34. http://harissa.com/D_forum/Culture_Tune/presentation.htm.

35. Jami'at al-Adab wa-al-Funun wa-al-'Ulum al-Insaniyya, *Histoire communautaire, histoire plurielle la communauté juive de Tunisie*, 35.

36. Hibou, *Force of Obedience*, 229.

37. Jami'at al-Adab wa-al-Funun wa-al-'Ulum al-Insaniyya, *Histoire communautaire*, 35.

38. Daniel Rivet, *Le Maghreb à l'épreuve de la colonisation*, 9–14.

39. Robert Ilbert, *Alexandrie, 1830–1930*.

40. The term "international gallery" is employed by Hugh Roberts in his article "The International Gallery and the Extravasation of Factional Conflict in Algeria," in his *The Battlefield: Algeria, 1988–2002, Studies in a Broken Polity*, 219–49.

41. Will Hanley, "Grieving Cosmopolitanism in Middle East Studies," 1349. *A Summer in La Goulette* depicts conviviality between Muslims, Jews, and Christians in the coastal town of La Goulette near Tunis just before the Arab-Israeli war of 1967.

42. Sami Zubaida, "Middle Eastern Experiences of Cosmopolitanism"; Hanley, "Grieving Cosmopolitanism," 1350.

43. Ibid., 1346.

44. Barthes, *Mythologies*, 142.

45. See, for example, Abdelhamid Larguèche, *Les communautés méditerranéennes de la Tunisie*.

46. See Rodd Balek, *La Tunisie après la guerre: Problèmes politiques*. Writing under the pseudonym of "Rodd Balek," Charles Monchicourt, an experienced member of the French Contrôle Civil who had served in Tunisia since 1898, distanced himself from the terms of "Sicilian peril" and "Italian invasion," suggesting that the Italian population of Tunisia should enjoy the full benefits of French citizenship. Italian citizenship rights, guaranteed in Tunisia by the 1896 conventions, are an anachronistic Levantine survival that should be abolished. The term "Sicilian peril" was employed by Jules Saurin, *L'invasion sicilienne et le peuplement français de la Tunisie*.

47. Gaston Loth, *Le peuplement italien en Tunisie et en Algérie*, 1–2, 429, 426. Loth's source for these data was Dr. Lucien Bertholon (1854–1914), sometime army doctor, anthropologist, and member of the Carthage Institute. Bertholon describes the foreign (Italian)

element of the population as "precious auxiliaries" for the French. See Lucien Bertholon, "Assimiler ou coloniser," 525. On Bertholon, see A. Arrouas, *Livre d'Or de la Tunisie*, 33.

48. Chatterjee, *Nation and Its Fragments*, 223, 224; Yves Chatelain, *La vie littéraire et intellectuelle en Tunisie de 1900 à 1937*, 6.

49. H. Kazdaghli, "À la découverte de la littérature italienne de Tunisie."

50. Ray Cashman, "Critical Nostalgia and Material Culture in Northern Ireland," 154.

51. *Réalités* 1245 (Nov. 5–11, 2009).

52. Robert Ilbert, "De Beyrouth à Alger: La fin d'un ordre urbain." Some of these cities, notably Alexandria and Tunis, had long-established city councils (the Tunis *baladiyya* dates from 1858) with a measure of autonomy, although Alexandria's municipal council was suspended in 1926, and after 1952 the city's governor was appointed by the central government. A similar situation existed in post-1956 Tunis, with the mayor nominated by presidential decree.

53. Cooper, *Colonialism in Question*, 18.

54. Hazem Kandil, "Revolt in Egypt," 46.

55. The publications of the "Memory Project" comprise S. Finzi, ed., *Architetture italiane di Tunisia, Memorie italiane di Tunisia, Mestieri e professioni degli Italiani di Tunisia*, and *Pittori italiani di Tunisia*; M. Pendola, ed., *L'alimentazione degli Italiani di Tunisia*; and S. Finzi and D. Laguillon Hentati, eds., *Écrivains et poètes italiens de Tunisie Scrittori e poeti italiani di Tunisi*. A more general work is that of M. Pendola, *Gli italiani di Tunisia: Storia di una comunità (XIX–XX secolo)*.

56. J. Clark Kennedy, *Algeria and Tunis in 1845: An Account of a Journey Made through the Two Regencies by Viscount Fielding and Capt. Kennedy*, 2:5, 42–43. See also Leon Carl Brown, *The Tunisia of Ahmad Bey, 1837–1855*, 227.

57. Kennedy, *Algeria and Tunis*, 2:18, 50.

58. Perkins, *History of Modern Tunisia*, 44.

59. *Le Colon Français*, Nov. 7, 1912.

60. Marinette Pendola, "La réprésentation des Italiens dans la Tunisie coloniale à travers la littérature."

61. Naval Intelligence Division (Royal Navy), *Geographical Handbook Tunisia*, 149.

62. See Laura Davì, "Entre colonisateurs et colonisés: Les Italiens de Tunisie (xixe–xxe siecles)."

63. Kyle Liston, "Migrando a Sud: Coloni italiani in Tunisia, 1881–1939, by Daniela Melfa."

64. Silvia Finzi, "Il Progetto della Memoria: Obiettivi e risultati."

65. http://www.euromedcaf.org/winner.asp?lang=ing&documentID=12731.

66. http://www.italianiditunisia.com preserves memories of the Italian community, while http://www.aideinternational.com, with its tinny MP3 version of the Italian national anthem, is a site created by former Italian residents of Egypt.

67. Finzi, "Il Progetto della Memoria," 5.

68. Daniela Melfa, "De l'italianité aux Italiens de Tunisie: Identité nationale et recherche historique."

69. Cooper, *Colonialism in Question*, 64.

70. Anthony Santilli, "Un mythe historiographique au service de deux nations: Les 'Italiens' d'Égypte au xixe siècle." Details of the career of Angelo Sammarco can be found in Anthony Gorman's *Historians, State and Politics in Twentieth Century Egypt*, 14–16.

71. Armando Sanguini, *Architectures italiennes de Tunisie*. See also Finzi, "Il Progetto della Memoria."

72. Henein Bey Henein in *L'Egypte: Aperçu historique et geographique gouvernement et institutions vie economique et sociale*, edited by Yusuf Qattawi, 382, quoted by Gorman, *Historians, State and Politics*, 178.

73. Daniela Melfa and David Bond, "All Things to All Men: Postcolonial History's Many Guises," 216.

74. Armando Sanguini, preface to *Architectures italiennes de Tunisie*.

75. Albert Memmi, *The Colonizer and Colonized*, 13–15.

76. Angelo Del Boca, *Italiani, brava gente? Un mito duro a morire*.

77. Michel Péraldi, Alain Tarrius, and Geneviève Marotel, *L'Aménagement à contretemps*, 118.

78. Pierre George, *Précis de géographie urbaine*, 157–60.

79. See, for example, Jellal Abdelkafi, *La médina de Tunis*, 102.

80. Justin McGuinness and Zubeir Mouhli, *Tunis, 1800–1950*, 75. See also Myriam Bacha, "La construction patrimoniale tunisienne."

81. Bacha, "La construction patrimoniale tunisienne," 120, 118.

82. McGuinness and Mouhli, *Tunis, 1800–1950*, 37.

83. Ibid., 75.

84. For "colonial city," see Péraldi, Tarrius, and Marotel, *L'Aménagement à contretemps*, 118. McGuinness and Mouhli generally avoid the term "colonial." Prosper Ricard's *Guide Bleu: Algérie, Tunisie, Tripolitaine, Malte* refers to the "modern European city."

85. Charles Bilas and Thomas Bilanges, *Tunis: L'Orient de la modernité*, 114, 309.

86. Sémia Akrout-Yaïche, ed., *Tunis patrimoine vivant: Conservation et créativité, Association de Sauvegarde de la Médina, 1980–2012*.

87. Christopher Bayly, *The Birth of the Modern World, 1780–1914*, 183–97; Veronica Della Dora, "The Rhetoric of Nostalgia: Postcolonial Alexandria between Uncanny Memories and Global Geographies."

88. Della Dora, "Rhetoric of Nostalgia," 210.

89. Ibid.

90. "Vers le cœur de la ville: La veine de sauvegarde."

91. *Archibat* 20 (2010): 53.

92. Roderick Beaton, *Byron's War: Romantic Rebellion, Greek Revolution*, 14.

93. Lord Byron, *Childe Harold's Pilgrimage: A Romaunt*, 2:831–82, stanza added in Athens, early 1811. On "preserver l'esprit des lieux," see Akrout-Yaïche, *Tunis patrimoine vivant*, 255.

94. Personal observation of the author, May 2010.

95. Svetlana Boym, *The Future of Nostalgia*, 49; David Lowenthal, "Past Time, Present Place: Landscape and Memory," 26, quoted in Della Dora, "Rhetoric of Nostalgia," 229.

96. Alaa al-Aswany, *The Yacoubian Building*, 164.

97. Rivet, *Le Maghreb à l'épreuve*, 284–90.

98. Ennahda Electoral Programme, 2011, http://www.sapereaude.se/val2011ennah da.pdf, 7–8.

99. http://www.leaders.com.tn/article/100-juifs-100-tunisiens?id=8355.

100. Stéphanie Pouessel, "Du fantasme d'une Tunisie tolérante à la transition démocratique: La bombe de l'anti-racisme," *La Presse*, June 19, 2012, http://www.lapresse .tn/19062012/51539/la-bombe-de-lanti-racisme.html.

101. Stéphanie Pouessel, "Les marges renaissantes: Amazigh, Juif, Noir."

102. http://www.timeshighereducation.co.uk/news/habib-kazdaghli-honoured-by -scholars-at-risk/2012520.article.

103. Pierre Nora, *Realms of Memory*, xxiv.

104. Herbert Butterfield, *The Whig Interpretation of History*, 131.

10. Majority and Minority Languages in the Middle East

1. Jonathan Owens, introduction to *Arabic as a Minority Language*, 1.

2. Bernard J. Spolsky and Elana Goldberg Shohamy, *The Languages of Israel: Policy, Ideology, and Practice*, 116–17. On the majority-minority relations of Hebrew and Arabic in Israel, see Yasir Suleiman, *A War of Words: Language and Conflict in the Middle East*. See also Rafael Talmon, "Arabic as a Minority Language in Israel."

3. Owens, introduction to *Arabic as a Minority Language*, 2–6.

4. The cultural implications of English's rise and the relationship of this trend to colonialism, including settler colonialism, have been explored at length. See Alastair Pennycook, *The Cultural Politics of English as an International Language*; Robert Phillipson, *Linguistic Imperialism*; Braj B. Kachru, *The Other Tongue: English across Cultures*; and James Belich, *Replenishing the Earth: The Settler Revolution and the Rise of the Angloworld, 1783–1939*.

5. Selma K. Sonntag, *The Local Politics of Global English: Case Studies in Linguistic Globalization*, 6.

6. Hannan Hever, *Producing the Modern Hebrew Canon: Nation Building and Minority Discourse*, 31.

7. Central Zionist Archives (CZA) DD1/1915, bolded text in the original. Original in four languages: Yiddish, Hebrew, Ladino, and German.

8. Meron Benvenisti, *Sacred Landscape: The Buried History of the Holy Land since 1948*, 56.

9. Many of the earliest language battles in the Yishuv focused on creating an all-Hebrew school system to replace the collection of foreign philanthropic institutions, religious academies, and missionary schools that were educating Palestine's Jewish youth. This process got under way with the creation of the Hebrew Teachers' Federation in 1903, the formation of the Gimnasya Herzliya in 1905, and the Reali School in 1913. Following actions against the French missionary schools, the decisive move to bar European language instruction occurred at the Haifa Technikum, whose governing board had proposed teaching scientific courses in German. See Arieh Bruce Saposnik, *Becoming Hebrew: The Creation of a Jewish National Culture in Ottoman Palestine*, 213–32; Margalit Shilo, "Milhemet ha-safot ki-tenu'ah 'amamit"; Yaakov Ben-Yosef, *Milhemet ha-safot: Ha-ma'avak le-'Ivrit, 1914*; Moshe Rinott, "Capitulations: The Case of the German-Jewish Hilfsverein Schools in Palestine, 1901–1914"; and N. Tamir, *Seminaristim be-ma'avak-'am: Sipur mi-yeme milhemet ha-safot be–Eretz Yisra'el.*

10. See, for example, an article in the school bulletin from the Carmi School in Haifa, from 1929 to 1930, in which an eighth grade girl worked hard on acquiring Hebrew until "the foreignness disappeared." "Ha-Shahar," Carmi School, Haifa, 1929–1930, Aviezer Yellin Education Archives, 3.147/12.

11. Benjamin Harshav, *Language in Time of Revolution*, 91, 133.

12. Cited in *Et-Mol* 8, no. 4 (1983): 16.

13. Tzvi Elpeleg interview, July 23, 1998, Oral History Division of the Hebrew University's Institute of Contemporary Jewry 31 (240), 1.

14. Oz Almog, *The Sabra: The Creation of the New Jew*, 140.

15. Menahem Ussishkin's comments, Protocol of the General Assembly of Teachers in Zikhron Yaakov, *Sefer ha-yovel alef*, 392, cited in Nurit Reichel, "Ben 'kartanut' le-'ofke-tarbut': Mekomah shel ha-haskalah ha-kelalit ba-Hinukh ha-'Ivri be–Eretz-Yisra'el, 1882–1935," 33.

16. Izhac Epstein, "Ha-hitrakzut ha-milulit be-hora'at ha-leshonot ha-zarot, Part 1," 87.

17. Ibid., 92–93.

18. Izhac Epstein, "Ha-hitrakzut ha-milulit be-hora'at ha-leshonot ha-zarot, Part 4."

19. Y. A. Zaydman, "Morim: Avot tehiyat ha-lashon," 86.

20. Fishel Shneurson, *La-psikhologiyah shel du ha-leshoniyut ba-aretz: Hakirah be-vate ha-sefer ha-'ironiyim be–Tel Aviv bi-shenot 1936–7, 37–8*, 2–3.

21. Liora R. Halperin, *Babel in Zion: Language Politics and Jewish Nationalism in Palestine, 1920–1948.*

22. Mordecai Ben Hillel Ha-Cohen, "Eretz Yisra'el tahat shilton-ha-tzava ha-Briti."

23. M. Schiller, 1927, cited in Shoshana Sitton, "Zionist Education in an Encounter between the British Colonial and the Hebrew Cultures," 110; Klausner, "Possibilities," *Ha-Shiloah* 31 (1915): 481–86, cited in ibid., 111.

24. Report: Central Council for the Enforcement of Hebrew, Aug. 27, 1941, CZA J1/2228/7.

25. Reichel, "Ben 'kartanut' le-'ofke-tarbut'," 3.

26. Roberta Kraemer and Elite Olshtain, "The Social Context of Second Language Learning in Israeli Schools"; H. Brosh, "The Sociocultural Message of Language Textbooks: Arabic in the Israeli Setting"; Bernard Spolsky, "Conditions for Second Language Learning in Israel"; Bernard Spolsky and Elana Shohamy, *The Languages of Israel: Policy, Ideology, and Practice*; Joel Walters, "The Anglos Are Coming, the Anglos Are Coming: English Language Instruction in Israeli Schools." On Israeli language policy more generally, see Spolsky and Shohamy, *Languages of Israel*.

27. Anat Helman, "'Even the Dogs in the Street Bark in Hebrew': National Ideology and Everyday Culture in Tel-Aviv," 360.

28. Y. S., "Le-she'elat anahnu u-shekhenenu," *Hed Ha-hinukh* 1, nos. 10–12 (1927): 169.

29. Letter from Ben-Zion Dinaburg, principal of the Hebrew Teachers' College, to Yosef Azaryahu, head of the Va'ad ha-Le'umi Department of Education, Nov. 15, 1939, CZA J17/320.

30. Ha-Cohen, "Eretz Yisra'el tahat shilton-ha-tzava ha-Briti," 231.

31. J. S. Bentwich, "The Teaching of English in Hebrew Secondary Schools" (Jerusalem, May 1941), 2, CZA J17/317.

32. Bet sefer le-mishar Safra, Tel Aviv, 1940, CZA DD1/3085.

33. Bentwich, "Teaching of English," 18.

34. On Levantinism, see Gil Z. Hochberg, *In Spite of Partition: Jews, Arabs, and the Limits of Separatist Imagination, Translation/Transnation*, 44–50.

35. *Here and There in the British Empire, with Illustrations*, 2–3.

36. Partha Chatterjee writes of the "moral privilege" of the West, saying that even when anticolonial movements challenge the West's supremacy, they maintain the perception that it encompasses theories of progress: "It is the epistemic privilege which has become the last bastion of global supremacy for the cultural values of Western industrial societies." Chatterjee, *Nationalist Thought and the Colonial World: A Derivative Discourse?*, 16–17. Prasenjit Duara writes that postcolonial nations are caught in a discursive framework that denies a history to postcolonial peoples, and thus denies them the prerequisites of nationalism and of freedom. Duara, *Rescuing History from the Nation: Questioning Narratives of Modern China*.

37. H. Y. Roth, "'Al ha-kivun ha-ratzui shel limude ha-Anglit," 143.

38. Ibid., 146, 145.

39. Ibid., 146, 147.

40. Kachru, *Other Tongue*, 1.

41. Ali A. Mazrui and Alamin M. Mazrui, *The Power of Babel: Language & Governance in the African Experience*, 128–32.

42. Alastair Pennycook critiques the idea, spread often by England, that English could be simply neutral. "To view it as neutral," he continues, "is to . . . assume that the apparent international status of English raises it above local social, cultural, political, or economic concerns. To view it as beneficial is to take a rather naively optimistic position on global relations and to ignore the relationships between English and inequitable distributions and flows of wealth, resources, culture, and knowledge." Pennycook, *Cultural Politics of English*, 23–24.

43. Sonntag, *Local Politics of Global English*, 8.

44. Ibid., 114.

11. The Chaldean Church between Iraq and America

1. During a lecture delivered at the University of Regensburg, the pope quoted an unfavorable remark about Islam made by the fourteenth-century Byzantine emperor Manuel II Palaiologos. The Vatican-published English translation of the quote was "Show me just what Muhammad brought that was new and there you will find things only evil and inhuman, such as his command to spread by the sword the faith he preached." See "Lecture of the Holy Father: Faith, Reason and the University, Memories and Reflections," *Libreria Editrice Vaticana*, Sept. 12, 2006, http://w2.vatican.va/content/benedict-xvi/en/speeches/2006/september/documents/hf_ben-xvi_spe_20060912_university-regensburg.html.

2. "Pope Names 23 Cardinals from 14 Countries," *Catholic News & Herald*, Nov. 30, 2007, http://issuu.com/catholicnewsherald/docs/cnh_issue_11_30_07/9.

3. Wilhelm Baum and Dietmar W. Winkler, *The Church of the East: A Concise History*, 112, 128.

4. No exact counts exist, and the (politicized) figures available from community sources are mostly misleading for two reasons: they operate with a political agenda that benefits from promoting a numerically larger-than-real image of the Chaldean minority and because, in order to augment the size of the minority, the figures available often temporarily overlook the social and religious distinctions between Chaldeans and Assyrians in order to represent them as one unified and sizable ethnoreligious population. See, for example, http://www.aina.org/faq.html.

5. Peggy Levitt and Nina Glick Schiller, "Conceptualizing Simultaneity: A Transnational Social Field Perspective on Society," 1026.

6. See, for instance, L. Dinnerstein and D. Reimers, *Ethnic Americans: A History of Immigration*, who argue that "the decline of foreign language in churches [in the United States] was indicative of the growing Americanization and loss of ethnicity in American religion in the twentieth century" (184). The late-nineteenth-century German Catholic church slogan "Language Saves Faith" (ibid.) is also indicative of the threat of assimilation perceived by certain ethnoreligious immigrants upon settling in the United States.

7. Stuart Hall, "Ethnicity: Identity and Difference," 15.

8. Werner Sollors, *Beyond Ethnicity: Consent and Descent in American Culture*, 35.

9. Benedict Anderson, *Imagined Communities: Reflections on the Origin and Spread of Nationalism*, 6.

10. Anthony O'Mahony, "The Chaldean Catholic Church: The Politics of Church-State Relations in Modern Iraq," 436.

11. The largest and oldest settled concentration of Chaldeans outside of Iraq can be found today in Southeast Michigan, where approximately 34,000–113,000 individuals are estimated to live (Walsh College of Business and United Way for Southeastern Michigan, *Chaldean Household Survey*; Josephine Sarafa, ed., "Chaldean Americans: Past and Present"; Mary Sengstock, *Chaldeans in America*; US Census Bureau, *Census 2000*.

12. See "Iraq."

13. For a detailed account of the various Christian missions and their schools in Iraq during the twentieth century, see Suha Rassam, *Christianity in Iraq: Its Origins and Development to the Present Day*. See also Joseph MacDonnell, *Jesuits by the Tigris: Men for Others in Baghdad*, for detailed descriptions of the arrival of the American Jesuits to Iraq upon the request of the Chaldean patriarch, their systematic expulsion between 1932 and 1969, and the nationalization of their two Vatican-sponsored schools in Iraq, Baghdad College and al-Hikma University.

14. Revolution Command Council Decree No. 251 of 1972, "Elimination of Racial Discrimination," recognized the cultural rights of Syriac-speaking citizens (paras. 3, 9, 6, and 7).

15. Alda Benjamen, "Assyrians in Iraq's Nineveh Plains: Grass-Root Organizations and Inter-communal Conflict," 13.

16. I. Younan, "Les chrétiens sous le poids de l'Islam dominant: Entre peur et compromis."

17. Anthony O'Mahony, "Christianity in Modern Iraq," 129.

18. O'Mahony, "Chaldean Catholic Church," 442.

19. According to O'Mahony, between 1961 and 1995 the number of Chaldeans and Assyrians in northern Iraq dwindled from 1 million to 150,000 owing to the war of attrition between the Kurds and the Iraqi army. See O'Mahony, "Chaldean Catholic Church," 438.

20. J. M. Mérigoux, *Va à Ninive! Un dialogue avec l'Irak*, 445–75.

21. "Iraq."

22. Rassam, *Christianity in Iraq*, 172.

23. O'Mahony, "Chaldean Catholic Church," 434.

24. Ibid., 438–44.

25. *Los Angeles Times*, Jan. 15, 2015.

26. J. F. Coakley, *The Typography of Syriac: A Historical Catalogue of Printing Types, 1537–1958*, 239.

27. "The History," in *Mother of God Church, 50th Anniversary, 1948–98: Celebrating the Historical Growth of the Chaldean Community in Mother of God Parish*.

28. A separate church-associated Chaldean transnational network was forming after World War II in San Diego, California, when a group of Chaldean young men who had received their education at the hand of the American Jesuits in Iraq were invited to San Diego to teach Arabic at the Army Language School to American officers who were to be stationed in the Middle East. Their diasporic community continued to grow in relative isolation from the family chain migration–based Chaldean communities in and around Michigan.

29. *Detroit Free Press*, Mar. 1, 1981, A1.

30. *Moses*, Mar. 31, 2003.

31. *Detroit Free Press*, Mar. 1, 1981, A15.

32. *San Francisco Chronicle*, Jan. 18, 1982, 5.

33. Arianne Ishaya, *Familiar Faces in Unfamiliar Places: Assyrians in the California Heartland, 1911–2010*, 173.

34. Relations with other adjacent Middle Eastern Christian churches (especially Lebanese and Syrian) and Catholic organizations are also developed and maintained, extending the social life of the Chaldean Church outside its strictly "ethnic" relationships.

35. Walsh College of Business and United Way for Southeastern Michigan, *Chaldean Household Survey*, 1.

36. *Chaldean News*, July 2005.

37. According to a *Chaldean News* article entitled "Father, Do You Have a Minute? Priest Shortage Hits Community Hard" (July 2004), the priest-parishioner ratio in Chaldean Michigan is 1:12,000. Citing Father Manuel Boji, the article attributes this unreasonably low figure to the Chaldean community's "preoccupation with material prosperity" that drives second-generation Chaldeans away from priesthood.

38. I discuss the role of Chaldean American secular institutions and their influence on the Chaldean Church in more depth in Yasmeen Hanoosh, "Fighting Our Own Battles: Iraqi Chaldeans and the War on Terror."

39. *New York Times*, Sept. 6, 2014.

12. Permanent Temporariness in Berlin

1. Ruth Mandel, *Cosmopolitan Anxieties: Turkish Challenges to Citizenship and Belonging in Germany*; Betigül Ercan Argun, *Turkey in Germany: The Transnational Sphere of Deutschkei*; Gökce Yurdakul, *From Guest Workers into Muslims: The Transformation of Turkish Immigrant Associations in Germany*; and Haldun Gülalp and Günter Seufert, eds., *Religion, Identity and Politics: Germany and Turkey in Interaction*, to name just a few.

2. Jörn Thielmann, "Islam and Muslims in Germany: An Introductory Exploration," 3–4.

3. Klaus Bade, "Versäumte Integrationschancen und nachholende Integrationspolitik," 49–56.

4. Thilo Sarrazin, *Deutschland schafft sich ab: Wie wir unser Land aufs Spiel setzen*, 59.

5. Annika Marlen Hinze, *Turkish Berlin: Integration Policy and Urban Space*, xxii.

6. *Frankfurter Allgemeine Zeitung*, Mar. 14, 2007.

7. Bade, "Versäumte Integrationschancen," 32; Ralph Ghadban, *Die Libanon-Flüchtlinge in Berlin: Zur Integration ethnischer Minderheiten*, 1.

8. Karin Rietz, "Integrationssenatorin Bluhm über den schwierigen Weg palästinensischer Flüchtlinge in die Berliner Gesellschaft."

9. Ghadban, *Die Libanon-Flüchtlinge in Berlin*, 2.

10. Sonia Haug, Stephanie Müssig, and Anja Stichs, *Muslim Life in Germany: A Study Conducted on Behalf of the German Conference on Islam*, 65; Frank Gesemann, *Zur Integrationsforschung in Deutschland: Komparative Darstellung ausgewählter Ansätze und Methoden*, 19.

11. Bade, "Versäumte Integrationschancen," 32.

12. Peter Von Bethlenfalvy, "Migrants in an Irregular Situation in the Federal Republic of Germany: The Psycho-social Situation of Unaccompanied Minors from Areas of Armed Conflict in Berlin, West," 243.

13. Klaus Hurrelmann and Michael Zürn, eds., *Hertie-Berlin-Studie, 2009*.

14. *Daily Star*, Jan. 27 2001.

15. Ralph Ghadban, "Sind die Libanon-Flüchtlinge noch zu integrieren?", 5–6.

16. Ghadban, *Die Libanon-Flüchtlinge in Berlin*, 86–87.

17. Cited in Meho Lokman and Farah Kawtharani, "The Kurdish Community in Lebanon and Their Future Prospects."

18. Mahmood Abbas et al., "The Socio-economic Conditions of the Palestinians in Lebanon"; Ghadban, *Die Libanon-Flüchtlinge in Berlin*, 97.

19. Mohamed Kamel Dorrai, "Palestinian Emigration from Lebanon to Northern Europe: Refugees, Networks and Transnational Practices."

20. Ghadban, "Sind die Libanon-Flüchtlinge noch zu integrieren?," 4–5.

21. Dorrai, "Palestinian Emigration," 25.

22. *Die Süddeutsche Zeitung*, Aug. 10, 2005.

23. Phillip-Asmus Riecken, *Die Duldung als Verfassungsproblem Unrechtmäßiger, nicht sanktionierter Aufenthalt von Ausländern in der Bundesrepublik Deutschland*, 24–26, 37–40.

24. Lydia Morris, *Managing Migration: Civic Stratification and Migrants Rights*, 30–31.

25. Ibid., 51.

26. Ibid., 31.

27. Ibid., 38.

28. Von Bethlenfalvy, "Migrants in an Irregular Situation," 241; Ghadban, *Die Libanon-Flüchtlinge in Berlin*, 9.

29. Von Bethlenfalvy, "Migrants in an Irregular Situation," 243.

30. Ghadban, *Die Libanon-Flüchtlinge in Berlin*, 9, 10.

31. Ibid.

32. Interview with Arnold Mengelkoch, Neukölln Mayor's Office, June 16, 2011; Jürgen Fijalkowski, "Die ambivalente Funktion der Selbstorganisation ethnischer Minderheiten: Das Beispiel Berlin," 164.

33. Joachim Genge and Imke Juretzka, *Ausschluss oder Teilhabe? Rechtliche Rahmenbedingungen für Geduldete und Asylsuchende*, 29.

34. Sarrazin, *Deutschland schafft sich ab*, 296.

35. Bassam Tibi, *Islamische Zuwanderung: Die gescheiterte Integration* and *Political Islam, World Politics and Europe: Democratic Peace and Euro-Islam versus Global Jihad*.

36. Frank Gesemann, *Migration und Integration in Berlin: Wissenschaftliche Analysen und politische Perspektiven*, 20.

37. Gesemann, *Integrationsforschung in Deutschland*, 5–7.

38. Gesemann, *Migration und Integration in Berlin*, 408–14.

39. Von Bethlenfalvy, "Migrants in an Irregular Situation," 241.

40. Rex Brynen, "Imagining a Solution: Final Status Arrangements and Palestinian Refugees in Lebanon"; Susan Akram, "Palestinian Refugees and Their Legal Status: Rights, Politics and Implications for a Just Solution."

41. Rosemary Sayigh, "Palestinians in Lebanon: Harsh Present, Uncertain Future," 45.

42. Ghadban, *Die Libanon-Flüchtlinge in Berlin*, 76.

43. Von Bethlenfalvy, "Migrants in an Irregular Situation," 241.

44. Gökce Yurdakul, *From Guest Workers into Muslims: The Transformation of Turkish Immigrant Associations in Germany*; Sener Aktürk, *Regimes of Ethnicity and Nationalism in Germany, Russia, and Turkey*; Hinze, *Turkish Berlin*.

Bibliography

Archival Sources

Archives Nationales, Pierrefitte-sur-Seine, Paris (AN)
Archives of the Sacred Congregation of the Propaganda Fide, Rome (SCPF)
Aviezer Yellin Archives of Jewish Education in Israel and the Diaspora, Tel Aviv
    (AYA)
Başbakanlık Arşivi, Istanbul
Central Zionist Archives, Jerusalem (CZA)
International Council on Monuments and Sites Documentation Centre, Charen-
    ton-le-Pont (ICOMOS)
Iraqi National Library and Archive, Baghdad (INLA)
Israel State Archives, Jerusalem (ISA)
Kattan and Son business records, private collection of Jack Kattan, Amman
Latin Parish Records, Bethlehem
Ministry of Defense
National Archives, Kew (TNA)
    Air Ministry and Royal Air Force (AIR)
    Colonial Office (CO)
    Foreign Office (FO)
Oral History Division of the Hebrew University's Institute of Contemporary
    Jewry, Jerusalem

Periodicals

Agence France Press
al-Ahram Online
Archibat
Architecture Méditerranéenne
Associated Press
'Ayn Shams Hatur

Bild Online
Bloomberg News
Bulletin de l'Alliance Israélite Universelle
Al-Burhan
Cable
Catholic Herald

Catholic News Service

Chaldean News

ClickonDetroit.com

Le Colon Français

Daily News Egypt

Daily Star

Detroit Free Press

Egyptian Chronicles

Egypt Today

Et-Mol

Filastin

Frankfurter Allgemeine Zeitung

Le Gaulois

Guardian

Haaretz

Al-Hasid

Al-Hayat

Hed Ha-Hinukh

Independent

Jerusalem Post

Los Angeles Times

Al-Misbah

Misr

Al-Misri al-Yawm

New York Times

NPR News

Al-Quds al-'Arabi

Al-Ra'i

Réalités

Al-Sawt al-ahali

Spiegel TV Online

Die Süddeutsche Zeitung

Tunisie Plus

Tunis Socialiste

Al-Yawm al-Sabi'

Yedi'ot Aharonot

Zinda

Works Cited

Abbas, Mahmood, Hussein Shaaban, Bassem Sirhan, and Ali Hassan. "The Socio-economic Conditions of the Palestinians in Lebanon." *Journal of Refugee Studies* 10, no. 3 (1997): 378–96.

Abbassi, Driss. *Quand la Tunisie s'invente: Entre Orient et Occident des imaginaires politiques.* Paris: Éditions Autrement, 2009.

'Abd al-Malak, Subhi, and Nabil 'Adli, eds. *Al-Nayruz . . . 'Id Misri Qadim.* Cairo: Mu'assasa Watani lil-Tiba'a wa al-Nashr, 2007.

Abdelkafi, Jellal. *La médina de Tunis.* Tunis: Alif, 1989.

Abdussalam, Ahmad. "Human Language Rights: An Islamic Perspective." *Language Sciences* 20, no. 1 (1998): 55–62.

Achcar, Gilbert. *Les Arabes et la Shoah.* Paris: Actes Sud, 2009.

———. *The Arabs and the Holocaust: The Arab-Israeli War of Narratives.* London: al-Saqi, 2010.

Ahmad, Jamal Mohammed. *The Intellectual Origins of Egyptian Nationalism.* London: Oxford Univ. Press, 1960.

Ahonen, Pertti. "Domestic Constraints on West German Ostpolitik: The Role of the Expellee Organizations in the Adenauer Era." *Central European History* 31, no. 1 (1998): 31–63.

Akarli, Engin. *The Long Peace: Ottoman Lebanon, 1861–1920.* Berkeley: Univ. of California Press, 1993.

Akçam, Taner. *The Young Turks' Crime against Humanity: The Armenian Genocide and Ethnic Cleansing in the Ottoman Empire.* Princeton, NJ: Princeton Univ. Press, 2012.

Akram, Susan M. "Palestinian Refugees and Their Legal Status: Rights, Politics and Implications for a Just Solution." *Journal of Palestine Studies* 31, no. 3 (2002): 36–51.

Akrout-Yaïche, Sémia, ed. *Tunis patrimoine vivant: Conservation et créativité, Association de Sauvegarde de la Médina, 1980–2012.* Tunis: Association de la Médina, 2013.

Aktürk, Sener. *Regimes of Ethnicity and Nationalism in Germany, Russia, and Turkey.* Cambridge: Cambridge Univ. Press, 2012.

Alexandropoulos, Jacques, and Patrick Cabanel, eds. *La Tunisie mosaïque: Diasporas, cosmopolitismes, archéologies de l'identité.* Toulouse: Presses Univ. du Mirail, 2000.

Ali, Nadje al-, and Nicola Pratt. *What Kind of Liberation? Women and the Occupation of Iraq.* Berkeley: Univ. of California Press, 2008.

Almog, Oz. *The Sabra: The Creation of the New Jew.* Berkeley: Univ. of California Press, 2000.

Alsagoff, Syed Mohsen. *The Alsagoff Family in Malaysia: A.H. 1240 (A.D. 1824) to A.H. 1382 (A.D. 1962).* Singapore: Mun Seong Press, 1963.

Amin, Muzaffar A. "Jama'at al-Ahali: Its Origin, Ideology and Role in Iraqi Politics, 1932–1946." PhD diss., School of Oriental Studies, Durham Univ., 1980.

Anderson, Benedict. *Imagined Communities: Reflections on the Origin and Spread of Nationalism.* Rev. ed. New York: Verso, 1995.

Angelica, Edzard-Karolyi. "Opinion publique et politique exterieure." *Politique Étrangère* 48 (1983): 761–62.

Aqbat Muttahidun ibn 'Abd al-Hakam, Abu al-Qasim. *Futuh misr wa-'akhbaruha.* Edited by Charles Torrey. Leiden: Brill, 1920.

'Arbawi, Muhammad al-Mukhtar al-. *Al-Barbar: 'Arab qudama.* Tunis: Matba' Fann al-Tiba'a, 2000.

Argun, Betigül Ercan. *Turkey in Germany: The Transnational Sphere of Deutsch-kei.* New York: Routledge, 2003.

Armanios, Febe. *Coptic Christianity in Ottoman Egypt.* New York: Oxford Univ. Press, 2011.

Armstrong, Megan. "De-centring the Reformation: Franciscans and Catholic Expansionism, 1500–1700." Unpublished manuscript, 2014.

Arrouas, A. *Livre d'Or de la Tunisie.* Tunis: n.p., 1932.

Aswany, Alaa al-. *The Yacoubian Building.* Cairo: AUC Press, 2004.

'Awad, Girgis Filuthaws. *Al-Nayruz: Al-Khutba alqaha Girgis Filuthaws fi ihtifal jam'iyat al-tawfiq al-fara'iya fi al-Iskandariya bi-ra's sana 1612 lil-shuhada'.* Cairo: Matba'at al-Tawfiq, 1895.

———. "Al-Nayruz: Ra's al-Sana al-Qibtiya wa al-Ihtifal bih." *Misr,* Sept. 10, 1901.

Bacha, Myriam. "La construction patrimoniale tunisienne." In *L'Année du Maghreb* 4 (2008): 99–122.

Bade, Klaus. "Versäumte Integrationschancen und nachholende Integrations-politik." In *Nachholende Integrationspolitik und Gestaltungsperspektiven der Integrationspraxis,* edited by Klaus Bade and Hans-Georg Hiesserich, 21–95. Göttingen: V&R Unipress, 2007.

Bagnall, Roger Shaler, and Klaas Anthony Worp. *Chronological Systems of Byzantine Egypt.* 2nd ed. Leiden: Brill, 2003.

Bahr, Samira. *Al-Aqbat fi al-Hayat al-Siyasiyya al-Misriyya.* Cairo: Maktabat al-Anglu al-Misriya, 1979.

Balek, Rodd. *La Tunisie après la guerre: Problèmes politiques.* Paris: Comité de l'Afrique Française, 1920.

Balibar, Etienne, and Emmanuel Wallerstein. *Race, Nation, Class: Ambiguous Identities.* London: Verso Books, 1991

Barada'i, Mustafa al-, and 'Adli Sharabi. "Al-Ihtifal bi-'Id al-Nayruz fi Jam'iyyat al-Tawfiq." In *Al-Nayruz . . . 'Id Misri Qadim,* edited by Subhi 'Abd al-Malak and Nabil 'Adli, 33–35. Cairo: Mu'assasa Watani lil-Tiba'a wa al-Nashr, 1962.

Baranowski, Shelley. *Nazi Empire: German Colonialism and Imperialism from Bismarck to Hitler.* Cambridge: Cambridge Univ. Press, 2011.

Barkey, Karen. *Empire of Difference: The Ottomans in Comparative Perspective.* Cambridge: Cambridge Univ. Press, 2008.

Barron, J. B., ed. *Palestine: Report and General Abstracts of the Census of 1922.* Jerusalem: Government of Palestine, 1923.

Barthes, Roland. *Mythologies.* Translated by Annette Lavers. London: Jonathan Cape, 1972.

Bar-Yosef, Eitan. "Bethlehem." In *Cities of God: The Bible and Archaeology in Nineteenth-Century Britain*, edited by David Gange and Michael Ledger-Lomas. Cambridge: Cambridge Univ. Press, 2013.

———. *The Holy Land in English Culture, 1799–1917: Palestine and the Question of Orientalism*. Oxford: Clarendon Press, 2005.

Bashkin, Orit. *New Babylonians: A History of Jews in Modern Iraq*. Stanford, CA: Stanford Univ. Press, 2013.

———. *The Other Iraq: Pluralism and Culture in Hashemite Iraq*. Stanford, CA: Stanford Univ. Press, 2008.

Bassiouney, Reem. *Arabic Sociolinguistics: Topics in Diglossia, Gender, Identity, and Politics*. Washington, DC: Georgetown Univ. Press, 2009.

Batatu, Hanna. *The Old Social Classes and the Revolutionary Movements of Iraq: A Study of Iraq's Old Landed and Commercial Classes and of Its Communists, Ba'thists and Free Officers*. London: Saqi, 2004.

Baum, Wilhelm, and Dietmar W. Winkler. *The Church of the East: A Concise History*. London and New York: Routledge Curzon, 2003.

Bayd, Salim al-. *Al-'Aqalliya al-barbariyya fi Tunis*. Tunis: al-Markaz al-'Arabi li-l-Dirasat al-Siyasiyya wa-l-Ijtima'iyya, 2011.

Bayly, Christopher Alain. *The Birth of the Modern World, 1780–1914*. Oxford: Blackwell, 2004.

———. "Representing Copts and Muhammadans: Empire, Nation, and Community in Egypt and India, 1880–1914." In *Modernity and Culture from the Mediterranean to the Indian Ocean, 1890–1920*, edited by Leila Fawaz, Christopher Alain Bayly, and Robert Ilbert, 158–203. New York: Columbia Univ. Press, 2002.

Beaton, Roderick. *Byron's War: Romantic Rebellion, Greek Revolution*. Cambridge: Cambridge Univ. Press, 2013.

Bedlian, Ara. "Christians in Iraq: Decreased Numbers and Immigration Challenges." In *Minorities in Iraq: Memory, Identity and Challenges*, edited by Sa'ad Salloum. Baghdad and Beirut: Masarat, 2013.

Beinin, Joel. *The Dispersion of Egyptian Jewry: Culture, Politics and the Formation of a Modern Diaspora*. Berkeley: Univ. of California Press, 1998.

———. "Lives of Struggle and Commitment of Social Justice." *Chronicles* 2, no. 1 (2006): 39–41.

Béji, Helé. *Le désenchantement national*. Paris: Maspero, 1982.

Belich, James. *Replenishing the Earth: The Settler Revolution and the Rise of the Angloworld, 1783–1939*. Oxford: Oxford Univ. Press, 2009.

Ben-Dor, Gabriel. "Minorities in the Middle East: Theory and Practice." In *Minorities and the State in the Arab World*, edited by Ofra Bengio and Gabriel Ben-Dor. Boulder, CO: Lynne Riener, 1999.

Ben-Ghiat, Ruth. *Fascist Modernities: Italy, 1922–1945*. Berkeley: Univ. of California Press, 2001.

Benjamen, Alda. "Assyrians in Iraq's Nineveh Plains: Grass-Root Organizations and Inter-communal Conflict." *TAARII Newsletter* (2011): 13–20.

———. "Negotiating the Place of Assyrians in Modern Iraq, 1960–1988." PhD diss., Univ. of Maryland, 2015.

Benmamoun, Elabbas. "Language Identities in Morocco: A Historical Overview." *Studies in the Linguistic Sciences* 30, no. 1 (2001): 95–106.

Benrabah, Mohamed. "The Language Planning Situation in Algeria: Historical Development and Current Issues." *Language Policy* 6, no. 2 (2007): 379–502.

Benvenisti, Meron. *Sacred Landscape: The Buried History of the Holy Land since 1948*. Berkeley: Univ. of California Press, 2000.

Ben-Yosef, Yaakov. *Milhemet ha-safot: Ha-ma'avak le-'Ivrit, 1914*. Tel Aviv: Otsar ha-moreh, hotsa'at ha-sefarim shel Histadrut ha-morim be-Yisra'el, 1984.

Berque, Jacques. *Le Maghreb entre deux guerres*. Paris: Le Seuil, 1962.

Bertholon, Lucien. "Assimiler ou coloniser." *Bulletins et Mémoires de la Société d'Anthropologie de Paris* 6 (1897): 509–36.

Bet-Shlimon, Arbella. "Kirkuk, 1918–1968: Oil and the Politics of Identity in an Iraqi City." PhD diss., Harvard Univ., 2012.

Beydoun, Ahmad. *La dégénérescence du Liban ou la réforme orpheline*. Paris: Sindbad, 2009.

Bilas, Charles, and Thomas Bilanges. *Tunis: L'Orient de la modernité*. Paris: Éditions de l'éclat, 2010.

Bloxham, Donald. *The Great Game of Genocide: Imperialism, Nationalism, and the Destruction of the Ottoman Armenians*. Oxford: Oxford Univ. Press, 2005.

Boogert, Maurits van den. "Millets Past and Present." In *Religious Minorities in the Middle East: Domination, Self-Empowerment, Accommodation*, edited by Anh Nga Longva and Anne Sofie Roald, 27–46. Leiden: Brill, 2012.

Boukous, Ahmed. "La langue berbère: Maintien et changement." *International Journal of the Sociology of Language* (Sociolinguistics in Morocco) 112 (1995): 9–28.

———. "Situation sociolinguistique de l'Amazighe." *International Journal of the Sociology of Language* (Berber Sociolinguistics) 123 (1997): 41–60.

Boym, Svetlana. *The Future of Nostalgia*. New York: Basic Books, 2001.

Braude, Benjamin. "Foundation Myths of the Millet System." In *Christians and Jews in the Ottoman Empire: The Functioning of a Plural Society*, edited by Benjamin Braude and Bernard Lewis, 1:69–88. New York: Holmes and Meier, 1982.

———. "The Strange History of the Millet System." In *The Great Ottoman-Turkish Civilisation*, edited by Kemal Çiçek, 2:409–18. Ankara: Yeni Turkiye, 2000.

Brosh, H. "The Sociocultural Message of Language Textbooks: Arabic in the Israeli Setting." *Foreign Language Annals* 30, no. 3 (1997): 311–26.

Brown, Leon Carl. *The Tunisia of Ahmad Bey, 1837–1855*. Princeton, NJ: Princeton Univ. Press, 1974.

Brynen, Rex. "Imagining a Solution: Final Status Arrangements and Palestinian Refugees in Lebanon." *Journal of Palestine Studies* 26, no. 2 (1997): 42–58.

Burke, Edmund, and Nejde Yaghoubian, eds. *Struggle and Survival in the Modern Middle East*. Berkeley: Univ. of California Press, 1993.

Butterfield, Herbert. *The Whig Interpretation of History*. New York: W. W. Norton, 1956.

Carter, Barbara Lynn. *The Copts in Egyptian Politics, 1918–1952*. Kent: Croom Helm, 1986.

Cashman, Ray. "Critical Nostalgia and Material Culture in Northern Ireland." *Journal of American Folklore* 119, no. 472 (2006): 137–60.

Catholic Near East Welfare Association. "The Assyrian Church of the East." http://www.cnewa.org/default.aspx?ID=1&pagetypeID=9&sitecode=HQ&pageno=3.

Cavatorta, Francesco, and Rikke Hostrup Haugbølle. "The End of Authoritarian Rule and the Mythology of Tunisia under Ben Ali." *Mediterranean Politics* 17, no. 2 (2012): 179–95.

Chalabi, Tamar. *The Shi'is of Jabal 'Amil and the New Lebanon: Community and Nation State, 1918–1943*. London: Palgrave Macmillan, 2006.

Chatelain, Yves. *La vie littéraire et intellectuelle en Tunisie de 1900 à 1937*. Paris: Geuthner, 1937.

Chatterjee, Partha. *Nationalist Thought and the Colonial World: A Derivative Discourse?* London: Zed Books for the United Nations Univ., 1986.

———. *The Nation and Its Fragments: Colonial and Postcolonial Histories*. Princeton, NJ: Princeton Univ. Press, 1993.

Chatty, Dawn. *Displacement and Dispossession in the Modern Middle East*. New York: Cambridge Univ. Press, 2010.

Clancy-Smith, Julia. *Mediterraneans: North Africa and Europe in an Age of Migration.* Berkeley: Univ. of California Press, 2011.

Clarence-Smith, William Gervase. "Middle Eastern Migrants in the Philippines: Entrepreneurs and Cultural Brokers." *Asian Journal of Social Science* 32, no. 3 (2004): 436–37.

Clark, Bruce. *Twice a Stranger: How Mass Expulsion Forged Modern Greece and Turkey.* London: Granta, 2006.

Coakley, J. F. *The Church of the East and the Church of England: A History of the Archbishop of Canterbury's Assyrian Mission.* Oxford: Clarendon Press, 1992.

———. *The Typography of Syriac: A Historical Catalogue of Printing Types, 1537–1958.* New Castle, DE: Oak Knoll, 2006.

Cole, Juan. "Iraq in 1939: British Alliance or Nationalist Neutrality toward the Axis?" *Britain and the World* 5, no. 2 (2012): 204–22.

Coller, Ian. *Arab France: Islam and the Making of Modern Europe, 1798–1831.* Berkeley: Univ. of California Press, 2010.

Conder, C. R. *The Future of Palestine: A Lecture Delivered for the Palestine Exploration Fund.* London: Palestine Exploration Fund, 1892.

Cooper, Frederick. *Colonialism in Question: Theory, Knowledge, Practice.* Berkeley: Univ. of California Press, 2005.

Coury, Ralph M. "The Politics of the Funereal: The Tomb of Saad Zaghlul." *Journal of the American Research Center in Egypt* 29 (1992): 191–200.

Dallenbach, Lucien. *Mosaïques: Un objet esthétique à rebondissements.* Paris: Le Seuil, 2001.

Daly, Okasha el-. *Egyptology, the Missing Millennium: Ancient Egypt in Medieval Arabic Writings.* London: UCL Press, 2005.

Darudi, Sa'id al-. *Hawl 'urubat al-barbar.* Casablanca: Manshurat Fikr, 2012.

Davì, Laura. "Entre colonisateurs et colonisés: Les Italiens de Tunisie (xixe–xxe siecles)." In *La Tunisie mosaïque: Diasporas, cosmopolitismes, archéologies de l'identité,* edited by Jacques Alexandropoulos and Patrick Cabanel, 99–115. Toulouse: Presses Univ. du Mirail, 2000.

Del Boca, Angelo. *Italiani, brava gente? Un mito duro a morire.* Vicenza: Neri Pozza Editore, 2005.

Della Dora, Veronica. "The Rhetoric of Nostalgia: Postcolonial Alexandria between Uncanny Memories and Global Geographies." *Cultural Geographies* 13 (2006): 207–38.

Dennis, Brad R. "Explaining Coexistence and Conflict in Eastern Anatolia, 1870–1878." PhD thesis, Univ. of Utah, 2015.

Dijkstra, J. H. F. *Philae and the End of Ancient Egyptian Religion: A Regional Study of Religious Transformation (298–642 CE)*. Leuven: Peeters, 2008.

Dinnerstein, L., and D. Reimers. *Ethnic Americans: A History of Immigration.* New York: Columbia Univ. Press, 1999.

Donabed, Sargon. "Iraq and the Assyrian Unimagining: Illuminating Scaled Suffering and a Hierarchy of Genocide from Simele to Anfal." PhD diss., Univ. of Toronto, 2010.

———. "Rethinking Nationalism and an Appellative Conundrum: Historiography and Politics in Iraq." *National Identities* 14, no. 2 (2012): 115–38.

Donabed, Sargon, and Shamiran Mako. "Ethno-cultural and Religious Identity of Syrian Orthodox Christians." *Chronos* (Sept. 1, 2009): 77–82.

Donzelot, Jacques. *The Policing of Families*. New York: Pantheon Books, 1979.

Doorn-Harder, Pieternella van, and Kari Vogt. *Between Desert and City: The Coptic Orthodox Church Today.* Oslo: Novus Forlag, 1997.

Dorrai, Mohamed Kamel. "Palestinian Emigration from Lebanon to Northern Europe: Refugees, Networks and Transnational Practices." *Refuge* 21, no. 3 (2003): 23–31.

Duara, Prasenjit. *Rescuing History from the Nation: Questioning Narratives of Modern China.* Chicago: Univ. of Chicago Press, 1995.

Dupont, Anne-Laure, and Catherine Mayeur-Jaouen. "Monde nouveau, voix nouvelles: États, sociétés, islam dans l'entre-deux-guerres." In *Débats intellectuels au Moyen-Orient dans l'entre-deux-guerres*, edited by Anne-Laure Dupont et Catherine Mayeur-Jaouen. Aix-en-Provence: Edisud, 2002.

Efrati, Noga. "Competing Narratives: Histories of the Women's Movement in Iraq, 1910–58." *International Journal of Middle Eastern Studies* 40, no. 3 (2008): 445–66.

———. "The Other 'Awakening' in Iraq: The Women's Movement in the First Half of the Twentieth Century." *British Journal of Middle Eastern Studies* 2 (2004): 153–73.

Eisenberg, Laura Zittrain. *My Enemy's Enemy: Lebanon in the Early Zionist Imagination, 1900–1948.* Detroit: Wayne State Univ. Press, 1994.

Eisenman, Robert H. *Islamic Law in Palestine and Israel: A History of the Survival of Tanzimat and Shar'ia in the British Mandate and the Jewish State.* Leiden: Brill, 1978.

Ellis, N. *Feasts of Light: Celebrations for the Seasons of Life Based on the Egyptian Goddess Mysteries*. Wheaton, IL: Theosophical Publishing House, 1999.

Elsasser, Sebastian. *The Coptic Question in the Mubarak Era*. New York: Oxford Univ. Press, 2014.

Ende, Werner. "Iraq in World War I: The Turks, the Germans and the Shi'ite Mujtahids' Call for Jihad." In *Proceedings of the Ninth Congress of the Union Européenne des Arabisants et Islamisants, Amsterdam, 1978*, edited by Rudolph Peters, 57–71. Leiden: Brill, 1981.

Ennaji, Moha. "Language Contact, Arabization Policy and Education in Morocco." In *Language Contact and Language Conflict in Arabic: Variations on a Sociolinguistic Theme*, edited by Aleya Rouchdy, 70–88. London: Routledge Curzon, 2002.

———. *Multilingualism, Cultural Identity, and Education in Morocco*. New York: Springer Science and Business Media, 2005.

———. "The Sociology of Berber: Change and Continuity." *International Journal of the Sociology of Language* 123 (1997): 23–40.

Epstein, Izhac. "Ha-hitrakzut ha-milulit be-hora'at ha-leshonot ha-zarot, Part 1." *Ha-Hinukh* 1, no. 2 (1911): 85–94.

———. "Ha-hitrakzut ha-milulit be-hora'at ha-leshonot ha-zarot, Part 4." *Ha-Hinukh* 1, no. 3 (1911): 168–74.

Fawaz, Leila Tarazi. *An Occasion for War: Civil Conflict in Lebanon and Damascus in 1860*. Berkeley: Univ. of California Press, 1994.

Fijalkowski, Jürgen. "Die ambivalente Funktion der Selbstorganisation ethnischer Minderheiten: Das Beispiel Berlin." In *Migration und Integration in Berlin: Wissenschaftliche Ergebnisse und Politische Perspektiven*, edited by Frank Gesemann, 163–83. Opladen: Leske & Budrich, 2001.

Fink, Carole. "Minority Rights as an International Question." *Contemporary European History* 9, no. 3 (2000): 385–400.

Finzi, S., ed. *Architetture italiane di Tunisia*. Tunis: Finzi, 2002.

———, ed. *Memorie italiane di Tunisia*. Tunis: Finzi, 2000.

———, ed. *Mestieri e professioni degli Italiani di Tunisia*. Tunis: Finzi, 2003.

———, ed. *Pittori italiani di Tunisia*. Tunis: Finzi, 2000.

———. "Il Progetto della Memoria: Obiettivi e risultati." *Polo Sud: Semestrale di studi\storici* 4, no. 1 (2014): 1–5.

Finzi, S., and D. Laguillon Hentati, eds. *Écrivains et poètes italiens de Tunisie Scrittori e poeti italiani di Tunisi*. Tunis: Finzi, 2009.

Firro, Kais. *Inventing Lebanon: Nationalism and the State under the Mandate.* London: Tauris, 2003.

――――. "Nationalism and Confessionalism: Shi'is, Druzes and Alawis in Syria and Lebanon." In *Religious Minorities in the Middle East: Domination, Self-Empowerment, Accommodation*, edited by Anh Nga Longva and Anne Sofie Roald, 245–65. Leiden: Brill, 2012.

Fischer, A., and A. K. Irvine. "Kahtan." In *Encyclopaedia of Islam*, edited by P. Bearman, Th. Bianquis, C. E. Bosworth, E. van Donzel, and W. P. Heinrichs. 2nd ed. Leiden: Brill Online, 2015.

Forsdick, Charles. *Travel in Twentieth-Century French and Francophone Cultures: The Persistence of Diversity.* Oxford: Oxford Univ. Press, 2005.

Freitag, Ulrike. *Indian Ocean Migrants and State Formation in Hadhramaut: Reforming the Homeland.* Leiden: Brill, 2003.

Freitag, Ulrike, and Israel Gershoni. "The Politics of Memory: The Necessity for Historical Investigation into Arab Responses to Fascism and Nazism." *Geschichte und Gesellschaft* 37, no. 3 (2011): 311–31.

Gal, Susan, and Judith Irvine. "Language Ideology and Linguistic Differentiation." In *Regimes of Language: Ideologies, Polities and Identities*, edited by Paul Kroskrity, 35–83. Santa Fe, NM: School of American Research Press, 1999.

Ganim, As'ad. *The Palestinian-Arab Minority in Israel, 1948–2000: A Political Study.* Albany: SUNY Press, 2001.

Genge, Joachim, and Imke Juretzka. *Ausschluss oder Teilhabe? Rechtliche Rahmenbedingungen für Geduldete und Asylsuchende.* Berlin: Der Beauftragte für Integration und Migration, 2009.

George, Pierre. *Précis de géographie urbaine.* Paris: PUF, 1961.

Gershoni, Israel. "Rethinking the Formation of Arab Nationalism in the Middle East, 1920–1945." In *Rethinking Nationalism in the Arab Middle East*, edited by Israel Gershoni and James Jankowski, 3–25. New York: Columbia Univ. Press, 1997.

Gershoni, Israel, and James P. Jankowski. *Egypt, Islam, and the Arabs: The Search for Egyptian Nationhood, 1900–1930.* New York: Oxford Univ. Press, 1986.

Gershoni, Israel, and Amy Singer. "Introduction." *Comparative Studies of South Asia, Africa and the Middle East* 28, no. 3 (2008): 383–89.

Gesemann, Frank. *Zur Integrationsforschung in Deutschland: Komparative Darstellung ausgewählter Ansätze und Methoden.* Berlin: Friedrich-Ebert-Stiftung, 2010. http://library.fes.de/pdf-files/akademie/berlin/07711.pdf.

————. *Migration und Integration in Berlin: Wissenschaftliche Analysen und politische Perspektiven*. Opladen: Leske + Budrich, 2001.

Ghadban, Ralph. *Die Libanon-Flüchtlinge in Berlin: Zur Integration ethnischer Minderheiten*. Berlin: Das Arabische Buch, 2000.

————. "Sind die Libanon-Flüchtlinge noch zu integrieren?" Lecture notes, Feb. 26, 2008. http://www.ghadban.de/de/wp-content/data/die-libanon-flucht linge2.pdf.

Ghar, Muhammad Abu al-. *Yahud misr: Min al-izdihar ila al-shatat*. Cairo: Dar al-Hilal, 2004.

Ginzburg, Carlo. *The Cheese and the Worms*. Translated by John Tedeschi and Anne Tedeschi. Baltimore: Johns Hopkins Univ. Press, 1992.

Gorman, Anthony. *Historians, State and Politics in Twentieth Century Egypt*. London: Routledge Curzon, 2003.

Greenberg, Ela. *Preparing the Mothers of Tomorrow: Education and Islam in Mandate Palestine*. Austin: Univ. of Texas Press, 2012.

Greene, Molly. *Catholic Pirates and Greek Merchants: A Maritime History of the Mediterranean*. Princeton, NJ: Princeton Univ. Press, 2010.

Gualtieri, Sarah. *Between Arab and White: Race and Ethnicity in the Early Syrian American Diaspora*. Berkeley: Univ. of California Press, 2009.

Guirguis, Laure. *Les copts d'Egypte: Violences communautaires*. Paris: Karthala, 2012.

Gülalp, Haldun, and Günter Seufert, eds. *Religion, Identity and Politics: Germany and Turkey in Interaction*. New York: Routledge, 2013.

Haarmann, U. "Watan." In *Encyclopaedia of Islam*. Leiden: Brill Online, 2012. http://referenceworks.brillonline.com.proxy.lib.ohio-state.edu/entries/en cyclopaedia-of-islam-2/watan-SIM_7891.

Habermas, Jürgen. *The Structural Transformation of the Public Sphere: An Inquiry into a Category of Bourgeois Society*. Cambridge, MA: MIT Press, 1991.

Ha-Cohen, Mordecai Ben Hillel. "Eretz Yisra'el tahat shilton-ha-tzava ha-Briti." *Ha-Shiloah* 41 (1923–24): 231.

Haddad, Fanar. *Sectarianism in Iraq: Antagonistic Visions of Unity*. New York: Columbia Univ. Press, 2011.

Haeri, Niloofar. "Form and Ideology: Arabic Sociolinguistics and Beyond." *Annual Review of Anthropology* 29 (2000): 61–87.

Hafiz, ʿAli Muhsin al-. *Min lahajat "Mahra" wa-ʾadabiha*. Musqat: Majallat al-Nahda al-ʿUmaniyya, 1987.

Haiduc-Dale, Noah. *Arab Christians in British Mandate Palestine: Communalism and Nationalism, 1917–1948*. Edinburgh: Edinburgh Univ. Press, 2013.

Hall, Stuart. "Ethnicity: Identity and Difference." *Radical America* 23, no. 4 (1991): 9–20.

Halm, Heinz. *Shi'ism*. Translated by Janet Watson and Marian Hill. Edinburgh: Edinburgh Univ. Press, 2004.

Halperin, Liora R. *Babel in Zion: Language Politics and Jewish Nationalism in Palestine, 1920–1948*. New Haven, CT: Yale Univ. Press, 2015.

Hamdani, Abu Muhammad al-. *Sifat jazirat al-'arab*. Edited by Muhammad al-'Akwa'. Riyadh: Dar al-Yamama li-l-Bahth wa-l-Tarjama wa-l-Nashr, 1974.

Hamza, Belgacem. "Berber Ethnicity and Language Shift in Tunisia." PhD diss., Univ. of Sussex, 2007.

Hamzah, Dyala, ed. *The Making of the Arab Intellectual: Empire, Public Sphere and the Colonial Coordinates of Selfhood*. London: Routledge, 2013.

Hanioğlu, M. Şükrü. "The Young Turks and the Arabs before the Revolution of 1908." In *The Origins of Arab Nationalism*, edited by Rashid Khalidi, 35–38. New York: Columbia Univ. Press, 1991.

Hanley, Will. "Grieving Cosmopolitanism in Middle East Studies." *History Compass* 6 (2008): 1346–67.

Hanna, Nelly. *Making Big Money in 1600: The Life and Times of Isma'il Abu Taqiyya, Egyptian Merchant*. Syracuse, NY: Syracuse Univ. Press, 1998.

Hanoosh, Yasmeen. "Fighting Our Own Battles: Iraqi Chaldeans and the War on Terror." In *Arab Detroit 9/11: Life in the Terror Decade*, edited by N. Abraham, A. Shryock, and S. Howell, 126–50. Detroit: Wayne State Univ. Press, 2011.

———. "The Politics of Minority: Chaldeans between Iraq and America." PhD diss., Univ. of Michigan, 2008.

Harshav, Benjamin. *Language in Time of Revolution*. Stanford, CA: Stanford Univ. Press, 1999.

Hart, D. M. "The Berber Dahir of 1930 in Colonial Morocco: Then and Now (1930–1996)." *Journal of North African Studies* 2, no. 2 (1997): 11–33.

Harun, Shihata. *Yahudi fi al-qahira*. Cairo: Dar al-Thaqafa al-Haditha, 1987.

Hassan, Sana S. *Christians versus Muslims in Modern Egypt: The Century-Long Struggle for Coptic Equality*. New York: Oxford Univ. Press, 2003.

Hassoun, Jacques, ed. *Histoire des Juifs du Nile*. Paris: Minerve, 1990.

Haug, Sonia, Stephanie Müssig, and Anja Stichs. *Muslim Life in Germany: A Study Conducted on Behalf of the German Conference on Islam*. Nuremberg: Federal Office for Migration and Refugees, 2009.

Helman, Anat. "'Even the Dogs in the Street Bark in Hebrew': National Ideology and Everyday Culture in Tel-Aviv." *Jewish Quarterly Review*, n.s., 92, nos. 3–4 (2002): 359–82.

Here and There in the British Empire, with Illustrations. London: Macmillan, 1902.

Hever, Hannan. *Producing the Modern Hebrew Canon: Nation Building and Minority Discourse*. New York: New York Univ. Press, 2002.

Heyberger, Bernard. *Les Chrétiens du Proche-Orient au temps de la Réforme Catholique*. Rome: École Française de Rome, 1994.

Hibou, Béatrice. *The Force of Obedience: The Political Economy of Repression in Tunisia*. Cambridge: Polity Press, 2011.

Hinze, Annika Marlen. *Turkish Berlin: Integration Policy and Urban Space*. Minneapolis: Univ. of Minnesota Press, 2013.

Hirschon, Renée. *Heirs of the Greek Catastrophe: The Social Life of Asia Minor Refugees in Piraeus*. 2nd ed. Oxford and New York: Berghahn Books, 1998.

Hizb, Lajnat Matbu' Shuhada' al-. *Shuhada' al-Hizb, Shuhada' al-Watan: Shuhada' al-Hizb al-Shuyu'i al-'Iraqi, 1934–1963*. 2nd ed. [Beirut?]: Hizb al-Shuyu'i al-'Iraqi, 2008.

Hoblos, Farouk. "Public Services and Tax Revenues in Ottoman Tripoli (1516–1918)." In *Syria and Bilad al-Sham under Ottoman Rule: Essays in Honour of Abdul-Karim Rafeq*, edited by Peter Sluglett and Stefan Weber, 115–36. Leiden: Brill, 2010.

Hochberg, Gil Z. *In Spite of Partition: Jews, Arabs, and the Limits of Separatist Imagination, Translation/Transnation*. Princeton, NJ: Princeton Univ. Press, 2007.

Holes, Clive, and Said Abu Athera. *Poetry and Politics in Contemporary Bedouin Society*. Reading, PA: Ithaca Press, 2009.

Hopwood, Derek. *The Russian Presence in Syria and Palestine, 1843–1914: Church and Politics in the Near East*. Oxford: Clarendon Press, 1969.

Hourani, Albert. *Minorities in the Arab World*. London: Oxford Univ. Press, 1947.

Hurrelmann, Klaus, and Michael Zürn, eds. *Hertie-Berlin-Studie, 2009*. Hamburg: Hoffmann und Campe Verlag, 2009.

Husri, Sati' al-. *Mudhakkirati fi al-'Iraq (1927–1924)* [My Memoirs in Iraq (1927–1941)]. Vol. 2. Beyrouth: Dar al-tali'a, 1968.

Ibn Abi l-Diyaf, Ahmad. *Ithaf ahl al zaman bi akhbar Tunis wa'Ahd al aman.* Edited by André Raymond. Vol. 2. Tunis: IRMC-ISHMN, 1994.

Ibn Khaldun, Abu Zayd 'Abd al-Rahman. *The Muqaddimah: An Introduction to History.* Translated by Franz Rosenthal. 3 vols. Princeton, NJ: Princeton Univ. Press, 1958.

Ibn al-Mujawir, Jamal al-Din. *Sifat bilad al-yaman al-musamma bi-ta'rikh al-mustabsir.* Edited by Oscar Löfgren. Beirut: Dar al-Tanwir li-l-Tiba'a wa-l-Nashr, 1986.

Ibn al-Sakkit, Abu Yusuf Ya'qub. *Islah al-mantiq.* 3rd ed. Cairo: Dar al-Ma'arif, n.d.

Ibrahim, Vivian. *The Copts of Egypt: The Challenges of Modernisation and Identity.* New York: I. B. Tauris, 2011.

Ibrahim, Zeinab, et al., eds. *Diversity in Language: Contrastive Studies in Arabic and English Theoretical Linguistics.* Cairo: American Univ. in Cairo Press, 2000.

Idrisi, Abu 'Abdallah al-. *Nuzhat al-mushtaq fi iftiraq al-afaq.* Edited by Fuat Sezgin. Leiden: E. J. Brill, 1970.

Ilbert, Robert. *Alexandrie, 1830–1930.* Cairo: IFAO, 1996.

———. "De Beyrouth à Alger: La fin d'un ordre urbain." *Vingtième Siècle Revue d'histoire* 32 (1991): 15–24.

"Iraq." *Proche-Orient Chrétien* 39 (1989): 346–48.

Ishaq, Emile Maher. "Coptic Language, Spoken." In *The Coptic Encyclopedia,* edited by Aziz S. Atiya, 2:604a–607a. New York: Macmillan, 1991.

Ishaya, Arianne. "Assyrian-Americans: A Study in Ethnic Reconstruction and Dissolution in Diaspora." *Nineveh Online,* n.d. http://www.nineveh.com/ASSYRIAN-AMERICANS.html#_ftn1

———. *Familiar Faces in Unfamiliar Places: Assyrians in the California Heartland, 1911–2010.* Bloomington, IN: Xlibris, 2010.

Iskander, Elizabeth. *Sectarian Conflict in Egypt: Coptic Media, Identity and Representation.* New York: Routledge, 2012.

Ismael, Tareq Y. *The Rise and Fall of the Communist Party of Iraq.* Cambridge: Cambridge Univ. Press, 2012.

Issawi, Charles. "The Transformation of the Economic Position of the Millets in the Nineteenth Century." In *Christians and Jews in the Ottoman Empire,* edited by Benjamin Braude and Bernard Lewis, 1:261–85. New York: Holmes and Meier, 1982.

Istakhri, Abu 'Ishaq al-. *Kitab masalik al-mamalik*. Edited by Fuat Sezgin. Frankfurt: Institute for the History of Arabic-Islamic Science, 1992.

Jami'at al-Adab wa-al-Funun wa-al-'Ulum al-Insaniyya. *Histoire communautaire, histoire plurielle la communauté juive de Tunisie*. Tunis: Centre de Publication Univ., 1999.

Joseph, John. *Muslim-Christian Relations and Inter-Christian Rivalries in the Middle East: The Case of the Jacobites in an Age of Transition*. Albany: SUNY Press, 1983.

Jumahi, Ibn Sallam al-. *Tabaqat fuhul al-shu'ara'*. Edited by Mahmud Shakir. Cairo: Dar al-Ma'arif, 1974.

Kachru, Braj B. *The Other Tongue: English across Cultures*. Second ed., *English in the Global Context*. Urbana: Univ. of Illinois Press, 1992.

Kandil, Hazem. "Revolt in Egypt." *New Left Review* 68 (2011): 17–55.

Karpat, Kemal H. *Ottoman Population, 1830–1914: Demographic and Social Characteristics*. Madison: Univ. of Wisconsin Press, 1985.

Kasser, Rodolphe. "Language(s), Coptic." In *The Coptic Encyclopedia*, edited by Aziz S. Atiya, 8:A145a–151b. New York: Macmillan, 1991.

Katz, I., and R. Kark. "The Greek Orthodox Patriarchate of Jerusalem and Its Congregation: Dissent over Real Estate." *International Journal of Middle East Studies* 37 (2005): 509–34.

Kaufman, Asher. *Reviving Phoenicia: The Search for Identity in Lebanon*. London: I. B. Tauris, 2004.

Kazdaghli, Habib. "À la découverte de la littérature italienne de Tunisie." *Attariq Aljadid*, Feb. 7, 2009.

———. "Histoire et mémoire." Public presentation, Univ. of Tunis, 1998. http://www.harissa.com/D_Histoire/histoireetmemoire.htm.

Kedourie, Elie. "The Jews of Baghdad in 1910." *Middle Eastern Studies* 7, no. 3 (1971): 355–61.

Kennedy, J. Clark. *Algeria and Tunis in 1845: An Account of a Journey Made through the Two Regencies by Viscount Feilding and Capt. Kennedy*. London: Henry Colburn, 1846.

Kenny, Kathy. "The Power of Place: Katrina in Five Worlds." *Jerusalem Quarterly* 35 (Autumn 2008): 8–9.

Khalidi, Rashid. *The Iron Cage: The Palestinian Struggle for Statehood*. Boston: Beacon Press, 2014.

Khater, Akram Fouad. *Embracing the Divine: Passion and Politics in the Christian Middle East*. Syracuse, NY: Syracuse Univ. Press, 2001.

————. *Inventing Home: Emigration, Gender, and the Middle Class in Lebanon, 1870–1920.* Berkeley: Univ. of California Press, 2001.

Khoury, Dina. *State and Provincial Society in the Ottoman Empire: Mosul, 1540–1834.* Cambridge: Cambridge Univ. Press, 1997.

Khoury, Philip S. *Syria and the French Mandate: The Politics of Arab Nationalism, 1920–1945.* Princeton, NJ: Princeton Univ. Press, 1987.

Kildani, Hanna. *Modern Christianity in the Holy Land.* Bloomington, IN: AuthorHouse, 2010.

Kraemer, Roberta, and Elite Olshtain. "The Social Context of Second Language Learning in Israeli Schools." *Israel Social Science Research* 9, nos. 1–2 (1994): 161–80.

Krämer, Gudrun. *The Jews in Modern Egypt, 1914–1952.* Seattle: Univ. of Washington Press, 1989.

Kuni, Ibrahim al-. *Al-Tibr.* Limassol: Tasili li-l-Nashr wa-l-'I'lam, 1992.

Kuroki, Hidemitsu. "Mobility of Non-Muslims in Nineteenth Century Aleppo." In *The Influence of Human Mobility in Muslim Societies,* edited by Hidemitsu Kuroki, 117–35. London: Kegan Paul, 2003.

————. "The Orthodox-Catholic Clash in Aleppo in 1818." *Orient* 29 (1993): 1–18.

————. "Zimmis in Mid-Nineteenth-Century Aleppo: An Analysis of Cizye Defteris." In *Essays in Ottoman Civilization: Proceedings of the XIIth Congress of CIEPO, Archiv Orientálníl,* 204–50. Prague: Academy of Sciences of the Czech Republic, Oriental Institute, 1998.

Lagnado, Lucette. *The Man in the White Sharkskin Suit: A Jewish Family's Exodus from Old Cairo to the New World.* New York: Harper, 2008.

Larguèche, Abdelhamid. *Les communautés méditerranéennes de la Tunisie.* Tunis: CUP, 2006.

————. "L'histoire à l'épreuve du patrimoine." *L'Année du Maghreb* (2008): 191–200.

Laskier, Michael. *The Jews of Egypt, 1920–1970: In the Midst of Zionism, Anti-Semitism, and the Middle East Conflict.* New York: New York Univ. Press, 1992.

Levenstein, Harvey. *Seductive Journey: American Tourists in France from Jefferson to the Jazz Age.* Chicago: Univ. of Chicago Press, 1998.

Levi, Tomer. *The Jews of Beirut: The Rise of a Levantine Community.* Bern: Peterlang, 2012.

Levitt, Peggy, and Nina Glick Schiller. "Conceptualizing Simultaneity: A Transnational Social Field Perspective on Society." *International Migration Review* 38, no. 3 (2004): 1002–39.

Liston, Kyle. "Migrando a Sud: Coloni italiani in Tunisia, 1881–1939, by Daniela Melfa." *Revue de l'Institut des Belles-Lettres Arabes* 2 (2008): 325–33.

Lorcin, Patricia. *Imperial Identities: Stereotyping, Prejudice, and Race in Colonial Algeria*. London: Tauris, 1995.

Loth, Gaston. *Le peuplement italien en Tunisie et en Algérie*. Paris: Librairie Armand Colin, 1905.

Lowenthal, David. "Past Time, Present Place: Landscape and Memory." *Geographical Review* 65 (1975): 1–36.

Lutfi, Huda. "Coptic Festival of the Nile: Aberrations of the Past?" In *The Mamluks in Egyptian Politics and Society*, edited by Thomas Philipp and Ulrich Haarmann, 254–82. Cambridge: Cambridge Univ. Press, 1998.

MacDonnell, Joseph. *Jesuits by the Tigris: Men for Others in Baghdad*. Boston: Jesuit Mission Press, 1994.

Maddy-Weitzman, Bruce. *The Berber Identity Movement and the Challenge to North African States*. Austin: Univ. of Texas Press, 2011.

Madun, Muhmmad 'Ali. *'Urubat al-barbar: Al-Haqiqa al-maghmura*. Damascus: al-Markaz al-'Arabi li-l-Ta'rib wa-l-Tarjama wa-l-Ta'lif wa-l-Nashr, 1992.

Magocsi, Paul Robert. *Historical Atlas of Central Europe*. Seattle: Univ. of Washington Press, 2002.

Makdisi, Ussama. *The Culture of Sectarianism: Community, History, and Violence in Nineteenth-Century Ottoman Lebanon*. Berkeley: Univ. of California Press, 2000.

Makko, Aryo. "The Historical Roots of Contemporary Controversies: National Revival and the Assyrian 'Concept of Unity.'" *Journal of Assyrian Academic Studies* 24, no. 1 (2010): 1–29.

Malaty, Tadros Y. *The Coptic Calendar and Church of Alexandria*. Wadi al-Natrun: Monastery of St. Macarius, 1988.

Mandel, Ruth. *Cosmopolitan Anxieties: Turkish Challenges to Citizenship and Belonging in Germany*. Durham: Duke Univ. Press, 2008.

Manqabbadi, Nagib Kirlus al-. "'Id li-Kull al-Misriyyin: 'Id al-Nayruz Ta'kid li-Huwiyyat-na wa Wahdat-na al-Wataniyya." In *Al-Nayruz . . . 'Id Misri Qadim*, edited by Subhi 'Abd al-Malak and Nabil 'Adli, 78–81. Cairo: Mu'assasa Watani lil-Tiba'a wa al-Nashr, 2007/1999.

Mansar, Adnen. "La personnalité nationale chez l'élite nationaliste en Tunisie et en Égypte (1956–1970)." In *Après l'independance parcours et discours*, edited by Michaël Béchir Ayari and Sami Bargaoui. Tunis: Arabesques Éditions, 2010.

Maqrizi, T. A. 'A. al-. *Al-Mawa'iz wa al-I'tibar bi-Dhikr al-Khitat wa al-Athar*. 3 vols. Cairo: Maktabat al-Madbuli, 1998.

Marikh, 'Adil Mihad. *Al-'Arabiyya al-qadima wa-lahajatuha*. Abu Dhabi: al-Majma' al-Thaqafi, 2000.

Mashala, Nur. "A Galilee without Christians? Yosef Weitz and 'Operation Yohanan.'" In *Palestinian Christians: Religion, Politics, and Society in the Holy Land*, edited by Anthony O'Mahony, 190–222. London: Melisende, 1999.

Masters, Bruce. *Christians and Jews in the Ottoman Arab World: The Roots of Sectarianism*. Cambridge: Cambridge Univ. Press, 2001.

———. "The Establishment of the Melkite Catholic Millet in 1848 and the Politics of Identity in Tanzimat Syria." In *Syria and Bilad al-Sham under Ottoman Rule: Essays in Honour of Abdul-Karim Rafeq*, edited by Peter Sluglett and Stefan Winter, 455–74. Leiden: Brill, 2010.

Mas'udi, Abu al-Hasan al-. *Muruj al-dhahab wa-ma'adin al-jawhar*. Edited by Yusuf Daghir. 4 vols. Beirut: Dar al-Andalus li-l-Tiba'a wa-l-Nashr, 1965.

Mati'i, Lama'i al-. *Mawsu'a 1000 Shakhsiyya Misriyya*. Cairo: Maktabat al-Dar al-'Arabiya lil-Kitab, 2006.

Mazower, Mark. "Minorities and the League of Nations in Interwar Europe." *Daedalus* 126, no. 2 (1997): 47–73.

Mazrui, Ali Al'Amin, and Alamin M. Mazrui. *The Power of Babel: Language & Governance in the African Experience*. Oxford, England: J. Currey, 1998.

McDowall, David. *A Modern History of the Kurds*. London: I. B. Tauris, 1996.

McGuinness, Justin, and Zubeir Mouhli. *Tunis, 1800–1950*. Tunis: ASM, 2004.

McGuire, Brian. "Lebanese Asylum Applicants in Denmark, 1985–1988: Political Refugees or War Emigrants?" In *The Lebanese in the World: A Century of Emigration*, edited by Albert Hourani and Nadim Shehadi, 661–86. London: I. B. Tauris, 1992.

Meho, Lokman, and Farah Kawtharani. "The Kurdish Community in Lebanon and Their Future Prospects." In *The Kurdish Question and the 2003 Iraq War*, edited by Mohammad Ahmed and Michael Gunter, 248–75. Costa Mesa, CA: Mazda, 2005.

Meier-Braun, Karl-Heinz. *Deutschland, Einwanderungsland*. Frankfurt: Suhrkamp Verlag, 2002.

Melfa, Daniela. "De l'italianité aux Italiens de Tunisie: Identité nationale et recherche historique." *Polo Sud: Semestrale di studi\storici* 3, no. 1 (2014): 65–81.

Melfa, Daniela, and David Bond. "All Things to All Men: Postcolonial History's Many Guises." *Revue de l'Institut des Belles-Lettres Arabes* 206 (2010): 213–31.

Memmi, Albert. *The Colonizer and Colonized.* Translated by Howard Greenfield. New York: Orion Press, 1965.

Mérigoux, J. M. *Va à Ninive! Un dialogue avec l'Irak.* Paris: Éditions du Cerf, 2000.

Mikhail, Kyriakos. *Copts and Moslems under British Control: A Collection of Facts and a Résumé of Authoritative Opinions on the Coptic Question.* London: Kennikat Press, 1911.

Miller, Catherine. "Linguistic Policies and the Issue of Ethno-linguistic Minorities in the Middle East." In *Islam in the Middle Eastern Studies: Muslims and Minorities*, edited by Usuki A. and H. Kato, 149–74. Symposium Series 7. Osaka: JCAS, 2003.

Mirkova, Anna. "Citizenship Formation in Bulgaria: Protected Minority or National Citizens?" *Journal of Muslim Minority Affairs* 29 (2009): 469–82.

———. "Landownership and Modernization in the Transition from Ottoman Imperial to Bulgarian National Rule (1877/78–1908)." PhD diss., Univ. of Michigan, 2006.

Morris, Lydia. *Managing Migration: Civic Stratification and Migrants Rights.* London: Routledge, 2002.

Moscrop, John James. *Measuring Jerusalem: The Palestine Exploration Fund and British Interests in the Holy Land.* London: Leicester Univ. Press, 2000.

Mother of God Church, 50th Anniversary, 1948–98: Celebrating the Historical Growth of the Chaldean Community in Mother of God Parish. Southfield, MI: n.p., 1998.

Muqaddam, 'Ahmad Sa'd Sa'id 'Ali. *Safahat min tarikh al-mahra.* Damascus: Maktabat Dar al-Fath, 2005.

Muqaddasi, Shams al-Din al-. *'Ahsan al-taqasim fi ma'rifat al-'aqalim.* Edited by Michael Jan de Goeje. Leiden: E. J. Brill, 1992.

Murray, M. A. "Nawruz; or, The Coptic New Year." *Ancient Egypt* (1921): 79–81.

Musallam, Adnan. *Folded Pages from Local Palestinian History in the 20th Century: Developments in Politics, Society, Press and Thought in Bethlehem in the British Era, 1917–1948.* Bethlehem: Wiam, 2002.

Nakash, Yitzhak. *The Shi'is of Iraq.* Princeton, NJ: Princeton Univ. Press, 1994.

Naval Intelligence Division (Royal Navy). *Geographical Handbook Tunisia.* London: HMSO / Oxford Univ. Press, 1945.

Nieuwenhuis, Tom. *Politics and Society in Early Modern Iraq: Mamluk Pashas, Tribal Shayks and Local Rule between 1802 and 1831*. The Hague: Mouton, 1982.

Nocke, Alexandra. *The Place of the Mediterranean in Modern Israeli Identity*. Leiden: Brill, 2009.

Nora, Pierre. *Realms of Memory*. New York: Columbia Univ. Press, 1997.

Nordbruch, Götz. "Bread, Freedom, Independence: Opposition to Nazi Germany in Lebanon and Syria and the Struggle for a Just Order." *Comparative Studies of South Asia, Africa and the Middle East* 28, no. 3 (2008): 416–27.

Norris, H. T. "Yemenis in the Western Sahara." *Journal of African History* 3, no. 2 (1962): 317–22.

Norris, Jacob. "Bethlehem: The Global Story of a Little Town." *History Today* 63, no. 12 (2013): 11–17.

———. "Exporting the Holy Land: Artisans and Merchant Migrants in Ottoman-Era Bethlehem." *Mashriq and Mahjar: Journal of Middle East Migration Studies* 2 (2013): 14–40.

Odisho, Edward Y. "City of Kirkuk: No Historical Authenticity without Multiethnicity." *Journal of Assyrian Academic Studies* (1981): 7.

Offrey, Charles. *Cette grande dame que fut la Transat*. Paris: Editions MDV, 1994.

O'Mahony, Anthony. "The Chaldean Catholic Church: The Politics of Church-State Relations in Modern Iraq." *Heythrop Journal* 45, no. 4 (2004): 435–50.

———, ed. *The Christian Communities of Jerusalem and the Holy Land: Studies in History, Religion and Politics*. Cardiff: Univ. of Wales Press, 2003.

———. "Christianity in Modern Iraq." *International Journal for the Study of the Christian Church* 4, no. 2 (2004): 121–42.

Owens, Jonathan. Introduction to *Arabic as a Minority Language*, edited by Jonathan Owens. Berlin: Walter de Gruyter, 2000.

Papaconstantinou, Arietta. "Historiography, Hagiography, and the Making of the Coptic 'Church of the Martyrs' in Early Islamic Egypt." *Dumbarton Oaks Papers* 60 (2006): 65–86.

Papastathis, Konstantinos, and Ruth Kark. "Orthodox Communal Politics in Palestine after the Young Turk Revolution (1908–1910)." *Jerusalem Quarterly* 56–57 (Winter 2013–Spring 2014): 118–39.

Pedersen, Susan. "The Meaning of the Mandates System: An Argument." *Geschichte und Gesellschaft* 32, no. 4 (2006): 560–82.

Pellegrin, Arthur. *Histoire de la Tunisie depuis les origines jusqu'à nos jours*. Tunis: Louis Namura, 1948.

Pendola, M., ed. *L'alimentazione degli Italiani di Tunisia.* Tunis: Finzi, 2005).

———. *Gli italiani di Tunisia: Storia di una comunità (XIX–XX secolo).* Umbra: Foligno, 2007.

———. "La réprésentation des Italiens dans la Tunisie coloniale à travers la littérature." In *Traces: Désirs de savoirs et volonté d'être, l'après-colonie au Maghreb,* edited by Fanny Colonna and Loïc Le Pape, 92–115. Arles: Actes Sud, 2010.

Pennycook, Alastair. *The Cultural Politics of English as an International Language.* Language in Social Life Series. Harlow, Essex, England: Longman Group UK, 1994.

Péraldi, Michel, Alain Tarrius, and Geneviève Marotel. *L'Aménagement à contretemps.* Paris: L'Harmattan, 1988.

Perkins, Kenneth. *A History of Modern Tunisia.* Cambridge: Cambridge Univ. Press, 2005.

Philipp, Thomas. *Acre: The Rise and Fall of a Palestinian City, 1731–1830.* New York: Columbia Univ. Press, 2002.

———. "Copts and Other Minorities in the Development of the Egyptian Nation-State." In *Egypt from Monarchy to Republic: A Reassessment of Revolution and Change,* edited by Shimon Shamir, 131–50. Boulder, CO: Westview Press, 1995.

———. *The Syrians in Egypt, 1725–1975.* Stuttgart: Steiner, 1985.

Phillipson, Robert. *Linguistic Imperialism.* Oxford: Oxford Univ. Press, 1992.

Piening, Günter. "Islam und Integrationspolitik am Beispiel Berlin." In *Integration und Islam: Migration, Flüchtlinge und Integration,* 184–93. Nuremberg: Bundesamt für Migration und Flüchtlinge, 2006.

Podeh, Elie. *The Politics of National Celebrations in the Arab Middle East.* New York: Cambridge Univ. Press, 2011.

Porath, Yehoshua. *The Emergence of the Palestinian Arab National Movement.* London: Cass, 1974.

Porter, Andrew. *Religious versus Empire? British Protestant Missionaries and Overseas Expansion, 1700–1914.* Manchester: Manchester Univ. Press, 2004.

Pouessel, Stephanie. "Les marges renaissante: Amazigh, Juif, Noir." *L'Annee du Maghreb* 8 (2012): 143–60.

Provence, Michael. *The Great Syrian Revolt and the Rise of Syrian Nationalism.* Austin: Univ. of Texas Press, 2005.

Pursley, Sara. "A Race against Time: Governing Femininity and Reproducing the Future in Revolutionary Iraq, 1945–63." PhD thesis, City Univ. of New York, 2012.

Qattan, Najwa. "The Damascene Jewish Community in the Latter Decades of the Eighteenth Century: Aspects of Socio-economic Life Based on the Registers of the Shari'a Courts." In *The Syrian Land in the 18th and 19th Century: The Common and the Specific in the Historical Experience*, edited by Thomas Philipp, 197–216. Stuttgart: Steiner, 1992.

———. "Dhimmis in the Muslim Court: Legal Autonomy and Religious Discrimination." *International Journal of Middle East Studies* 31 (1999): 429–44.

Qattawi, Yusuf, ed. *L'Egypte: Aperçu historique et geographique gouvernement et institutions vie economique et sociale*. Cairo: L'Institut Français, 1926.

Raafat, Samir W. *Maadi, 1904–1962: Society & History in a Cairo Suburb*. Cairo: Palm Press, 1994.

Raheb, Viola, ed. *Latin Americans with Palestinian Roots*. Bethlehem: Diyar, 2012.

Rasheed, Madawi al-. *Iraqi Assyrian Christians in London: The Construction of an Ethnicity*. Lewiston, NY: Mellen Press, 1998.

Rassam, Suha. *Christianity in Iraq: Its Origins and Development to the Present Day*. Herefordshire: Gracewing, 2005.

Reichel, Nurit. "Ben 'kartanut' le-'ofke-tarbut': Mekomah shel ha-haskalah ha-kelalit ba-Hinukh ha-'Ivri be–Eretz-Yisra'el, 1882–1935." PhD diss., Tel Aviv Univ., 1994.

Reid, Donald Malcolm. "Indigenous Egyptology: The Decolonization of a Profession?" *Journal of the American Oriental Society* 105, no. 2 (1985): 233–46.

———. *Whose Pharaohs? Archaeology, Museums, and Egyptian National Identity from Napoleon to World War I*. Cairo: American Univ. in Cairo Press, 2002.

Ricard, Prosper. *Guide Bleu: Algérie, Tunisie, Tripolitaine, Malte*. Paris: Hachette, 1927.

Riecken, Philipp-Asmus. *Die Duldung als Verfassungsproblem: Unrechtmässiger, nicht sanktionierter Aufenthalt von Ausländern in der Bundesrepublik Deutschland*. Berlin: Duncker & Humblot, 2006.

Rietz, Karin. *Integrationssenatorin Bluhm über den schwierigen Weg palästinensischer Flüchtlinge in die Berliner Gesellschaft*. Press release, Berlin Senate, Oct. 21, 2010. http://www.berlin.de/rbmskzl/aktuelles/pressemitteilungen/2010/pressemitteilung.57099.php.

Rinott, Moshe. "Capitulations: The Case of the German-Jewish Hilfsverein Schools in Palestine, 1901–1914." In *Palestine in the Late Ottoman Period: Political, Social, and Economic Transformation*, edited by David Kushner. Jerusalem: Yad Izhak Ben-Zvi, n.d.

Rippen, Andrew. "Syriac in the Qur'an: Classical Muslim Theories." In *The Qur'an in Its Historical Context*, edited by Gabriel Reynolds, 249–61. New York: Routledge, 2008.

Rivet, Daniel. *Le Maghreb à l'épreuve de la colonisation*. Paris: Hachette, 2002.

Rivlin, Benjamin. "Berque's le Maghreb entre deux guerres." *Journal of Politics* 30, no. 2 (1968): 558–59.

Roberts, Hugh. *The Battlefield: Algeria, 1988–2002, Studies in a Broken Polity*. London: Verso Books, 2003.

Roberts, Nicholas. "Dividing Jerusalem: British Urban Planning in the Holy City." *Journal of Palestine Studies* 22, no. 4 (2013): 7–26.

Robinson, Shira. *Citizen Strangers: Palestinians and the Birth of Israel's Liberal Settler State*. Stanford, CA: Stanford Univ. Press, 2013.

Robson, Laura. *Colonialism and Christianity in Mandate Palestine*. Austin: Univ. of Texas Press, 2011.

Rodrigue, Aron, and Nancy Reynolds. "Difference and Tolerance in the Ottoman Empire." *Stanford Electronic Humanities Review* 5, no. 1 (1996). http://www.stanford.edu/group/SHR/5-1/text/rodrigue.html.

Roth, H. Y. "'Al ha-kivun ha-ratzui shel limude ha-Anglit." *Moznayim* 16, nos. 1–6 (1943): 143–47.

Rouchdy, Aleya, ed. *Language Contact and Language Conflict in Arabic: Variations on a Sociolinguistic Theme*. London: Routledge Curzon, 2002.

Rubin, Aaron. *The Mehri Language of Oman*. Leiden: Brill, 2010.

Sabella, Bernard. "Palestinian Christian Emigration from the Holy Land." *Proche-Orient Chrétien* 41 (1991): 74–85.

Sadiq, Rami 'Ata. *Sahafat al-Aqbat wa Qadaya al-Mujtama' al-Misri*. Cairo: al-Majlis al-'A'la lil-Thaqafa, 2009.

Sajdi, Dana. *The Barber of Damascus: Nouveau Literacy in the Eighteenth-Century Ottoman Levant*. Stanford, CA: Stanford Univ. Press, 2013.

Sami, Rufa'il. "'Id al-Nayruz: Tarikh wa Wataniyya wa 'Aqida." In *Al-Nayruz . . . 'Id Misri Qadim*, edited by Subhi 'Abd al-Malak and Nabil 'Adli, 91–94. Cairo: Mu'assasa Watani lil-Tiba'a wa al-Nashr, 2007.

Sammur, George. *Bayt Lahm 'Abr al-Tarikh*. Bethlehem: Wiam, 2007.

Samuel, Herbert. *Report of the High Commissioner on the Administration of Palestine, 1920–1925*. London: HMSO, 1925.

Sanguini, Armando. *Architectures italiennes de Tunisie*. Tunis: Éditions Finzi, 2000.

Santilli, Anthony. "Un mythe historiographique au service de deux nations: Les 'Italiens' d'Égypte au xixe siècle." *Polo Sud Semestrale di studi storici* 3, no. 1 (2014): 15–35.

Saposnik, Arieh Bruce. *Becoming Hebrew: The Creation of a Jewish National Culture in Ottoman Palestine.* New York: Oxford Univ. Press, 2008.

Sarafa, Josephine, ed. *Chaldean Americans: Past and Present.* Bloomfield Hills, MI: St. Thomas the Apostle Chaldean Catholic Diocese of America, n.d.

Sarrazin, Thilo. *Deutschland schafft sich ab: Wie wir unser Land aufs Spiel setzen.* Munich: Deutsche Verlags-Anstalt, 2010.

Saurin, Jules. *L'invasion sicilienne et le peuplement français de la Tunisie.* Paris: Augustin Challamel, 1900.

Sayigh, Rosemary. "Palestinians in Lebanon: Harsh Present, Uncertain Future." *Journal of Palestine Studies* 25 (1995): 37–53.

Schellner, Ludwig. *Reisebriefe aus heiligen Landan.* Cologne: n.p., 1910.

Schlaepfer, Aline. *Les intellectuels juifs de Bagdad: Discours et allégeances (1908–1951).* Leiden: Brill, 2016.

Schreier, Joshua. *Arabs of the Jewish Faith: The Civilizing Mission in Colonial Algeria.* New Brunswick, NJ: Rutgers Univ. Press, 2010.

Sciolto, Giovanni. "Tunisi—Tel Aviv tra normalizzazione e antisemitismo." Master's thesis, Univ. degli Studi di Catania, 2012.

Sebag, Paul. *Tunis: Histoire d'une ville.* Paris: L'Harmattan, 1998.

Sedra, Paul. "Writing the History of the Modern Copts: From Victims and Symbols to Actors." *History Compass* 7, no. 3 (2009): 1049–63.

Sengstock, Mary. *Chaldeans in America.* Lansing: Michigan State Univ. Press, 2005.

Shahri, 'Ali 'Ahmad al-. *Lughat 'Ad.* Abu Dhabi: al-Mu'assasa al-Wataniyya li-l-Taghlif wa-l-Tiba'a, 2000.

Shami, Seteny. "'Aqalliya/Minority in Modern Egyptian Discourse." In *Words in Motion: Towards a Global Lexicon*, edited by Carol Gluck and Anna Lowenhaupt Tsing, 152–73. Durham, NC: Duke Univ. Press, 2009.

Shatzmiller, Maya. "Le mythe d'origine Berbère: Aspects historiographiques et sociaux." *Revue de l'Occident Musulman et de la Méditerranée* 35, no. 1 (1983): 145–56.

Sha'ul, Anwar. *Qissat hayati fi wadi al-rafidayn.* Jerusalem: Manshurat rabitat al-djami'iyyin al-yahud al-nazihin min al-Iraq, 1984.

Shavit, Yaacov. "The Mediterranean world and 'Mediterraneanism.'" *Mediterranean Historical Review* 2, no. 3 (1988): 96–117.

Shawkat, Sami. *Hadhihi ahdafuna*. Baghdad: Matba'at al-tafayyud, 1939.

Shilo, Margalit. "Milhemet ha-safot ki-tenu'ah 'amamit." *Katedrah* 74 (1995): 87–119.

Shneurson, Fishel. *La-psikhologiyah shel du ha-leshoniyut ba-aretz: Hakirah be-vate ha-sefer ha-'ironiyim be–Tel Aviv bi-shenot 1936–7, 37–8*. Tel Aviv: Seminariyon mehkar la-psikhologiyah u-pedagogiyah refu'it sotzialit, 1939.

Shoshan, Boaz. *Popular Culture in Medieval Cairo*. Cambridge: Cambridge Univ. Press, 1993.

Shoufani, Elias. *Rihla F'il Rahil: Fusul Min al-Dhakira . . . Lam Taktamul*. Beirut: Dar al-kunuz al-adabiya, 1994.

Shukri, Subhi. "Fi al-Ihtifal al-Kabir bi-'Id al-Nayruz." In *Al-Nayruz . . . 'Id Misri Qadim*, edited by Subhi 'Abd al-Malak and Nabil 'Adli, 40–48. Cairo: Mu'assasa Watani lil-Tiba'a wa al-Nashr, 1973.

Silberman, Neil Asher. *Digging for God and Country: Exploration, Archeology, and the Secret Struggle for the Holy Land, 1799–1917*. New York: Alfred A. Knopf, 1982.

Sitton, Shoshana. "Zionist Education in an Encounter between the British Colonial and the Hebrew Cultures." *Journal of Educational Administration and History* 29, no. 2 (1997): 108–20.

Sluglett, Peter. "Aspects of Economy and Society in the Syrian Provinces: Aleppo in Transition, 1880–1925." In *Modernity and Culture from the Mediterranean to the Indian Ocean*, edited by Leila Tarazi Fawaz and C. A. Bayly, 144–57. New York: Columbia Univ. Press, 2002.

———. *Britain in Iraq: Contriving King and Country*. New York: Columbia Univ. Press, 2007.

———. "The British, the Sunnis and the Shi'is: Social Hierarchies of Interaction under the British Mandate." *International Journal of Contemporary Iraqi Studies* 4 (2010): 257–73.

———. "An Improvement on Colonialism? The 'A' Mandates and Their Legacy in the Middle East." *International Affairs* 90, no. 2 (2014): 413–27.

Sluglett, Peter, and Marion Farouk-Sluglett. "Some Reflections on the Sunni/Shi'i Question in Iraq." *British Journal of Middle Eastern Studies* 5, no. 2 (1978): 79–87.

Sluglett, Peter, and Nadine Meouchy, eds. *The British and French Mandates in Comparative Perspective*. Leiden: Brill, 2004.

Sluglett-Farouk, Marion, and Peter Sluglett. *Iraq since 1958: From Revolution to Dictatorship*. New York: I. B. Tauris, 2003.

Smith, Woodruff D. *The Ideological Origins of Nazi Imperialism.* New York: Oxford Univ. Press, 1989.

Soffer, Arnon. "Lebanon: Where Demography Is the Core of Politics and Life." *Middle Eastern Studies* 22 (1986): 197–205.

Sollors, Werner. *Beyond Ethnicity: Consent and Descent in American Culture.* New York: Oxford Univ. Press, 1986.

Sonntag, Selma K. *The Local Politics of Global English: Case Studies in Linguistic Globalization.* Lanham, MD: Lexington Books, 2003.

Spalinger, A. "The Limitations of Formal Ancient Egyptian Religion." *Journal of Near Eastern Studies* 57, no. 4 (1998): 241–60.

Spector, Stephen. *Evangelicals and Israel: The Story of American Christian Zionism.* New York: Oxford Univ. Press, 2008.

Spolsky, Bernard. "Conditions for Second Language Learning in Israel." *English Teachers' Journal* 47 (1994): 45–54.

Spolsky, Bernard, and Elana Goldberg Shohamy. *The Languages of Israel: Policy, Ideology, and Practice.* Tonawanda, NY: Multilingual Matters, 1999.

Stavrou, T. G. *Russian Interests in Palestine, 1882–1914.* Thessaloniki: Institute for Balkan Studies, 1963.

Stillman, Norman A. *The Jews of Arab Lands in Modern Times.* New York: Jewish Publication Society, 1991.

Stransky, Thomas. "Origins of Western Christian Missions in Jerusalem and the Holy Land." In *Jerusalem in the Mind of the Western World, 1800–1948,* edited by Yehoshua Ben-Arieh and Moshe Davis. Westport, CT: Praeger, 1997.

Suleiman, Yasir. *Language and Identity in the Middle East and North Africa.* London: Curzon Press, 1996.

———. "Language and Political Conflict in the Middle East: A Study in Symbolic Sociolinguistics." In *Language and Society in the Middle East and North Africa: Studies in Variation and Identity,* edited by Yasir Suleiman, 10–37. London: Curzon Press, 1999.

———. "Nationalism and the Arabic Language: A Historical Overview." In *Arabic Sociolinguistics, Issues and Perspectives,* edited by Yasir Suleiman, 3–24. Surrey: Curzon Press, 1994.

———. *A War of Words: Language and Conflict in the Middle East.* Cambridge: Cambridge Univ. Press, 2004.

Suyuti, Jalal al-Din al-. *Al-Mutawakkili.* Edited by 'Abd al-Karim al-Zubaydi. Beirut: Dar al-Balagha, 1988.

Talmon, Rafael. "Arabic as a Minority Language in Israel." In *Arabic as a Minority Language*, edited by Jonathan Owens, 199–220. Berlin: Mouton de Gruyter, 2000.

Tamcke, Martin. "Johann Worrlein's Travels in Palestine." In *Christian Witness between Continuity and New Beginnings: Modern Historical Missions in the Middle East*, edited by Martin Tamcke and Michael Marten. Münster: Transaction, 2006.

Tamir, N. *Seminaristim be-ma'avak-'am: Sipur mi-yeme milhemet ha-safot be-Eretz Yisra'el*. Tel Aviv: Yavneh, 1963.

Tariqi, Salim al-. *Rihla fi 'alim al-'ibl*. Tunis: Manshurat al-Mutawassit, 2006.

Telhine, Mohammed. *L'Islam et les musulmans en France: Une histoire de mosques*. Paris: Harmattan, 2010.

Terry, Janice J. "Community and Political Activism among Arab Americans in Detroit." In *Arabs in America*, edited by Michael Suleiman, 241–54. Philadelphia Temple Univ. Press, 1999.

Thielmann, Jörn. "Islam and Muslims in Germany: An Introductory Exploration." In *Islam and Muslims in Germany*, edited by Ala al-Hamarneh and Jörn Thielmann, 1–29. Leiden: Brill, 2008.

Thompson, Elizabeth. *Colonial Citizens: Republican Rights, Paternal Privilege, and Gender in French Syria and Lebanon*. New York: Columbia Univ. Press, 2000.

Tibawi, A. L. *British Interests in Palestine, 1800–1901: A Study of Religious and Educational Enterprise*. London: Oxford Univ. Press, 1961.

———. "Russian Cultural Penetration of Syria: Palestine in the Nineteenth Century." *Journal of the Royal Central Asian Society* 52 (1966): 166–82.

Tibi, Bassam. *Islamische Zuwanderung: Die gescheiterte Integration*. Munich: Deutsche Vertrags-Anstalt, 2002.

———. *Political Islam, World Politics and Europe: Democratic Peace and Euro-Islam versus Global Jihad*. London: Routledge, 2007.

Tripp, Charles. *A History of Iraq*. Cambridge: Cambridge Univ. Press, 2007.

Tumas, Tuma. "Awraq Tuma Tumas." *Thekriat* (2006). http://www.al-nnas.com/THEKRIAT/15jsf1.htm.

Twayq, Salih. *Dhikrayat wa khawatir*. Jerusalem: Manshurat rabitat al-djami'iyyin al-yahud al-nazihin min al-Iraq, 2011–12.

US Census Bureau. *Census 2000*. Summary File 3. Matrices PCT15 and PCT18. https://www.census.gov/prod/cen2000/doc/sf3.pdf.

Vella, Christina. *Intimate Enemies: The Two Worlds of the Baroness de Pontalba*. Baton Rouge: Louisiana State Univ. Press, 2004.

"Vers le cœur de la ville: La veine de sauvegarde." *Architecture méditerranéenne (Revue internationale d'architecture)* (1997).

Vester, Bertha Spafford. *Our Jerusalem: An American Family in the Holy City, 1881–1949.* London: Evans Brothers, 1951.

Viruega, Jacqueline. *La bijouterie parisienne, 1860–1914.* Paris: L'Harmattan, 2004.

Von Bethlenfalvy, Peter. "Migrants in an Irregular Situation in the Federal Republic of Germany: The Psycho-social Situation of Unaccompanied Minors from Areas of Armed Conflict in Berlin, West." *International Migration* 21 (1983): 238–59.

Walsh College of Business and United Way for Southeastern Michigan. *Chaldean Household Survey.* Bloomfield Hills, MI: Chaldean American Chamber of Commerce, 2007.

Walters, Joel. "The Anglos Are Coming, the Anglos Are Coming: English Language Instruction in Israeli Schools." *Jewish Education* 50, no. 1 (1982): 16–21.

Ways, 'Abd al-Majid Yasin al-. *Fiqh al-'arabiyya wa-sirr al-lugha al-mahriyya.* Sana'a: Sana'a Univ. Press, 2004.

Weiss, Max. *In the Shadow of Sectarianism: Law, Shi'ism and the Making of Modern Lebanon.* Cambridge, MA: Harvard Univ. Press, 2010.

Wendell, Charles. *The Evolution of the Egyptian National Image: From Its Origins to Ahmad Lutfi al-Sayyid.* Berkeley: Univ. of California Press, 1972.

Wer, Enam al-. "Arabic Between Reality and Ideology." *International Journal of Applied Linguistics* 7, no. 2 (1997): 251–65.

White, Benjamin Thomas. *The Emergence of Minorities in the Middle East: The Politics of Community in French Mandate Syria.* Edinburgh: Edinburgh Univ. Press, 2011.

Wien, Peter. *Iraqi Arab Nationalism: Authoritarian, Totalitarian and Pro-Fascist Inclinations, 1932–1941.* London and New York: Routledge, 2006.

Winter, Stefan. "The Nusayris before the Tanzimat in the Eyes of Ottoman Provincial Administrators, 1804–1834." In *From the Syrian Land to the States of Syria and Lebanon,* edited by Thomas Philipp and Christoph Schumann, 97–112. Beirut and Würzburg: Orient Institut der DMG, 2004.

———. *The Shi'is of Lebanon under Ottoman Rule, 1516–1788.* Cambridge: Cambridge Univ. Press, 2010.

Wood, Michael. "The Use of the Pharaonic Past in Modern Egyptian Nationalism." *Journal of the American Research Center in Egypt* 35 (1998): 179–96.

Y. S. "Le-she'elat anahnu u-shekhenenu." *Hed Ha-Hinukh* 1, nos. 10–12 (1927): 169.

Yaffe, Nurit. *The Arab Population of Israel, 2003.* Jerusalem: Central Bureau of Statistics, 2003.

Yavuz, M. Hakan. "Warfare and Nationalism: The Balkan Wars as a Catalyst for Homogenization." In *War and Nationalism: The Balkan Wars, 1912–1913, and Their Sociopolitical Implications*, edited by M. Hakan Yavuz, Isa Blumi, and Edward J. Erickson, 31–84. Salt Lake City: Univ. of Utah Press, 2013.

Yehuda, Zvi. "Haham Başı (Chief Rabbi)." In *Encyclopedia of Jews in the Islamic World*, edited by Norman A. Stillman. Leiden: Brill Online, 2014.

Younan, I. "Les chrétiens sous le poids de l'Islam dominant: Entre peur et compromis." *Actualité Religieuse dans le Monde* 15, no. 51 (1991): 19.

Youssef, Ahmad Abdel-Hamid. *From Pharaoh's Lips: Ancient Egyptian Language in the Arabic of Today.* Cairo: American Univ. in Cairo Press, 2003.

Youssef, Youhanna Nessim. "The Coptic Calendar." In *The Blackwell Companion to Eastern Christianity*, edited by Ken Parry, 450–57. Malden, MA: Blackwell, 2007.

Yurdakul, Gökce. *From Guest Workers into Muslims: The Transformation of Turkish Immigrant Associations in Germany.* Newcastle: Cambridge Scholars Press, 2009.

Zaydman, Y. A. "Morim: Avot tehiyat ha-lashon." In *Sefer ha-yovel shel histadrut ha-morim*, 77–93. Tel Aviv: Merkaz histadrut ha-morim be–Eretz Yisra'el, 1956.

Ziegler, Robert. "The Containment and Diffusion of History in Huysmans' Saint-Séverin." In *Correspondances: Studies in Literature, History, and the Arts in Nineteenth-Century France*, edited by Keith Busby. Amsterdam: Rodopi, 1992.

Zubaida, Sami. "Contested Nations: Iraq and the Assyrians." *Nations and Nationalism* 6 (2000): 363–82.

———. "Middle Eastern Experiences of Cosmopolitanism." In *Conceiving Cosmopolitanism: Theory, Context and Practice*, edited by Steven Vertovec and Robin Cohen, 32–41. New York: Oxford Univ. Press, 2002.

Contributors

JOEL BEININ is the Donald J. McLachlan Professor of History and a professor of Middle East history at Stanford University. He has written or edited ten books, most recently *Workers and Thieves: Labor Movements and Popular Uprisings in Tunisia and Egypt* (2015). In 2002 he served as president of the Middle East Studies Association of North America.

ALDA BENJAMEN received her PhD in modern Middle Eastern history from the University of Maryland in 2015. Her dissertation, "Negotiating the Place of Assyrians in Modern Iraq," contextualizes Assyrians in Iraqi history by analyzing their role in leftist movements of the twentieth century. She has been a fellow at the American Academic Research Institute in Iraq and holds a master's degree from the Near and Middle Eastern Civilizations Department at the University of Toronto in Syriac studies.

DAVID BOND is a doctoral candidate in the Department of Near Eastern Languages and Cultures at the Ohio State University. He has studied at the universities of Oxford and Tunis. Between 2001 and 2010 he was editorial coordinator of the *Revue de l'Institut des Belles-Lettres Arabes* in Tunis, a city with which he has engaged artistically in a number of exhibitions.

LIORA R. HALPERIN is an assistant professor of history and Jewish studies at the University of Colorado. Her research focuses on Jewish cultural history, Jewish-Arab relations in Ottoman and Mandate Palestine, language ideology and policy, and the politics surrounding nation formation in Palestine in the years leading up to the creation of the state of Israel in 1948. Her first book, *Babel in Zion: Jews, Nationalism, and Language Diversity in Palestine, 1920–1948*, was published in 2015.

YASMEEN HANOOSH is an assistant professor of Arabic studies at Portland State University and a literary translator. Her research interests include Arabic literature, especially the post-2003 Iraqi novel, and Iraq's Christian minorities and their transnational communities.

SAMUEL LIEBHABER is an associate professor of Arabic at Middlebury College. He received his master's degree in comparative semiotics (2000) and his PhD in Arabic literature from the University of California (2007). He has published a translation of the first-ever written collection of poetry in the Mahri language, *The Diwan of Hajj Dakon* (2011), as well as articles on Mahri poetry and language in a number of scholarly journals. He is also the author of the Mahri Poetry Archive, an online resource for Mahri poetry, society, and history: http://sites.middlebury.edu/mahripoetry/. Beyond his work in al-Mahra and Yemen, he has scholarly interests in classical Arabic literature, bedouin vernacular poetry, and the language minority communities of the Middle East and North Africa.

HIROKO MIYOKAWA is a researcher on Coptic studies at the Institute of Asian Cultures of Sophia University, Tokyo. Her research primarily focuses on the formation of ethnoreligious identity among Coptic Christians and its links to Egyptian nationalism.

JACOB NORRIS is a lecturer in Middle Eastern history at the University of Sussex. He completed his PhD at the University of Cambridge in 2010, followed by a postdoctoral fellowship at Pembroke College, Cambridge, from 2010 to 2013. His book *Land of Progress: Palestine in the Age of Colonial Development, 1905–1948* was published in 2013. His current research focuses on the town of Bethlehem and its global connections in the nineteenth and early twentieth centuries.

LAURA ROBSON received her PhD in modern Middle Eastern history from Yale University in 2009 and is currently an associate professor in the Department of History at Portland State University in Oregon. She is the author of *Colonialism and Christianity in Mandate Palestine* (2011), as well as a number of articles on ethnic and religious minorities in the Arab Middle East.

ALINE SCHLAEPFER holds a PhD in Arabic studies from the University of Geneva. Her research interests focus on modern Arab intellectual history, the history of Arab nationalism, and the history of Jews in Arab lands. After being a visiting research student at the School of Oriental and African Studies in London, she was a lecturer at the University of Geneva and is now a research affiliate at the American University of Beirut, where she lives. She is the author of *Les intellectuels juifs de Bagdad: Discours et allégeance (1908–1951)* (2015).

PETER SLUGLETT is director of the Middle East Institute at the National University of Singapore. He taught at Durham University in England for nineteen years before moving to the United States in 1994, where he was a professor of Middle Eastern history at the University of Utah until 2011. His main research interests are the history of Iraq, Lebanon, and Syria in the nineteenth and twentieth centuries. He is coauthor, with the late Marion Farouk-Sluglett, of *Iraq since 1958: From Revolution to Dictatorship* (2001); author of *Britain in Iraq: Contriving King and Country* (2007); and editor of *The Urban Social History of the Middle East, 1750–1950* (2008). He was president of the Middle East Studies Association of North America in 2012–13.

LUCIA VOLK is a professor of international relations and Middle East and Islamic studies at San Francisco State University. She is the author of *Memorials and Martyrs in Modern Lebanon* (2010), about the politics of memory in Lebanon, and the author and editor of *The Middle East in the World: An Introduction* (2015). She is currently working on a study of Arab migrants and refugees who live as part of the Muslim minority in Germany.

Index